MW01232261

DEC 1 3 2013

A UNION FOREVER

A volume in the series

The United States in the World

edited by Mark Philip Bradley, David C. Engerman, and Paul A. Kramer

A list of titles in this series is available at www.cornellpress.cornell.edu.

A UNION FOREVER

The Irish Question and U.S. Foreign Relations in the Victorian Age

David Sim

PEABODY INSTITUTE
LIBRARY
DANVERS, MASS.

Cornell University Press
Ithaca and London

DEC 1 3 2013

Copyright © 2013 by Cornell University

All rights reserved. Except for brief quotations in a review, this book, or
parts thereof, must not be reproduced in any form without permission in
writing from the publisher. For information, address Cornell University
Press, Sage House, 512 East State Street, Ithaca, New York 14850.

First published 2013 by Cornell University Press
Printed in the United States of America

Library of Congress Cataloging-in-Publication Data

Sim, David, 1985– author.
    A union forever: the Irish question and U.S. foreign relations in the
Victorian age / David Sim.
        pages cm. — (The United States in the world)
    Includes bibliographical references and index.
    ISBN 978-0-8014-5184-3 (cloth : alk. paper)
    1. United States—Foreign relations—Ireland. 2. Ireland—
Foreign relations—United States. 3. United States—Foreign relations—
Great Britain. 4. Great Britain—Foreign relations—United States.
5. United States—Foreign relations—19th century. 6. Irish question.
7. Ireland—Politics and government—19th century. I. Title.
    E183.8.I6S56   2013
    327.730417'09034—dc23   2013021194

Cornell University Press strives to use environmentally responsible
suppliers and materials to the fullest extent possible in the publishing
of its books. Such materials include vegetable-based, low-VOC inks
and acid-free papers that are recycled, totally chlorine-free, or partly
composed of nonwood fibers. For further information, visit our website
at www.cornellpress.cornell.edu.

Cloth printing   10 9 8 7 6 5 4 3 2 1

"*What to that redoubted harpooner, John Bull, is poor Ireland, but a Fast-Fish? What to that apostolic lancer, Brother Jonathan, is Texas but a Fast-Fish? And concerning all these, is not Possession the whole of the law?*"

—Herman Melville, *Moby Dick* (1851)

Contents

Acknowledgments   ix

Introduction: An Atlantic Triangle   1

1. Challenging the Union: American Repeal and U.S. Diplomacy   11
2. Ireland Is No Longer a Nation: The Irish Famine
   and American Diplomacy   39
3. Filibusters and Fenians: Contesting Neutrality   69
4. The Fenian Brotherhood, Naturalization, and Expatriation: Irish
   Americans and Anglo-American Comity   97
5. Toward Home Rule: From the Fenians to Parnell's Ascendancy   129
6. A Search for Order: The Decline of the Irish Question
   in American Diplomacy   153

Epilogue: Rapprochement, Paris, and a Free State   175

Notes   187
Bibliography   243
Index   259

Acknowledgments

This book owes much to the patience, generosity, and insight of many people. In particular, I'd like to thank Jay Sexton for his assistance and sagacity throughout the project's progress. Despite inflicting much impenetrable prose and numerous bewildering arguments on him over the years, he agreed to act as my supervisor and has been unfailingly supportive. Special thanks also go to Donald Ratcliffe, Gareth Davies, Stephen Tuck, Martin Crawford, Adam Smith, David Gleeson, Eric Rauchway, Kevin Kenny, Peter Onuf, Lizabeth Cohen, and Richard Carwardine for innumerable conversations, book recommendations, and scholarly advice. Ian Tyrrell, Frank Brinkley, Daniel Peart, and Steve Tuffnell all read drafts of sections of the manuscript (the more masochistic read a whole draft), and I thank them for their suggestions. I'd also like to thank Michael McGandy, Sarah Grossman, David Engerman, Kate Babbitt, and the anonymous readers at Cornell University Press for their help. Their comments improved the book immeasurably.

I've also benefited from feedback and questions received at various seminars and conferences, particularly those held by the Rothermere American Institute, the Institute of Historical Research, the Society for Historians of the Early American Republic, and, of course, the Association of British

American Nineteenth Century Historians, which unfailingly puts on the best conference of the year.

Gratitude is also due to Nigel Bowles, Jane Rawson, Judy Warden, and all at the Rothermere American Institute for their support and assistance over the years. The conviviality and friendship of Seb Page, Ed Adkins, Huw David, Jon Sudbury, Mandy Izadi, and the rest of the Institute's group of graduate students did much to mitigate the isolation that can characterize graduate study. Seb, in particular, has had to put up with me for years. He was there when I started out on this project, and he provided valuable material at its end. I believe I owe him a drink or two.

Parts of chapter 3 originally appeared as "Filibusters, Fenians, and a Contested Neutrality: The Irish Question and U.S. Diplomacy, 1848–1871," published in *American Nineteenth Century History* in December 2011. My thanks to Bruce Baker for permission to reproduce that material.

For their financial assistance, I thank Corpus Christi College, Oxford; the Association of British American Nineteenth Century Historians' Peter J. Parish Memorial Fund; and the Gilder Lehrman Institute of American History. In addition, the Rothermere American Institute provided invaluable funds in the form of a one-year doctoral fellowship. A teaching post at Pembroke College gave me the time and space to complete my research, and special mention should go to Adrian Gregory, Gemma Allen, Mike Finch, and Peter Claus for making what could have been a hard slog a real pleasure. Phill, Jonny, Frank, Nils, and Juliet provided friendship, perspective, new records, coffee, and books that weren't about history. Crucially, none of these involved being in the archives. I can hardly thank them enough. Special thanks also to John Duddy, Juliet Grames, Anna Sproul, and Katie and Mike Marino for putting me up during my research trips.

I thank John, Ann, and Katherine Duddy for their generosity and support, and, of course, I thank my wife, Claire. Not only did she make valuable suggestions after reading the manuscript from start to finish, but her love, patience, and encouragement have been unstinting. I'd imagine that she now knows far more about nineteenth-century American diplomacy than she ever wanted to, for which I can only apologize. Finally, I'd like to express my gratitude to my grandmother, Mair, and to my parents, Janice and Ian. Their continuing love and support have underwritten everything I've done.

A UNION FOREVER

Introduction

An Atlantic Triangle

In the autumn of 1851, shiploads of Irish migrants disembarked on New York's quays with every tide, attracting the curiosity—and sometimes the antipathy—of the city's citizens. As the gravity of the Irish famine became apparent to U.S. audiences in late 1846, a slew of articles, lectures, and publications sought to diagnose Ireland's ills and explain the avalanche of displaced people arriving in the United States. One of the city's newest journals, the *New-York Daily Times*, reprinted an article from a Washington, D.C., newspaper that noted that

> among the subjects which momentarily rise to excite the interest of mankind, perhaps there is not one other combining so much to awaken or exercise reflection as the great Western Island of Europe. . . . With all its claims to attention, there are few parts of Europe . . . less known than Ireland, in proportion to its intrinsic importance and relative position.[1]

The *Times* article had been prompted by a visit to Ireland made by the U.S. minister to London, Abbott Lawrence. As a Whig from Massachusetts who was keen to promote transatlantic trade, Lawrence reflected the newspaper's conviction that "giving efficacy to the natural resources yet dormant in Ireland" would be important to the commerce and politics of the United States.[2] In terms of both migration and commercial potential, Ireland occupied an important place in the thoughts of American statesmen and newspapermen. It also occupied the minds of American citizens who were troubled by British rule in Ireland, deeming it an affront to republicanism and a black mark against Britain's supposedly liberal constitution. On the same day that the *Times* reprinted the article testifying to the perplexing hold that Ireland exercised on the American mind, it also reported a meeting held in Philadelphia "in favor of [William] Smith O'Brien, and the other Irish exiles" who had been banished to Britain's antipodean colonies for their role in the abortive 1848 Irish uprising.[3] Some Americans were clearly most sympathetic to the aspirations of Irish separatists.

This book investigates the implications of this sympathy and asks how Irish and Irish American nationalists attempted to make use of it to recast the United States' relationship with Great Britain. No sovereign Irish nation emerged as a consequence of their efforts. In fact, Irish American agency had the paradoxical effect of breeding closer Anglo-American relations over the long term. Nonetheless, the manner and consequences of their failures are worthy of scrutiny. First, they illustrate the openness of U.S. foreign policy to the influence of nonstate actors, particularly in the middle decades of the nineteenth century, when Anglo-American tensions made collusion with Irish nationalism an attractive proposition. Second, the changing place of Irish nationalism in U.S. political and diplomatic thought highlights a fundamental ambivalence about the prospect of other peoples emulating the U.S. model of republican revolution. Americans in the nineteenth century often talked confidently (if blandly) about the international spread of republican virtue, but in practice such views were heavily qualified by religion and ethnicity. Finally, this book details the process by which British and American statesmen built stronger transatlantic ties through the marginalization of revolutionary Irish nationalism. By 1890, when this study concludes, the dream of annexing American power to Irish goals seemed fanciful. The final achievement of an independent Irish state in the 1920s owed little to any innate American sympathy with Irish republicanism and rather more to the immediate context of the world made (or unmade) by the Great War.

Though we have a number of exceptional studies of Irish America, we have few that seriously historicize Irish nationalism and its complex connections with the American Union over the long nineteenth century.[4] This is surprising. Contemporaries appreciated that neither the American Union nor the Anglo-Irish union were stable entities whose futures could be taken for granted, and they thought about both deeply, often in connection with one other. This book captures this uncertainty by offering a synthesis of a transnational, bottom-up approach to Irish American nationalism with attention to the words, intentions, and actions of elite statesmen. This uncertainty has to be central to our understanding of Irish nationalism and U.S. diplomacy and to our study of the nineteenth-century United States more generally.

The Irish Question and the Early Republic

Throughout the early nineteenth century, Americans of a variety of political persuasions expressed faith in a progressive interpretation of history. They believed that liberty would gradually spread around the globe and that Ireland would eventually achieve some form of national independence. There were a number of reasons why nineteenth-century Americans might have been persuaded by this. One was that proponents of Irish self-governance could point to the prior existence of an Irish Parliament that had been bribed out of existence at the turn of the nineteenth century under a fraudulent Act of Union.[5] Another was that they could identify such widely known figures as Edmund Burke and Henry Grattan to support the contention that Ireland produced statesmen of substance who might populate another Irish Parliament to good effect.

In addition, observers of Anglo-Irish relations drew on Revolutionary-era connections between Ireland and colonial America to suggest a deep-rooted affinity between two provinces subject to the dictates of the London metropole.[6] These connections were more than sentimental but were certainly drawn a little crudely. American-Irish affinity owed much to Irish resolutions in support of American grievances during the 1770s. After the outbreak of hostilities in the spring of 1775, the Continental Congress sent an address to the people of Ireland detailing the perfidy of the British ministry and expressing hopes for Ireland's "friendly disposition."[7] Colonial leaders viewed events in Ireland through the lens of their own Revolution. For instance, in Irish attempts to assert legislative independence John Adams saw the "foundations of another Revolution, [which] will effect a total Independence of Ireland on England."[8] If the British failed to adopt ameliorative measures, he suggested, "Congress may have an Ambassador at the Court or Congress of Ireland, in a very short Time."[9]

No revolution followed. However, members of the Society of United Irishmen, exiled to the United States after the failure of their 1798 uprising, perpetuated the hope that the Irish political nation would emulate the success of the American Revolution. The elite among them—Protestant and professional—integrated (albeit with some friction) into the new nation's politics, and historians are increasingly coming to investigate their contribution to political culture, to the new republic's Anglophobia, and to the increasingly abrasive political competition between Federalists and Republicans at the turn of the nineteenth century.[10] These immigrant United Irishmen, groused one Federalist, were by and large "the most God-provoking Democrats on this side of Hell."[11] It did not follow, however, that American interest in Irish affairs was wholly a partisan matter. In the 1820s, when the dominant figure in Irish politics, Daniel O'Connell, campaigned successfully for Catholic rights within the United Kingdom, his efforts attracted attention across the political spectrum.[12] Numerous "Friends of Ireland" societies throughout the United States forwarded funds and passed resolutions of support for the O'Connellite movement, and they celebrated the success of the cause in the spring of 1829.

From the 1840s onward, a group of young urban nationalists under the banner of "Young Ireland" consciously added another layer of association with the United States. Focusing their energies on Ireland's cultural and political resurrection, they were increasingly disillusioned with what they perceived as the impotent parliamentarianism and overbearing Catholicism of Daniel O'Connell, and they looked to the United States for a model of nonsectarian self-governance that might be translated for Irish conditions.[13] Cheering U.S. territorial aggrandizement at the expense of Great Britain and unperturbed by the spread of chattel slavery in the American southwest, "Young Irelanders" sought to emancipate the transatlantic image of Ireland from the celebrated abolitionism of O'Connell.[14] Their faith in the cohering power of national culture and their opposition to British rule attracted U.S. intellectuals, journalists, and artists who, like their Irish counterparts, resented what they interpreted as the continued dependence on Britain for cultural affirmation.[15] And this "Young America," like Young Ireland, emerged at a time when Anglo-American tensions were growing more acute.

American interest in the political status of Ireland inevitably entailed an engagement with British constitutional and imperial politics. Historians are increasingly attentive to the continued deep cultural, material and political entanglement of the United States with British imperialism after 1783 and to the impact that this had on the new nation's foreign policy. Britain's abolition of slavery throughout the empire in 1834 injected new anxieties into Anglo-American relations, as American slaveholders and their allies contemplated the implications of an antislavery British foreign policy. This study of the Irish question and U.S. statecraft begins with the resulting competition between a slaveholding republic and an abolitionist empire as context.

Ireland occupied an ambiguous place in Americans' thoughts about global politics. Perceived to be neither wholly of the Old or New Worlds—a potential wedge for republican revolution in Europe yet apparently desperately poor, Catholic, and hopelessly dependent upon British power—Ireland offered both a damning indictment of British governance and hope for future reform. Identifiably a "nation" in cultural and historic terms but lacking statehood, riven by sectarian tensions, and characterized by diasporic diffusion, Ireland captured American attention but confounded easy classification.

Historians of U.S. foreign relations have generally paid little attention to the political salience of the Irish question as a destabilizing factor in Anglo-American diplomacy. Where they *do* identify Irish nationalist sentiment as an influence on American statecraft, they present it in unchanging, ahistorical terms. In other words, they replicate those nationalist, anti-British pieties that have been so ably contextualized and challenged by historians of modern Ireland over the past quarter-century.[16] In doing so, they miss an important story. Through the antebellum, Civil War, and Reconstruction years, Irish nationalists used the United States as a base from which to contest Ireland's partnership in the Anglo-Irish Union. And more than this, many hoped to connect their own aspirations for an independent, republican Ireland with the growing power of the American republic. However, efforts designed to bring on a confrontation between the United States and Great Britain had unintended consequences and made Irish American nationalists ironic agents of Anglo-American conciliation in the final third of the nineteenth century. In response to insurgent Irish nationalism, British and American statesmen worked to address contentious questions regarding citizenship, neutrality, and extradition and to craft a new Anglo-American order.

The Irish Question and Transnationalism

In late June 1842, the Whig governor of New York, William Henry Seward, wrote to William Stokes, a representative of Philadelphia's Friends of

Ireland, informing him that he would be unable to accept an invitation to speak at their Fourth of July celebrations. Though he was unable to attend, Seward acknowledged that the invitation was "very gratifying."[17] "You shew me so much kindness as to acknowledge me as one of the fast friends of Ireland[']s freedom," Seward wrote.[18] "So indeed I desire to be and I mourn that a country so eminent for genius and heroism should find need in this enlightened age for sympathy so humble as mine."[19] Seward then reconsidered his language, crossing out "country" and inserting the word "people." Perhaps this signified nothing more than an able politician tightening his prose. More likely, the choice of "people" over "country," and "a people" over "people," indicated his appreciation of diasporic realities. Attuned to the changing demographics of the largest U.S. city, Seward's language of peoplehood allowed him to connect Irish constitutional politics and the battle against proscriptive anti-Catholicism.[20]

Nineteenth-century Irish American nationalism was inescapably transnational. Yet there were tensions implicit in building and maintaining Irish nationalist movements across national borders, and Ireland-based nationalists sporadically felt resentment at perceived American dictation. Specifically, members of the Irish Republican Brotherhood (IRB), Ireland's revolutionary directory, were prone to feel themselves the victims of a kind of economic imperialism: those in the United States were the principal suppliers of funds for agitation, and as such, they felt that they should have a correspondingly significant say in the direction of Irish activities.[21] At the very least, the U.S.-based nationalists of the Fenian Brotherhood and, later, Clan na Gael acted with considerable autonomy—their chagrined IRB counterparts might say with considerable recklessness—in formulating plans for an Irish uprising.[22]

This study's approach demands consideration of the Roman Catholic Church—another transnational enterprise with claims upon migrant Irishmen and women—and the antipathetic reactions that it generated among Americans concerned about immigrants' fitness for republican citizenship. Central to this book are changes in how Americans thought about the global meaning of their revolution and its applicability to other peoples. Americans' doubts about Catholics' capacity for republican self-governance were as old as the United States itself, but during this period these doubts competed with a faith in the universal applicability of republican rule. Of course, "Irish" and "Catholic" were not synonyms throughout. As David Noel Doyle notes, it was as a consequence of the overwhelmingly Catholic famine exodus that Americans generally came to think of Ireland and the Irish as essentially Catholic.[23] Further complicating matters is the gap between the Catholicism casually associated with Irish aspirations to self-governance and the often anticlerical stance of Irish American nationalists who rejected "priests in politics."[24] Paradoxically, though these nationalists generated much opposition from the Catholic hierarchy in Ireland, they were themselves not immune to nativist and anti-Catholic suspicions in the United States.

Finally, a transnational approach can help us see more clearly the seemingly hegemonic power of American nationalism. Historians generally have been attentive to how appeals to national tradition have been used to mute challenges to power on the grounds of race, gender, and class, but American nationalism also had the capacity to subsume competing nationalisms. Time and again, Irish American nationalists saw allying their cause with American power as necessary if they were to achieve their ends. This asymmetric relationship strengthened Irish nationalism where the two were aligned but left it vulnerable when U.S. statesmen reassessed their interests in light of the compelling bonds of Anglo-American cultural and commercial exchange.

The Irish Question and U.S. Diplomacy

An investigation of the relationship between Irish nationalism and U.S. diplomacy over the half-century following 1840 allows us to see changes in how American statesmen conceptualized their nation—and their nation's republicanism—in relation to the wider world. In the 1840s, Daniel O'Connell's transnational campaign to repeal the Anglo-Irish Union, the subject of the first chapter, elicited broad enthusiasm and paeans to Ireland's contribution to the American Revolution, and this romantic rhetoric of revolutionary sympathy continued to frame American conceptions of the Irish question throughout the century.

This identification with aspirations to republican self-determination was qualified by skepticism about the viability of any Irish republican project, particularly in the aftermath of the disastrous 1848 uprising in Ireland. It also competed with an emergent sense of Anglo-Saxon kinship, fueled in the late 1840s by novel racial theorizing and a sense of Anglo-American liberal exceptionalism. As chapter 2 discusses, these ideas found expression in the provision of charity for the Crown's subjects in Ireland, who were suffering under the fearful weight of the Great Famine.

Though the mass migration that followed the famine was channeled by the preexisting structures of Irish America, the horror of those years and the exile of Young Ireland ideologues after the failed 1848 uprising nurtured a reformulation of Irish nationalism in the United States. This reformulation ushered in a distinct period in the U.S.-Irish connection that lasted from the late 1840s to the early 1870s. Anglo-American tensions meant that the newly aggressive assertion of Irish separatist sentiment found, on occasion, a most sympathetic audience. Prior to the American Civil War, fears about British abolitionist imperialism and the fragility of the American Union meant that Irish nationalists were valued fellow travelers. From the end of the conflict until the 1871 Treaty of Washington, strategic sympathy helped sustain a myth of general U.S. support for Irish efforts against British authority. Such sympathy inspired the Irish Republican Brotherhood and its U.S. corollary, the Fenian Brotherhood. Chapter 3 investigates Irish separatists' attempts to exploit U.S. neutrality legislation to plan a militant insurgency in Ireland in the 1850s and 1860s. Chapter 4 details an attempt to drive the United States and Great Britain apart by engineering a controversy over citizenship and expatriation.

The uses that American statesmen might make of Irish nationalism narrowed during the post–Civil War years. The conclusion of agreements on, first, the status of naturalized Irish Americans and, second, the definition of neutrality in international law shrank the political space in which Irish American nationalists could act. The grounding of Anglo-American peace on a firmer basis in the 1870s proved a profound disappointment to Irish American nationalists. Conversely, with these sources of transatlantic contention resolved, American statesmen had little incentive to dance with Irish nationalism. As the penultimate chapter suggests, those in the United States who sympathized with Irish home rule increasingly used southern reconciliation within the Union as a lesson in the virtues of a federal salve for separatist tendencies.

The failures of the Fenian Brotherhood, capped by a discreditable raid on British North America in 1870, appeared to confirm that Irish separatism was a doomed enterprise. Both British and American statesmen saw value in marginalizing factious transnational nationalism as a disruptive element in the Atlantic world. In the decades following the Civil War a growing community of transatlantic liberals espoused a discourse of civilization in which the United States and Great Britain were united by a commitment to progressive, liberal governance. For these ideologues, the Irish question was increasingly viewed as a troublesome impediment to greater

Anglo-American harmony rather than through the prism of the global application of republican values. As the final chapter suggests, these views were strengthened by the campaign of dynamite terrorism conducted against British cities by Irish American nationalists in the 1880s. Irish nationalists had not only failed in their objectives, they had also provided an incentive for liberal statesmen to address areas of continuing tension and to build an international legal structure that would contain violent transatlantic nationalists. Ultimately, Irish American nationalists found their ability to insert themselves into Anglo-American relations curtailed: by the end of the 1880s it was clear that the influence of Irish nationalism on U.S. diplomacy had decreased markedly since the Civil War. It was now a domestic political factor to be weighed rather than a potential lever for international confrontation.

In terms of domestic partisanship, one might expect Ireland and the Irish question to be an issue of concern for Democrats and rather less so for Whigs and Republicans. The former were closely associated with Irish voters, not least because the latter parties carried the taint of nativism.[25] Yet a striking feature of American conceptions of Ireland during the nineteenth century is the extent to which Whigs and, later, Republicans thought seriously about the Irish question. This was partly a function of oppositional politics, but there was also something more substantive to Whig-Republican interpretations. Both were committed to freeing the United States from what they saw as its commercial dependency on Great Britain, and to this end, both promoted the "American system," an interlocking cluster of economic policies including the development of internal communications, a protective tariff for domestic industries, and the cultivation of a market for domestically produced goods.[26] Henry Carey, the great economic theorist of American Whiggery, repeatedly invoked the condition of Ireland to demonstrate the unedifying consequences of British economic hegemony.[27] Britain "fastened upon Ireland, by coercion, the same system which it seeks to fasten upon us by coaxing," he argued.[28] Democrats, by promoting free trade, promoted "the British system," while Whigs worked to maintain "the American protective policy, the same policy precisely as Ireland maintained so long as it had the power."[29] The implications for American voters were clear, and it was a theme to which Whigs and Republicans would return throughout the period. Though both parties engaged with the Irish question unevenly at different times and in different contexts, it is important to emphasize that the Democratic Party had no monopoly on pro-Irish sentiment or on anti-British rhetoric and policy.

Finally, the American profiles of the two figures who bookend this study—Daniel O'Connell and Charles Stewart Parnell—tell us much about the way that nineteenth-century Americans thought about nationhood. In his eulogy on the death of O'Connell, William Seward spoke of "the Man who for a time becomes substituted for a Nation, is clothed in our regard with the national attributes.... DANIEL O'CONNELL was the imperson-ation of [the Irish] people, 'A Nation in a Man compris'd.' In this consists the secret of the interest he excited while living, and his fame now that he lives no more."[30] O'Connell and Parnell's celebrity tells us something significant about the popular method of conceptualizing nationhood in a liberal Atlantic world that venerated Garibaldi, Kossuth, Bismarck, Glad-stone, and other "representative men" as nation-builders on the progressive edge of history.[31] Their elevated status, however, can obscure the activities of a multitude of other Irish and Irish American nationalists who sought, in various ways, to exploit the foreign policy of the United States to secure an Ireland free of British rule.

Our transatlantic protagonists—Irish American nationalists—were not the dupes of scheming politicians. They comprised organized and moti-vated groups that sought to manipulate the foreign policy of the United States for their own ends. At the same time, American statesmen sought to manipulate the Irish question—the governance of the island of Ireland—to further their own diplomatic goals. The attractiveness of this mutual con-nivance was as much a function of the state of Anglo-American relations as it was of the strength and vibrancy of separatist politics in Ireland and Irish America. This was as true at the end of the century as it was in the 1840s, when Daniel O'Connell set about building a transatlantic movement in support of a renegotiated Anglo-Irish relationship.

Chapter 1

Challenging the Union

American Repeal and U.S. Diplomacy

In the 1840s, Daniel O'Connell headed a transatlantic campaign for the repeal of the Act of Union between Britain and Ireland. That campaign received significant American support and had an important impact on U.S. domestic politics in the early years of the decade. Mutual suspicion shaped Anglo-American relations, a result of a series of geopolitical confrontations, not least concerning the United States' annexation of the Republic of Texas. British statesmen were alarmed by what they perceived as the unnecessarily aggressive expansionism of the United States, and many Americans feared that British foreign policy was driven by antislavery zealots who wished to see the end of the peculiar institution in the United States. In this interpretation of global competition, Britain, jealous of the threat to her own power that the United States represented, sought to promote abolition as a means of fracturing the American Union. Even those who did not subscribe to this reading of Anglo-American competition framed their interpretations of Irish agitation with the conflict between an abolitionist empire and a slaveholding republic in mind. For the more cynical, Britain's efforts to promote American disunion might be met by stirring disunion in her own backyard via the Irish question.

How did this transatlantic competition complicate Irish American politics? Historians have rightly focused on the entangled stories of Irish politics and transatlantic abolitionism, though in explaining the ultimate collapse of the repeal movement they have generally placed too much emphasis on Daniel O'Connell's antislavery politics and too little on his professions of loyalty to the British throne. Through 1843 and 1844, reports from England suggested to U.S. statesmen that Irish discontent limited British freedom of action. At the same time, the prospect of further Anglo-American tension—perhaps even conflict—encouraged many proponents of repeal to dwell on the benefits that might accrue to Ireland. Yet Daniel O'Connell's apparent emergence as an agent of British abolitionist imperialism in the New World undermined this possibility and embarrassed his followers in both the United States and Ireland, shattering the transnational network.

Despite this eventual foundering, repeal agitation was a significant feature of the American political landscape during the mid-1840s. Indeed, we cannot fully understand Anglo-American relations without it. Although Irish independence was never an official desideratum of U.S. foreign policy, the repeal movement spoke to important continuing debates about transatlantic abolition, American disunionism, and the threat of British imperial power.

Daniel O'Connell and the Progress of the Repeal Movement

In the decade after Catholic emancipation, Daniel O'Connell spent much of his parliamentary career acting in loose concert with the British Whigs. Though pressed by others to bring forward a motion for a repeal of the Act of Union in 1834, he was generally reluctant to push the issue of Irish home rule because of the benefits that flowed from continued Whig governance. More responsive to Irish grievances than their Tory counterparts, Whigs, particularly under Prime Minister Melbourne, opened up increasing numbers of Irish offices to Catholics and turned to O'Connell and his followers for advice on legislation and appointments.[1] However, with the Tories appearing likely to return to power in 1840, O'Connell again took up the question of repeal.[2]

The first branch of the Loyal National Repeal Association (LNRA)—its name a testament to constitutional ambiguities—was established by O'Connell and his followers in Dublin in August 1840. They placed great faith in the power of moral suasion and employed the tactics that had proved successful in effecting Catholic emancipation in the 1820s. Repealers sought to build a cohesive, self-disciplined body that would present the Irish people's demand for self-governance to the British Parliament. Local associations corresponded with the central organization in Dublin, forwarding accounts of activities and (most important) funds to sustain the agitation. Associations held public demonstrations and parades to generate and sustain mass interest and to present British authorities with the spectacle of organized national sentiment. As with later formulations of Irish home rule, "repeal" was left a protean term. It could, in theory, capture the aspirations of a coalition of nationalists—moderate and advanced, Catholic and Protestant—and both critics and supporters of Ireland's socioeconomic order. Broad in audience, it was also ambiguous in aspiration: the cry of "repeal" represented as much "an invitation to treat" extended to the British government as it did a specific program of demands.[3] In its capaciousness, O'Connell aimed to project the image of a truly national movement whose moderation, legality, and moral force would influence public opinion both in Britain and internationally.[4]

By 1843, the repeal campaign had brought significant pressure to bear on the ministry of Robert Peel, who came to power when Melbourne resigned in August 1841. A series of "monster" meetings in the summer of 1843 was due to culminate with a gathering at Clontarf, County Dublin, but at the eleventh hour, the meeting was proscribed by the British government. Even though they bowed to the demands of the authorities, O'Connell and a number of other repealers were arrested on a charge of conspiracy and in May 1844 were sentenced to a year's imprisonment. Though the repeal campaign was renewed after their convictions were quashed that September, it was not pursued with the same verve. O'Connell's age (he was in his late 60s), his lack of assertiveness, and his willingness to resume alliance with the British Whigs troubled younger, more assertive nationalists. These nationalists took the sobriquet "Young Ireland" in sympathy with other romantic nationalist movements emerging across Europe and the United States. They were disillusioned by O'Connell's loyalism and his absolute repudiation of violence; they saw his pacific parliamentarianism as fruitless and, by extension, degrading to Irish manhood. Their defection to a new, more radical organization, the Irish Confederation, in January 1847; the devastation of the Irish famine; and O'Connell's death in May of the same year brought to a close this period of high-profile constitutional agitation.

The repeal campaign captured considerable attention in the United States, particularly from 1843 to 1845. Again, seeking to replicate the successes of the Catholic emancipation campaign, O'Connell and his supporters looked to the United States to provide both moral and financial support, supplementing and supporting the agitation in Ireland and Britain. They established a transnational "greater Ireland" network in which each provincial corresponding association was held in the same relationship to the central association in Dublin.[5] This network, which elided distinctions between Charleston, London, New York, Manchester, and Cork, did not last beyond the repeal campaign itself, but during its brief existence it allowed the demonstration of significant American support for Irish self-government.[6]

What is perhaps most surprising about this support is its robustness in the face of O'Connell's continued public expressions of antislavery sentiment. His abolitionism was no secret in 1840, and he had long argued that antipathy to slavery was an integral part of Irish national identity.[7] Indeed, American audiences were particularly well acquainted with O'Connell's distaste for the company of slaveowners. In 1838, he had engaged in a very heated and very public exchange with the U.S. minister to London, a Virginian planter named Andrew Stevenson, during which he accused Stevenson of being a slave-breeder and thus beneath "the civilized inhabitants of Europe."[8] In short, O'Connell was no enigma when it came to the question of slavery, yet American enthusiasm for the repeal campaign was undimmed.

Though neglected by most historians of antebellum politics, the movement for Irish repeal became something of a cause célèbre in the United States during the 1840s. Testifying to its prominence, during the summer months of 1843, 27-year-old Gansevoort Melville, an aspiring Democratic politician (and the elder brother of a peripatetic seaman, Herman) decided that championing the cause of Irish repeal was an excellent way to embark upon a career in American public life. Gansevoort would have had no special reason to take an interest in Ireland—indeed, his uncle warned him against "unseemly meddling with the Papists"—but, distressed by the sight of poor Irish immigrants arriving at the docks of New York, he threw himself into the burgeoning repeal movement.[9] Speaking at rallies in and around New York City, he helped raise funds and maintain the cause in the public eye. Melville earned himself a reputation as a strong speaker and a popular advocate for the repeal of the Union.[10] And young Gansevoort was no eccentric in attaching himself to the movement for Irish home rule. By the summer of 1843, there was an extensive and active network of repeal associations throughout the United States.

The development of a network of repeal associations in the United States was more or less coincident with events in Ireland. The first associations formed under American initiative were those of Boston, in October 1840, and Philadelphia and New York, both in December of the same year.[11] Branches in Savannah, Albany, Natchez, St. Louis, Baltimore, Charleston, New Orleans, Cincinnati, and other U.S. towns and cities followed.[12] Remittances were welcomed from these autonomous American associations, though members of American branches could not become full members of the LNRA. In Dublin, remittances from within the British Empire were recorded in one accounting book and those from the United States in another. As Daniel O'Connell's son, John, noted, repealers were "deeply grateful . . . for [Americans'] generous assistance [but] it was impossible for them to enrol as members any natives of a foreign country."[13] This was an implicit statement of imperial loyalty and, we can assume, was intended to deflect accusations of unwanted American influence in the constitutional politics of Great Britain and Ireland.

Historians have debated the composition of the American repeal associations. Thomas Mooney, a contemporary correspondent of Ireland's leading nationalist newspaper, the Dublin *Nation*, commented that rather than drawing on long-established populations of Irish migrants, the impetus for American repeal organizations was strongest among "as yet but infantine" communities of workingmen and small businessmen.[14] He suggested that recently "denationalized" Irish, "scattered abroad as exiles," constituted a large mass of attendees at repeal meetings, implying that the political education they had received during the agitation for Catholic emancipation cast a shadow in the United States.[15] In reality, we simply don't know the migration histories of men and women who attended repeal meetings. In terms of class composition, a rough survey of the *Nation's* coverage of American LNRA meetings suggests that the various associations were relatively heterogeneous, attracting lawyers, newspaper editors, shopkeepers, artisans, and workingmen.[16] The most recent historian of the American repeal movement suggests that it drew support from a representative cross-section of Irish-America.[17]

Though the amounts collected at repeal meetings were in the words of one historian "unimpressive [and] meager" compared with the later Parnellite organizations in the United States, they are significant in highlighting the ease with which an ostensibly national campaign could be successfully extended from a central metropolis—in this case, Dublin—to a loosely federated periphery—the urban centers of the United States.[18] Given Irish immigrants' reflexive hostility to the nativist undertones of many evangelically inspired reform crusades, it was a touch ironic that, as one historian of American nativism notes, the repeal associations exhibited much of the "raucous emotionalism of . . . Protestant revivals."[19] Though repealers were somewhat less likely to be fired by the evangelical zeal of the Second Great Awakening, there were undoubted parallels between the transnationalism of the repeal movement and that of other reform interests in the early Victorian Atlantic world.

With O'Connell's announcement that 1843 would be "Repeal year," American interest surged.[20] Aspirations to Irish home rule carried great currency in the United States because they resonated with certain elements of U.S. political culture. There was an assumed historical and ideological sympathy between the United States and Ireland, built of strident allusions to Irish service during the Revolution, the sympathetic Revolutionary-era oratory of Edmund Burke, and Ireland's "strong claim" on American aid in her own anti-imperial struggle.[21] In addition, upheavals in the Irish economy precipitated by the end of the Napoleonic Wars brought greatly increased migration from Ireland to the United States. In the three decades after 1815, between 800,000 and 1,000,000 Irish emigrants left for North America, and the majority went to the United States.[22] As Kerby Miller has argued, many of these immigrants interpreted their movement in the language of exile, and the circulation of these ideas in the United States reinforced convictions about the destructive consequences of British imperialism.[23] Finally, reflexive rhetorical Anglophobia came easily to many U.S. statesmen, particularly those of a Democratic persuasion, and championing the cause of Irish nationalism—constitutional or otherwise—was a low-risk means of demonstrating one's patriotic and anti-British credentials.[24]

In the early 1840s, the importance of this rhetorical stance was amplified by three contingent factors: first, the impassioned debate over the republic's foreign policy and, by extension, the question of British influence on the North American continent; second, the impending presidential election of 1844; and third, President John Tyler's related attempt to build a political coalition independent of the Democratic and Whig party machines.

In the early 1840s, President Tyler's administration became increasingly concerned about British designs in the newly independent Republic of Texas. In 1841, Tyler sent Duff Green (a supporter of South Carolina senator John Calhoun's presidential ambitions) as an unofficial agent to England with instructions to report on Britain's intentions in the American southwest, among other things. Christened the "ambassador of slavery" by John Quincy Adams, Green suggested that Lord Aberdeen, the British foreign secretary, sought to spread abolition to Texas.[25] A free-labor, cotton-producing Texas, feared Green, would compete economically with the American South and might prove a haven for runaway slaves.

Moreover, the perception that Britain's experiment with Caribbean emancipation had proved a disaster heightened fears that Britain had a strong economic interest in undermining slavery in the United States.[26] These concerns made their way into formal diplomatic correspondence as Tyler's administration became increasingly beholden to the anxieties of southerners over the future of slavery, which was threatened both by abolitionists at home—supposedly encouraged by their British counterparts—and by apparent antislavery imperialism abroad. In September 1843, Abel P. Uphsur, Tyler's secretary of state, wrote a remarkably agitated dispatch to the U.S. minister in London, Edward Everett, detailing his belief that "the abolition of domestic slavery throughout the continent & islands of America, is a leading object of present policy in England."[27] Recent scholars have stressed the sincerity of these fears, though not their accuracy: historians have discerned no serious British plan to take a stand on Texas annexation. Certainly heightened tensions created a climate in which a robust expression of U.S. strength in opposition to the antislavery machinations of Great Britain dovetailed neatly with support for Irish repeal. As one leading repealer argued in September 1843, support for Ireland's attempts to end her unjust Union with Britain was justified by Britain's "constant efforts to disrupt our Union ... [and] to *diplomatize* the dissolution of the American Confederacy" over the issue of slavery.[28] He continued:

> If it be right for English philanthropists ... to interfere with the peculiar institutions of the Southern States, it cannot be wrong in an American philanthropist to advocate the cause of the Irish people.[29]

No statesmen seriously considered committing the United States to intervention—diplomatic or otherwise—on behalf of Ireland, yet plenty of politicians were keen to make their sympathies with repeal publicly known. In 1844, the unremitting cycle of U.S. elections was coupled with intraparty factionalism. The untimely death of William Henry Harrison just one month after his 1841 inauguration brought John Tyler to the White House. Tyler alienated many Whig Party grandees through his determined adherence to a strict reading of the Constitution and his opposition to Henry Clay's "American System" of a national bank, internal improvements, and the disbursement of funds from the sale of Western lands.[30] Simultaneously, his apostasy from the Democratic Party (he was the only senator to vote against Andrew Jackson's 1833 Force Bill) left him with few political options. Unable to secure his position at the head of one party and persona non grata in the eyes of the other, he sought to establish a new machine to support his ambitions for the presidency in 1844.

Not coincidentally, John Tyler's son, Robert Tyler, had positioned himself as a pivotal figure in the Philadelphia repeal movement. A powerful and popular speaker, the younger Tyler was a regular feature at the city's repeal meetings and in September 1843 was elected president of the National Repeal Convention, held in New York.[31] He spoke of the "wonderful contrast" between the "wise and constitutional arrangements" of the "[American] Union," with the "anomalous Union of force" perpetrated by Great Britain, "extorted by the dagger and the rack, or purchased by . . . bribery."[32] The Tylers, historian David Noel Doyle has argued, were "a power in search of a constituency," and, like Gansevoort Melville, Robert Tyler calculated that Irish repeal was an issue to be associated with: it was intimately bound up with the extension of liberal rights and national self-definition—all, importantly, in opposition to British power.[33] Tyler had an appetite for the sentimental that he indulged to good effect in front of enthusiastic repeal crowds:

> [There is] a bond of sympathy . . . stretching across the Atlantic from our own beloved land to the far-off shores of the Emerald Isle. . . . The fervent hopes . . . of Irish hearts ascended to Heaven during the darkest day of our political history; the patriotic judgments of Irish minds are incorporated in the sacred frame-work of our Republican institutions; and many an Irish soul has breathed its last sigh upon the encrimsoned battle-field in defense of our country's rights.[34]

Robert Tyler's long and peculiar career in American Irish nationalism began with this involvement in the repeal movement. As will be seen, he involved himself in increasingly radical attempts to secure Irish independence before the Civil War, belying the cynicism attributed him by Doyle. However, his connection with Irish American politics in the early 1840s was more ambivalent. Diarist Sidney George Fisher recorded attending a dinner party with Tyler in June 1844. After eating, Tyler

made a set speech, quite a harangue . . . in which liberty, slavery, Irish repeal, the feudal system, the reformation, English ambition and American
interests, the Texas question & the Democratic Party were strangely min-
gled. . . . He declared to us openly that he did not care for the Irish, that his
object was not their benefit but the injury of England . . . the dismember-
ment of the British Empire, because he thought it was both the interest &
intention of England to injure America, to agitate the slave question here.[35]

This manipulation of the Irish question for diplomatic advantage was not
unique to the Tylers, as Fisher lamented: "Unhappily these are the opinions
of a large & powerful party in this country, whose efforts to get up a war
feeling are constant, and whose topics are English encroachment [and] English influence."[36]

President Tyler did not involve himself in the repeal movement as directly as his son, but he made it known that he was "no half-way man"
on repeal but was rather its "decided friend."[37] In addition, he attended a
major repeal event in New York at which "very inflammatory resolutions
were passed" declaring that "the government of G. Britain has ever evinced,
both in her foreign & domestic policy, a rapacious & cruel disregard for the
rights & interest of the People."[38] Given his son's very public connection
with the Pennsylvania Repeal Association, John Tyler's sympathies required
little further elaboration.

Democratic contenders for the presidency felt that their interests would
be similarly well served by exploiting the cause of Irish repeal. Martin Van
Buren, a favorite for the 1844 nomination, wrote an "admirable, explicit,
and temperate" message to the repealers of Georgia sometime in the autumn of 1843.[39] A later missive spoke of his general hope for the success
of O'Connell's campaign.[40] As the front-runner for the nomination, Van
Buren exhibited the same caution in approaching the repeal question as
he did that of Texas annexation, yet he clearly deemed it unwise to remain
altogether silent on the issue.[41]

In September 1843, Senator John Calhoun, an early rival to Van Buren,
was strongly advised by one Pennsylvanian correspondent to distance himself from those who attacked repeal, even if he could not bring himself to
make a positive public statement on the subject.[42] Calhoun chose to em-
ploy his Scots-Irish ancestry to make a point about his natural sympathy
with Irishmen everywhere, as had Andrew Jackson when approached for a
public statement upon the propriety of repeal.[43] Not seeking high office,
Old Hickory could make explicit what was left unsaid in many other letters

of support. Penned in 1842, Jackson's letter suggests an uneasy balance between moral support for O'Connell's campaign and qualms over the propriety of Americans intervening in Old World politics. Stating that "there is nothing more grateful to my feelings than the anticipation . . . that the day is not far distant, when without violence or civil commotion, Ireland will regain the principles she lost in 1800," Jackson then qualified his support:

> It is proper for me to say that I [express my hopes] . . . without meaning to transcend that maxim which teaches us not to interfere offensively with the internal affairs of other nations. The preservation of the principle on which this maxim rests is far more important to the good of mankind than any benefit which can possibly be obtained by a departure from it.[44]

Doubtless slavery and fears of British abolitionism reinforced Jackson's convictions on this point.

Less reticent than Jackson was Richard M. Johnson, another presidential hopeful, whose exuberant politicking brought him harsh criticism from

Figure 1. As this cartoon suggests, some Americans believed that Tyler's support for the abolitionist Daniel O'Connell was degrading. "American Sympathy and Irish Blackguardism" (1843), lithograph by Edward Williams Clay, LC-USZ62-13213, www.loc.gov/pictures/item/2008661403/, Library of Congress Prints & Photographs Online Catalog, Library of Congress, Washington, D.C.

the abolitionist *Liberator* and the mocking contempt of Henry Clay.[45] Lewis Cass and James K. Polk, likewise, made appropriate expressions of "pious hopes" for the future redemption of Ireland.[46]

In contrast with the multiplicity of candidates offered by the Democratic Party, the Whigs retained their internal cohesion: their May 1844 national convention unanimously elected Henry Clay as the party's candidate for the presidency. Whigs generally seemed to be far more nuanced in their assessment of Anglo-Irish constitutional politics, which is perhaps surprising, given their growing association with organized nativism.[47] This did not mean that they were always more sympathetic to the Irish cause, simply that they spoke in less hackneyed terms about Ireland and the repeal campaign and were less cynical in its manipulation. A strain of pessimism ran through John Quincy Adams's interpretation of the movement, for instance. He concurred with Andrew Jackson in the expression of sympathy with Irish "national aspirations," though doubted that these would be fulfilled by the repeal agitation.[48]

By contrast, New York's William Henry Seward was a leading proponent of repeal, and his public addresses on the subject were arguably the most sophisticated of any American politician. Seward was the keynote speaker at numerous repeal rallies, perhaps most notably at a major meeting at Albany in January 1844. His career to that point illustrates his immersion in the Irish American politics of New York State. He had cultivated close relations with Roman Catholic bishop John Hughes, despite the opprobrium of many in his own party.[49] Moreover, Seward had briefly toured Ireland in the early 1830s and had been deeply affected by Irish "poverty and wretchedness."[50] In one emotional letter home, he wrote that had he sat in the Irish Parliament of the late eighteenth century, he "would have seen English armies wade in blood" before assenting to the Act of Union.[51] Supported by his political associate Thurlow Weed and William Erigena Robinson, a young journalist with the *New York Tribune*, Seward became the fulcrum of repeal agitation in the state. Irish-born and Yale-educated, Robinson found in the repeal movement the beginnings of a sustained engagement with Irish American nationalism that was to last throughout his life. Weed traveled through Ireland in 1843, providing Seward with first-hand information on the development of the repeal movement in Dublin.[52] "The American who travels with unbandaged eyes through Ireland," he commented, "deserves no credit for being a Repealer."[53]

For his early and zealous advocacy of Irish repeal, Seward received public acclamation in Dublin from Daniel O'Connell himself.[54] Yet Seward was no tub-thumping demagogue. His writings and speeches on Irish constitutional politics were able, qualified, and infused with an appreciation of diasporic politics. He argued that just as Irishmen did not receive justice at the hands of the British government, so they got a raw deal in the New World, calumniated and despised by nativists. In a letter to the Philadelphia Friends of Ireland he noted that

> I have . . . endeavoured to soften the asperities of those national prejudices which alienate the native from any citizen adopted from Ireland—Yet it is not because I am . . . desirous of being esteemed as peculiarly an advocate of Ireland or Irishmen. . . . Liberty is the inalienable right of man . . . and public and social respect . . . the earthly duty of our race. Tyranny over one country or one individual is a wrong against . . . mankind. . . .
>
> That the efforts of the Friends of Ireland to ameliorate the condition of her exiles here and to restore national rights at home may be carried with success and that here and in the British empire . . . there may be "one law" for the native born and the stranger is the true wish.[55]

Seward blended an appeal to universal rights with a description of Irish justice as being "the earthly duty of our race," though it is not entirely clear what he meant by "our race."[56] It seems fair to suggest that Seward saw no Celtic essentialism at work in Irish claims to self-governance. Rather, he spoke in Burkean tones of the "organic changes" that "become necessary to every state from the inevitable progress of civilization," and of the desirability of enlightened British imperial reform to prevent "civil war" between England and Ireland.[57] Again, the use of the phrase "civil war" does not suggest the existence of two racially distinct blocs. Certainly he placed the inhabitants of Ireland firmly within the pale of enlightened nations, contrasting them with the "distant and [power]less barbarian."[58]

The New York clique was not anomalous in its appreciation of the subtleties of Irish repeal. Kentuckian Henry Clay also grasped the ambiguities of the movement far more clearly than the Tylers did. Like John Quincy Adams, he was doubtful of its eventual success. In private correspondence with William Erigena Robinson, Clay wrote:

> I yield to no one in this Country in ardent feelings for Ireland . . . but I am not satisfied as to the propriety of any American Statesman taking part on the mere question of Repeal. . . . If Ireland had declared her Independence,

and had manifested a capacity to maintain it . . . her case would then be like those of the Spanish American Republics and Greece . . . *But I do not understand the present aim of O'Connell & his friends to be Independence*, but a mere alteration of the conditions of the connection between Ireland and England. Have the people of the U. States any legitimate right to intervene on such a domestic question?[59]

Clay, like Jackson, saw that sympathy with Irish repeal might be so qualified by respect for international law as to be meaningless. Yet still he recognized the political value in confessing an interest in the morality of repeal. Clay was well aware that the presidential election of 1844 would be a close one, and his supporters sought advantage by attempting to gain Irish voters for the Whig Party. A pamphlet entitled *Fifty Reasons why the Honorable Henry Clay Should Be Elected President of the United States* was published at Baltimore in the run-up to the election, presenting Clay's whole-hearted commitment to religious toleration, his support of a "free and untrammelled Ireland," and a denunciation of Van Buren's "selfish non-committal letter" to the repealers in Georgia.[60]

However, Clay's private letter suggests that what appealed to Robert Tyler about the repeal agitation—the possibility of reciprocal intervention in British affairs—was, for Clay, a central objection to courting repeal. Clay was concerned by what he saw as Britain's "grasping ambition" and the shadowy influence that she exercised behind abolitionism in the United States, though he remained unconvinced by the claims of Tyler and his associates that the British were actively scheming to abolish Texan slavery.[61] It seemed to many Americans hypocritical to complain of British meddling in the New World, particularly directed at American slavery, and yet actively support a potentially revolutionary movement in the Old World. According to the *New Orleans Bee*, this idea had particular resonance in the slaveholding South:

We are continually and justly . . . exhibiting a sensitiveness at the effects made by Great Britain to agitate in this country question of domestic policy which concern us alone; but . . . if we wish to act consistently, we should equally discourage and repress the attempt of individuals among us to interfere in the government . . . of Great Britain. When we wax indignant at the arrogant intermeddling of British emissaries in the South, they will . . . point to our agitation of the repeal of the Irish Union, as an example of officiousness, which they only imitate.[62]

Tyler saw Britain's unwelcome interference as an argument for, rather than against, championing Irish repeal. William Seward, by contrast, saw advantages in reciprocal Anglo-American criticism. He believed that if American institutions were insufficiently robust they ought to be reshaped. "To fear retaliation by any foreign[er] is to distrust our own virtue," he argued.[63] Collapsing distinctions between the Old World and the New, Seward spoke of the desirability of enlightened British rule in the same way Daniel O'Connell did, emphasizing justice, restitution, and respect for the power of moral opinion: "Shall [we] repress our sympathies for Ireland? . . . Shall we fear to give offence to England? That country would need only such a manifestation of American pusillanimity to encourage the spirit of aggression," he declared at a national repeal meeting in October 1843. "Are we afraid of retaliating sympathies which may disturb systems of oppression among ourselves?" Again, universalism was his theme:

> Let it come! Let freedom, universal freedom, come over this hemisphere as we desire to extend it over the other. The sympathetic love of liberty . . . reveals itself in the singular results that the restoration of Ireland connects itself even by contrary and opposing agencies with emancipation in America, and the Liberator of Ireland becomes by unforeseen necessity the champion of universal liberty.[64]

Others abstracted Irish repeal from the framework of Anglo-American diplomatic contention and stressed the moral power of the argument for repeal. The movement's theological liberalism, strict legalism, and moral rectitude impressed many: O'Connell was seen as bringing order out of anarchy. Irish repealers, wrote Thurlow Weed, were "a moral power."[65] In the summer of 1843, at the height of the agitation, the U.S. minister to Great Britain, Edward Everett, sent a formal despatch noting the movement's singular force. "The state of Ireland is certainly very peculiar," he wrote. "It may be doubted whether history presents another example of a movement extending to such vast numbers, and brought to united action by such organization, yet skilfully kept within the pale of the law."[66]

Likewise, the leading journal of the exuberant, expansionist Young Americans was impressed by the "power of Public Opinion" and noted that "the movement now so deeply agitating Ireland is . . . too remarkable a passage of contemporaneous history, not to arrest strongly the notice and interest of the general observer."[67] Young Americans, of course, had their own reasons for taking a deep interest in Irish nationalism, but they were correct to identify the movement's moral core as key to its broad public currency. Both Democratic Young Americans and Whigs such as Seward could agree that there were deep moral motives for supporting repeal: the campaign's symbolic power was underwritten by the parallels between the postcolonial United States and the still-colonial Ireland. "Their cause . . . is as sacred and as dear to humanity . . . as our own," Seward pronounced. "It is the common cause of all Mankind."[68]

Impressed by the political spectacle, American repealers were largely shielded from the internal tensions of the Irish movement, which centered on O'Connell's unremitting constitutionalism and his immersion in British-Catholic politics. Indeed, some Americans projected an essential republicanism onto O'Connell's moderate formulation of repeal, and the most ardent persuaded themselves that Ireland would be the point from which Europe would be revolutionized and republicanized.[69] Yet for all the enthusiasm for the repeal movement in the United States in 1843 and 1844, it is important to remember that this support was broader than it was deep. No one suggested that American interests might be set aside in favor of promoting Irish ends. Rather, support was augmented by the assumption that Irish and American interests were congruent and that Irish home rule and American interest went hand in hand. And just as Americans discussed Irish repeal, so Irishmen thought deeply about their relationship with the United States.

Ireland, Abolitionism, and Nativism

Daniel O'Connell shared Seward's commitment to the universalism of the struggle for liberty but was a far more strident opponent of slavery.[70] As historian Bruce Nelson suggests, O'Connell's conception of Irish history, which "made Irishness synonymous with opposition to oppression wherever it reared his head," led him to an atypical, *outward*-looking nationalism, whose principles "allowed (even compelled) him to choose internationalism over nationalism at critical moments."[71] To observers in the United States, Daniel O'Connell's position within the dynamic transatlantic network of Irish, British, and American abolitionists rendered his supporters vulnerable to charges of disloyalty, even disunionism. He was personally and ideologically connected with the Garrisonian wing of the abolitionist movement throughout the 1830s and was committed to immediate abolition.[72] The connection between abolition and Irish repeal was stated explicitly by William Lloyd Garrison, who claimed to support "the repeal of the Union between England and Ireland . . . for the same reason [its immorality]" that he supported "the repeal of the Union between the [free states of the] North and the [slaveholding states of the] South."[73] Garrisonians recognized O'Connell's political capital among recently arrived Irish migrants and sought to use it to draw them away from the pro-immigrant Democratic Party.[74]

The most concrete expression of this Garrisonian-O'Connellite nexus was "An Address of the People of Ireland to Their Countrymen and Countrywomen in America," signed by 70,000 individuals, which called on the transplanted Irish to "continue to love liberty—hate slavery—*cling by the abolitionists*, and in America you will do honor to the name of Ireland."[75] The address was presented at Faneuil Hall in January 1842, and the initial response from Boston's Irish community was deemed overwhelmingly positive, leading Garrison to hope that the "stupendous conspiracy" between southern slaveholders and "the pseudo-democrats" of the North would be broken.[76] As months passed, though, it became apparent that Irish immigrants had little interest in allying themselves with a movement steeped in evangelical Protestantism that was so vocal in its attacks on their adopted home. The Catholic press defensively questioned the authenticity of the address.[77] Irish immigrants themselves were angered by the presumption that they would be subject to the dictates of Dublin (and London), arguing that they took their new citizenship—and the duties that accompanied it—deeply seriously.[78]

Why did American abolitionists believe that Irishmen who had so thoroughly embraced the "negrophobia" of the Democracy (as the Democratic Party was commonly called) would perform a volte-face and fall in behind the movement to abolish slavery in the United States?[79] The answer has much to do with O'Connell's success in perpetuating a historical narrative of the antithetical relationship between Ireland and slavery.[80] In addition, the Hibernian Anti-Slavery Society, established 1837, was disproportionately strong and very active in the international antislavery community, considering the political weight of Ireland in other contexts.[81] It seems plausible to suggest that the abolitionist appeal was predicated on a false conflation of O'Connell's antislavery sentiments with those of the Irish population as a whole. Abolitionists who traveled to Great Britain and Ireland in the 1830s and early 1840s may have attended mass meetings, but their principal point of contact was with other individuals who thought as they did. The extrapolation of popular opinion from the views O'Connell expressed (and the acclamation that he received) was understandable, if myopic. Indeed, a recent historian of Ireland and abolitionism has noted that antislavery politics had comparatively shallow roots when viewed in a broader British context.[82]

In the United States, debate over the proper relationship of abolition to repeal proved disruptive. A dispute over the abolitionist address undermined the first national convention of repeal associations in January 1842. The divisive response it received prompted O'Connell to be more circumspect in his criticism of American slavery. For about a year, historian Bruce Nelson writes, O'Connell sought a "workable compromise," whereby he might make known his antislavery sentiments without undermining the U.S. network of repeal associations.[83] But this position was made increasingly untenable by tensions within the Dublin Repeal Association, and here it is worth noting the limitations of the contemporary and historiographical focus on Daniel O'Connell at the expense of other actors. Despite the Carlylean tone repealers in the United States used, O'Connell was not Ireland, and he did not have free rein in setting the pace of repeal agitation.

Irish abolitionists were uneasy about money from slaveholders underwriting repeal activities. In particular, the increasingly significant role played by the pro-slavery Robert Tyler troubled those leaders of the Hibernian Anti-Slavery Society, such as James Haughton, who were prominent in the LNRA. Haughton was set on breaking the "unholy alliance" of repeal and slaveholder money.[84] O'Connell had addressed a personal note of thanks to Robert Tyler for his efforts on behalf of repeal, something that revolted Haughton.[85] "A man who holds men in chains," Haughton wrote, "must be, in heart and soul, a despot. . . . It is impossible that this man [Tyler] can care one farthing for freedom or for Ireland."[86]

Such domestic pressures prompted O'Connell to step up his attacks on U.S. slavery, with significant transnational consequences. In May 1843, O'Connell delivered a speech, widely published in the United States, in which he called on all Irishmen to either denounce slavery or cease to consider themselves true Irishmen.[87] This prompted the Philadelphia Repeal Association to split into antislavery and anti-abolitionist camps.[88] However, as historian Angela Murphy has noted, both halves of that society continued their correspondence with—and remittances to—the central association in Dublin.[89] Though O'Connell's rhetorical attacks on U.S. slavery provoked strident responses from his southern supporters, they did not preclude continued support or, importantly, continued donations. In July 1843, the Charleston Repeal Association called O'Connell's speech a "base and malignant libel upon the people of the South" and voted for its own dissolution.[90] Yet by the end of the year, the association had reconstituted itself, though O'Connell's antislavery tone had not slackened.[91] Indeed, it had intensified: in September 1843, the Cincinnati Repeal Association delivered a stinging denunciation of O'Connell for his interventionist abolitionism and criticized him for addressing them as Irishmen rather than as Americans. This prompted the Irish leader to respond with a point-by-point rebuttal of what he thought of as an unnatural defense of slavery by men from a northern state.[92]

Perhaps O'Connell's repudiation of this northern defense of slavery would have proved more damaging to the American repeal cause had it not reached the United States at the same time as news of the Irish authorities' long-anticipated clampdown on the Repeal Association.[93] On October 7, 1843, the authorities at Dublin Castle issued a proclamation prohibiting the following day's mass meeting at Clontarf. O'Connell submitted to the prohibition and issued a proclamation to the people of Ireland, urging peaceful acquiescence.[94] Despite this show of conciliation, O'Connell and eight others were later arrested and charged with conspiring sedition against the government. These arrests boosted American interest. A letter from Robert Tyler to the Dublin Repeal Association stated that O'Connell's conviction in February 1844 gave the American movement "a newer strength and a fresher spirit" and that "all differences of opinion in respect of other questions" were cheerfully forgotten.[95] In short, the drama in Ireland overshadowed the divisive slavery issue among American repealers.[96]

These waves of excitement did not, of course, occur in a political vacuum. As more politicians expressed their support for the repeal movement, a backlash against it emerged. One New York newspaper criticized O'Connell as a corrupt politician who was duping his followers for his own financial benefit. Another asked, "What care American politicians for repeal of the Irish Union?"[97] In addition, a controversy concerning religion and public education reached a flash point. In New York, Bishop Hughes had sought to secure public funding for Catholic parochial schools and the removal of anti-Catholic texts that were used in public education. A similar effort in Philadelphia, in the context of increasing economic competition along ethnic lines, provided the catalyst for rioting in the spring and summer of 1844.[98] Though the lawlessness was widely condemned, opposition to the perceived influence of Rome and Ireland was not restricted to the fringes of American politics. That May, the Whig Party selected Theodore Frelinghuysen, "probably the most illustrious lay evangelical in the country" and a noted critic of the influence of Rome in American politics, as their candidate for vice-president.[99]

Freshly organized nativist groups anticipated a new electoral alignment centered on the issues of immigration, religion, and naturalization.[100] One such group, the American Party, argued that there was a direct correlation between enthusiasm for the repeal movement and the growth of their party.[101] Certainly, the prospect of intervention, if only financial or rhetorical intervention, in the controversies of Old World politics did little to assuage the fears of native-born Americans who doubted the loyalty of recent Irish Catholic migrants.[102] One early propagandist of the American Party asserted that the "primary cause of [the] fierce outbreaks" of violence in Philadelphia in 1844 was the nativist belief that repeal was a banner beneath which the Irish deviously sought to involve the United States in the affairs of Great Britain and Ireland. Another suggested that repeal was simply a means to gratify the anti-British sentiments of recent Irish immigrants.[103]

This interpretation was echoed by Lewis Levin, an American Party founder, ideologue and, between 1845 and 1851, a member of Congress from Philadelphia.[104] Levin cited a "conspiracy [originating] behind the mask of Repeal to fix absolutism on the United States" as his motivation for forming the party. He even went so far as to issue a pamphlet denouncing the "fallacies of Irish Repeal."[105] Arguing that the disparity between English and Irish power was so marked as to make O'Connell's attempts at repeal suspicious, Levin argued that "[O'Connell] is too sagacious not to mean something. . . . This cunning demagogue, has made Repeal of the Irish Union, the means of *concentrating* a religious and political power, unsurpassed in the history of the world."[106] Levin believed he had divined a plot to foist Catholic governance on a naive and unsuspecting American public. Nativists were troubled that the leading Democrat and Whig presidential candidates had taken pains to point out their support for a free Ireland. As much might be expected of the corrupt Democratic Party, but William Seward's aggressive courting of the Catholic vote in New York City was especially galling.

Yet as a testament to the near-ubiquitous acknowledgement of Irish claims to (at the very least) better governance, Levin wrote: "Who would not raise a voice for Ireland? Who would not strike a blow for Ireland[?]"[107] Interestingly, Levin articulated a relatively sophisticated argument in favor of Irish home rule that eschewed both sentimentalism and demagoguery. The "virtuous credulity" of the Irish patriot was being cynically exploited, he argued, by the "selfish and designing O'Connell."[108] Levin claimed to admire the "sublimity in Irish suffering," though he condemned what he saw as the deadening effects of the Irish priesthood.[109] Moreover, he used the ambiguity of repeal as a stick with which to beat O'Connell. Levin argued that the Irish leader aimed, at best, for an Irish Parliament under the British monarch: "a *Republic* is not dreamed of—O'Connell hates all Republics."[110] But O'Connell was not Ireland. Hostility to his person, to his abolitionism, and to his Catholicism did not mean implacable opposition to the idea of an independently governed Ireland. Levin's nativist case for Irish home rule certainly had an internal logic: a better governed Ireland— even an independent Ireland—would mean that Irish Catholics would stay at home, preserving the purity of a Protestant American republic. More generally, nativists had a conflicted sense of the repeal movement. The low opinion that nativists had of the intellectual and political independence of Irish immigrants meant that they were deemed the dupes of scheming Democratic politicians, sustaining slavery through their ignorance and servility to urban demagogues, *and* dupes of the abolitionist O'Connell, sent forth to constitute an well-organized antislavery fifth column within the ranks of the republic's voters.

The uncertain status of Irish immigrants in a new land has been central to historiographical interpretations of the declining repeal movement following its early organizational dynamism.[111] One historian has described Irish Catholics as generally retreating from political confrontation following the Philadelphia riots of the summer of 1844, but repeal associations continued to meet throughout the year, offering financial support to the Dublin organization as it dealt with O'Connell's trial, conviction, imprisonment, and eventual acquittal.[112] A number of historians have seen nativism as an unavoidable function of O'Connell's antislavery politics because his attacks on U.S. slavery and his invocation of an essentialist understanding of Irishness left Irish immigrants open to charges of disloyalty to their adopted home. Such attacks made it expedient for Irishmen to distance themselves from the dictates emanating from Dublin. But the persistence of repeal in the United States suggests that the nexus of abolition and repeal is an insufficient explanation for the ultimate collapse of U.S. repeal associations. O'Connell was always openly an abolitionist, yet the movement flourished.[113] And as Angela Murphy has highlighted, repeal associations could learn to live with his attacks on slavery. The man was not the whole campaign, and vice versa. The issue of slavery was profoundly destabilizing, but in isolation it did not fatally undermine the status of American repealers. It was only when paired with the geopolitical contest over Texas that the repeal movement in the United States crumbled. It was O'Connell's self-positioning as an agent of British abolitionist imperialism that prompted the collapse of American repeal.

The Foreign Policy of Slavery and the Irish Question

The U.S. minister to London, Edward Everett, kept the Tyler administration informed of developments in Ireland. Everett first mentioned the repeal agitation in his despatch of May 16, 1843, and through the year reported on the "great anxiety" and general sense of crisis that the progress of O'Connell's movement bred within the British political establishment.[114] Irish grievances, discontent in Wales, "the schism of the Church in Scotland; the pervading agitation on the subject of the corn laws, the growing divisions in the church, and the wide spread distress among the laboring classes in England" united "to produce a state of things in Great Britain of no ordinary embarrassment and gravity."[115] By mid-1843, the constitutional instability of Great Britain led Everett to believe that the Peel administration might countenance checking "further agitation . . . at the point of the bayonet."[116]

This theme of instability—of fluidity in British domestic and constitutional politics—was central in the missives of Duff Green, who acted as President Tyler's unofficial agent in England until the autumn of 1843.[117] The relationship between Green and Everett was hardly a smooth one. Everett understandably felt that Green's presence suggested the Tyler administration's lack of confidence in his own ability to prosecute U.S. interests. This was not altogether untrue. The U.S. minister confided to British foreign secretary Lord Aberdeen that he and the administration did not see eye to eye on the issue of slavery (Everett described the peculiar institution as a "shocking anomaly") and privately members of the administration concurred that Everett was not up to the task of rebuffing what they assumed to be the imperial prosecution of an abolitionist agenda.[118] Writing to John Calhoun in November 1843, Secretary of State Abel Upshur stated that Texas was now "emphatically *the* question of the day. . . . The preservation of the Union . . . depend[s] upon it."[119] Everett was not the man to command the issue, however, as he was "from the wrong side of Mason & Dixon."[120] "We should be represented in England," Upshur wrote, "by some one who understands domestic slavery as it exists among us, & who can properly appreciate its bearing, upon other great interests of the U[nited]

States."[121] Duff Green, by contrast, was very much attuned to those great interests.[122] "England," he claimed in a letter to Calhoun, "having abolished slavery, & thereby raised the price of labour in her colonies was bound as an act of justice to her Colonial subjects to abolish slavery everywhere."[123] Everett described Green as "full of the designs of the British Government on Texas & antislavery" and criticized him for promoting the annexation of the Texan republic to boost Calhoun's electoral chances.[124]

For Green, the situation in Ireland was critical to achieving American goals, both expansionist and economic. Ireland acted as a black hole, drawing the strength of the British ministry and, as such, British statesmen would be helpless to prevent the extension of the boundaries of the U.S. republic to include Texas and territory in the Pacific Northwest. In addition, the free trade goals of the Tyler administration might be advanced if Irish issues catalyzed opposition to Peel's premiership. Though Green believed repeal to be "a hopeless and obsolete idea," he thought that any further repression in Ireland would provoke such political instability that the free trade British Whigs would be brought to power.[125] Thus the economic goals of U.S. diplomacy would be indirectly furthered by events in Ireland.

Irish disorder (and continued Anglo-Russian tensions over the Oregon boundary) meant that late 1843 offered a window of opportunity to secure various diplomatic goals, the most important of which, according to the Tyler administration, was the annexation of Texas. "Now . . . is the time to press our measures," wrote Green. "Annex Texas, and urge our rights to Oregon. . . . The Irish and Russian questions put them in that position that they cannot quarrel with us now."[126] He urged that an explicit defense of slavery be made central to U.S. foreign policy. Believing that the Cincinnati repealers' rejection of O'Connell's May 1843 address revealed deep antipathy to abolitionism in the northern states, Green argued that annexation ought to be pitched to the American public "upon the ground of the danger of permitting Texas to become a refuge for runaway slaves."[127] To Green, dissension within the transatlantic repeal movement indicated the integrative and nationalist potential of Texas annexation.

But there were two fallacies here. The first is that, as has been seen, the repeal network did not fold. The second was that the U.S. public did not appreciate the framing of Texas annexation as an explicitly pro-slavery measure. John Calhoun, who in February 1844 replaced Abel Upshur as secretary of state, sought to justify the annexation of Texas as a response to British schemes for abolition on the borders of the United States.[128] But when his treaty of annexation was transmitted to the Senate, "the whole thing blew up in the administration's face" as senators, alienated by Calhoun's strident defense of slavery, voted down the measure.[129]

Yet it still seemed possible that a less stridently proslavery framing of Texas annexation might succeed, especially if continued discontent in Ireland undermined British opposition. With Daniel O'Connell's acquittal in August 1844, it appeared to Everett that any renewed Irish agitation would be undertaken with "increased fervor & violence."[130] Some Calhounites prayed for exactly this. The prospect of an Anglo-Irish conflagration gave annexationists hope for a second window of opportunity to join Texas to the United States. For instance, John Hogan, a correspondent of Calhoun, argued that in the event of the seemingly imminent Anglo-Irish collision,

> England would be compelled to with[h]old her interference in the Slavery and Texas questions by properly directing her attention to her own internal affairs in keeping an eye to the movements of Mr. O[']Connell in Ireland[,] the imprisonment of whom is well worthy of attention. . . . [It] is a tremendous weapon now in Europe and likely to become still more so for the reason that England could do nothing better calculated to embroil her with the Catholic Countries of Europe."[131]

For Hogan, Ireland was an important component in balance-of-power politics in Europe that would act as a restraint on British action.

For Irish repealers, the implications of this position cut both ways. Proponents of Irish self-governance appeared to have a strong hand to play and believed that Ireland had the capacity to destabilize British imperial and domestic politics. Yet any concessions that were achieved were likely to be granted by a British government. This placed a premium on loyalty and on the idea that repeal might be a measure that would *strengthen* the British state—and the British Empire—by removing a source of irritation and a site of potential violence. O'Connell's recognition of this conditioned his repeated protestations of loyalty to the British Crown.

By contrast, the more advanced nationalists in Dublin cheered from the sidelines at the prospect of American expansion at the expense of British interests. In 1844, Thomas Davis, Thomas Meagher, and other Young Irelanders became increasingly frustrated at O'Connell's apparent willingness to grant that concessions by the British government might produce a union that could work for loyal Catholics.[132] These more assertive nationalists welcomed the aggression of the United States, and editorials in the *Nation*, under the direction of Young Irelander Charles Gavan Duffy, became increasingly strident in their articulation of a nationalist foreign policy that celebrated American expansion. This vicarious celebration was at least in part predicated on the idea that a belligerent American foreign policy might provoke a military reaction from Great Britain. Any Anglo-American war would either give Britain good cause to make concessions to Ireland in terms of its own governance or would result in Ireland seizing her own constitutional destiny by force. The realism of this logic, of course, might be debated. Still, the election to the presidency of James K. Polk, a committed expansionist, occasioned editorials that trumpeted the imminence of Texan annexation, the accession of Oregon to the Union, and the possibility of Canada falling into American hands.[133]

Despite internal divisions over the desirability of Texan annexation, funds continued to flow from U.S. repeal associations. Chastened by his experience of the disruptive potential of abolitionist sentiment, Thomas Mooney, in his "Letters from America" series in the *Nation*, was clear that the loose structure of greater Ireland was its commanding virtue. "If you suffer the Friends of Ireland in America to manage their part of the Repeal agitation . . . the work will be well done," he wrote in the aftermath of mass repeal meeting in Albany.[134] Mooney saw that the unstructured federation of individual associations was the key to maintaining the profitable relationship between Irish America and Ireland, yet cracks in the Irish movement were becoming more prominent. These had the potential for deleterious consequences in the United States. One conflict concerned the substantive end that repealers should aim for. Following his acquittal in September 1844, O'Connell increasingly advocated some form of Anglo-Irish federalism, much to the disgust of nationalist Young Irelanders, who dismissed this as ensuring Ireland's continued moral and political subjection to England.[135]

Simultaneously, there was increasing criticism from those who thought that O'Connell was still too supine in receiving remittances from American slaveholders, particularly once Polk's narrow election victory prompted John Tyler's attempt to expand the sphere of slavery by annexing Texas.[136] Abolitionist James Haughton was the most public in pushing O'Connell to denounce Tyler's statecraft in the strongest terms. In March 1845 he wrote a letter to Gavan Duffy, editor of the Dublin *Nation*, arguing that "our countrymen in the United States are still led astray by . . . Robert Tyler, *the Slaveholder*" and that Irishmen ought to be guided by the conviction that slavery was a sin against God everywhere and at all times.[137] Haughton believed that Tyler was no more than a hack politician who was cynically exploiting Irish patriotism to deliver votes for the Democratic Party. "Let us keep ourself unsullied by coming into contact with such men as Robert Tyler," Haughton declared.[138] The moral cost of Tyler's support was too great to countenance. Privately, Haughton pushed O'Connell to make a clear statement on the extension of the slave republic. In late January 1845, he wrote, "I wish you had given the Tyler the thrashing he so richly deserves. The system sustained by him and his compeers is so infernal that it is difficult even to think of it with christian patience. . . . I think sheep stealing a much more honourable occupation."[139] O'Connell replied that he abhorred the principles of slavery as much as ever:

> Indeed, if it was possible to increase my contempt of slave-owners and the advocates of slavery, my sentiments are more intense now than ever they were, and I will avail myself of the first practical opportunity of giving utterance to them, especially in connection with the horrible project of annexing Texas to the United States. . . . I will . . . avail myself of the first favourable opportunity to express my indignation on the subject, so as to give my sentiments circulation in America.[140]

He made good on this promise in March 1845 in a speech responding to Polk's bullish inaugural of that month.[141] O'Connell promised that Ireland would stand proudly in support of British antislavery diplomacy in the event of war with the United States. He proclaimed that the British

> can have us . . . the throne of Victoria made perfectly secure—the honor of the British Empire maintained—and the American eagle, in its highest pride of flight, be brought down. Let them but . . . give us the Parliament in College Green, and Oregon shall be theirs, and Texas shall be harmless.[142]

Prior to this speech, the *Nation* had warned that O'Connell's recent focus on federalism and loyalty to the British Crown had dampened American repeal enthusiasm, though remittances continued to be received from the United States.[143] But by making manifest what he saw as the all-pervasive conflict between the abolitionist empire and the slaveholding republic, O'Connell effectively shattered the struggling U.S. repeal associations.

He also embarrassed his Young Ireland allies at home. Only weeks before, the *Nation* had boasted of the power Ireland exercised in restraining Britain from acting as she saw fit in relation to the United States. "Our secession from the policy and feelings of the empire is beginning to be felt," claimed one editorial.[144] "Irish neutrality" meant that Texas became part of the United States against British wishes, and Oregon could only follow.[145] Reporting Polk's inaugural, the *Nation* crowed,

> The Tories protest to Heaven that the conduct of America is unbearable, and they bear it. Ha! gentlemen, where is Ireland now? You dare not fight, because Ireland is discontent. . . . Verily, these Americans are "making hay while the sun shines"—making States while Ireland is malcontent.[146]

O'Connell's speech undermined his Young Ireland allies. Though he couched his commitment to the Crown in conditional terms, his pacific course after Clontarf, his arrest, trial and release; his flirtation with federalism; and his seemingly obsequious courting of British public opinion did little to suggest that his implicit threat of disloyalty amounted to much.[147]

In the United States, O'Connell's speech confirmed nativist fears of an Irish fifth column. Arguing the immorality of slavery was one thing—Irish Americans could parse his commentary or suggest that there was a divergence between "O'Connell" and "Ireland" and that loyalty to the latter was not slavishness to the former. This was not a critique of the U.S. domestic institution, however, but a promised intervention into Anglo-American diplomacy on the side of Great Britain.[148] The Boston Repeal Association argued that O'Connell's "eccentricities" did nothing to dampen their enthusiasm and that it supported "PRINCIPLES NOT MEN," but to slight effect.[149] Thomas Mooney commented sadly that "the declaration of war against America by Ireland has annoyed the citizens of this Republic much more than the declaration to the same effect by England."[150] To so many, O'Connell *was* Ireland. "Our country has been treated abroad as a nation of serfs," wrote Mooney, "with one mighty man at its head."[151] An "open repudiation" of O'Connell was exceptionally damaging to the self-conception of Irishmen abroad and to the cause of Irish home rule in the United States.[152] Southern repeal associations dissolved, this time permanently, to the applause of nativist observers. Northern associations were critical of their southern counterparts and suggested that they were in thrall to the "slave power," but they themselves severely curtailed their activity in the face of nativist pressure. In both the North and the South, repeal associations were responsive to the politics of their respective regions.[153] O'Connell's later commentary on Oregon (that he would join with Great Britain to "set America at defiance") only confirmed the death of Irish repeal in American politics.[154] Daniel O'Connell's affirmation of imperial loyalty in the cause of abolitionism undermined the careful balance between center and periphery that had characterized the repeal network during the preceding half-decade. Promising Irish agency versus American expansion, he opened U.S.-based repealers to charges of disloyalty to the republic.

Ireland remained a factor to consider in American statesmen's interpretations of Britain's ability to project her power in the New World. During the increasingly heated Anglo-American tension over the Oregon Territory in the spring of 1846, Louis McLane, Everett's successor as minister to Great Britain, noted that "unhappy, miserable Ireland, stands as an almost insurmountable obstacle in the way of every thing. . . . It is difficult to exaggerate the difficulties of the Irish question. . . . English statesmen [are] . . . more dependent upon *O'Connell* at this moment for the Government of Ireland than upon anything else."[155]

Yet Daniel O'Connell had deemed Irish and American interests divergent. His version of liberal imperialism eroded his position at home among more advanced nationalists. Simultaneously, the allegiance of Irish Americans to their adopted country drew their support away from the repealers and encouraged a hypernationalism that tied anti-British sentiment to aggressive expansionism. The story of Irish repeal in the United States highlights the tensions inherent in building a transnational movement that sought to draw strength from its position between competing empires. It also reveals the conflicting demands of allegiance—British imperial, American national, and Irish would-be national—that buffeted Irish American citizens in the Atlantic world of the 1840s and how these influenced the contest between antislavery Great Britain and the expansionist, slaveholding United States.

Through the winter of 1845–1846, members of Congress debated expansion in the Pacific Northwest. Polk's aggressive diplomacy had provoked a bullish reaction in the English press and raised the prospect of a war with Great Britain.[156] On January 6, 1846, in the midst of these debates, Representative Felix Grundy McConnell, a Democrat from Alabama, made an unorthodox suggestion to extend the scope of America's territorial ambition. Celebrating a universal spirit of expansionism and glossing over the profound divisions that Polk's policies had engendered, McConnell spoke in cosmic terms. He hoped to project "the blessings of our free institutions in every practicable quarter of the universe."[157]

> While we hail the admission of Texas . . . into our Union, and view with
> unaffected pride and satisfaction the patriotic resolution of the Executive

Government and Congress of the United States to uphold our title to Oregon, and also observe the growing desire to incorporate Mexico, Yucatan, California, &c., in the confederacy, [we resolve] that *Ireland* is fully entitled to share the blessings of our free institutions.[158]

Assuming a correspondence between the experience of British rule and republican sympathies, McConnell spoke of Ireland "as a nation [which has] . . . always cherished the democratic principle of republican government."[159] He desired that the House "receive with due attention . . . any communication . . . from that high-minded and liberty-loving people, with a view to effect such an object."[160] McConnell's suggestion was howled down, but it is interesting that a *southern* Democrat should make such a plea so soon after O'Connell's abolitionist statecraft had prompted a vitriolic response in the United States. Most likely, Felix McConnell conceived his resolution as nothing more than a means of Democratic tub-thumping (he made no mention of Daniel O'Connell or the repeal movement). Few took his suggestions seriously—though Thomas Steele, one of O'Connell's lieutenants, used their reception in Dublin as an opportunity to reassert Irish loyalty to the British Crown.[161] Clearly, few in Congress thought Ireland a proper element of a debate on the Anglo-American contest over U.S. expansion.

Between McConnell's January 1846 speech and the Irish rebellion of September 1848, American interest in the Irish question would peak again. This time it would not be as a consequence of the transnational agency of Irish nationalists but in response to the cataclysm of famine.

Chapter 2

Ireland Is No Longer a Nation

The Irish Famine and American Diplomacy

The Irish famine is rarely viewed as an event of consequence in the history of U.S. foreign relations. This is short sighted, for the transnational significance of the famine was apparent to contemporary U.S. statesmen, to whom it offered the opportunity to demonstrate U.S. power in the heart of the British imperial system, and to the U.S. public, who donated large sums in private philanthropy to aid those starving in Ireland.

For free trade Democrats, the famine confirmed their indictment of the British imperial system of protectionism and gave rise to exuberant predictions of U.S. economic ascendancy. Buoyed by the success of tariff reductions at home and encouraged by Britain's apparent pusillanimity over U.S. territorial expansion, Democrats interpreted the Irish famine as an opportunity to demonstrate the nation's burgeoning power in Britain's backyard. Irish dependence on imports of food from the United States bred a new confidence and confirmed the Democrats' faith that the United States had gained parity with the great imperial power and was being treated with due respect.

This assertion of U.S. political and commercial ascendancy was matched by a kind of general moral ascendancy as the famine sparked unparalleled philanthropic activity on the part of the U.S. public. Throughout the

Union, citizens formed relief committees to collect and forward money, food, and clothes to Ireland. Whigs in particular were active in promoting Irish charity as a means of improving Anglo-American relations. The more evangelically inclined among them saw such philanthropy as a way of atoning for the sin of the Mexican-American War. Whig members of Congress introduced resolutions to send federal funds to aid the famine relief effort in Ireland. Though the constitutional scruples of the Polk administration weighed against official relief, Congress agreed to the use of two naval vessels for the purpose of delivering food to Ireland. Famine relief demonstrated the ability of the United States to project both commercial and moral power in the Old World.

Throughout the famine years, Irish nationalist discourse was marginal in U.S. public discourse. Though people had shown extensive interest in the progress of O'Connell's repeal agitation earlier in the 1840s, many observers saw the famine as confirmation of the futility of pressing for Irish nationhood. Even the most hostile of Anglophobes now argued that Ireland should look for amelioration within a British imperial context. By the early 1850s, the Irish question was a subject of Anglo-American rapprochement, rather than a contentious issue that had the capacity to complicate Anglo-American relations.

The Famine in the Democratic Mind

First observed in Ireland in September 1845, the fungus *Phytophthora infestans* caused potatoes to rot, making them unfit for human consumption.[1] Because of the overwhelming importance of the potato to the Irish diet, famine followed. Historians estimate that between 1.1 and 1.5 million people died of starvation and the diseases that accompanied it in the decade following 1845.[2] The fungus most likely came from the eastern United States, where the potato crops of 1843 and 1844 had been almost wholly destroyed.[3] Though the blight initially caused greater destruction of crops in other parts of Western Europe, Ireland's distinctive socioeconomic structure ended up magnifying the problem over time. Explosive demographic growth over the previous century and the concurrent increase in demand for land had stimulated production of the potato as a staple crop, deepening Irish dependence on continued cultivation.[4] "Nowhere else in Europe," writes one historian, "did so high a proportion of the population come to rely on the potato for its food."[5]

The American press first reported the blight in November 1845. The Boston *Pilot*, a leading Irish American daily, reported that "in Ireland matters look appalling."[6] In response, Bostonians organized a great public meeting in the second week of December, but this was an isolated event.[7] Irishmen urged their U.S. friends, family, and associates to focus on sending money for political activities rather than organizing charitable relief funds.[8] In the United States, as in Great Britain, there was no sense of imminent catastrophe despite reports of the partial failure of the potato crop. In part, this was because of imperfect knowledge. A commission appointed by the British government was unable to accurately ascertain the extent of the shortfall in the harvest of 1845.[9] In addition, there was nothing apparently exceptional in the failure of the Irish potato crop. In the popular imagination, Ireland was a land of scarcity, and there was little indication that the reduced harvest of 1845 would prove any more devastating than previous food shortages.[10] Despite a brief mention of scarcity in Ireland during a debate in Congress on the revision of the tariff in June 1846, it was not until early 1847 that Congress seriously discussed the subject of the Irish famine.[11]

The concerted U.S. relief effort did not start until late 1846, when the severity of conditions in Ireland became apparent after a second crop failure. Prior to this second failure, there was little sense of crisis in Ireland. Ironically, in late 1845 and early 1846, the Americans who were most aware of the forbidding aspects of a failed harvest were those who were most likely to be assured by the steps taken by Robert Peel's government to ameliorate conditions.[12] Acting with little fanfare, Peel initiated a secret purchase of £100,000 worth of foodstuffs from the United States through the agency of the transatlantic financial house Baring Brothers. In total, the British government spent £185,000 and imported 20,000 tons of maize and oatmeal by August 1846.[13]

This, though, was insufficient to spare Ireland the "horrible winter of 1846–47 [when] so many deaths occurred that the government was obliged to amend the Poor Law and allow public relief outside the workhouses."[14] Though historians have often contrasted the response of John Russell's Whig ministry unfavorably with that of its predecessor under Robert Peel, both talked about the famine in providentially inflected tones and both were concerned to limit public expenditure.[15] Despite Peel's early intervention in the grain market, ministers generally shied away from overt interference with private enterprise. Conforming to the idea that Irish property ought to support Irish poverty, in mid-1847 Russell's government reformed the poor law to throw the burden of public relief on local poor law unions in Ireland, who struggled to cope. Mass starvation, evictions, migration, and death followed.[16]

Irish distress seemed to promise the trade reforms that Democrats so ardently sought. Writing in September 1846, long before the full horrors of the famine were evident, secretary of the U.S. legation James Henry McBoyd wrote of the transformative potential of the "disastrous failure of the potatoe [*sic*] crop."[17] Polk's administration had sought British trade liberalization—the repeal of Britain's antiquated system of Navigation Laws and the reduction of duties on American imports—as a valuable corollary to its reduction of duties under the revised tariff of 1846.[18] Improved Anglo-American relations, Democrats believed, would both promote and be promoted by deeper commercial ties. With the British Whigs committed to immediate and total removal of the Corn Laws and Robert Peel a convert to gradual repeal, both parties explicitly linked a liberal commercial policy with an improved Anglo-American diplomatic dialogue.[19] The prospect of Irish destitution, it was hoped, might catalyze this reform.

The precise impact of famine relief on the relationship between British free trade and improved Anglo-American relations has been much debated by historians. Scholars no longer draw a straight line between the British need for food importations and conciliation over the Oregon Territory.[20] However, this is not to suggest that economic concerns were negligible in shaping responses to the famine. The potential for the development of Ireland as an economic client undoubtedly proved an important component in Americans' interpretations of Anglo-Irish conditions. On his arrival in London, the new U.S. minister, George Bancroft, fielded the "anxious inquiries" of British Members of Parliament concerned about the ever-more-prized supplies of Indian corn from the United States: "such is the famine in Ireland and such the scarcity in England consequent on the failure of the potato crop."[21] In this he concurred with the reports of Thomas Gilpin, the U.S. consul at Belfast. Gilpin foresaw a doubling in American exports to Ireland and the long-term cultivation of American trade: in his mind, Irish dependence on the potato might be replaced by a dependence on American corn.[22] In addition, Bancroft described the integrative impact of the British government's spending on Irish aid: money allocated for public works schemes would inevitably form "a tribute to the great valley of the West," meaning the Mississippi River valley, as Irish workers spent their income on the cheapest food available to them.[23] Clearly, Irish scarcity might have both short- and long-term implications for the U.S. economy.

The famine represented more than a commercial opportunity. It vindicated Democratic conceptions of British dependence on America's agricultural output. Statesmen such as George Bancroft and Secretary of the Treasury Robert Walker propounded a theory of political economy that stressed the essential interdependence of British and American production. Where Whigs fretted over continued U.S. reliance on goods manufactured in Europe, Democrats followed Jefferson in emphasizing the dependence of European states—especially Britain—on American agriculture as their own soil deteriorated and their cities expanded.[24] Protectionism spelled ruin, argued Walker in his annual report of December 1846, and events in Ireland had overtaken British policy.[25]

This commercial interdependence had political consequences. It militated against Old World—and by "Old World," Democrats generally meant "British"—interference in the New World. As Walker's annual reports outlined, it also worked against the perpetuation of a colonial economic relationship with Great Britain. Though the United States might continue to rely upon British imports for finished manufactured goods, they were, unlike Ireland, not powerless economic satellites. Instead, Democrats argued, grain from the West and cotton from the South inverted this relationship, making Britain reliant on American production for her economic wellbeing and, by extension, her social and political stability. Such dependence, Democrats believed, could breed harmonious international relations. Trade liberalization, noted Calhounite politician James Henry Hammond, was "the omen of Peace & a benevolent intercourse between two . . . great nations."[26]

The Young American *Democratic Review* spoke in more exhilarated tones of the "practical annexation of England" in July 1846, brought about by exhaustion of British soil and by global technological innovations—railroads and canals—that "have brought the great valley of the Mississippi as near London as a few years since was that of the Tweed."[27] Beneath this rhetoric of "annexation" lay a complex understanding of complementary commercial and diplomatic interests and a burgeoning, loosely defined sense of Anglo-American community of which free trade and prosperity were the common currency. For the *Democratic Review*, the United States was escaping its economic (and cultural) postcolonial dependency on Great Britain. The liberalization of trade, British pusillanimity over Texas annexation, compromise on the Oregon Territory, and now Britain's pressing need for American imports in the face of Irish famine served as proximate causes of a blossoming Anglo-American parity in the realm of international relations.

Reduced barriers to trade and increased commercial exchange were two indicators of a better-integrated Atlantic economy. A third was the mass migration of Irishmen and women fleeing the destitution of the famine. As they made their way across the Atlantic, George Bancroft was pleased to report that "the worst of the population, the apathetic and incorrigibly idle, stay behind. The enterprising, despairing of Ireland, quit their old country, and look with hope to the New World."[28] Essential to this process were remittances from Irishmen and women already in the United States, which, one American traveler in Ireland remarked, utterly astonished local postmasters.[29] An 1850 survey suggested that as many as 75 percent of fares were funded by money from the United States, and one historian has estimated that, in the period 1850–1855, an annual *average* of £1.2 million (the equivalent of about $6.7 million) was remitted, facilitating emigration on an incredible scale.[30]

Whatever their financial means, almost 1.5 million sailed to the United States from Ireland in the ten years following 1845, representing roughly 70 percent a total emigration from Ireland of 2.1 million.[31] In Ireland, wrote one observer, "humanity seems to be the principal surplus commodity in port."[32] As both capital and migrants left for the United States, U.S. commercial power was augmented. In addition, John Calhoun noted that the "great demand for . . . agricultural products" was of particular value in helping to fund the first year of the war with Mexico.[33] "The immense sums which the misery of Ireland extorts" were incredible, wrote Bancroft.[34] The money allocated by the British government to relieve distress in 1847 equaled "the entire expense of the whole administration of the Federal Government . . . for two years, as conducted in 1845."[35] The famine augured the financial ruin of Britain, argued Bancroft, and the crisis entailed Britain's dependence on U.S. agricultural production, just as Walker had suggested. In a February 1847 despatch, when the spectacle of Irish distress was perhaps at its most graphic, he wrote to James Buchanan:

> The measures for Ireland will attract your attention. The duty on corn is abrogated until November next. . . . The usual industry of the country has been interrupted, and more than one fourth of the people of Ireland have been led to look for employment and support, to the Treasury of the United Kingdom. . . . Years must pass before the evils consequent on this state of things can be remedied; and all seem to agree, but in a good measure, for years to come, Ireland and this island, in part, will be dependent

on America for food. . . . Every body here perceives the benefits that will come to our country, which, as it is the most free, is fast tending to become the most opulent country in the world.[36]

In a private letter to Buchanan of the same date, he commented on the army of officials involved in distributing charity, arguing that "the moneys required by the misery of the pauper population of that wretched island . . . will sweep away every trace of the economy of the past years" and would produce such a dependence on governmental assistance as to "foster & increase the evil" of pauperism in Ireland.[37] Fundamentally, Bancroft saw the famine as illustrating the inferiority of the British system of political economy and as an opportunity to demonstrate and extend the commercial supremacy of the United States.

In diplomatic terms, Bancroft saw the condition of Ireland as limiting Britain's autonomy. He believed that British statesmen were deeply perturbed by U.S. commercial strength at a time of economic and political dislocation in Europe. Even had the British wanted to oppose the territorial expansion of the United States, Irish problems produced a "great disinclination of England to interfere."[38] Bancroft saw immense diplomatic capital in the material dependence on the United States that the Irish crisis bred. "You may be certain," he wrote, "that the embarrassments attending the settlement of Ireland have become so formidable, that for this reason, among others, England will be careful not to come into collision with the United States."[39] Though Lord John Russell and Henry Labouchere, chief secretary for Ireland, spoke in "the warmest manner" of U.S. philanthropy, Bancroft warned against interpreting this as meaning that Britain cheerfully approved of U.S. expansion.[40] Rather, "her consciousness of her inability [to interfere] effectually" bred a feigned indifference to U.S. territorial gains.[41] Irish famine and European instability convinced Bancroft of an asymmetry in Anglo-American commercial relations. "Lord John Russell is resolved on friendship with the United States; & England is conscious that such friendship is necessary," he concluded.[42] "We can do without England better than E[ngland] can do without us."[43]

Alongside opportunity came diagnosis. In his most extensive despatch on the causes of the famine, Bancroft wrote of the "great questions" that remained unresolved. The minister played the Marx of the Irish laboring classes, pointing to an ineffective political superstructure in Ireland that was dissociated from the realities of British commercial development.

England's prosperity has outgrown the system of government through the landed interest. The Towns now sway . . . the House of Commons. And yet English legislation is not lifted out of the forms which the landed interest had established. Collisions are therefore impending. . . . The same element lies at the bottom of the Irish question. The abolition of entails; the facility for the subdivision and sale of lands, the substitution of working proprietors for idle absentee proprietors, the placing of Irish burdens upon Irish property, which is chiefly owned by the English gentry, these are the measures which the industrial classes of England demand, which the landed interest resists, and which if carried into effect, will place Ireland implacably on the side of further popular, and even radical reforms in England.[44]

Irish distress was therefore symptomatic of a deep malaise within the British constitution.

Of course, Bancroft was not the only individual who provided a U.S. audience with news of and commentary on the progress of the famine. Along with newspaper reports, sometimes reprinted from British newspapers, and the correspondence (and, increasingly, the physical presence) of those who had experienced the famine first hand were a growing number of published accounts written by those who had traveled in Ireland. Though of course open to the charge that as travelers, they molded their accounts to fit their a priori assumptions, such writers contributed to "the creation of a famine spectacle" that prompted humanitarian sympathy in the United States.[45]

Most prominent among these travelers was Asenath Nicholson, an antislavery activist and advocate of vegetarianism and temperance.[46] Born in Chelsea, Vermont, but a New Yorker from the 1830s, she first traveled to Ireland in June 1844.[47] She was interested in the condition of the Irish poor in both Ireland and the United States, having visited the slums of New York City's Five Points District during a cholera outbreak in 1832.[48] Though she used her travels as an opportunity for proselytism, distributing Bibles in both English and Irish, she undertook them in an investigative spirit, hoping to present a compassionate and moving account of the famine to her audience. In 1850, she published an account of her travels in famine-stricken Ireland as the third part of her study of Irish history, *Lights and Shades of Ireland*. It was republished as a separate volume, *Annals of the Famine in Ireland*, a year later, suggesting that the public's appetite for her philanthropic work was greater than it was for her missionary endeavors.[49] Nicholson saw inequality as the fundamental problem in Irish society.

Poverty, she argued, had sapped the industry of the people and encouraged passivity in the face of suffering.[50] For the British and Irish elite, she noted, the spectacle of poverty engendered a discourse that saw the lowly Irish as active agents in their own degradation while blinding them to the failings of the British imperial state. In this she preempted the nationalist critique of Irish starvation, writing that it was a "mockery" to talk of "God's Famine [as] there was not a week . . . but there was sufficient food for the wants of that week, and *more* than sufficient," yet Britain failed in her imperial responsibilities.[51]

Like Nicholson, William Balch traveled through Ireland and presented his findings for an U.S. audience. Balch was a Universalist minister and another transplant to New York. Perhaps surprisingly for one who took the trouble of making a trip to Ireland, Balch had dabbled in nativism during the early 1840s.[52] His journey around Ireland in 1848 reinforced his sense of American exceptionalism and, more generally, his belief that republicanism was the only natural form of government, which he contrasted with the distorting and abnormal form of aristocratic rule that the British exercised in Ireland.[53] In landholding, religion, and the provision of education, Balch argued that American social and political relations were distinctive and superior.[54] Ireland demonstrated the evils of Old World political theory in microcosm.

This sense of political-institutional supremacy had its apparent apotheosis in the commercial vibrancy of the United States, which was ever more evident as the country emerged from the economic dislocation that followed the Panic of 1837. And from this exceptional economic bounty, argued many Americans, came an imperative for Americans to use their providentially ordained wealth for humanitarian relief in Ireland. Nicholson wrote that Americans sent food out of gratitude for God's munificence and suggested that Britain "call on [her] transatlantic sister" in order to feed the starving Irish.[55] The role of Providence was a common theme in conceptions of American aid: Providence determined American abundance just as it dictated Irish destitution.[56] Rather than dictating passivity, however, this interpretation emphasized the obligations of charity. Because the United States could afford relief, they should send it, argued the Boston *Daily Atlas*, an argument that was often repeated in the early months of 1847.[57] Interpretations of U.S. commercial supremacy, then, cut both ways. Those with an eye to a U.S. economic sphere of influence saw the famine as presenting an enticing vista of commercial opportunity. For others, the buoyancy of the U.S. economy—and the great profits to be made from shipping western grain to Europe—fused with a culture of politicized evangelicalism to demand a humanitarian response to Irish suffering. That response was overwhelming.

Money from America

As historian Oliver MacDonagh has noted, "Americans . . . were very well informed of the progress of distress in Ireland.[58] Their reaction was remarkable. The importance of private philanthropy was increased by the Russell ministry's emphasis on public fiscal restraint. Central to that philanthropy was the Religious Society of Friends, the Quakers, who "were the major organizers and conveyors of Irish relief in the United States as well as [in] England and Ireland."[59] Their charity was certainly the best documented, and their *Transactions of the Central Relief Committee during the Famine in Ireland* provide an invaluable historical resource for students of the famine.[60]

One explanation for the prominence of Quakers in relief efforts from the United States is their apparent nonsectarianism (though Quakers were not immune to anti-Catholic sentiment.)[61] Nativist suspicions militated against non-Catholic citizens making donations via a specifically "Irish" or "Roman" network of remittance, and the Society of Friends was an acceptable alternative.[62] For Catholic communities, Roman Catholic bishop John Hughes acted as an intermediary.[63]

Perceiving the inadequacy of the efforts of the British government, Dublin's Central Relief Committee (a private committee of philanthropic Friends) made contact with Quakers in London, New York, and Philadelphia to establish a charitable network that would forward funds to purchase food for the starving Irish.[64] In early December 1846, Jonathan Pim, a secretary for the Central Relief Committee, wrote to Jacob Harvey, a leading New York Quaker, of the "appalling effects" that might follow "the almost total failure of the potato crop."[65] Pim urged Harvey to circulate an address calling for charitable contributions, pointing out that Quakers in London were already contributing large subscriptions to the central fund.

At the end of December, Harvey reported that the Philadelphia Quakers were active in promoting philanthropy and that arrangements had been made to set up a mechanism for channeling remittances. He was especially struck by the amount of money remitted by Irish immigrants to their friends and families back home. He noted that he had done some cursory research on "those houses that give small drafts to the poor Irish" and had found that remittances from such households were "greater than ever before known at this period."[66] He expressed his amazement:

> I am happy to say that the poor labouring Irish themselves are doing their duty fully. Without any public meetings or addresses, they have been silently remitting their little savings. . . . These drafts are from £1, upwards; they probably average between £4 and £5. . . . I had ascertained from five [financial] houses here, that within the past sixty days they had received and remitted from the poor Irish, eighty thousand dollars. . . . I have collected further returns. . . . The sum total remitted since November 1st amounts to 150,000 dollars, or £30,000 sterling! . . . For the whole year 1846 . . . I have received returns from the five principal [banking] houses, and the sum total is 650,000 dollars, or £130,000 sterling. There are four houses yet to hear from.[67]

A second calculation in March 1847 revealed an even greater total. "The Irish emigrant remittances for Jan. & Feb. in small bills—to their families & connections from Boston, New York, Philada. & Baltimore—is $623,000," wrote Harvey. "There is no mistake about it. I have taken pains to come at the truth & I am under the mark."[68] To give these amounts some context, using Harvey's conversion rate, the Irish in these various urban centers raised £130,000 in 1846 and about the same amount again the first two months of 1847 (a total of approximately $1.3 million in modern terms). The *total amount* donated by the principal British philanthropic association was £430,000 (just over $2 million in modern terms).[69]

How much was remitted in all from the United States? William Lloyd Garrison suggested that £50,000 (approximately $240,000 in 1847) had been sent between the initial call for funds in December 1846 and the middle of February 1847.[70] An American visitor to Ireland estimated that, altogether, £200,000 ($959,000) had been sent via the Quakers' philanthropic network.[71] The lack of clarity perhaps reflects the multiplicity of routes that money could take from the United States to Ireland. Remittances from the Irish in the United States, outside the Quakers' ledger books, are a complicating factor (and, as noted, potentially a very large one). John Francis Maguire, an Irish MP visiting the United States in 1868, estimated that over the previous twenty-five years £24,000,000 ($115,000,000), had been transmitted in this way, though the evidence he relied on is unknown. This would give an average annual remittance just short of £1,000,000 ($4,790,000).[72] More chronologically precise, historian Kerby Miller follows Timothy Sarbaugh in estimating that almost $1,000,000 worth of provisions were donated in response to the famine.[73] Though "America sent much money and many ship-loads of provisions" that did not pass through the distribution network of the Society of Friends, we can at least quantify a minimum level of philanthropy by referring to the statistics provided in the Society's *Transactions*.[74]

In addition to this cargo, the Society forwarded another £16,000 ($76,700) in financial relief between April 1847 and July 1848. In total, the Society recorded just short of £150,000 ($719,000) in aid.[75]

Table 1. Quantities and money value of shipments from the United States to Ireland

Shipped at	Quantity (Tons)	Value (with approximate 1847 U.S. dollar equivalent)
New York, NY	4,658	£62,372.12s.2d.($299,000)
Philadelphia, PA	2052	£27,446.15s.8d.($132,000)
New Orleans, LA	453	£6,786.12s.8d.($32,500)
Newark, NJ	410	£6,739.13s.4d.($32,300)
Baltimore, MD	361	£4,028.17s.4d.($19,300)
Richmond, VA	252	£3,727.14s.10d.($17,900)
Charleston, SC	171	£1,650.15s.2d.($7,910)
Alexandria, VA	126	£2,010.15s.5d.($9,630)
New Orleans, Boston, &c., per William Rathbone, Liverpool	1,067	£15,551.4s.6d.($74,500)
Ditto, U.S. consul at Cork	220	£1,978.4s.0d.($9,480)
Apalachicola, FL, per ditto at Liverpool	37	£238.11s.3d.($1,140)
Other ports in the United States	103	£1,288.15s.3d.($6,170)
Port unknown, per Rawlins and Son, Liverpool	1	£26.16s.6d.($125)
Total	9,911	£133,847.7s.7d.($642,000)

Source: Transactions of the Central Relief Committee of the Society of Friends During the Famine in Ireland, in 1846 and 1847 (Dublin: Hodges and Smith, 1852), 334. Pound to dollar conversions calculated using Lawrence H. Officer and Samuel H. Williamson, "Computing 'Real Value' over Time with a Conversion between U.K. Pounds and U.S. Dollars, 1830 to Present," Measuring Worth website, www.measuringworth.com. Using Officer and Williamson's calculations, £133,847 in 1847 equals approximately $14,200,000 in modern (2013) terms.

The Politics of Relief

With American newspapers saturated by coverage of the terrible poverty experienced in Ireland, leading U.S. politicians gathered in an unofficial capacity in Washington, D.C., on February 9, 1847. The meeting, which was chaired by Vice President George Dallas, attracted a long list of senators and representatives: one from each state and a delegate each from the District of Columbia and the Wisconsin Territory. In addition to numerous celebrated statesmen, Thomas Ritchie, editor of the administration's mouthpiece, *The Union*, and William Erigena Robinson, the Washington correspondent of Horace Greeley's *New-York Tribune*, were also present, serving as two of the meeting's eight secretaries.[76] In transmitting news of the meeting to London, Richard Pakenham, the British minister to the United States, stated that he had "no doubt" that aid from the United States would prove "considerable."[77]

The group passed resolutions that established a new network for channeling collections to major ports for shipping in collaboration with the existing arteries of Quaker benevolence.[78] Committees for accepting donations of food and clothing were established at New York and New Orleans. The meeting further resolved to recommend "to the inhabitants of all the cities, towns and villages in the United States" that they "immediately . . . appoint committees to receive contributions and make collections to be forwarded."[79] The collection of relief was therefore neither wholly centrally directed nor entirely dependent on spontaneous, bottom-up organization. National coordination directed and made more effective the extraordinary levels of local charity throughout the United States.

The resolutions and circulars this meeting generated consciously framed the relief efforts as national.[80] One Philadelphia newspaper pointed out that the interest in alleviating Irish suffering was not limited by class and was explicitly nonsectional.[81] It is instructive that Pakenham's correspondence detailed a united American effort to aid Ireland alongside descriptions of rancor in Congress about the Mexican-American War and the Wilmot Proviso.[82] Southerners, like northerners, took up the cause of famine philanthropy. In one week Charlestonians forwarded £1,300 (approximately $6,200); the fund-raising was led by the city's Hibernian Society.[83] The society received provisions from the state's interior, aided by the "South Carolina [Rail] Road [who] transported [donations] free of charge to the city."[84] The leading historian of the Irish in the south notes that $14,000 and 400 bags of corn were donated, though this arguably underestimates the extent of donations as this represents only what had been collected by the middle of March 1847. At any rate, it is important to note that famine aid was a *national* movement at a time of pervasive sectional tensions. It was not exclusively a northeastern phenomenon.[85]

The generosity of private individuals and associations in the United States contrasted favorably with the actions of the federal government. Despite the involvement of several prominent politicians in charitable efforts to alleviate the Irish famine, U.S. involvement remained a venture of private associations that lacked the official sanction of the U.S. government. Coincident with the meeting in Washington D.C., a Whig congressman from New York, Washington Hunt, announced his intention to bring a relief bill before the House the following day.[86] The bill requested that the U.S. government appropriate $500,000 to spend on "articles of subsistence" and provide transportation to ship it to the suffering in Ireland.[87] The resolution was referred to the Committee of the Whole but was never seriously debated. With the end of the congressional session looming, members were locked in debate about the possibility of seizing land from Mexico and the future of slavery in the potential new territories. Charles J. Ingersoll, a Pennsylvania Democrat, tried to pressure Congress to consider the motion to no avail.[88] Hunt made one last "strong effort" to salvage his bill, "but the House refused."[89]

In the closing days of February, John Crittenden, a Kentucky Whig, introduced a bill in the Senate with the same provisions. Emphasizing precedent—the United States had purchased $50,000 worth of aid to send to Venezuela in the aftermath of an earthquake in 1812—Crittenden spoke of the great "moral spectacle" of aid "tendered" in liberal spirit, "in the name of the Government of the United States to that of Great Britain" to alleviate suffering in Ireland.[90] He drew on familiar arguments, speaking of humanitarian duty, the familial connections between the United States and Ireland, and the philanthropic obligations that American abundance created. Alluding to the possibility that some might raise constitutional objections to the bill, he argued that "it would be strange . . . if our Constitution was so fashioned and framed as to interdict the exercise of Christian charity."[91] Moreover, he made his political intentions clear. He hoped that such a gift from one government to another would render war more infrequent and improve international relations.

Senators John M. Clayton, Daniel Webster, John Calhoun, and Lewis Cass, among others, spoke in favor of the bill. Webster spoke of being "delicate" in offering aid and blunted Crittenden's language of intergovernmental conciliation, replacing the reference to "the Government" with "the people" of the United States.[92] Calhoun, who was often associated with a strict reading of the Constitution, favored the bill and even suggested broadening the scope of relief, arguing that reports of food shortages in France justified American attention. Some senators were nonetheless troubled by the constitutionality of such measures. A proposal to replace direct financial aid with the use of American naval vessels garnered some support but was voted down.[93] Ultimately, the Senate passed Crittenden's resolution by twenty-seven votes to thirteen. Support for the bill came from seventeen Whig Senators and ten Democrats. Partisanship rather than geography characterized opposition to the bill: eleven Democrats and only two Whigs (William S. Archer of Virginia and George E. Badger of North Carolina) voted against it. Interestingly, both Democratic senators from New York voted against the resolution, suggesting that something more than simply courting Irish votes was involved.

The bill faced greater opposition when it was sent to the House. Nativist leader Lewis Levin was again a central figure. He saw the bill as nothing more than "food for party vultures" and suggested that it be referred to the Committee on Ways and Means.[94] With only a few days remaining in the final session of the twenty-ninth Congress, Levin's measure was designed to kill the bill without bringing it to a vote. The attempt was successful. Robert C. Winthrop, a Massachusetts Whig, and John Wentworth, an Illinois Democrat, failed in their attempts to force the bill to the floor of the House. Winthrop, a member of the Ways and Means Committee, believed that the real reason the committee did not report the bill to the House was because "a general 'understanding' existed among the members that, if the bill passed, President Polk would veto it."[95] One Whig newspaper reported that "the Loco-foco majority dares not strike down the bill in the face of day; but they strangle it in the dark" so they could avoid responsibility for vetoing a proposition "to feed their starving kindred in Ireland."[96]

The allegation that President Polk intended to veto the bill was true. Polk noted the progress of the relief bill in his diary, and in the Cabinet, he "stated unequivocally" that he would veto any such measure that came before him on constitutional grounds, despite his personal sympathy with the suffering in Ireland.[97] Polk claimed to have discarded his veto message once it became clear that the House would not put him in the undesirable position of having to deny humanitarian aid to the Irish, but copies of it remain in his private papers.[98] On the back of one he had scrawled: "It turned out the Bill did not pass the Ho.Repts—Had it passed . . . I should have sent in this *veto* message."[99] In it he expressed his doubts over the constitutionality of the measure, arguing that "the power is certainly not to be found in the expressly enumerated grants of the Constitution; and I am at a loss to discover the express power to which it is a 'necessary and proper' incident."[100] Moreover, he felt that such a measure would set a dangerous precedent and might retard private benevolence:

> The world has never witnessed a more beautiful spectacle than that which is now presented throughout the length and breadth of our happy land. . . . I entertain serious doubts whether in the end such an assumption [of charitable work] would not reduce instead of increase the aggregate amount of donations.[101]

It's entirely possible that Polk slyly used the issue of Irish famine relief as a means of asserting authority over his Cabinet. Though he had committed himself to serving only one term as president, he was increasingly aggravated by the ambitions of his Cabinet associates. In particular, he suspected Secretary of State James Buchanan of prioritizing his own political ambitions over the collective good of sound Cabinet decision-making.[102] Polk instructed both Buchanan and his secretary of the navy, James Young Mason, to read and revise his text. The section extolling the great spectacle of aid from the United States was Mason's; Buchanan tightened some of the language. A copy in the latter's hand is extant in Polk's papers.[103] Polk himself never referred to the political uses of these drafts, but it seems plausible to suggest that he saw some value in keeping them.

The *Jamestown* and America's Contested Philanthropy

Though Democrats stalled the relief bill in the House, Congress approved the use of two naval vessels, the *Jamestown* and the *Macedonian*, to ship private donations to Ireland on the "last stormy day of the session."[104] Those who had voted against Crittenden's resolution defined the measure as distinct from financial aid as it represented only "the use" of government property rather than its permanent transfer.[105] William Lloyd Garrison claimed that "a petition . . . from our [Boston's] merchants to Congress" prompted the resolution, as did Robert Bennet Forbes, who captained the *Jamestown* on its resultant voyage to Cork.[106] Forbes, in fact, was emphatic in stressing his own agency in bringing about the measure, and his correspondence reveals the competition between the merchants of Boston and those of New York for the leadership of Irish relief efforts.[107]

A romantic figure who was largely uninhibited by modesty, Forbes left considerable correspondence about his voyage to Ireland. He also published a memoir, *The Voyage of the Jamestown*, on his return. These allow us to reconstruct the preparation and conduct of the relief mission and use his visit to gauge the impact of transatlantic philanthropy on Anglo-American relations. In accordance with the instructions of Congress, Secretary of the Navy John Mason placed the *Jamestown* under Forbes's command and gave him responsibility for outfitting the ship. He also confirmed that, as expected, there would be no naval officer present on board: the ship was put at Forbes's disposal purely to facilitate private actions.[108] As a sloop of war, the *Jamestown*'s armament had to be removed before she could be loaded with provisions. Once this was done, loading began on St. Patrick's Day, March 17, 1847, in the main conducted by the Irish immigrant workers of the Laborers' Aid Society.[109] Loaded with Indian meal, bread, corn and other provisions, the ship set sail on the March 28 and anchored at Cove (today's Cobh), County Cork on April 12.[110] Ten days later, its cargo discharged, the *Jamestown* set out on its return voyage to Boston.[111]

Unsurprisingly, Forbes received a rapturous welcome on his arrival in Ireland. The citizens of Cove presented him with an address expressing their "sincere and lively gratitude to the great American people, for their generous sympathy" and "honor to the citizens of Massachusetts . . . [for their] assistance in the present afflicting condition of our unhappy country."[112] Forbes and his crew were somewhat embarrassed to be the guests of honor at a sumptuous dinner, the munificence of which contrasted starkly with the deprivation that surrounded them.[113] Forbes diplomatically commented on "the kindness of the Corkonians" and, on leaving, he was treated to a series of speeches giving thanks for the *Jamestown* mission and his part in it. He received "addresses from all quarters . . . [and] a beautiful Litho[graph] of the Ship . . . [and] an engraving beautifully framed of the Tower of Mr. Connor, erected to the great Father Mathew."[114]

Forbes's ability to plug into elite networks was central to the effective distribution of American philanthropy. Distributing goods and money was a collaborative effort that depended on the agency of British government officials; religious association networks, particularly the Society of Friends; and, on occasion, U.S. minister to Great Britain George Bancroft.[115] Forbes traveled with letters of introduction to the lord lieutenant and the chief secretary for Ireland, both written by one of Bancroft's predecessors,

Edward Everett.[116] From other sources he carried letters of introduction to John Murphy, the bishop of Cork, and to the temperance leader Theobald Mathew.[117] Within the British political elite, Forbes's principal contact was William Rathbone, a Liberal ex-mayor of Liverpool with a keen interest in Irish affairs. Rathbone was heir to a highly successful shipping business with a diverse portfolio, including a substantial interest in Southern cotton.[118] Most likely, Rathbone and Forbes's personal connection sprang from the involvement of both families in the lucrative trade with China. Through Rathbone, Robert Forbes could make contact with the world of Anglo-American high finance: the Rathbones had built a close relationship with Joshua Bates, the American-born senior partner at Barings Bank in London.[119] Bates was a pivotal figure in the overlapping worlds of Anglo-American finance and diplomacy, and Forbes made use of his substantial political capital to ensure a quick turnaround at Cork.[120] With the help of Bates and Rathbone—and with the "cordial and efficient" intercessions of the British government—approximately 4,000 barrels of kiln-dried Indian meal, 1,000 barrels of peas and beans, and 5,000 bushels of Indian corn were unloaded and distributed.[121]

Just as the U.S. federal government played an auxiliary role in philanthropy through the loan of naval vessels, so the British government supplemented American beneficence through freight remittances, expedited treasury procedures, and the provision of naval assistance.[122] The high price of Irish and British foodstuffs convinced U.S.-based relief organizers that it was more cost effective to ship food from the United States than it was to forward money.[123] There were also suggestions that the improvident Irish might squander any money sent to them.[124] However, transporting tangible goods added tariff and freight costs to the expense of shipping. This cost, though not prohibitive, ate into the sums collected for famine relief. In late February 1847, the Irish Relief Committee of New York wrote to Dublin offering to pay the freight on goods shipped to Ireland, but as it transpired, its generosity was not needed.[125] In response to inquiries, U.S. minister Richard Pakenham was able to confirm that the British government would "pay the freight of any provisions or clothing, which benevolent persons in the United States may send to Ireland . . . on proof being afforded that the articles were purchased from the produce of private subscription, and have been appropriated to charitable objects."[126]

The British government took pains to show its gratitude. Richard Pakenham had paid great attention to American philanthropic efforts, and his positive reports prompted Lord Palmerston to append a note of thanks to

a February 1847 despatch. In it he instructed Pakenham "to take every opportunity of saying how grateful Her Majesty's Government & the British
Nation at large feel for their kind & honorable Manifestation of Sympathy . . . for the sufferings of the Irish People."[127] Anglo-American cooperation over famine aid bred a correspondingly friendly tone. Though
Forbes doubted that the British ministry were as enthusiastic about the
reception of American charity as they appeared to be—on the back of a
note of thanks from Lord John Russell, he had scrawled the single word
"laconic"—others were more willing to believe that British warmth was
sincere.[128] Bancroft reported that although the British reaction to U.S. territorial acquisition remained cool, Russell had expressed himself both in
public and private with great amiability and gratitude for U.S. philanthropy
in response to the famine. In addition,

> [Chief Secretary for Ireland] Mr. Labouchere . . . spoke to me in the warmest
> manner, expressing his satisfaction both with reference to the amount, which
> is here universally acknowledged to be considerable, and still more, with ref-
> erence to the friendly feeling which the movement manifested, and which,
> he observed, appeared to pervade all classes of our society, and all parts of
> our country. His manner, and his words, were as satisfactory as possible.[129]

Thus Bancroft added the "good feeling" fostered by American aid to his
interpretation of U.S. commercial ascendancy.[130] A British correspondent
of John Calhoun rejoiced at "the strength of kindred feeling between
two people" that was manifested by "the benevolent on your side of the
Atlantick."[131]

Lord Palmerston expressed his interpretation of famine aid clearly and
unreservedly as an expression of Anglo-American conciliation:

> It might indeed have been Expected that a generous & high minded na-
> tion would deeply commiserate the sufferings which an awful visitation of
> Providence has inflicted upon so large a Population descended from the
> same ancestors as themselves. . . . [This] active & Energetic assistance . . . re-
> flects the highest Honor upon our Transatlantic Bretheren [and] must
> tend to draw closer and to render stronger and more lasting those Ties of
> Friendship and Mutual Esteem which Her Majesty's Government trust
> will ever bind together The Two great Branches of the anglo saxon Family
> separated indeed by Geographical Position but united by common Interest
> to which every succeeding year must add Extension & Force.[132]

Similarly, the lord lieutenant of Ireland, Lord Bessborough, found "consolation" in the fact that the great calamity of the famine came with the silver lining of affording "the occasion for the development of that charitable sympathy on the part of a great and a sister nation, which is the strongest assurance of mutual good will."[133]

The familial language and Anglo-Saxon racialization of Palmerston's note raise the question of how far responses to the famine were conditioned by race. There was great contemporary interest, both scholarly and popular, in ethnological, phrenological, and racial theories.[134] Ralph Waldo Emerson, for one, spoke in exuberant tones of "the Saxon, the colossus who bestrides the narrow Atlantic" and disparaged the poverty-stricken Irish, replicating the antipathy toward the Irish that his hero, Thomas Carlyle, manifested in his own works.[135] Others were less certain in their racial categorizations, speaking of Irish "Celts" as belonging to the same division of the "Caucasian race" as the Anglo-Saxons or folding various Europeans into a valorized "American" race.[136] An ideology of Anglo-Saxon brotherhood may well have provided underpinned famine relief for some, but this characterization took place at an individual rather than a collective level. Public relief efforts were not couched in this language. Far more common were ideas about the enervating effect of Catholicism and the endemic poverty engendered by the evils of British landholding in Ireland, both of which appeared to contemporaries to be confirmed by the famine.

Turning from motivation to effect—the blossoming good feeling that Palmerston's note of thanks points to—it seems entirely plausible to suggest that American benevolence was seen as giving a fillip to Anglo-Saxonist ideas. Certainly American statesmen of such diverse political backgrounds as Robert Walker and Abbott Lawrence spoke of closer Anglo-American relations underpinned by racial affinity in the early 1850s.[137] As will be seen, many American statesmen talked of the death of Irish nationality (and by extension, we might assume, Irish nationalism) consequent on the famine and mass migration that followed. For them, the famine seemed to be a watershed moment, after which Ireland might be incorporated more fully into the British imperial system. This in turn would remove a major impediment to Anglo-American rapprochement and clear the way for Britain and the United States, as Lawrence put it, to give "not only . . . their language, but their laws to the world, and defy the power of all *despots* on the face of the Globe."[138]

In keeping with the British government's conciliatory attitude, Robert Forbes's visit is striking for its lack of subversiveness or rather for Forbes's desire to avoid seeming to be subversive of British power in Ireland. In part, this was accomplished by diminishing the profile of Irish agency and rendering philanthropy as a series of transactions between American and British actors. On occasion, however, the consensual patina of the Anglo-Irish-American relationship was disrupted by partisan concerns. Alongside the banal thanks of so many, various groups addressing Forbes took the opportunity to press their own interpretations of the famine, revealing limits to the bonhomie of transatlantic philanthropy.[139] Forbes left accounts of at least three such instances. First, an address from the citizens of Cork spoke of their gratitude for receiving American "generosity . . . *undogged by any conditions*," and their earnest desire "to live in benevolent amity with the rulers of the British Empire."[140]

Then, on April 17, Forbes received an address from the Tenant League of Cork. Proclaiming the nobility of American aid when the commercial advantages of the famine might have proved more alluring, the Tenant League placed responsibility for the terrible suffering at the feet of the system of landholding that prevailed in Ireland. Though "our land is fruitful; our clime genial; our people frugal and laborious; and our Sovereign gracious yet we perish," they argued, pointing to the "*Monster* . . . Landlordism" that had "crept into the Councils of State [and] shackled our beloved Queen with laws of his own making."[141] Forbes thanked William Trenwith, secretary of the league, for his address but excused himself from responding immediately, stating that he had "no sympathy with party politics."[142] In a later letter to Trenwith he spoke in vague terms about his hopes that "those who are in power" would come together to promote social reform.[143] Forbes wrote weakly that "it cannot be that a good Providence has brought about this dispensation of famine and pestilence without some good end" and concluded by wishing that Trenwith had conveyed his address "more privately . . . to give more a more suitable time for its hearing."[144] Forbes's discomfort was evident.

Finally, Thomas Francis Meagher presented Forbes with an address the day before the *Jamestown* set out on its return voyage to the United States. Meagher, with John Mitchel, William Smith O'Brien, and other Young Irelanders, had parted with Daniel O'Connell's Repeal Association and, in January 1847, had formed the Irish Confederation as a more assertive nationalist body.[145] Meagher's address challenged the marginal status of Irish nationalist politics during Forbes's visit. In response, the Bostonian thanked him in very uncertain terms:

> I acknowledge myself . . . so little acquainted with the different political parties in Ireland, that I am not aware how or exactly for what purpose this confederation is constituted, but Sir, as an American & a citizen of that part of the United States, *which is really free*, I must say, that the sound of "confederation" is grateful to my ears—& I take it for granted that it must imply a bond of unity—against some existing or part evil, & whether evils of government, or of fanaticism, or the not lesser evils of intemperance, I am happy that the body, which you represent, is uniting to assert the *rights of men who should be free*—I say that Sir—without any knowledge of your Constitution or bye laws—I trust I am not heading on ground which an impartial man, coming with relief to all grades & parties should not occupy—I have endeavoured Sir to believe that the mission of the Jamestown will serve to unite all parties & all creeds even more than sweet charity has already united them.[146]

Reflecting on his time in Ireland, Forbes thought that "so much was said of a political nature while expressing the gratitude of Irishmen, that the sympathies of Englishmen & especially the British Government were somewhat dampened."[147] For some, Forbes's own personality was seen as problematic. Though he claimed he wanted to eschew "all [personal] glorification," Forbes, wrote Edward Everett, lacked "the requisite tact for the [philanthropic] work, & I saw at first glance, that his doings in Ireland would not suit the meridian of London."[148] However, Everett weighed "some ostentation" on Forbes's part against "a little coldness" from Britain and concluded that, overall, "the good has been done."[149] Forbes and his hosts certainly spoke a mutual language of providentialism, of American benevolence, and of sanguine hopes for the effects of future British governance in Ireland. He even went so far as to criticize "the good people of Cork and Cove" and, remarkably, hoped that the famine might promote greater anti-sectarian, nonpartisan interaction.[150] "[The people] expect too much," he argued. "They should forget political animosities, and unite in the great work of the regeneration of Ireland."[151]

Given the widespread knowledge of—and support for—the repeal movement in the United States earlier in the decade, the absence of Irish nationalist politics in discussions about the provision of aid is striking. In part, this is a consequence of the incredible human cost of the famine.

Understandably, Irish suffering was seen as an issue that was beyond constitutional politics. Moreover, repeal in the United States had largely collapsed
by 1846. One or two groups continued to meet, but in general the public
meetings that were organized in response to the famine were independent
of an Irish American nationalist constituency.[152] The *Brooklyn Daily Eagle*
reported that the chair of one local meeting had groused that "a great deal
of money had been sent to Ireland in the name of repeal," but he "did not
know that the people were any better for it."[153] Given the low standing of
repeal after O'Connell's declarations of fidelity to British abolitionist diplomacy, it seems plausible to suggest that this independence from nationalist
politics encouraged rather than retarded giving.

Even in diagnosing the causes of the famine, Americans shied away from
the more aggressive interpretations later offered by nationalist ideologues.
Throughout this period of astounding philanthropy, there seemed to be
little correlation between charity and support for Irish nationalism. Speakers at famine aid meetings celebrated the absence of political dissension,
and while they might criticize British imperial rule, they framed palliatives
in imperial rather than national terms.[154] Reform rather than revolution
was to be looked for.

Other observers were more interested in American moral supremacy.
William Balch, for instance, was clear that transatlantic charity represented
a triumph of the American social and political system over the institutions of Great Britain. "Our charity has not been thrown away," he trumpeted.[155] "How much more glorious is a victory thus gained over the
prejudices and hatred of an arrogant and hostile nation, than one won by
the sword in battle!"[156] Referring to those who were concerned that such
actions would constitute an affront to British pride, he wrote: "Let others
carp about the indignity to Britain's sense of honor. . . . No matter! It is
an offence which ought to come—a rebuke which she should receive."[157]
Likewise, American newspapers trumpeted the "sublime spectacle" of "this
young people giving alms to the Old World."[158] U.S. benevolence offered
"a commentary on our institutions, which will be felt throughout Europe," noted one southern newspaper.[159] "Is not this triumph of humanity
as far above the paltry triumphs of diplomacy and of arms as the sublime
heights of God's glory are above the defeated and plotting spirit of evil?"[160]
Just as Bancroft saw in the famine an opportunity to project U.S. commercial power, some believed that the famine offered the United States
the opportunity to "extend the influence of her moral empire" in the Old
World.[161]

Famine and the Apparent Death of Irish Nationhood

What was the significance of American benevolence? Most obviously, American philanthropy generated pro-American sentiment in Ireland. American aid was received in the most positive terms. "Were it not for the america provision half ireland was dead Long since," wrote one Irish-woman.[162] The Dublin *Nation* contrasted American and English concep-tions of the famine and spoke glowingly of "the establishment of a cordial understanding between [Ireland] and the United States."[163] The Irish Con-federation took the opportunity of sending Vice-President Dallas a letter of thanks that emphasized the historic links between the two "countries," ex-pressing hope that "the current of trade . . . shall continue to flow when the occasion of its first direction [the famine] shall have happily passed away" and hinted at "future relations important to both countries" that would follow on this commercial intercourse.[164] The United States was seen as a land of opportunity and abundance even before famine-era philanthropy, and American benevolence perpetuated and strengthened this perception. During William Balch's visit to Ireland, when crowds learned of his nation-ality, they swarmed around him, offering their gratitude for food from the United States.[165] Yet not all shared in this good feeling. The fervor aroused by American charity washed away antipathy to American slavery, lamented Irish abolitionist James Haughton, who went so far as to advocate rejecting donations from southern relief committees.[166]

From an American perspective, the Whig response to the famine is of particular interest. As noted, the Senate vote authorizing the use of the *Jamestown* and the *Macedonian* received overwhelmingly disproportionate support from Whig members. Moreover, Whig merchants and politicians led the efforts of Bostonians to raise money and collect provisions." Edward Everett and Abbott Lawrence, both Whigs, served on the city's Committee of Relief.[167] Both men had strong ties to U.S.-British political relations: Everett had served as minister to Great Britain from 1841 to 1845 and Lawrence would serve in this capacity from 1849 to 1852. Undoubtedly partisan interest in supporting aid that was opposed by President Polk and administration Democrats in Congress was strong, and Boston was a dis-proportionately Whig city. More enlightening is the support that famine aid received from the Whig press and the way that Whigs conceived of the relationship between their philanthropy and their domestic political con-cerns. As mentioned, Whig newspapers commented on the obligation of

articles reporting the "depopulation of Ireland," the "Celtic Exodus" to the United States, and the prodigious change in the "balance of power" that would inevitably follow.[183]

The seemingly terminal failure of Irish nationalism in 1848 only confirmed one of the most striking aspects of the famine relief efforts: the marginal presence of any discourse of Irish self-determination in the United States. Even before the uprising, Meagher and his confederates were very much outside the tent looking in on the Anglo-American niceties surrounding the delivery of the *Jamestown's* consignment. Failure, disillusionment and exile made many feel that it no longer seemed to make sense to speak of an "Irish nation." In William Balch's view, Ireland had been converted into "the manufactory of a race which is spreading itself . . . among all the nations of the earth," but which in the aggregate could never constitute an independent nation.[184]

Ireland's apparent status as an Anglo-American ward was confirmed by an unofficial approach the United States made to the British government during the winter of 1851–1852. Secretary of State Daniel Webster instructed Massachusetts Whig Abbott Lawrence, the minister to Great Britain from 1849 to 1852, to ask for the release of various Young Ireland prisoners who had been exiled to Van Diemen's Land after the 1848 uprising.[185] In this, the Fillmore administration undoubtedly sought to dampen pro-Irish agitation in the United States while courting the support of Irish American voters.[186] The State Department received letters and petitions advocating some formal representation on behalf of the exiles from mass meetings, state governors, legislatures, and even from members of Congress.[187] President Fillmore received a delegation of prominent Irish Americans in January 1852, though the meeting had little impact on government policy.[188] Daniel Webster did not share the popular enthusiasm for foreign intervention that had been aroused by the visit of exiled Hungarian nationalist Louis Kossuth's 1851 visit to the United States, and recognized that the case of the Van Diemen's Land Irishmen "was not deemed one proper for official interference of any kind."[189] Despite this, he believed that an Anglo-American concord might be fashioned whereby the prisoners' release would be secured contingent on their emigration to the United States.

Webster, a conservative Massachusetts Whig like Lawrence, invested in this idea because of the domestic political benefits it might bring. Yet the proposal also suggests a broader perspective: Webster believed Britain and the United States could reach an unofficial diplomatic agreement that would marginalize the disruptive influence of the Irish question on transatlantic diplomacy. This hope was predicated on the growing amiability that characterized relations with Great Britain in the late 1840s. As Abbott Lawrence wrote in his second despatch from London, he was received "not only with courtesy, but with great kindness" by the British ministry, and as we have seen, he was enthusiastic about the potential implications of closer Anglo-American relations.[190] In May 1850, he confided to Secretary of State John Clayton that he believed there had never been "so much good feeling" displayed toward the United States.[191] "High & honor[a]ble feelings" between the countries spurred the "march of civilization," he argued. "The ties that should bind these two great nations together, it appears to me are becoming stronger every day."[192]

Lawrence recognized that partisanship imposed limits on this good-naturedness and that great tact was essential in approaching the British government about the release of the Irish prisoners.[193] Lawrence's conservatism made him an especially well-suited emissary, but his task was complicated by the concurrent actions of the U.S. Congress, which acted under the impression that the Fillmore administration had declined to take up the subject.[194] With the 1852 elections approaching, the presidential game was "being played *deeply*," wrote one observer.[195] At the opening of the December 1851 session, Senator Henry Foote, a Democrat from Mississippi, introduced a resolution requesting that Fillmore open correspondence with the British government concerning the possibility of releasing William Smith O'Brien and Thomas Francis Meagher "and their immediate associates."[196]

Beyond the competition for Irish votes, the congressional debate that followed is interesting for the care taken to frame any interposition in terms conducive to good Anglo-American relations. Senator James Shields, an Irish-born Democrat from Illinois, amended Foote's resolution to make it more sensitive to British sentiments, disclaiming "all intention of interfering in any way in the internal affairs of the Kingdom of Great Britain and Ireland."[197] Any clemency would be regarded "as a new proof of the friendly disposition of the British Government towards our Republic," and could do nothing to stir Irish revolutionism, as Britain "has nothing to fear from Irish agitation now."[198] It was purposeless to talk of the dangers of Irish nationalism, as "Ireland is at this moment as feeble, helpless, and hopeless, as the most anti-Irish heart can desire. Her nationality is gone. . . . She has no future," Shields continued.[199] "Ireland is . . . no longer a nation."[200] As such, Ireland's future lay within the structure of the British Empire. "I have arrived at the conclusion that the present policy of Ireland is, to abandon all idea of a political separation from England," he argued.

Her old nationality is gone. . . . Her policy now is to make the most of her present political connection, and to avail herself of all the . . . advantages of the British Empire. She should cooperate. . . . She should throw her whole weight into the scale of liberalism. Her movement should be an imperial one.[201]

Despite this conciliatory tone, Abbott Lawrence griped about meetings on the subject of the Irish exiles in the United States, concerned that American politicking might undermine the effectiveness of his representations to the foreign secretary.[202] Those representations ultimately failed. Conservative prime minister Lord Derby rejected Lawrence's argument that because British law had been vindicated, "international advantages" and decreased discontent in Ireland would follow clemency.[203] He noted that the prisoners had already received clemency—they had not been executed—and voiced his fear that should John Mitchel and his co-revolutionists make their way to the United States, "they would be received by the great Irish population there as Martyrs . . . which, instead of creating good feeling between the two Countries, would produce an opposite result."[204] Though he was unable to give Webster the electoral fillip he desired, Abbott Lawrence's unofficial representations demonstrate how Irish nationalism could be made the object and subject of improved Anglo-American relations. In contrast with the Irish agency evident in Daniel O'Connell's transnational repeal campaign, Lawrence's letters suggest the intentional marginalization of disruptive Irish nationalism in Anglo-American relations.

In other ways, Abbott Lawrence's time in London was a consummation of the trends of conciliation and commercial opportunity outlined above. The good state of Anglo-American relations that he identified aided the formulation of the Clayton-Bulwer Treaty, which promised mutual self-denial with regard to building or controlling a transisthmian canal.[205] And, as noted, they encouraged the State Department to believe that the United States might be able to mediate the release of Irish state prisoners. In late 1851, Lawrence became the first U.S. minister to Great Britain to make an extensive tour of Ireland. His despatches outlined the persistent poverty of the country and the continued mass migration to the United States. He also highlighted that the country had become a net *importer* of foodstuffs since 1845.[206] Yet all this was as much an opportunity as cause for lamentation. Lawrence outlined several commercial proposals, particularly the development of commercial trade through the harbors of Galway, Bantry Bay, Foynes, and Cove (recently renamed Queenstown), which would promote the better integration of Ireland into an Anglo-American commercial world.[207]

In Lawrence's and Bancroft's correspondence from London, in Forbes's descriptions of his time in Ireland, and in U.S. commentary on the famine, Ireland's ills were interpreted as a function of imperial governance. Few Americans had any intention of intervening to alter that imperial relationship. Rather, the famine was seen as an opportunity to project American philanthropy and, implicitly, American power in the British archipelago. Moreover, a rebuilt Ireland that was emancipated from British mercantilism and socioeconomically reconstructed through migration and changed landholding patterns was perceived to offer great potential as a future market for American produce, even while it remained part of the British Empire. A paternalistic interpretation of Irish nationhood followed in which the national projects of repealers and Young Irelanders alike were interpreted as sorry if romantic failures. The famine and its aftermath offered a chance for the reconstruction of Ireland and for the removal of a destabilizing factor in Anglo-American political relations.

Chapter 3

Filibusters and Fenians

Contesting Neutrality

The years from the late 1840s to the early 1870s—from the onset of the
Great Famine migration to an emergent Anglo-American rapprochement—
constitute a distinct period in the relationship between the United States
(and U.S. statesmen) and Irish American nationalism. Considering U.S.
foreign policy during the Civil War era through the lens of Irish nationalism enriches our understanding of the North Atlantic world, particularly
in relation to the ambiguities of transatlantic neutrality and immigrant
citizenship. Moreover, the tensions generated by Irish filibustering in the
United States and questions of expatriation and naturalization in these
years highlight the important role of nonstate actors who sought to challenge and shape U.S. foreign policy and, conversely, how those in official
positions sought to manipulate Irish nationalism to forward their own diplomatic ends.

Viewing the evolution of Irish American nationalism in the context of
American foreign policy highlights both the seductive dream of linking
the power of the U.S. government to the goals of Irish nationalism and the
Faustian dimensions of such a connection. Lacking the capacity for autonomous action to secure an Ireland free of British rule, Irish Americans understood that they needed support from elsewhere, and allying themselves

with a sympathetic U.S. government seemed essential. Yet this connection rendered distinctively Irish goals vulnerable to cooptation. As long as U.S. grievances with Great Britain remained, manipulating the Irish question seemed like an attractive option. However, growing Anglo-American conciliation in the early 1870s—partly prompted by the disruptions of transatlantic Irish nationalism—left Irish American nationalists marginalized in the larger currents of global diplomacy.

Irish American nationalism was not static. As numerous historians attest, the migration of the late 1840s and early 1850s profoundly reshaped how nationalists thought about the Anglo-Irish connection. In particular, exiled Young Ireland leaders such as John Mitchel, Michael Doheny, and Thomas D'Arcy McGee played a significant role in forging a nationalist narrative of the famine as a deliberate project on the part of the British government. In doing so, they sought to make vengeful anti-British feeling central to Irish American nationalism.

This intellectual evolution had practical consequences. In 1856, a group of Irish Americans in Cincinnati were charged with violating the U.S. neutrality law by attempting to set in motion a filibustering expedition to Ireland.[1] Those who were arrested, like their more well-known counterparts in the postwar Fenian Brotherhood, attempted to exploit what they saw as U.S. ambivalence about enforcing its neutrality legislation. Both groups sought to carve out the necessary geopolitical space for what they saw as the noble goal of Irish liberation.

This space increased markedly as the United States pressed its grievances about British conduct during the Civil War. In this process, the Fenian Brotherhood proved a valuable diplomatic tool for American statesmen. But paradoxically, as Irish American nationalists exploited the unsettled postbellum environment, they provided a compelling argument for compromise that proved useful to statesmen on both sides of the Atlantic.

Remaking Irish American Nationalism

Militant Irish American nationalism predated the great waves of famine migration in the early 1850s. Though William Smith O'Brien, leader of the July 1848 uprising, issued a "curiously ambivalent appeal for Irish American support," the Irish Confederation sent agents to the United States to encourage U.S. residents to provide material support for their cause, and both native- and Irish-born Americans organized to promote republican insurrection in Ireland, "moral force [having] been tried and tried in vain."[2] Even in the context of a broad public appetite for news about the 1848 European revolutions and a growing enthusiasm in some quarters for overseas filibustering, interest in Ireland was striking.[3] The Irish Republican Union in New York City, the Irish League and the Emmet Club in New Orleans, and a similar group known as the "Boston Confederation" issued calls for men and munitions with the intention of forming an Irish brigade that might aid republican insurrection in Ireland.[4] Horace Greeley, editor of the *New York Tribune*; Roman Catholic Bishop John Hughes; and the ubiquitous Robert Tyler all involved themselves in a financial or an organizational capacity, as did William Seward, the former governor of New York State.[5] And, as they had done in during the War of 1812 and would do again in the 1860s, U.S.-based Irish nationalists talked loosely about the possibility of marching on Canada as a means of striking a blow against the British Empire.[6]

However, the Irish uprising was a failure, and the headiness of mid-1848 turned to disillusionment, even embarrassment.[7] The first reports of O'Brien's stand at Ballingarry, County Tipperary, were so pathetic that Horace Greeley dismissed them as British propaganda, as did a meeting of 20,000 Friends of Ireland.[8] They were, however, painfully accurate. Joseph Denieffe, a historian of (and participant in) mid-nineteenth-century Irish nationalist movements, bluntly described the 1848 debacle as "to Americans, inexplicable."[9] A mortifying failure, the uprising damaged the reputation of revolutionary Irish nationalism both domestically and internationally.[10]

The trauma of the famine and the great demographic changes it brought about ushered in a new and distinct period in relations between Ireland, the United States, and Great Britain. Famine migration was heavy—perhaps 1.8 million traveled from Ireland to North America in the period 1846 to 1855—and, in contrast to previous emigration, migrants were overwhelmingly Catholic and were from areas of Ireland that were generally less economically developed.[11] As noted, nationalism that advocated physical force predated famine migration, but it was given a boost by the arrival of "disabused, romantic, assertive, and articulate" Young Irelanders who laid the blame for the cataclysm squarely at the door of the British government.[12] Thomas D'Arcy McGee, for instance, summarized famine deaths as "2,000,000 ministerial murders."[13] Nationalists such as McGee attributed Irish poverty to plundering absentee English landlords, and they accused the British government of intentionally discouraging Irish industry and promoting emigration.[14]

The experience of famine—and of political impotence—allowed, even demanded, a renewed commitment to a revolutionary Irish nationalism heavily imbued with a hatred of all things English. John Mitchel, a gentlemanly Young Ireland journalist driven by a passionate hatred of Great Britain, was perhaps the most zealous propagator of the idea that the British had intentionally promoted the famine.[15] As Brian Jenkins notes, "He, more than anyone else, successfully imprinted the terrible charge of genocide on the Irish historic memory" through his lectures and his journalism.[16] His contemporaries—men such as McGee, Thomas Francis Meagher, Michael Doheny, and John Savage—also profoundly influenced the trajectory of Irish American nationalism.[17]

In this they were supported, ironically, by the very group they blamed for the failure of the 1848 uprising: the clergy.[18] Though collectively the Catholic hierarchy formally denounced insurrection, individual priests in both Ireland and the United States were more ambivalent.[19] Irish American clerics were as likely as their secular counterparts to espouse anti-English sentiments. John Hughes, for one, was an early proponent of the view that there had been more than sufficient food in Ireland to support the population.[20] He argued that the British government had intentionally promoted Irish suffering and was "justly responsible for the death by starvation of one million . . . Irishmen."[21] Though the exiles of 1848 often exhibited strong anti-clerical sentiments, their characterization of the Roman Catholic clergy as unremittingly opposed to revolution in Ireland was a crude one.

Nativism also played an important role in reshaping Irish American nationalism. The anti-Catholic hostility manifested in the nativist riots in Philadelphia in 1844, which was a growing feature of politics in the antebellum United States (and beyond), was catalyzed by the mass migration the famine precipitated. Nativists fretted over the moral character of Catholic immigrants, papal opposition to free schools and free inquiry, and the voting power of Catholics, whom they feared would follow the dictates of Rome.[22] A number of historians have demonstrated the role that nativism played in providing a hothouse context for the germination of both constitutional and revolutionary strands of Irish nationalist self-identity among Irish immigrants in the United States.[23]

In yoking the famine experience to a vengeful anti-British ideology, Young Irelanders accused British statesmen of feigning interest in the welfare of the American slave while at the same time neglecting the plight of the impoverished Irish peasant. This was one way that Young Irelanders sought to mobilize popular opinion in the United States against Great Britain. In representing an oppressed nation (Ireland) to an overseas imperial rival (the United States), they provided a rough inversion of the activities of African American speakers who traversed Great Britain in the antebellum period testifying to the horrors of American slavery and seeking to enlist British support for its abolition.[24] In both instances, a small cadre of activists presumed to speak for a broader constituency and framed a strategy for liberation that reached beyond the nation's boundaries. In both instances the attempts were of limited success, divorced as they were from the broader structures of Anglo-American relations.[25]

The sleight of hand involved did not pass without notice. Frederick Douglass, who sympathized with Irish struggles for independence, mocked the attempt to see American slavery and British oppression as equivalent. "The Irishman is poor," he argued in 1850, "but he is *not* a slave. . . . I cannot believe that [the British Parliament] will ever sink to such a depth of infamy as to pass a law for the recapture of Fugitive Irishmen!"[26] For Douglass, Irishmen were the victims of great injustice, and in certain, strictly delineated ways, their condition was comparable with that of African Americans. But, he argued, it was facetious and disingenuous to speak of "Irish slavery."[27] Still, as a correspondent of John Calhoun argued, Ireland proved a "perplexing issue" for British humanitarians who reflexively criticized American slavery, and the situation brought home the scriptural injunction to "take out the mote from thine own eye, and then shalt thou see clearly."[28]

Of all the Young Ireland immigrants, John Mitchel presented the headiest cocktail of violent anti-British, anti-abolitionist, and pro-slavery rhetoric. His pro-slavery views made him particularly popular with southerners and southern sympathizers. In 1853, he escaped from the penal colony he had been sentenced to in Van Diemen's Land, and migrated to New York. Two years later, he moved to eastern Tennessee.[29] Until late 1865, Ireland's most celebrated émigré remained largely aloof from the practical implications of the nationalist world he had rhetorically constructed but, he did establish a newspaper—the New York *Citizen*—with Thomas Francis Meagher. Mitchel suggested that Irish-Americans should organize a filibustering mission to Ireland with the aim of establishing a provisional republican government, and he wrote to "make clear and plain to naturalised Irishmen . . . what they might lawfully and conscientiously do in the direction of liberating their native country from British dominion."[30] However, both lawfulness and conscientiousness were elastic concepts—particularly given contemporaries' enthusiasm for filibustering—and in the mid-1850s a number of groups began planning to establish an Ireland independent of British rule.

The Cincinnati Filibusters

Irish Americans' most conspicuous attempt to challenge Anglo-American peace prior to the Civil War came in 1855–1856, two years before the formation of the more widely known Irish Republican Brotherhood and its American corollary, the Fenian Brotherhood.[31] On January 4 and 5, 1856, twenty men were arrested in Cincinnati on a charge of violating the U.S. Neutrality Act of 1818.[32] They were members of a nationalist group named the Robert Emmet Club, the Cincinnati branch of a nationwide organization, the Irish Emigrant Aid Society, which was based in Boston.[33] Its name alluded to the free-soil Massachusetts (later New England) Emigrant Aid Society, and like its namesake, it sought to shift the balance of power in a territory by promoting the migration of sympathetic individuals. Instead of sending antislavery advocates to Kansas, the Irish Emigrant Aid Society hoped to capitalize on England's entanglement in the Crimean War by encouraging the "emigration" of Americans to Ireland to foment revolution.[34] Just as the Irish Republican Union and others had done in 1848, the Irish Emigrant Aid Society sailed close to the wind on the issue of its legality. Its president, Robert Tyler, denied accusations that he and his associates were engaged in what he termed "filibusterism" and argued that at a recent convention the society had placed itself "on undoubted principles of sound constitutional and national law."[35] Tyler, who by 1848 was a leading organizer for the Democratic Party in Pennsylvania (and a strong supporter of James Buchanan), stridently outlined the contingent nature of the society's activities:

> It is certainly not *impossible*, that, in the complication of the political events of the future, the United States may be drawn into . . . conflict with England. . . . One may be full of regret when contemplating such an idea. . . . But if the British Government *will threaten* . . . to castigate this Union into its views of the settlement of political questions essentially affecting the future peace, prosperity and liberties of this American Continent[;] . . . if . . . England will insist . . . in trampling under her feet the old Monroe doctrine, so dear to the pride and so material to the interests of our citizens; if, with shouts of war from the London *Times* . . . she will continue to send her heavy armed squadrons to our coasts, as if to hint at intimidation; if her press will engage . . . in a steady and systematic [abolitionist] effort to procure a dissolution of this Confederacy, and to embroil

us in general anarchy and fraternal bloodshed; if she will send her crimps and servants into our territory to violate our Neutrality laws, by surreptitiously enlisting our citizens [into her armies][;] . . . [if England will have war] *we will endeavor to serve our Government with the utmost zeal and efficiency in that war—that's all.*[36]

Tyler's rousing rhetoric did not reassure all. The Cincinnati Emmet Club had come to the attention of the city's nativist organization, the American Protestant Association (APA) and, as important, its activities had alarmed the local British consul, Charles Rowcroft. A sometime novelist who had spent part of the 1820s living in Van Diemen's Land, Rowcroft was a recent appointment to a new position (as late as 1852 the British government had decided against opening a consulate in Cincinnati.)[37] His inexperience perhaps explains why he reported the Emmet Club to the authorities rather than demonstrating the circumspection other consuls exhibited in areas of Irish American nationalist activity.

In statements Rowcroft secured, witnesses accused the Emmet Club—which was led by Edward Kenifeck, William G. Halpin, and Samuel Lumsden, all delegates to the national Emigrant Aid Society—of actively recruiting men and seeking to buy arms in order to support an impending uprising in Ireland.[38] This was true. At a national convention held in New York in December 1855, the delegates had decided that $1,000,000 ought to be raised—half in the South and half in the North—to consolidate the organization and contract for guns. Samuel Lumsden, who was appointed "Chief Director for Ohio," had pledged $1,000 of his own money.[39] In private correspondence with Robert Tyler, Lumsden advocated impressing "on the minds of all the officers of State Directories the wisdom as well as the necessity of arming and drilling the Clubs. Muskets and bayonets can be contracted for wholesale. 100.000 armed and drilled men would in 6 or 9 months present a terrible front."[40] With rumors about Irish nationalist activity circulating, Consul Rowcroft decided to pay local nativists to spy on the club and bring its activities to the attention of U.S. Circuit Court judge Humphrey Leavitt. Arrest warrants were issued on the ground that an expedition to Ireland was to set off imminently.[41]

Nativist sentiment was intimately bound up with the prosecution of the Irish American organization. The bulk of the evidence was brought by John Barber, an engineer employed at a Cincinnati builder's yard. He and two associates joined the Emmet Club in order to report on its activities. They attended club meetings and provided details of the club's efforts to organize smaller societies, purchase arms, and send men to Ireland.[42] An Ulsterman by birth, Barber was a member of the APA, as were his two friends.[43] His nativist zeal was sincere, and he claimed to have burned his own naturalization papers when he infiltrated the Emmet Club, arguing that "I'd no right to remain an American citizen, and do such a rascally thing."[44] His evidence strongly suggested that the Emmet Club was planning for an imminent invasion of Ireland.

Drawing on Barber's reports, the publications of the Emigrant Aid Society, and the connections between that national body and the local Robert Emmet Club, the prosecution argued that the defendants had violated the U.S. Neutrality Act of 1818. Passed with an eye to restraining privateers in the conflict between Spain and her colonies in Central and South America, the law's provisions largely dealt with the rights and obligations of American citizens during a time of conflict.[45] Only one section dealt with neutrality during peacetime. This stated that

> if any persons shall, within the territory or jurisdiction of the United States, begin or set on foot, or provide or provide the means for, any military expedition or enterprise, to be carried on from thence against the territory of [any power] . . . with whom the United States are [at] peace, every person, so offending, shall be deemed guilty of a high misdemeanor.[46]

The club's design to overthrow British government in Ireland was clear, the prosecution stated. Prosecutors argued for a strong lineage between the designs of the Emmet Club, however "impracticable . . . wild and utterly extravagant" they might be, and those of the United Irishmen of 1798.[47] In doing so, they sought to invoke the historical memory of that uprising as irredeemably anarchic, sectarian, and repressive. Such horror, the prosecuting attorneys suggested, legitimated both the anti-Catholic bias evident in John Barber's testimony and Charles Rowcroft's involvement in the trial. They asked what humane patriot could stand by and allow the bloody terror that the defendants' quixotic plans would unleash.[48]

Tensions between the city's nativist and immigrant (particularly Irish) populations had been running high for some time.[49] Cincinnati's economy and society had been profoundly shaped by rapid industrialization and mass immigration: according to the federal census of 1850, 47 percent of a total population of about 115,000 was foreign born.[50] By 1851, after massive famine migration, perhaps as many as 12 percent of Cincinnatians were Irish-born.[51] The Irish American community there had demonstrated its nationalist sympathies by organizing a fund in sympathy with the Young Irelanders in 1848 and reception committees for John Mitchel and Michael Doheny in the 1850s.[52]

And Cincinnati was a violent city.[53] Anti-black and anti-abolitionist mobs frequently took to the streets in the antebellum years. In the 1850s, the common pattern of violence between urban Irish and black populations was supplemented by anti-Irish hostility and increasing conflict related to the stringent Fugitive Slave Law of 1850.[54] Violence had characterized municipal elections in April 1855.[55] During the Emmet Club trial, Barber experienced mob intimidation outside the courtroom, and on one occasion, he was shot at by an unidentified assailant.[56] The comparative lack of ethnic segregation in Cincinnati gave the city a compressed public geography, breeding conflict.[57] The American Protestant Association and the Robert Emmet Club held their meetings in the same civic hall, and undoubtedly such proximity aided Barber and his associates when it came to identifying Club members for arrest.[58] It also gave Barber a public profile that rendered him vulnerable to the ire of Cincinnati's Irish community.

Before joining the club, Barber had made himself known to the British consul. Rowcroft compensated Barber with $100 and agreed to hold the minutes of the club meetings he attended.[59] Rowcroft corresponded with the British minister in Washington, John Crampton, who in turn alerted the British foreign secretary, Lord Clarendon, in London. Clarendon had received news of Irish Clubs springing up elsewhere, but the British government had been assured by the U.S. secretary of state, William Marcy, that the U.S. government was taking all suitable steps to monitor the activities of potential filibusters.[60] Rowcroft remained anxious, and the prosecution had little compunction about declaring itself "quite willing to state that this prosecution was set on foot" by the consul.[61] They also noted that, as President Pierce's Democratic administration appeared to be tolerant of filibustering missions in Central America, it was up to the courts to enforce the law and restrain expeditions that would compromise the long-term reputation of the United States.[62] Such toleration bred a misapprehension among the Irish in America, argued prosecutor John Probasco. Their "fatal mistake,"

is to forget that they are no longer Irishmen; that they are no longer subjects of England, but owe loyalty to this republic only. They must not remain a distinct class in the body politic, having separate political interests, and forever looking to a nationality across the ocean.[63]

Taken on their own, the machinations of the Robert Emmet Club were troubling enough, but more alarming, argued the prosecution, was the broader culture of filibustering that appeared to be tacitly encouraged by elected officials. There was a need to "curb this lawless enthusiasm," argued Probasco, as "everywhere around there are unquiet spirits [and] every day brings intelligence of some violation of our neutrality laws."[64] The Neutrality Act appeared weak, and anyway the Pierce administration was apparently reluctant to enforce its provisions. To John Crampton, it seemed that the "extreme democratic doctrines" of Young America that urged intervention "in the Affairs of Foreign Nations in support of Democratic and Republican principles" were in the ascendancy under Pierce's watch.[65] And some of Pierce's Democratic Party rivals were no more restrained: Lewis Cass and Stephen Douglas, both of whom had reputations for favoring such intervention, were each seeking the party's nomination in 1856.[66] Charles Rowcroft (incorrectly) suggested that the president owed his election in 1852 to the votes of Irishmen and claimed that he was so concerned to protect his reelection prospects that he would do nothing to stop the actions of Irish associations engaged in illegal acts.[67]

Disregard for American neutrality was even more pervasive. Consul Rowcroft himself was simultaneously implicated in an "amateurish" scheme to induce men living in the United States to migrate to British North America for the purpose of enlisting in the British army, in violation of U.S. neutrality law.[68] Colluding with an "exiled Hungarian noble" and Mexican War veteran, Gabriel de Korponay, Rowcroft agreed to recruit up to 1,000 troops for service in the Crimea.[69] Rowcroft was arrested for his involvement in the scheme.[70] There were two neat ironies here. First, information of Rowcroft's implication in this scheme was made public by Cincinnati's United Irishman Society, a fraternal organization whose members included many who would later be involved in the Cincinnati filibuster scheme.[71] Second, Britain's need to recruit overseas was amplified by the depopulation caused by the famine in Ireland. The pool from which Parliament could draw soldiers for the British army was depleted, and it felt compelled to pass the Foreign Enlistment Act in December 1854, prompting John Mitchel to note with glee that the British government was reduced to scrabbling for men overseas.[72] Both John Crampton, the British minister at Washington, and Charles Rowcroft were unsure about the legality of recruiting under the act but were pushed to action by Foreign Secretary Lord Clarendon.[73] Rowcroft was right to be worried; after a short courtroom appearance, he was released on a $2,000 bond pending further trial.[74]

The Irish filibusters had better luck: they were exonerated. Three factors contributed to their acquittal. The first was the defense's strategy of drawing on stereotypes about the Irish. In 1850s American popular culture, the stock figure of the improvident, alcohol-soaked Irishman contrasted with the idealization of "poor Erin." In the Cincinnati courtroom, the defense drew on this caricature: the Irishman's love of his homeland and his emotionalism and childish irrationality were offered as exculpatory factors. Though plans for Irish liberation might be foolish, they were not sinister, the defense argued. "Miserable is that interpretation of our laws," argued William Groesbeck, the principal attorney for the defense, "that would put men in a dungeon because they hope their mother land may be free."[75] Such rhetoric drew upon a static conception of Irish colonial nationalism that mirrored that of the thirteen colonies before the American Revolution, and it convinced Judge Humphrey Howe Leavitt.[76] Indeed the judge himself drew on a language of romantic Hibernophilia in stating that he "censure[d] no Irishman for sympathising with his native land, and ardently desiring the restoration of the rights of its people."[77]

Second, the defense argued that the Emmet Club's plans were merely conditional. One witness testified that "*in the case of war between the United States and Great Britain*, we expected to equip ourselves . . . and offer our services to the United States to fight under the American flag for the freedom of our native land."[78] Other than that, the club served to do no more than "unite Irishmen in a bond of brotherhood."[79] Judge Leavitt accepted the idea that their actions were predicated only "upon certain contingencies," specifically an Anglo-American war, in the absence of which the defendants could not be said to have violated the Neutrality Act.[80] The law was simply not strong enough to prosecute the kinds of activities the Irishmen were accused of engaging in. Though he argued that "there can be no such thing as a divided national allegiance," the Neutrality Act did not extend to limiting the freedom of speech or association of those who anticipated future Anglo-American difficulties.[81]

Of ultimate importance, then, was the capaciousness of the Neutrality Act. Attorney William Groesbeck explicitly argued that his clients did indeed desire an opportunity to use violent means to bring about a free Irish state, but he stated that they could prepare for such an eventuality and yet remain within the boundaries laid out by the act. "Even if five thousand men should leave this country for Ireland, taking arms with them, with the intention of mingling with the people there and inciting them to revolt," he argued, "we could not punish the five thousand, or any one of them, under this law," as no military expedition actually existed.[82] In addition Groesbeck drew upon the familiar concept of "the Union," arguing that if abolitionists might plot the disunion of the United States "with impunity," might not the Irish do the same with regard to their own Union?[83] Somewhat paradoxically, he also argued that the openness and publicity that characterized the club's activities—a dig at the city's secretive nativist organizations—belied any subversive intent.[84]

Groesbeck's opinions chimed with those of Attorney General Caleb Cushing. When John Crampton pressed William Marcy on the problem of Irish would-be revolutionaries, Marcy requested Cushing's input. His response was candid:

> The organization . . . of combinations to aid or abet rebellion in another, or in any other way to act on its political institutions, is undoubtedly a violation of national amity and comity, and an act of wrongful interference with the affairs of other people. But there is no law in the United States to forbid this. . . . We do not punish such proceedings, until the spirit of interference which induces them reaches its natural consummation, that of attempts to interfere in the affairs of foreign countries by force.[85]

This suggests an important ambivalence in Irish American nationalism. Carried to their successful conclusion, the actions of the Robert Emmet Club would inevitably be subversive of the geopolitical order. An independent Irish nation established in part because of American forbearance would, of course, be a fundamental challenge to the British Empire and would likely provoke war between Great Britain and the United States. Yet rather than presenting their activities as revolutionary, the defendants, unsurprisingly, positioned their desire for Irish independence as a logical corollary to their love of American liberty. As the campaign for Irish repeal had demonstrated, this argument had broad purchase in mid-nineteenth-century America. However, this argument from consonance and contingency—that Irish and American nationalism were compatible and that only in the event of a break between Britain and the United States would the revolutionary character of the former become apparent—could limit the political space in which Irish nationalism could operate. American nationalism had the capacity to absorb and neuter the disruptive tendencies of radical Irish nationalism, whatever the defense might argue about the congruity of support for an independent Ireland and a strict devotion to the obligations U.S. citizenship.

For Judge Leavitt, it was necessary to dismiss the case against the Irish filibusters, though he believed that the publicity about the proceedings might have a beneficial effect. "The time and labor" involved in putting forth the case was valuable, he argued, insofar as it forced the public mind (particularly the Irish American mind) to contemplate the proper obligations of citizenship and the relationship that ought to exist between legal membership in a political community—through naturalization—and affinity with an alternative nationalism.[86] In the case of Ireland, this was a particularly difficult question: the Irish nation was widely conceived of as an historic or cultural entity yet it was clearly not a nation-state. Allegiance to "Ireland" differed from, say, allegiance to papal authority or allegiance to another state in the family of nations.

The question of what a policy of neutrality really meant was another issue. How far did adherence to that policy preclude Irish (or Cuban or Nicaraguan) nationalist activity? This was a pressing question. Under Pierce, federal authority over foreign policy seemed to atrophy, as expedition after expedition successfully thumbed their noses at government proscription and set off for Central or South America. The connections between Irish and Central American filibustering were more than cultural: at a November 1855 meeting of the Emmet Club, Lumsden reported that an investigative mission to New Orleans had revealed that "arms that had been intended for a recent Cuban expedition could be bought at $7.50 a piece, which would shoot five times without reloading."[87] The Cuban mission in question may well have been John Quitman's abortive effort of March 1855, which was postponed as a consequence of Franklin Pierce's quiet diplomacy and, as important, because Quitman's allies in Congress had failed in their efforts to repeal the U.S. neutrality laws.[88]

All this was especially distressing to northerners who viewed the contrast between the flimsy response to Caribbean filibustering and the brutal assertion of federal power in the form of the Fugitive Slave Act as evidence of the government's willingness to secure the future of southern slavery. Federal weakness also exercised John Crampton, who wrote home of the limitations of federal law. In reporting the outcome of the trial of the

Emmet Club, Crampton sardonically noted that restraints on action would apply only if war existed between the United States and Great Britain. He added that

> although [the judge] admits that it is worthy of consideration "whether the organization in question might not have the effect of bringing about that contingency," he evidently does not think that this is an offence which would be reached by the Neutrality Laws of the United States.[89]

The failed prosecution of the Cincinnati filibusters had two distinct effects on the politics of the Irish Emigrant Aid Society. Contrary to Samuel Lumsden's promise that "nothing could be more fortunate for the Cause" than publicity, the Cincinnati trial promoted internal dissension.[90] The society was already afflicted by factionalism. Various 1848 exiles jockeyed for positions of leadership because those with the greatest political capital—John Mitchel and Thomas Francis Meagher—had distanced themselves from the various nationalist groups in America's urban centers.[91] Mitchel became disillusioned with the infighting of Irish American nationalists in New York and with what he saw as an overbearing Catholic hierarchy in that city.[92] Meagher, it seems, yearned for a quieter life: he pursued his law practice, became an American citizen, and married into the New York elite.[93] Others, like Thomas D'Arcy McGee, felt alienated from life in the United States and sought a change; McGee turned first to ultramontanism and, ultimately, to a new life in British North America.[94] By the summer of 1856, some members believed Samuel Lumsden and other Ohioans were cashing in on their supposed "martyrdom" to enhance their position within Irish American circles.[95] Such factionalism would prove an enduring feature of Irish diasporic nationalism.

Second, the trial's conclusion prompted a turn to domestic politics. Minister Crampton wrote home that he felt "little doubt" that the society's energies were increasingly directed toward U.S. partisan politics, specifically Robert Tyler's "organization of the Irish vote in the interest of the Democratic Candidate at the next Presidential election."[96] However, the Irish clubs did not see domestic and transatlantic ends as antithetical. Just as they had no intention of being passive actors in the diplomatic drama being played out between the United States and Great Britain, so they had little inclination to sit on the sidelines of presidential politicking. Instead, they sought an anti–Know Nothing, conservative (i.e., anti-abolitionist) candidate to support for the 1856 presidential election. "It is about time for us to have a finger in the pie," wrote one society delegate.[97]

But who to back? Society members believed that leading contender, James Buchanan, was too soft toward Great Britain as a result of the time he had spent as minister to London and, referring to a mythical garment that slowly poisoned its wearer, they argued that a Franklin Pierce candidacy offered only a "Nessus like shirt."[98] Samuel Lumsden advocated the candidacy of Virginian Henry Wise.[99] Wise's description of Know-Nothings as "lousy, godless [and] Christless" appealed to Lumsden.[100] Moreover, the Ohioan argued that "a Southern man" was needed.

> No more Northern men for us now. . . . [They] have no sympathy with oppressed nations, and care little for the downfall of republican princi[ples]. . . . [They] truckle with great despotic nations—like England & France; and do not recognize with promptitude young struggling Republics. They are generally steeped in abolition schemes—seeking to exalt the Negro and debase the Irishman—because [they are] profitable . . . looking to give the right to vote to the Negro, and take it from the Irishman.[101]

All this pointed to the evolution of fierce devotion to the American Union on the part of Irish Americans; an antipathy to the materialist, anti-Irish proclivities of an urban northern elite; and staunch anti-abolitionism.[102] This intellectual cocktail had praxis: Lumsden suggested that the clubs be used as a "conservative armed force of loyal citizens" to oppose the spread of the "rabid 'isms'" that threatened the American Union.[103] The apparent fragmentation of federal authority—the struggle to enforce the Fugitive Slave Act in the face of abolitionists inspired, as Lumsden saw it, by imported British abolitionist doctrines—encouraged him to think that the clubs might wield influence in U.S. domestic politics even as the same national fractures over the politics of slavery facilitated the kind of filibustering projects the Irishmen were planning.[104]

For British observers such as Charles Rowcroft, the most important aspect of the failed prosecution of the Emmet Club members was the hollowed-out character of the Neutrality Act as presented by Judge Leavitt. As noted, Rowcroft had been arraigned under that act for his alleged involvement in British recruitment in mid-1855. That law was now shown to be "a farce," according to Rowcroft, and should it be allowed to "bear hard on the case of the British Enlistments . . . it would be a monstrous injustice and disgraceful to the American people."[105] Bear hard it did, though, and on May 29, 1856, after months of correspondence with the British government, Franklin Pierce informed Congress that he had "ceased to hold intercourse" with British Minister John Crampton as a result of British enlistment activities.[106] Simultaneously, the U.S. government revoked Rowcroft's exequatur as well as those of his counterparts in New York and Philadelphia.[107]

In the years before the Civil War crystallized animosity about the meaning of neutrality, mutual suspicion shaped Anglo-American relations. To British eyes, U.S. tolerance of Irish filibusterism was another instance of America's anarchic disregard for international law, and to Americans, Great Britain's traducing of U.S. neutrality in the enlistment affair suggested arrogance and a disregard for U.S. sovereignty. Within a broad context of imperial competition in Central America and the ever-wider divisions that characterized U.S. domestic politics, nonstate actors such as the Robert Emmet Club sought to complicate Anglo-American relations.[108] The prospect of large numbers of Irish emigrants returning from America "to create disturbances" troubled Lord Clarendon, despite U.S. Minister James Buchanan's reassurances.[109] Charles Rowcroft's doleful courtroom plea for a plain "exposition of the Neutrality Law . . . as should put a stop to the further progress of the societies" was symptomatic of an uncertain contest about the meaning of neutrality.[110] The seething zeal of the Fenian Brotherhood, which was founded in 1858 and expanded greatly during the American Civil War, helped this contest become a crisis.

Fenians, Neutrality, and Reconstruction

In 1858, James Stephens and Thomas Clarke Luby traveled to the United States to put remittances from America to their organization on a formal, regular basis.[111] Both were founding members of the Irish Republican Brotherhood (IRB), a clandestine organization that aimed to generate a disciplined, sustainable network of revolutionists dedicated to "the Irish Republic, now virtually established."[112] In this, the IRB would be aided by men, arms, and money organized by the Fenian Brotherhood in the United States and Canada.[113] John O'Mahony and Michael Doheny, two 1848 insurrectionists, had suggested this model of operation to Stephens the year before, and his visit was intended to lay the groundwork for continued links between the United States and Ireland. His American travels left him cold. "There is no *spiritual* life in this people," he wrote. "It might consequently, be fairly asserted that there is not—in the high & holy sense of the word—a single *patriot* amongst all the millions of these States!"[114] He was similarly dismissive of James Buchanan ("a Yankee development of the Artful Dodger"), John Mitchel (who lacked a "profound knowledge" of the Irish people) and Thomas Francis Meagher (a mere "rhetorical hero"), each of whom he met during his brief tour.[115]

John O'Mahony, by contrast, was impressed by the separate schools, parishes, and press that Irish American communities maintained and by the strong links these communities maintained with Ireland. He was excited by the vitality of Irish American life.[116] In the spring of 1859, O'Mahony launched a Fenian newspaper, the *Phoenix*, and openly declared a "Fenian Fund" to be in existence. With Stephens's support, he established himself as the "head center" of the North American movement. (The word *Fenianism* would later come to signify advanced Irish nationalism in both the United States and Ireland.)[117] The Fenian Brotherhood set about organizing to support the insurrection that, Stephens argued, would prove imminent if only sufficient funds could be forwarded from the United States.[118] However, the outbreak of the Civil War upset these calculations: by 1863, the IRB was languishing for the lack of funds from America.[119]

The secession of the South and the onset of the Civil War married the question of neutrality with that of the rights of belligerents. On May 13, 1861, Queen Victoria issued a Proclamation of Neutrality, a natural reaction to the incipient conflict between the northern and southern states but one that brought outrage from the U.S. North.[120] The London *Times*, for one, was unimpressed by northern indignation. The United States had exhibited a "constant disregard of international courtesy" in its toleration—even promotion—of violent expansionism and filibustering in the years before 1861, the paper argued, and it was poor form to complain when international law ran its natural course.[121] Nevertheless, the British Proclamation prompted a great ratcheting up of Anglo-American tensions.

Like Ireland, the nascent Confederate States of America was a geographically self-contained region that attempted to advance a claim to self-determination on cultural, political, and historic grounds. For the confederacy, the question of international recognition—and particularly British recognition—was of great significance, just as it was to the Union government.[122] Union statesmen—foremost among them Secretary of State William Henry Seward—accused the British government of precipitously blessing the Confederacy with the rights of a belligerent power. As a consequence, he argued, Britain needlessly raised Confederate hopes of recognition, prolonging the conflict and producing a terrible loss of blood and treasure. Britain's neutrality was biased, Seward argued, and covered a multitude of sins.[123] In addition, the Union navy's seizure of the *Trent*, a British steamship, precipitated a major international crisis that came close to tipping the United States and Great Britain into conflict.[124] With a lack of tact, Archbishop John Hughes of New York, returning via Ireland from a diplomatic mission to Rome in 1861, alluded to these Anglo-American tensions and suggested that "events [were] occurring calculated to bring the wrongs, the miseries, the sufferings of the Irish people under consideration elsewhere."[125] For their part, Irish and Irish American nationalists closely monitored Anglo-Union relations. Even moderate, constitutional nationalists were driven to declare that they were friends of the United States and that they would refuse to aid Britain should war develop between the two powers.[126]

Furthermore, Union voices accused the British government of turning a blind eye to the construction of Confederate ships in British ports—most notoriously the *Alabama*, a commerce raider—and of tolerating Confederate subversives on Canadian soil. The former issue, in particular, festered during the half-decade after the Civil War. As will be seen, the continuing failure of the British and American governments to resolve the issue shaped political and diplomatic machinations inside and outside Congress.[127] Conversely, British Members of Parliament seized on rumors that the federal government was recruiting troops in Ireland and an apparently suspicious bump in migration rates during 1863–1864, to suggest that, unlike the Pierce administration, Lord Palmerston's government was insufficiently rigorous in confronting Union violations of British neutrality.[128] These issues led to further transatlantic uneasiness. Well before Appomattox, Seward had darkly predicted that at the close of the war, "it would be difficult to enforce upon citizens of the United States the performance of international obligations that Europe has refused to observe in regard to ourselves."[129] Lord Palmerston, commenting on the "very hostile spirit" exhibited toward Britain, told Queen Victoria that he expected that "the Northern states . . . will either make war against England or make inroads into your Majesty's North American possessions which would lead to war" after the conclusion of the Civil War.[130] Likewise, the possibility of postbellum U.S. aggression drove politicians in British North America to consider confederation as a means of strengthening the colonies' defenses, a possibility that enthused Canadian Fenians who saw U.S. ambition as key to generating favorable conditions for an Irish revolution.[131]

The Civil War proved a mixed blessing for Irish nationalists. The conflict depressed remittances to Ireland, limited the ability of the IRB to raise funds, and, obviously, divorced Union and Confederate Fenians.[132] Though Irish and Irish American newspapers proudly reported the exploits of Irish soldiers in both the Union and Confederate armies, many found that their enthusiasm waned as casualties mounted and emancipation became an official war aim.[133] In both the North and the South, the evolving contest over the meaning of the war within Irish communities dovetailed with debate about the appropriateness of secession as an analogy for Irish separatism.[134] A Confederate-Irish identification was superficially attractive, yet many Irish Americans viewed the Union—and most lived *in* the Union—as the best hope for a free Ireland.[135] This left Union-supporting Irish American nationalists with something of an intellectual quandary, How could they support disunionism in the case of Ireland but oppose it in the case of the Confederacy?[136] John Mitchel criticized Unionist Irishmen who mistakenly believed that "the repeal of one union in Europe depends on the enforcement of another union in America."[137] Nonetheless, it seemed to Irish separatists that U.S. power allied to war-related grievances against Great Britain was the best means of generating favorable conditions for an Irish insurrection. The sanguine John Devoy, the preeminent leader of Irish American physical-force nationalism through the later decades of the century, believed that had an Irish uprising taken place during the winter of 1865–1866, the United States would surely have gone to war with Great Britain as a consequence of its Civil War grievances.[138] Likewise, in his recollections, John O'Leary noted the great encouragement that he and his associates had drawn from the possibility of an Anglo-American rupture over the *Alabama* claims.[139]

Finally, large numbers of Irishmen gained military experience during the Civil War. Although the IRB was increasingly ambivalent about Irish service in American armies because of high casualty rates, in the longer term such service cultivated an Irish American military elite.[140] Military service also went some way toward countering charges that the Irish were disloyal or could not be assimilated in the United States (though in 1870 a British traveler could argue that "in no part of the world are the virtues of the Irish so little appreciated" as in the United States).[141] Whatever his personal qualms about enlistment, IRB leader James Stephens made a tour of Union camps in the spring of 1864, raising funds and establishing new Fenian "circles."[142]

Stephens announced that 1865 would be the IRB's year of action, and after much vacillation, "several scores" of American veterans traveled to Ireland in the autumn of 1865 under the pretense that they were returned emigrants. The authorities in Ireland expected more to arrive imminently.[143] In the United States, the Fenian Brotherhood was quite open in its planning for insurrection. The arrival of Irish American soldiers would test American neutrality, noted a nervous London *Times* editorial: "We have to deal with a secessionist conspiracy, while they have to adopt the attitude of a neutral state."[144]

There was no Irish uprising in 1865, and in September of that year the authorities in Ireland moved to arrest the leadership of the IRB and suppress their leading newspaper.[145] At the close of the year, the Fenian Brotherhood split in two over control of finances and the expediency of attacking Britain's North American territory, yet its continued vibrancy alarmed British authorities.[146] Arguably, the decision to move against the leaders of the IRB in Dublin increased the influence of Irish Americans in the transatlantic world of Irish nationalism.[147] Moreover, Fenians were becoming increasingly assertive in the politics of Irish Canada, and the apparent short-term impossibility of acting in Ireland made an attack on British North America more attractive.[148] Despite concerns in Britain that the U.S. government was not doing enough to prevent Fenian activities, Frederick Bruce, the British minister in Washington, followed a course of conciliation that was based on a series of logical propositions. He believed, probably correctly, that British interests were best served by the restoration of ex-Confederate states to Congress because southern representatives would temper northern hostility over the *Alabama* reparations. Bruce identified President Andrew Johnson's limited reconstruction policy as the most likely to lead to such a speedy restoration, and therefore he sought to avoid putting Johnson in the unenviable position of having to act against the Fenian Brotherhood.[149] Were he to be pressed into doing so, the argument went, Johnson's more radical opponents in Congress would gain political capital and prevent the readmission of southern states.

Aware of the potential value of the Irish vote in the autumn 1866 elections (and with the growing appreciation that those elections would dictate the direction of Reconstruction), Johnson and his administration gave the appearance of colluding with the Fenian Brotherhood.[150] Following various representations, Johnson made a show of releasing John Mitchel, who had been imprisoned for his work as a Confederate editor, and the administration did nothing to prevent Fenians from purchasing large quantities of arms.[151] Moreover, Bernard Doran Killian, a prominent Fenian organizer, reported an autumn 1865 conversation with William Seward in which the secretary of state intimated that the United States would "acknowledge accomplished facts" in the event of a successful Fenian raid on British North America.[152] Killian, as historian David Wilson notes, is the only source scholars have for this conversation, and recent work by Peter Vronsky suggests that far from tacitly endorsing the Fenians' activities, U.S. authorities privately worked with the British government, represented by Frederick Bruce, to limit the brotherhood's significance.[153]

Figure 2. John Mitchel spent time acting as the financial agent for the Fenian Brotherhood in Paris after his release from prison in 1865. This portrait, from sometime in the mid-1840s, portrays him as a youthful Young Ireland journalist. John Mitchel, *Jail Journal* (1854; repr., Dublin: M. H. Gill & Son, 1913), ii.

Many assumed that the federal government *did* support Fenian ambitions. Thomas Sweeny, who meticulously planned a Canadian invasion
strategy by reading accounts of the Revolution and the War of 1812, noted
that various prominent Washingtonians sympathized with the brotherhood
and that "the United States government . . . was perfectly well aware" of
the Fenians' purchases of arms and the uses to which they would be put.[154]
Archbishop Spalding of Baltimore was so convinced that the federal government smiled upon the Fenian Brotherhood that in November 1865 he
resisted a papal proscription of the brotherhood, arguing that

> as the organization waxed strong during the war under government influ-
> ence or encouragement & as political motives would be likely to foster it
> for some time yet, as a sort of standing menace to England, we thought
> that any public condemnation would tend to stimulate its growth, perhaps
> to irritate the government.[155]

And Frederick Bruce, whatever his role in sharing intelligence with Johnson and Seward, was aware that there were limits to the federal government's ability to control events. If the Fenians' Canadian designs were to
succeed, he noted anxiously, "great pressure would be brought to bear on
this Govt to recognise these adventurers as belligerents . . . in retaliation for
the losses the Confederate Cruizers [*sic*] inflicted on American Shipowners
during the Civil War."[156]

Did Killian make up—or distort—his conversation with Seward? Perhaps. But it seems entirely plausible to suggest that Johnson and Seward
hedged their bets and that Killian was reporting Seward's words truthfully.
Or it may be that timing is the decisive factor: in early 1865, the situation
in Ireland seemed more threatening and U.S. public opinion was arguably more belligerent toward Great Britain than it would be the following
spring. Perhaps had the Fenians acted in late 1865, they would have found,
first, that the U.S. government was more willing to look favorably on their
actions and, second, that their anti-British politics resonated more closely
with the public mood in the United States.

The fruits of such a widespread faith in tacit government endorsement
were two raids on Canadian soil in mid-1866. As noted, the Fenian Brotherhood had split into two factions. One, led by John O'Mahony, favored
supporting action in Ireland alone. The other, led by William R. Roberts
(later a New York congressman and minister to Chile in Grover Cleveland's
first administration), favored acting against Britain by attacking Canada.[157]

Ironically, it was the O'Mahony wing, which was anxious about being out-flanked by the Roberts faction, that moved first against Canada, launching a disastrous raid at Campobello Island, New Brunswick, in April 1866.[158] Various members of the Johnson administration sought to avoid responsibility for acting against the Fenians, and it was left to General George E. Meade to seize Fenian caches and publicly assert that he intended to enforce the U.S. neutrality law.[159] This was followed by a more serious and better-co-ordinated raid that was organized by Thomas Sweeny and launched from Buffalo, New York, by the Roberts faction on the morning of June 1, 1866. The raid was led by John O'Neill, a capable, hardened Civil War cavalry-man who had developed a reputation as an effective anti-guerilla specialist, and the Fenians had initial success against Canadian militiamen, though they were forced to fall back when reinforcements were cut off and a much larger and more professional British and Canadian force threatened.[160]

Again, the Johnson administration responded in a halting and half-hearted way, but when he issued a proclamation proscribing Fenian ac-tivities after O'Neill's raid, the president opened himself to charges of bad faith.[161] William Roberts described the administration's actions as "unex-pected and repressive," while John O'Neill bluntly characterized the gov-ernment's proscription as "treachery."[162] Even after Johnson's proclamation, one Fenian leader declared that within a few days "Congress will . . . repeal the neutrality laws or extend to us belligerent rights."[163]

President Johnson's move against the Fenians sparked a domestic politi-cal contest over U.S. neutrality. Johnson's Radical Republican opponents, alienated by the president's veto of the Civil Rights Act of April 1866, and anti-Johnson Democrats used the Fenian issue as a way to embarrass the administration. In the House, Sydenham Ancona, a Democrat from Penn-sylvania, and Robert Schenck, a Republican from Ohio (and later minis-ter to London) introduced resolutions questioning the value of the U.S. neutrality legislation.[164] Reader Clarke and Rufus Spalding, both Ohio Republicans, demanded information on Fenian prisoners who had been arrested during the raids on Canada.[165] The focus on the limits and mean-ing of American neutrality culminated in a report by Nathaniel P. Banks, chair of the Foreign Affairs Committee, on modifying the 1818 Neutrality Act. Banks argued that the 1818 act "disregards the inalienable rights of the people of all nations." The law, he argued, served as a creature of British influence in the United States by suppressing anticolonial insurrections.[166] Banks, who had been explicitly tasked with assessing the Neutrality Act alongside resolutions of sympathy with Ireland, recommended "a critical and liberal revision" to bring the U.S. law into line with the more limited obligations of international law and the more constrained provisions of comparable British acts.[167] "It is incredible that it should have been thought necessary to permanently suppress, as crimes . . . transactions which are not punished as crimes elsewhere [i.e. in Britain], for the benefit of nations inimical if not hostile to us, and against States struggling for independence and liberty in emulation of our own example," Banks claimed. No longer should American law be predicated on weakness vis-à-vis British power, he concluded, arguing that the United States ought to boldly proclaim its support for revolutions that imitated its own.[168]

As this might suggest, Radical Republicans were increasingly keen to court Irish voters. James Stephens assumed that Banks and Roberts had struck some kind of deal for the Irish vote, and Roberts rather ostentatiously appeared on the floor of Congress, talking with various representatives.[169] However, neither could deliver what they promised. Banks drafted bill on neutrality revision that passed the House but, as expected, was buried by the Senate Committee on Foreign Affairs, which Radical Republican Charles Sumner chaired.[170] Moreover, there was no monolithic "Irish vote" for Roberts to deliver, and even had there been, the Fenian Brotherhood was crippled by factionalism.[171] Yet collusion was superficially attractive to both Fenian leaders and politicians. While the London *Times* might be confident that Britain's "hold on Ireland [was] too firm to be shaken by any filibustering agitation," Banks held out the possibility that U.S. foreign policy might be made more sympathetic to any future Fenian filibustering.[172] In October 1866, Frederick Bruce wrote to Lord Stanley, a Conservative who was the new foreign secretary, to highlight the continuing faith of Fenians that in the event of an Irish uprising, the Irish Republican Brotherhood could secure the same recognition of belligerent rights that the British had extended to the confederacy in May 1861.[173]

Simultaneously, Minister Charles Francis Adams suggested that the confluence of U.S. congressional politics and Fenian insurrection was a dangerous one. In an informal interview with Stanley, he stated that with respect to the *Alabama* claims, "my government was disposed to deal in a most amicable spirit . . . [but] the main point was to reopen the matter. . . . The state of the popular feeling in America was such as evinced by the proceedings in Congress, as to lead to an apprehension of a repeal of the neutrality laws if there was no other recourse."[174] Adams's time in London was, perhaps unsurprisingly, thoroughly conditioned by his experience of Civil War diplomacy, especially by British toleration of the construction of

Confederate cruisers. He recorded in his diary that although he believed that the Anglophobia of Americans was predicated on a series of misunderstandings, "we apprehend the truth all too well. We have to thank England for not a single really energetic act of good will."[175] Seward too recognized this fundamental fact, writing that, as the *Alabama* controversy festered, "it is to be expected that time will add to the strength of the interest which demands that projected modification of our neutrality laws."[176] (This despite his private conviction that "the conduct of the Irish during the War in spite of their military service, has not rendered them popular.")[177] Seward believed there might be value in using congressional agitation as a means of levering concessions from Britain. Ironically, the ascendancy of the Radical Republicans after the elections in the fall of 1866 aided him in this, allowing him to paint the administration as a restraining influence. It would be far better for the British ministry to deal with Seward than with the more wild-eyed congressmen who might be elevated to power at the next presidential election.[178]

Conversely, American toleration of Fenian activities, bred by dissatisfaction at the still-unresolved Civil War claims, led to British attempts to mitigate her *Alabama* misdemeanors. In 1870, looking back over a decade of Fenian activities in the United States, William Gladstone wrote to Lord Clarendon of the advantages of conducting "a very careful collection & dispassionate review of all the facts . . . which illustrate the case of Fenianism in America."[179] He went on:

> In the Alabama case, what an arbiter would probably find against us is insufficiency or miscarriage of preventive measures. He would have a nice point to determine in what seems to me to be the American contention, viz. that every such failure invests the foreign State injured thereby with a claim for compensation. A case substantially parallel, & in its development stronger & more varied, might be brought out in the inquiry about Fenianism & the U.S. Govt?[180]

Unsurprisingly, conservative commentators condemned the Johnson administration's willingness to use the Fenian invasions of Canada as a means of exacting revenge on the British government "for her *Alabamas* and *Floridas*" as the "vulgar satisfaction of a petty spite."[181] The raids offered an "opportunity, of which Mr. Seward somewhat hesitatingly availed himself" to set "an example of how neutrality should be understood and maintained."[182] This hesitation and the willingness of congressmen to use the Fenian Brotherhood in their anti-British diplomacy were significant as more than a demonstration of the corrosive effects of partisan politics on the statecraft of the United States. Coupled with widespread talk in the United States about the possibility—even the likelihood—of imminent Canadian annexation, a realignment of the Atlantic world seemed to be in motion that fostered hope among Irish nationalists.[183] This possibility prompted deep anxiety among Canadian politicians and, though support for Canadian federalism predated post–Civil War Fenian agitation, such fears reinforced the conviction that confederation was a necessary protective measure against the volatile compound of Fenianism and U.S. politics.[184]

The issue of neutrality was manipulated, then, by both camps of the Republican Party for domestic gain and by the Fenian Brotherhood as a way of linking the threat of U.S. diplomatic—and possibly military—power to Irish ends. Paradoxically, the seeming power Fenians gained by linking their goals with U.S. interests was contingent upon inaction. As demonstrated during the Canadian raids, when the brotherhood looked to the Johnson administration to make good on its tacit endorsement of Fenian activities, the superficiality of that link was exposed. Though Banks argued that the 1818 Neutrality Act was too strict because it placed burdens on U.S. citizens beyond those required by the norms of international law, it was actually the contrast between the open field of insurrection-planning in the United States (and the seeming convergence of Fenian and U.S. interests) and the hard world of Anglo-American geopolitics that proved so disillusioning for members of the brotherhood.

The strength of the Fenians lay in their sublimation of Irish goals in U.S. interests. This required them to create a permanent state of imminence: revolution had always to seem impending, never actualized. Fenian autonomy was circumscribed by the consequences of both acting and *not* acting. In order to maintain organizational discipline, Fenian leaders felt compelled to display activity in either a Canadian or an Irish context, but viable activities entailed consequences that weakened the brotherhood from both within and without. For instance, the first raid on Canada, directed by the Killian and O'Mahony wing of the Brotherhood, was provoked by a fear that the other wing of the Fenian movement, led by Thomas Sweeny and William Roberts, would act first.[185] Sweeny himself was convinced his invasion plans would ultimately fail and only put them into action because he believed that the disintegration of the movement that would follow *not* acting would be worse.[186]

The impulsive immediatism of the Fenian movement in the United States—its great fear of inertia—set it at odds with the longer-term cultivation of republican sentiment in Ireland.[187] James Stephens had long protested against the fitful "Knavish cry" of "English difficulty, Irish opportunity" that had proved "the chronic bane of Ireland" and was dismissive about the possibilities of an Irish American filibustering mission in the event of an Anglo-American conflict.[188] The autonomy of the Fenian Brotherhood deeply frustrated Stephens, who deemed time spent doing anything but supplying money for the IRB a waste. He also deeply disliked direction from the United States and resented the persistent desire of Fenians to confirm that his reports on the state of Ireland were accurate.[189]

In sum, the viability of the Fenian Brotherhood depended on a paradox: it relied on a *lack* of action married to a demonstration of potential political muscle even as its internal cohesion and broader political capital depended on being seen to be "up and doing." In Ireland, the IRB's uprisings in February and March 1867 were something of an embarrassment, as was a later filibustering mission from the United States that landed in April of the same year.[190] Though even a more serious uprising would not have caused the Johnson administration to abandon its *Alabama* claims in favor of a war against Great Britain, the illusion had proved tenacious.

Johnson's successor, Ulysses S. Grant, was relatively unconcerned with protecting his position among Irish voters (many of whom were increasingly disillusioned by the failures of the Fenian Brotherhood anyway) and proved more assertive in enforcing the Neutrality Act.[191] In discussions with leading Fenians, he made clear that he had no intention of tolerating the brotherhood's Canadian ambitions, a stance that earned him the British government's appreciation.[192] Likewise, Secretary of State Hamilton Fish exhibited little sympathy for Irish American nationalism. One historian suggests that he went so far as to systematically undermine the Fenian Brotherhood by supplying British authorities with information about their activities.[193] The Ten Years' War between Cuba and Spain (1868–1878) and the Franco-Prussian War (1870–1871) presented the immediate context for the U.S. government's assertion of a robust neutrality. The Grant administration sought to "enforce the principles [of neutrality], the alleged violation of which constituted its claim against England for indemnity."[194] Such stringency, prompted by the desire to protect the integrity of America's *Alabama* claims against Britain, made the Anglo-American collisions that fed Irish nationalist hopes less likely.

One fruit of the Grant administration's approach was a reassessment of the scope and meaning of neutrality in Anglo-American relations. In 1870, the British government, prompted by anxiety over the potential "construction of future *Alabamas* in Yankee shipyards" should Britain be dragged into a continental war, moved to tighten her neutrality laws, undermining Banks's argument for reciprocal laxness in the enforcement of international norms.[195] Clarity was the order of the day. The Treaty of Washington, which was concluded in May 1871, defined stronger obligations for neutral parties. During the negotiation, Britain (reluctantly) dropped her indirect claims arising out of the Fenian raids in Canada.[196] "The reception of the late treaty," noted Gladstone, "has been what was most to be desired in the practical interests of peace & goodwill. It is certainly to the great honour of the two Anglo-Saxon countries that they should first have rendered such a striking homage to the value of arbitration as a means of settling international disputes."[197] The resolution of outstanding causes of irritation greatly reduced the prospect that Irish discontent could successfully be yoked to U.S. foreign policy. Tensions arising out of the Civil War had temporarily encouraged a public opinion that was receptive to Irish nationalist ambitions. Rapprochement between Britain and the United States—and the edifying spectacle of two powers resolving grievances through arbitration—marginalized (though it did not eliminate) the disruptive potential of Irish nationalism in American politics.[198]

From the early 1850s to the early 1870s, Irish nationalists both encouraged and hoped to benefit from ambiguity over the meaning of American neutrality. At times they acted in concert with American politicians, hoping for a conjunction of U.S. grievances, Irish aspirations, and the power of the United States. Despite some condescension in the historiography, aligning Irish radical nationalism with American interest was a viable goal. As U.S. interests were redefined in the late 1860s and early 1870s, however, the asymmetry of the relationship became distressingly evident, and the Fenians' plan of gaining belligerent rights in a conflict with Great Britain dwindled.

Chapter 4

The Fenian Brotherhood, Naturalization, and Expatriation

Irish Americans and Anglo-American Comity

As we have seen, Fenians seized upon the capaciousness of the 1818 U.S. Neutrality Act to contest British rule in Ireland. British recognition of the Confederacy as a belligerent power, American claims for reparations for damage done by British-built Confederate ships, and the seeming toleration—even promotion—of Fenian activities by politicians in the United States fueled antagonism between the United States and Britain in the years after 1865. Fenian actions were predicated on the hope that sympathetic U.S. legislators would extend to Ireland the recognition that Britain had extended to the Confederacy during the Civil War. More quixotically, some hoped that the United States would use an Irish war against Britain as an opportunity to mobilize her own military power against the British Empire, specifically in Canada. A collusive U.S.-Irish assault on empire had an internal logic, so Fenian thinking went, and would prove mutually beneficial.

This did not occur, yet the movement of Irish nationalists across the Atlantic further strained the unsettled relations of the United States with Great Britain by aggravating the vexed issues of naturalization and expatriation. The arrest of Irish Americans on their return to Ireland raised the question of the reach of British law. Irish nationalists in Irish jails, sympathizers at political rallies in the United States, and representatives on the floor of Congress argued that Irish Americans had been incarcerated for acts committed in American cities or simply for coming from the United States at a time of extreme concern about the security of British rule in Ireland.

Even more problematically, these arrests brought forth contests regarding citizenship and subjecthood. British law made no provision for individuals to divest themselves of allegiance to the land of their birth. This had long been a major source of contention between Britain and the United States and had served as a proximate cause of the War of 1812 when the British navy impressed naturalized American citizens that Britain claimed as subjects.[1] Moreover, during that conflict the British government issued a notorious proclamation that said that former subjects—most likely immigrants from Ireland—bearing arms against the Crown would be executed as traitors.[2]

In the 1860s, the British state still did not recognize Irish who took up American citizenship after migration to the United States as U.S. citizens. In the absence of arrest and incarceration, this was of academic significance. However, Irishmen who returned to their place of birth with the aim of fomenting revolution, either as part of a coordinated expedition or individually, inevitably brought themselves within the scope of British law. Like native-born Americans, naturalized Irishmen appealed for intervention from U.S. authorities in Britain and Ireland—particularly Charles Francis Adams, the U.S. minister in London, and William West, the U.S. consul at Cork—and, ultimately, from the federal government in Washington. When the authorities at Dublin Castle refused U.S. consuls the right to visit U.S. citizens in Irish jails and, more significantly, denied the right of expatriation to Irish citizens, they asserted a doctrine of perpetual allegiance, stating that those born under the jurisdiction of the British Crown remained its subjects. British law assigned no value to the adoption of U.S. citizenship.

The conflict over expatriation and naturalization, argued the *North American Review* in April 1868, was "the last weighty question of international law [and] assumed the form of a conflict between the New and the Old World, between new and old ideas, between the doctrine of progress and the belief in precedent."[3] The *Review*'s construction of the problem masked the agency of Fenian nationalists in actively working to bring the question into the open in order to galvanize domestic support in the United States and engineer a rupture between the United States and Great Britain. But it hinted at the response of intellectuals and statesmen on both sides of the Atlantic who disputed the argument that the Fenian

Brotherhood offered a viable solution to Ireland's woes, and who saw in the Irish question an opportunity for transatlantic rapprochement on the subject of citizenship. The expatriation debate of the mid- to late 1860s was therefore not a product of disinterested speculation but a reaction to the pressure of Irish American nationalists.[4] The dispute provoked a change in British law; in 1870 Parliament declared that "a British-born subject may, by certain formalities, divest himself of his birth-allegiance, and adopt another citizenship."[5]

The Fenian Brotherhood failed in its objectives in Ireland and the United States, but in both countries the actions of Irish American nationalists reshaped the legal construction of citizenship. This cases of four incarcerated Irish Americans—George Archdeacon, Patrick Condon, William Nagle, and John Warren—illustrate the conflict over naturalization as a progressively more acute problem in statecraft for the United States and Great Britain. As in the case of the ambiguous construction of neutrality, Irish nationalist goals gained traction from their connection with more definably "American" diplomatic goals. This left those Irish Americans who sought to engineer a transatlantic rupture adrift when the British and U.S. governments settled the issue of citizenship amicably in May 1870.

Prelude, 1848

As noted, the contest between British and American conceptions of national belonging was not new. Nor was it novel in relation to Irish nationalist activity. In September 1848, George Bancroft, then minister to London, forwarded to Washington a copy of an act empowering the lord lieutenant of Ireland to apprehend and detain "such persons as he may suspect of conspiring against Her Majesty's person and Government," under which several U.S. citizens had been arrested.[6] The arrest of two men in particular—James Bergen, a Connecticut-born insurance agent who lived in New York, and Richard F. Ryan, a member of the Cincinnati bar—drew the attention of the U.S. government.[7] Thomas Nicholas Redington, the under-secretary of state for Ireland, freely admitted to George Bancroft that the Irish authorities were paying special attention to U.S. visitors as apprehension of an insurrection in Ireland grew through the summer of 1848. Information had been received—from what quarter Redington did not specify—that "a considerable number of citizens of the U. States ... might be expected in Ireland as Agents of the sympathizers with the Revolutionary

Party."[8] British intelligence suggested that Mexican-American War veterans were about to arrive in Ireland with the intention of aiding an anticipated insurrection.[9]

As Bancroft feared, the British government turned to the "inadmissable and exploded notion" of perpetual subjecthood.[10] Authorities in London were irate at U.S. tolerance of Irish revolutionary associations. The Polk administration was similarly enraged by the revelation that the Dublin constabulary had been directed specifically to arrest all individuals coming from the United States and "to seize, search, and examine their luggage, their persons, and the linings of their clothing."[11] When it became clear that the release of Bergen and Ryan was unlikely, Bancroft wrote to Lord Palmerston to declare that the U.S. government viewed the "doctrine of perpetual allegiance" as a "badge of servitude."[12]

The authorities eventually released the two men on the condition that they leave the country.[13] Bancroft optimistically suggested that their release represented the "practical renunciation of the doctrine of perpetual allegiance" by Great Britain.[14] Despite their liberation—and against Bancroft's better judgment—the Polk administration insisted on a formal remonstrance to the British government.[15] This, which Bancroft presented on January 26, 1849, drew on Roman, European, British, and U.S. law to critique a feudal notion of servitude and assert emphatically that "naturalized American Citizens are not subjects of Great Britain."[16] Notwithstanding the flurry of interest that accompanied these cases, neither the United States nor Great Britain sustained the controversy surrounding validity of naturalized U.S. citizenship. And with no naturalized Americans sitting in British or Irish jails and with unrest in Ireland largely quelled, tensions eased.

Irish Americans and Diplomatic Tact

The Fenian agitation of the mid-1860s revived the issue. Between September 1865 and the failed uprising of spring 1867, waves of arrests of suspected agitators (including many Irish Americans) crystallized the transatlantic contest over citizenship regimes. This was particularly the case following the suspension of habeas corpus in February 1866. Men were returning to Ireland from Britain and the United States at an alarming rate with weapons increasingly in evidence, and the Liberal cabinet agreed that the ordinary legal provisions were insufficient to meet the challenges posed by Irish agitation, particularly if that agitation was supplemented by resources from the United States.[17] Irish Lord Lieutenant John Wodehouse noted that those coming from the United States were "imbued with Yankee notions, thoroughly reckless, and possessed of considerable military experience" and thus were particularly dangerous.[18]

U.S. minister Charles Francis Adams formed his own impression of conditions in Ireland.[19] In August 1865, he replicated the tour that Abbott Lawrence had conducted fourteen years earlier. He noted the increased numbers of British troops but confessed that he had "never anticipated any difficulty that would prove serious," though he expressed his concern about the role sympathy within the United States played in maintaining "secret disaffection" in Ireland.[20] More troubling than mere sympathy, however, was the increasing number of U.S. citizens in Ireland, specifically U.S. citizens in Irish jails who were making demands on his attention. Adams's duties with regard to imprisoned Irish Americans were complicated by intense interest in their fate in the United States.

We know as much as we do about interned Irish Americans because of the political heat their cases generated. In response to a request from the House of Representatives for information on the alleged arrest of "peaceable citizens of the United States, engaged in no unlawful act," Secretary of State William Seward compiled a list of twenty-one U.S. citizens who had been held in Dublin following the suspension of habeas corpus and another five who had been held elsewhere in Ireland.[21] In addition, he forwarded a mass of correspondence to Congress detailing the efforts of the Johnson administration on behalf of these prisoners.

William West, the U.S. consul at Dublin, was convinced that these prisoners were determined to amplify any disagreement the United States had with British authorities. In offering legal assistance to the prisoners, he wrote, "nothing will be done that can in the slightest degree attach any complicity or approval on the part of our government . . . there being already, evidently, a desire to have Americans mixed up in [the politics of the Irish Republican Brotherhood], and if possible our government also."[22] West, a "good natured, conceited, chattering" Irish American lawyer, was placed in the uncomfortable position of intermediary between outraged arrestees and increasingly exasperated Irish authorities.[23]

One of the first cases to engage his attention was that of George Archdeacon, who was arrested on September 23, 1865, as part of the British government's suppression of the Irish Republican Brotherhood. Archdeacon, a naturalized American citizen, was a returned migrant. He protested his innocence, claiming that he had come to Ireland in 1862 in order to collect money owed to his wife but lacked the means to return to the United States. In order to make ends meet, he had become a book and newspaper agent, selling copies of the IRB newspaper *Irish People*.[24] His correspondence with William West detailed his indignation at the Irish authorities' rejection of his status as a U.S. citizen. Archdeacon, who claimed to have been a citizen since 1854, dismissed West's complacent assertion that he would "be fairly and justly dealt with as a subject of Great Britain, which its government recognizes you and every other native-born person found on her soil to be."[25] Dissatisfied with West's course, Archdeacon informed the consul that he intended to write to both William Seward and the eminent New York jurist Charles O'Conor for a fuller exposition of the rights and obligations of U.S. citizenship.[26] Moreover, he urged that his correspondence with West be made public.

> If . . . myself [and] others . . . (being natives of this country,) are still held by Britain as subjects, then . . . our solemn oaths in public American courts that we owe no allegiance to any foreign prince or potentate, more especially none to Queen Victoria, of whom we *were* subjects, becomes a mockery and a delusion.[27]

In this we can see the emergence of a novel political tactic: the public letter from a British or Irish prison. Various Fenian prisoners would make use of this over the next few years.

Despite holding to a doctrine of perpetual allegiance, Irish authorities permitted naturalized Irish Americans to contact the U.S. consul, and they were receptive to West's informal interventions on behalf of naturalized Americans, including George Archdeacon.[28] Contradicting the prisoner's continued protestations of innocence, Thomas Larcom, the under-secretary for Ireland, presented West with evidence that George Archdeacon had spent his years in the British Isles as an active member of Liverpool's Fenian community and had worked as an agent of the 1863 Fenian convention in Chicago, which sought to fund revolution in Ireland.[29] In all, it seemed that the authorities made a compelling case.

West's course was marked by caution. He acknowledged the strong evidence presented against Archdeacon but suggested that holding a naturalized U.S. citizen who was an agent of *Irish People* alone among hundreds of other such agents lacked diplomatic tact.[30] In dealing with U.S. citizens arrested under writs of habeas corpus, West wrote, my government will not . . . go so far as to require the production of . . . evidence. . . . It is not its desire or purpose to screen offenders. At the same time it will, I am sure, use its best efforts to maintain the enjoyment of the same rights in the persons of our innocent citizens within this part of the kingdom that we concede to British subjects under similar circumstances in the United States.[31]

This was hardly the bold assertion of U.S. power on his behalf that Archdeacon had sought.

Ultimately, in April 1866, the Irish authorities approved George Archdeacon's discharge on condition that he not return to Britain or Ireland for three years.[32] Though he had tried to intercede on Archdeacon's behalf, William West later explained that he had "carefully avoided any allusion to the question of allegiance, believing that the subject was not within the scope of my consular duties."[33] The British authorities' willingness to allow West informal interviews with Archdeacon and the compelling evidence of West's complicity in Fenian activities probably made a more robust demand for respect for U.S. citizenship unnecessary. In addition, West was right to say that he would have been going beyond his consular remit were he to press the twin issues of expatriation and naturalization. Adams's unwillingness to push hard for the rights of naturalized U.S. citizens was similarly simple: his faith in the imminent demise of Fenianism as a result of government suppression made him prepared to sidestep controversy. He phlegmatically accepted that "summary measures . . . [may] give side blows to the innocent."[34] When British authorities suspended the requirement of the writ of habeas corpus as a condition of arrest in February 1866, the number of U.S. citizens in British jails increased, making it progressively more difficult for West and Adams to avoid bringing questions of expatriation and naturalization to the fore.

A Working Arrangement

The British authorities suspended the requirement of writs of habeas corpus in February 1866 because of growing alarm over conditions in Ireland. The real threat presented by the Fenian Brotherhood and the Irish Republican Brotherhood was unclear, but the connection between these two groups and demobilized U.S. troops deeply troubled British authorities. Though the promised 1865 uprising had not materialized, there were

serious debates among brotherhood leaders about the possibility of an uprising in the spring of 1866.[35] The marginalization of IRB leader James
Stephens—who was accused of fighting shy—gave the more assertive Irish
Americans greater influence over any uprising.[36] Charles Francis Adams
was pessimistic about peace in Ireland, reporting in his diary "a swelling
mass of disaffection" there, "awaiting only a difficulty with some external
power to make its force felt."[37] Radical nationalists evidently hoped that
that external power would be the United States; the Fenian Brotherhood
there worked "to bring on a complication between the two countries."[38]

As Charles Francis Adams had predicted, another sweep of arrests that
took place in February 1866 focused on those coming from the United
States as potential revolutionaries.[39] During the state trials of autumn
1865, the prosecution had unequivocally outlined a theory of perpetual
allegiance. This panicked U.S. citizens in Dublin, who flooded the city's
consulate in fear of their own arrest.[40] One of these was William Halpin.
Now employed as a Fenian agent, Halpin traveled back and forth between
Ireland and the United States, delivering reports and transmitting funds.[41]
He was, in short, exactly the kind of individual the Irish authorities were
seeking to pin down. He somewhat disingenuously complained to West:

> Yesterday some forty citizens of the United States were arrested and cast
> into prison by the police without even an investigation. I know some of
> the parties arrested, and I am confident no criminal charge can be sus-
> tained against them. The evident desire of the Irish executive is to . . . cast
> into prison every American citizen in the country under the feigned belief
> that they are connected with the Fenians. . . . To incarcerate citizens of the
> United States simply because they are strangers, without trial or investiga-
> tion, is a crime which I trust the United States will not tolerate. I write you
> this in anticipation of my own arrest.[42]

Under his signature, Halpin detailed his military rank (he had served during the Civil War with the 15th Kentucky volunteers.)[43] Appending this
to his letter was more than a polite formality. Arrests under the suspension of writs of habeas corpus snared a large number of men who had
served in the American armies, both Union and Confederate. In letters
to the State Department from (and on behalf of) those arrested, military
service was a prominent theme, and Fenian propagandists argued that it
should guarantee attentive assistance from U.S. officials.[44] They pushed at an
open door, as William Seward—in a despatch clearly designed for domestic

consumption—openly acknowledged that "faithful service in the armies or navy of the United States during the rebellion constitutes an enhanced claim" to assistance from the U.S. government.[45]

Charles Francis Adams was well aware of the potential power that arrested Irish Americans wielded, whether they had military experience or not. A "good deal of prudence" would be required to thwart the "strong desire on the part of the arrested to bring on a complication with this [the British] government, or else to raise the popular sympathy at home."[46] Simultaneously, William West realized that the issue of expatriation would now prove impossible to avoid, even without the agency of Irish American prisoners. Where Under-Secretary Thomas Larcom identified nine U.S. citizens in Irish jails, West claimed he could compile a list of "fifty or sixty, if not more."[47] Armed with proof of naturalization, West applied to see various prisoners but was rebuffed. This refusal raised "in the most unqualified manner the issue between our government and this," West informed Adams.[48] Expecting that Irish American nationalists would make good use of the controversy, West wrote to Adams of his fear that they would "force us into a quarrel with this country, in order to gratify their own private ends, and their malignant spirit against England."[49]

In London, Adams had his own problems with the British ministry. Negotiations over the *Alabama* claims had stalled, and Adams was increasingly frustrated with the slipshod manner with which British politicians dealt with U.S. matters.[50] Not only had the British government refused the rights of naturalized citizens to contact U.S. consuls, but all U.S. citizens arrested under the suspension of writs of habeas corpus had been refused the right to see the evidence against them. Alert to the political capital that might be generated by unscrupulous politicians in the United States, the "serious" problem of both native-born and naturalized citizens being held as potential "Fenian conspirators" without specific charges brought against them troubled Adams deeply.[51] Adams was focused on the claims of the United States related to the Civil War and was extremely wary of other issues, like Fenian prisoners, that might complicate the U.S. case against Great Britain or that might exacerbate transatlantic tensions to the extent that settling the claims would be impossible.[52]

In Dublin, all West could do was assure incarcerated U.S. citizens that the "grave and vexed question" of their allegiance was under discussion between Adams and the British government. The U.S. minister warned Foreign Secretary Clarendon of the political ramifications of imprisoning Americans without trial and the unjust distinction the British government was making between native-born and naturalized citizens.[53] Recognizing that British law limited Clarendon's freedom of action when it came to the issue of allegiance but making clear that the U.S. government would brook no compromise on the matter, Adams suggested that the best course would be to "avoid a collision, by endeavoring so far as was practicable to evade making the issue."[54] "If the men in dispute could be released . . . on condition of their good behaviour, or of their quitting the country," he wrote to Seward, "the difficulty might be removed."[55]

The need to remove the difficulty was acute, as Adams noted, because of the political acumen of imprisoned Irish nationalists. "They are . . . astute enough to be capable of contriving means of raising a complication between the two nations, out of the questions that may follow from the abuse of the extraordinary powers of repression now resorted to here."[56] William Seward concurred, noting that the present unsettled state of relations between the United States and Great Britain gave Irish Americans unusual power to transform contention over a relatively small issue—the arrest and imprisonment of a few individuals—into a matter of grave national interest.[57]

The solution that Adams and Clarendon reached in March 1866 was candid yet informal. Clarendon had been keen to impress upon the Irish authorities the desirability of avoiding a "wrangle" with the United States over allegiance, and he was aware that cooperation to marginalize Irish nationalists was mutually advantageous.[58] Clarendon offered a commitment to release naturalized citizens in cases where their connection with treasonable activities was slight, and those who were native-born were to be set free on "condition of their disappearing."[59] By the second week of May, Adams could report to Washington that "the implied promise of the government has been faithfully carried out . . . so that persons in whose behalf representations have been made are continually in process of liberation, on the condition of their departure from the kingdom."[60] Without the threat of rebellion, Adams had "little doubt of the anxious desire of the ministry to be relieved as rapidly as possible of the burden imposed upon them by the suspension of the *habeas corpus* act."[61]

However, the success of the policy of conditional releases was contingent on the prisoners concerned accepting those conditions. West told Seward that some prisoners refused their conditional liberation, expecting instead that the U.S. government would insist upon their release as a matter of right.[62] Of those, the most troublesome was Patrick J. Condon, a resident of New York who had served as a captain with the 63rd New York State

Volunteers.[63] He was arrested in Dublin on February 23, 1866, and moved to the city's Kilmainham Gaol three days later. From there, he applied to the protection of the U.S. consul.[64] As with the applications of other arrested Americans, West's application for intervention was rejected by the Irish authorities. Writing to Condon on April 28, West outlined the compromise position that Adams and Clarendon had reached and explained that the issue of allegiance would, most likely, not be settled definitively in the near future. In the interim, he might receive an offer of conditional liberation, which he could accept or reject as he saw fit.[65] Condon's response was firm:

> As this question, I have no doubt, of allegiance, will cause a dispute be-
> tween both governments, I . . . will abide the issue, well believing that my
> government will take a bold and dignified stand on this important ques-
> tion. . . . It will be useless to require any conditions [of me] short of allow-
> ing me to be a free agent of my own actions.[66]

Lord Lieutenant John Wodehouse decided in early July that Condon's "del-icate" health and the prison time that he had already served justified his re-lease, even though he was "seriously implicated in the Fenian conspiracy."[67] As Thomas Larcom detailed it, Condon's release was contingent on him "forthwith leaving Ireland for America, and being accompanied to the ves-sel by the police. . . . If he is again found in Ireland he will be arrested."[68]

Disappointed by his failure to provoke controversy between Britain and the United States, Condon turned his attention to engineering a dispute between William West and the U.S. government. He accused the consul of acquiescing in his conditional release rather than asserting the rights of U.S. citizenship. Ought prisoners to assume that "grave and pressing reasons have urged upon [the government] the humiliating necessity of consent-ing to have its citizens . . . marched like common malefactors through the thoroughfares of a foreign country?" he asked.[69]

Despite his evident anger, Condon resigned himself to accepting the conditions of his release, arriving back in the United States on August 10.[70] There, like George Archdeacon, he wrote to the president, accusing Wil-liam West of "flunkeyism," of being insufficiently robust in demanding the rights due to U.S. citizens abroad, and of being a "hireling of the British government."[71] Contrary to their hopes, Archdeacon and Condon found little in the way of political traction back in the United States. A lull in Fenian activity followed the abortive Canadian raids of April and June 1866. Moreover, domestic sympathy with the Fenians, as mentioned, was

Figure 3. Patrick Condon photographed at Mountjoy Prison in 1866. Thomas A. Larcom Photographs Collection, 1857–1866, volume 2, November 1866, Manuscripts and Archives Division, The New York Public Library, Astor, Lenox, and Tilden Foundations.

something of an abstraction: Ireland's wrongs might be acknowledged and the legitimacy of the Fenian Brotherhood affirmed, but this did not mean that Americans and their representatives would assent to the application of U.S. power to Irish ends.

There was widespread optimism in the United States that the threat from Fenianism had been averted. Though Andrew Johnson's proclamation against the Fenian raids seemed halting and irresolute when viewed from the United States, it had a reassuring impact in Great Britain. In July 1866, William West referred in the past tense to the "Irish-American Fenian conspiracy of 1866" and commented on the beneficial diplomatic effects of the U.S. suppression of the Canadian invasion.[72] Likewise, Charles Francis Adams accepted the gratitude of elite Englishmen and women, though he slyly noted that the United States had only done its duty in proscribing rebellion. He left implicit the uncomplimentary comparison with British recognition of Confederate rebels.[73]

Though British anxieties remained, particularly in connection with the rumored departure of IRB leader James Stephens from New York for Ireland, the use of U.S. police power against Fenian forces in North America had a salutary effect.[74] As alarm about an impending winter outbreak receded in February 1867, Charles Francis Adams could report that more generous measures were likely in connection with men who were still being held as Fenian prisoners.[75] Anticipating the resumption of normal legal forms as the suspension of habeas corpus lapsed, Adams noted that the danger "seemed to be over" and that the government desired "to gradually get rid of the offenders on lenient terms."[76] Yet consular reports from New York in early 1867 detailed the departure of a number of leading Fenians for Ireland, and simultaneously British authorities received worrisome news of the extent of Fenian organization in British cities. Following an attempted IRB raid on Chester Castle and a botched uprising in Kerry, the government renewed its suspension of habeas corpus.[77]

Fenians, Jail, and Epistolary Influence

On March 8, 1867, Charles Francis Adams reported that "another attempt at insurrection" had taken place three days earlier.[78] "The newspapers contain frequent allusions to persons found among the insurgents, alleged to be Americans or American Irish," he noted, "but as yet Mr. West has not reported to me more than four or five cases of arrest in which his interposition has been solicited."[79] The uprising was a confused and halting affair, planned by a "Directory" of Irish U.S. officers that included Thomas Kelly, John McCafferty, and Patrick Condon. In December 1866, this cadre of impatient Fenians had ousted James Stephens as head of the Irish Republican Brotherhood, and they had determined on a March uprising. They hoped to maintain an insurrection long enough to elicit substantial support in men, arms, and money from their supporters in the United States.[80] A poor communication structure, which was weakened by arrests under the continued suspension of habeas corpus; a clear preponderance of British power in Ireland; and reliable inside information on the insurgents' plans stymied the insurrection, though its extent and organization impressed even unfavorable observers.[81]

Contending with "a factious Senate and a delirious representative chamber," Secretary of State Seward framed his response to news of the insurrection with a domestic audience in mind.[82] His letter to Adams of March 28 offered an exposition of the logic of Irish rebellion and noted the manifest concern of U.S. citizens about events in Ireland. An organized insurrection, he noted, "is intensely expected by many citizens. . . . That expectation excites a profound sympathy among adopted citizens . . . [and] it is equally manifest that the sympathy of the whole American people goes with such movements."[83] This sympathy, he argued, was a logical corollary of U.S. discontent with the British presence in North America and with the actions of the British government with regard to the confederacy.[84] He enclosed a copy of Congressman Nathaniel P. Banks's resolution of sympathy with the people of Ireland but made no mention of the likely resurrection of the issue of perpetual allegiance.

Seward claimed, perhaps disingenuously, that the failure of Irish insurrection had not dented the abstract sympathy that animated the interest of the U.S. public in events in Ireland. Indeed, such affinity had been inflamed by the death sentences passed at the trials of three Fenian prisoners who claimed U.S. citizenship: Thomas Bourke, Patrick Dolan, and John McCafferty.[85] The "traditional sympathy with the revolution in Ireland is increased by the convictions of natural justice, and therefore it is now . . . almost universal," he wrote to Adams.[86] Ironically, in at least two of these cases, the prisoners were ex-Confederate volunteers. All three, noted Adams, had "very doubtful antecedents."[87] McCafferty, a native of Sandusky, Ohio, had rendered "gallant service" for the South and, said Adams, had "little sense of the value of truth."[88] As such, the minister continued, he was receiving in Ireland only what had been due him in the United States.[89] Bourke was an "obstinate rebel" who had refused to take the oath of allegiance at the close of the Civil War.[90] Ultimately all three were granted clemency; the Conservative Lord Stanley, the new foreign secretary, intimated that U.S. public opinion was an important consideration for the British government.[91]

Another potential source of concern was the arrival of a filibustering mission from the United States in April 1867. The *Jacmel* sailed from New York on April 12, 1867, carrying with it "a party of 40 or 50 men."[92] Renamed *Erin's Hope* in the course of the transatlantic voyage, the vessel carried 2,000 muskets, with ammunition, for distribution on landing.[93] The expedition was led by James E. Kerrigan, who escaped arrest and, it can be presumed, returned safely to the United States.[94] Historian Sean McConville offers a charitable assessment when he suggests that the episode demonstrated the Fenians were capable of "bold and brave ventures" but lacked "the mastery of necessary detail to carry them through."[95] In truth, the expedition appears almost implausibly farcical.

The *Jacmel* mission ended with the ship sailing round the Irish coast while the men on board debated whether to land in Ireland—they had already been made aware of the failure of the March risings—or return to the United States.[96] The majority of those aboard decided on the former. As historian R. V. Comerford has suggested, the expedition revealed "the extent to which the fenians had allowed their hopes to outrun reality."[97] Among the filibusters arrested shortly after landing were John Warren and William J. Nagle, who came ashore at Dungarvan, County Waterford.[98] Though Lord Naas, the chief secretary for Ireland, opposed the prosecution of these "trumpery pirates" because of the trouble it might bring with the United States, Warren and Nagle were committed for trial as leading organizers of the expedition.[99] The imprisonment and subsequent trials of both men provoked great interest in the United States, and their conduct while in prison caused a number of problems for William West and Charles Francis Adams.

Both John Warren and William Nagle claimed U.S. citizenship, and both asserted that they were in Ireland to visit family and friends.[100] Nagle hailed from Niagara County in upstate New York. One of four brothers who had served under arms for the Union during the Civil War, he had risen to the rank of colonel with the 88th New York Infantry.[101] Though there was initially some confusion over Warren's provenance, it was eventually established that he had been born in County Cork.[102] In a written statement presented in court, Warren claimed to have been naturalized as a U.S. citizen in Massachusetts in October 1866, though, as the *New York*

Tribune later noted, he "might just as well hand [the British government] an old ballad" as his naturalization papers for all the notice that was taken of them.[103]

The incarcerated men were not without a voice, nor were they without influence. In a letter to his father, William Nagle made clear his intention to raise the general issues of naturalization and the detention of U.S. citizens by the Irish authorities. Following his arrest with John Warren on June 1, 1867 he complained that

> no evidence of any kind is shown or charge made, other than "suspicion," which is applied as a general rule to all Americans. . . . It would be well for you to take immediate steps to bring my case before the notice of the people, and have the subject brought before Congress at the coming session in July. This is not exclusively an individual case, but becomes a question of right involving the liberty of every American citizen that sets foot on this soil. I ask the government of my country . . . to secure to me that liberty which is my birthright, and of which I am now deprived . . . by an authority I do not recognize—a government to which I owe no allegiance, and whose laws I have in no way infringed upon.[104]

Nagle was evidently aware of the U.S. government's attempts to secure his release; he complained specifically about Charles Francis Adams's lax efforts to carry out Seward's instructions.[105]

Like William Nagle, John Warren sought to focus domestic political opinion on his case. Writing to the *Dublin Weekly News* from his Kilmainham cell, he called public attention to his incarceration. Though published in an Irish newspaper, Warren's audience was unmistakably American. "My case is your case," he proclaimed. The bearing of the returned Irish American—a solid republican with "a good coat . . . [and] square-toe[d] shoes]"—was, he argued, sufficient to arouse the ire of British authorities in Ireland, and land an innocent U.S. citizen in jail.[106] He also corresponded directly with anti-administration members of Congress in an attempt to make his case an issue of partisan contention, and excerpts from his correspondence made their way into speeches in Congress.[107] Such letter-writing deeply troubled the Conservative Marquess of Abercorn, the new lord lieutenant, who was so perturbed by the accusations of ill treatment that filled letters from Irish American prisoners to U.S. politicians that he suggested curtailing letter-writing privileges. Lord Stanley wisely overruled him.[108]

Warren sought to fuel the belief that Irish Americans were being arrested for acts done in the United States. In addition, he argued, they might

Figure 4. John Warren photographed at Mountjoy Prison in 1866. Thomas A. Larcom Photographs Collection, 1857–1866, volume 2, November 1866, Manuscripts and Archives Division, The New York Public Library, Astor, Lenox, and Tilden Foundations.

be arrested for acts *not* done there, for there was "nothing to prevent a Massey or a Corydon [two informers at the state trials] to swear he saw him at a public meeting in America, saw an Irish bond hanging up behind his counter, or saw a name to correspond with his published through the press as having spoke or written in favor of republicanism."[109] Warren claimed that the incarcerated Irish American could expect little help from his representatives: William West was too busy "playing billiards" with the Irish authorities up at Dublin Castle and Minister Adams was negligent of his republican duties.[110] "And thus it is," raged Warren, "between the diplomacy and the red-tapeism and the toadyism and the flunkeyism. The *habeas corpus* suspension acts may have expired, and you crawl into existence again . . . with a cauldron of vengeances burning in your breast, and no increased love for your own government."[111] He concluded by arguing that the failure of U.S. representatives overseas to act mandated action in the United States to validate the rights of expatriation and naturalization in the face of British defiance.

In transmitting a copy of Warren's letter to the government at Washington, Adams stated that it was quite evident that arrested individuals were attempting to "excite a public feeling in America . . . to force the two governments into a conflict on the questions thus raised by them on their arrest and imprisonment."[112] Frederick Bruce, the British representative in Washington, took the political dimensions of the potential crisis seriously enough to telegraph London to urge the release of Nagle and Warren, and September 11th Seward repeated the recommendation, directing Adams by telegram to "urge [the] prompt release of Nagle and Warren," adding that "[the] affair is embarrassing."[113]

The introduction of telegraphic communication increased the speed of diplomatic correspondence. Soon after the completion of the first transatlantic cable, one newspaper chose to play on the supposed naivety of Irish immigrants by publishing a cartoon entitled "An Irish-American Idea of the Use of the Atlantic Telegraph Cable." It depicted an Irishman, surrounded by his family, pulling on the Atlantic cable and proclaiming, "Be Jabers! We've got the Ould Country now, and we'll annix it fast and no mistake!"[114] Although the cartoon was clearly less than respectful of Irish immigrants, its central image was a sound one. The Atlantic telegraph had the potential to greatly improve communications between migrants and their families and to facilitate the remittances that were central to the domestic economy of so many in Ireland.[115] In addition, it very clearly illustrated the integrative potential of commercial and technological development that Abbott Lawrence had celebrated during his 1851 trip to Ireland.[116] In addition, by speeding up diplomatic transmissions, the transatlantic telegraph might serve as a means of amplifying diplomatic pressure.

Those in sympathy with Irish nationalists hoped that the advent of the transatlantic telegraph would make more effective the projection of U.S.

power on the other side of the Atlantic. A New York City meeting on the subject of imprisoned Irish Americans trusted that "the Atlantic cable will be used to remind an oppressive power of the greatness of the United States," for the United States "is too powerful to allow a government conventionally called civilized to treat in a barbarous manner American citizens."[117] Similarly, one member of Congress spoke of how the telegraph multiplied the bonds of affection between Ireland and the United States— and of course the transatlantic telegraph terminated in western Ireland—as a "wire that is insulated from the rest of the world thrills unceasingly with electric love from shore to shore."[118] Without doubt, the highly charged political atmosphere surrounding the arrest of naturalized Americans put a premium on the considered diplomacy of representatives in Washington and London if a diplomatic crisis—or worse—was to be averted.

John Warren Takes the Stand

The trial of Irish Americans in autumn 1867 provoked great controversy in the United States. On November 25, 1867, Representative William Erigena Robinson gave a strident speech in Congress on the subject of U.S. citizens arrested in Ireland.[119] Robinson, now a Democrat from New York, requested—and received—the previous two years' worth of correspondence on the subject.[120] Moreover, he called for the impeachment of Charles Francis Adams for "neglect of duty" in "failing to secure [prisoners'] rights as . . . citizens."[121] This was an early indication of the hostility toward Adams that would exist amongst Irish nationalists through the next decade and a half.[122] As Adams himself noted, his qualified defense of Fenian defendants had earned him "a great deal of hostility in the United States" and damaged his political prospects.[123] When the Boston *Pilot* later suggested that the minister might make a viable vice presidential candidate, one correspondent replied that he "bears the name immortalized in '76, but disgraced in '67."[124] Clearly Adams's pragmatic dealings with Lords Clarendon and Stanley did little to bolster his standing with the Irish American press or with those who sympathized with the incarcerated citizens.

To Adams, Robinson's actions fell neatly into what he perceived as a pattern of deranged political activity in the United States. "Wretched electioneering claptrap" excited by the "politically fitful, capricious and untrustworthy" Irish population in the United States was one symptom of the country's decaying political morality, he claimed.[125] The likely enfranchisement of former slaves, the weak spines of U.S. statesmen and, particularly, the attempted impeachment of Andrew Johnson left Adams disillusioned with civic life in the United States.[126] Referring to the prospect of his own impeachment, the minister wrote, simply: "Have men gone mad in America?"[127] He would hardly have been encouraged by the mass meetings held in the United States in support of imprisoned Americans, particularly John Warren and William Nagle.[128]

However, Warren and Nagle's agency in the case of their own incarceration was a double-edged sword. Ironically, their ability to raise awareness of their plight and gain political traction in the United States came at the price of diminished sympathy in Great Britain. As Seward noted, the publication of Warren's letters "beyond a doubt . . . has a tendency to counteract a favorable disposition on the part of her Majesty's government in his case."[129] Here, the concerns of imprisoned Irish Americans and those of the State Department were beginning to diverge. In his despatch of September 20, 1867, Seward was adamant that the issue with which he was most preoccupied was that of the arbitrary arrest of U.S. citizens traveling in Britain "for matters of speech or conduct occurring exclusively within the United States, and which are not forbidden by local or international law."[130] Seward referred directly to the arrests growing out of the *Jacmel* expedition. Like Adams, he was certain that because those involved had been arrested as soon as they set foot on Irish soil, no act of hostility to the British government could have taken place within the government's jurisdiction.[131]

Seward chose to focus his attention on the "arbitrary and indefinite imprisonment" of U.S. citizens rather than the invidious distinction between native and naturalized citizens.[132] Why he should do this is not immediately apparent. It is possible that he was more perturbed by the prospect of Americans being arrested and committed for trial arbitrarily and for acts that apparently took place in the United States (if at all). Yet it seems that shrewd political calculation might also have led to this decision, as it permitted Seward to channel discontent over the arrest of Irish Americans in a direction that limited the disruptive potential of Irish American grandstanding while pressing the British government to redress an identifiable wrong: the detention of U.S. citizens indefinitely without trial. Seward's complaint was met with the news that those still in Irish jails, including Warren, Nagle, and William Halpin, had been committed to stand trial.[133]

The prospect of courtroom appearances addressed Seward's primary concern—that of arbitrary detention without trial—but threatened to revive the possibility of a controversy over naturalization in two ways. First, it offered a very public forum in which Warren, Nagle, Halpin, and others could assert their defiance of British courts. Second, legal procedure forced decisions about *how* the prisoners were to be tried upon the Irish authorities. This was problematic: because the prisoners asserted that they were aliens, they could request that half of their juries be composed of U.S. citizens. In addition, the definitions of crimes against the Crown were distinct in the case of native-born and naturalized American citizens. The nature of the offense was contingent upon a prisoner's citizenship. One practical manifestation of this was the postponement of William Nagle's trial on the grounds that "the evidence to fix upon him, as an alien, an overt act, must clearly prove this act to have been committed within the British jurisdiction," suggesting that this degree of proof was not demanded in the case of John Warren, who was born in Ireland.[134]

Warren's trial, which began on October 30, 1867, lasted three days. Because of his prominent role in the *Jacmel* expedition, he was indicted for "feloniously and wickedly . . . intend[ing] to deprive and depose our Lady the Queen from the style, honour, and royal name of the imperial Crown" and intending to "levy war against the Queen [in] Ireland."[135] Warren pleaded not guilty and his counsel made the appropriate application for a mixed jury. This provoked extensive courtroom debate about the propriety and wording of the request.[136] This application, Charles Francis Adams believed, was part of an evident plan "to effect the object so long desired by parties concerned with these movements in Ireland, of raising a difficulty between the two countries on the question of the right of expatriation."[137] When the request was rejected, Warren protested against being tried as a British subject. "I instruct my counsel to withdraw from the case," Warren stated, "and I place it in the hands of the United States Government; which has now become the principal."[138] In withdrawing, Warren's counsel assured the Court that "this is not a hasty determination on the part of the prisoner."[139] (In fact, Warren's intentions were known to William West in advance and the consul had taken it upon himself to appoint a Dublin barrister to report on the trial as it progressed.)[140]

The jury took just twenty minutes to convict Warren on the charge of treason-felony.[141] As he was born in Ireland, the prosecution had only to prove that the Fenians were responsible for the Dublin uprising of March 1867 and that, at that time, Warren had been a member of the "Fenian confederacy."[142] This done, "a recent decision of the highest court of criminal jurisprudence in this country" dictated that Warren "would be answerable" for "acts done by others who were co-conspirators . . . as if he were there bodily present doing the act himself."[143] U.S. Attorney General Henry Stanberry assured William Seward that the proceedings had been in accordance with the law: Warren had no right to a mixed jury, and because he was being tried in a British court, British law fixed the status of his citizenship.[144] In short, Stanberry noted, nothing was done that would not also have been done in a U.S. court.

On November 16, John Warren was sentenced to fifteen years' penal servitude.[145] From his Kilmainham cell he wrote an open letter directly to Congress. He complained that he had been convicted in connection with an uprising that had taken place while he was in the United States—implicitly challenging the ability of the United States to protect her citizens—and alleged that the British courts had wholly ignored his "U.S. citizenship, and consequently your right to confer it."[146] More damning, as "England has ignored ... [my] citizenship ... the government of the United States, as represented by Mr. Johnson, Mr. Seward, and Mr. Adams appeared to coincide in this enforcement."[147]

Though John Warren was ultimately convicted, his actions—and those of his co-defendants—indicate that Irish nationalists were not passive subjects of high diplomatic negotiation. Rather, they were agents active in shaping—or at least attempting to shape—the political response to their own arrests and incarceration. Warren's intention was very obviously to make his citizenship and, more generally, the questions of expatriation and naturalization domestic political issues in the United States. The pressure that he exerted clearly had an effect, if not the result he desired. After his conviction, Secretary of State Seward continued to press for his liberation, noting that anti-British sentiment aroused by the cases of arrested Irish Americans was considerable and detrimental to healthy relations between Great Britain and the United States.[148] More broadly, the incarceration of Warren and Nagle catalyzed a debate about the nature of citizenship and the protection of naturalized Americans abroad.

The Slow Trudge toward Comity

Warren's highly publicized conviction inspired political agitation in the United States. Following the trial, John Savage—newly elected as head of one wing of the Fenian Brotherhood—demanded a definitive statement on the status of naturalized citizens abroad from the secretary of state.[149] In a letter to Seward, he argued that Warren's conviction represented "an insolent commentary on and defiance of the compact entered into between the United States and its adopted citizens. . . . If the doctrine is admitted, then we are not a country, but a colony of Great Britain."[150] At a mass meeting held in Boston's Faneuil Hall in December 1867, 6,000 citizens met under Fenian auspices to urge Congress to "pass an act declaring the rights of all citizens, native and adopted, to the fullest legal protection while traveling in foreign countries."[151] In addition, they called upon "the Executive to maintain and enforce this principle at all hazards, as we deem it essential to the sovereign and independent character of the nation."[152] The meeting's resolutions made clear that the ability to create and defend citizenship was an integral part of U.S. independence and that in anticipation of British resistance, the United States ought to use its power to enforce this claim.

The impact of John Warren's and William Nagle's attempts to engineer a confrontation between Great Britain and the United States over the issue of naturalization was, in part, contingent on the activities of Irish nationalists in the British Isles. The accidental killing of a policeman in Manchester on September 18, 1867 in the course of a botched attempt to rescue Thomas J. Kelly severely curtailed the possibility that the British government would deal leniently with Irish Americans still in custody. (Kelly had ousted Stephens as the leader of the IRB in December 1866.)[153] The British press claimed that the "Yankee Irish," who were free and easy in their use of firearms, were to blame for introducing a new level of casual violence to Britain's cities.[154] British intransigence might well have increased the likelihood of a collision, especially as it was compounded two months later by "a tragically naive attempt" to liberate an IRB prisoner held in Clerkenwell Prison in London.[155] An effort to blow up a prison wall that resulted in the death of seven members of the public "dangerously strained" English public opinion and convinced the British government that it was fighting a serious terrorist threat.[156] In sum, the events of autumn 1867 did much to undermine any remaining Fenian sympathies in Great Britain.

Charles Francis Adams believed that British forbearance had been exhausted. "It may be doubted whether at any time since the discovery of the scheme of Guy Fawkes" had there been such "panic spread among families throughout this community as at this time," he noted.[157] William Seward claimed that there was continuing—even increasing—sympathy for Irish nationalism in the United States during this period, but there is evidence to suggest the contrary.[158] The Fenians' "atrocious programme" was "foolish, reckless, and wicked," declaimed a *New York Times* editorial.[159] The paper argued that the bomb at Clerkenwell revealed the hollow center of Fenian nationalism, which now stood only for "unreasoning hate and indiscriminate violence."[160] Though the events at Manchester and Clerkenwell forestalled the revival of a program of negotiated releases (such as had been agreed between Charles Francis Adams and Lord Clarendon in March 1866), they did little to dent the growing sense that a bilateral resolution to the problem of expatriation needed to be found. As the controversy over the incarceration of naturalized U.S. citizens grew through late 1867, both Lord Stanley's Tory ministry and the Johnson administration started to think about reforming their citizenship laws.

Naturalization and expatriation had been central issues during the *Jacmel* trials. But as the London *Times* had gleefully noted, American protests against the British doctrine of perpetual allegiance were hypocritical: U.S. law made no provision for expatriation.[161] Citing James Kent, Daniel Webster, and General Halleck as legal authorities, the newspaper argued that "very few propositions are better established . . . than . . . that a natural-born subject cannot transfer his allegiance from one sovereign to another at pleasure. . . . No doubt whatever exists as to the doctrine of our own law, which is here identical with that of the United States."[162] The intimation was clear: the authority of the United States to speak on the natural right of expatriation existed only in the abstract. In practice the legal scaffolding of expatriation in the United States was the same as that of Great Britain.

In his annual message to Congress on December 3, 1867, Andrew Johnson described this "singular and embarrassing conflict of laws" relating to expatriation:

> The executive department of this Government has hitherto uniformly held, as it now holds, that naturalization in conformity with the Constitution and laws of the United States absolves the recipient from his native allegiance. The courts of Great Britain hold that allegiance to the British Crown is indefeasible, and is not absolved by our laws of naturalization.[163]

Referring to the citation of U.S. authorities during John Warren's trial, Johnson noted that British judges referred to "courts and law authorities of the United States in support of that theory against the position held by the executive authority of the United States."[164] Ambiguity surrounded the status and rights of naturalized citizens and, as important, "impair[ed] the national authority abroad."[165] Some legislative resolution was imperative in order to align principles and practice in the United States.

The hope that Britain and the United States might reach a reciprocal agreement on naturalized citizenship was influenced by broader diplomatic trends. In the year following Johnson's message, agreements were reached with a number of European states.[166] Perhaps of greatest significance was the agreement negotiated with the North German Confederation, a product of Minister George Bancroft's diligence and close friendship with Otto von Bismarck, then the confederation's chancellor.[167] The case of British law was more pressing, however. Fenianism continued to dominate the substance of Charles Francis Adams's communications with the British government, and the heart of the problem was the question of expatriation. The issue was "one of the most threatening . . . to the peace of the two countries," wrote Minister Adams in mid–December 1867, yet the issue could not be addressed unilaterally.[168] Were Bancroft's Prussian successes to be repeated in Great Britain, a major cause of Anglo-American dissension would be removed.

Adams' hopes were fueled by the appearance in the London *Times* of a series of articles under the pseudonym Historicus. The actual author was William Vernon Harcourt, a patrician Liberal with a strong interest in international law.[169] During the Civil War, Harcourt had demonstrated evident Union sympathies and had written numerous articles for the London *Times* that advocated strict neutrality and strongly argued against recognition of the confederacy. As a member of William Gladstone's reform ministry of 1868 to 1874, he favored the disestablishment of the Irish Church and pardons for Fenians convicted of criminal offences. In a series of articles written during the Fenian agitation, he displayed a commitment to Anglo-American rapprochement and a willingness to apply the lessons of the U.S. Civil War to Britain's own secession crisis. For instance, he pointed to the granting of clemency for Confederates at the close of the conflict as an example that might condition Britain's response to Irish political crimes.[170]

The first article by "Historicus" appeared in the second week of December 1867. It spoke candidly of Britain's "irrational and intolerable" position, which espoused a theory of perpetual allegiance that properly belonged to feudal times.[171] Harcourt proposed that a mixed commission of English and U.S. lawyers and statesmen be empowered to suggest mutual revisions. Such an enlightened approach to a contentious transatlantic topic would encourage the U.S. government to act more strongly against Fenian agitators, he argued, as "the more clearly such men are recognized as American citizens the more directly responsible the American Government would be for their conduct abroad."[172] Adams heartily approved of the article and an accompanying editorial and was encouraged "that some-thing may be done to harmonize the rule as well here as at home into one system."[173] At the time of writing, Harcourt and the Liberals were in opposition, but the Conservatives shared their aspirations for revision. To this end, in May 1868, a royal commission was established to investigate the minutiae of British citizenship law and make appropriate suggestions to Parliament.[174] Though changing the law would prove a prolonged opera-tion, Lord Stanley confessed, the British government "no longer held to the doctrine of indefeasible allegiance."[175] It took some time for legislation to catch up with principle, but by the middle of 1868, both government and opposition were committed to reform.

By the summer of 1868, William Seward was also willing to make a mutual accord on the issue of naturalization a diplomatic priority for the administration. In June, Reverdy Johnson, a Unionist Democrat from Mary-land, was appointed to succeed Charles Francis Adams as the minister in London. Johnson's instructions, penned by Seward, described naturalization as "the most important question requiring attention" and stated that some resolution was a prerequisite for the discussion of other outstanding con-troversies between Britain and the United States.[176] Seward informed the new U.S. minister that "irritation and jealousy, produced by the unsatisfac-tory condition of the naturalization laws . . . [had] marked the proceedings of both houses throughout the whole of the last session of Congress."[177] The secretary of state was concerned that the contention over naturaliza-tion and expatriation had so inflamed passions that the prospect of settling the *Alabama* claims had been adversely affected. Tempers remained high in Congress through December 1868, when William E. Robinson delivered another impassioned speech in which he declared that "these claims [re-garding Irish American prisoners] are of transcendently greater importance than the Alabama claims: one is of greenbacks, gold, and such trash; the other is life, honor, self-respect, and everything that makes a nation nobly grand or ignobly base."[178]

The 1868 presidential election provided politicians with another reason to keep the issue of the rights of U.S. citizens front and center. Reconstruc-tion politics were being fiercely, even violently, contested, and electoral advantage was desperately sought. Robinson, for one, sought to capitalize on the publicity surrounding his 1867 speech on the rights of U.S. citizens abroad by issuing it as a pamphlet.[179] At its national convention at Tammany Hall, New York City, the Democratic Party declared its support for equal rights and protection for naturalized and native-born citizens at home and abroad; the assertion of American nationality, which shall command the respect of foreign powers . . . and the maintenance of the rights of naturalized citizens against the absolute doctrine of immutable allegiance and the claims of foreign powers to punish them for alleged crimes committed beyond their jurisdiction.[180]

Likewise, the Republican convention at Chicago spoke of opposing the British "doctrine . . . that because a man is once a subject, he is always so."[181] This "must be resisted . . . as a relic of the feudal times, not authorized by the law of nations, and at war with our national honor and independence":[182]

Naturalized citizens are entitled to be protected in all their rights of citizenship, as though they were native-born; and no citizen of the United States, native or naturalized, must be liable to arrest and imprisonment by any foreign power, for acts done or words spoken in this country; and, if so arrested and imprisoned, it is the duty of the Government to interfere in his behalf.[183]

One stumbling block—the absence of a U.S. legal framework by which individuals could divest themselves of their native citizenship—was removed by the passage of an Expatriation Act on July 27, 1868. The act declared that "the right of expatriation is a natural and inherent right of all people" and, in conformity with this sentiment, "any declaration . . . or decision of this government which denies, restricts, impairs, or questions the right of expatriation, is hereby declared inconsistent with the fundamental principles of this government."[184] Historians have suggested that the act was an important corollary to the right of jus soli citizenship embodied in the Fourteenth Amendment, which was officially promulgated by Seward the following day, July 28, 1868, but this seems suspect.[185] The date of the promulgation was arbitrary, determined by the date the requisite number of states ratified the amendment. In addition, had the two documents—creating a right to citizenship rooted in nativity, in the case of the amendment, and the qualification of this right via the assertion of a right to expatriation, in the case of the Expatriation act—been intimately bound together, the act might have emerged during Congress's consideration of the amendment's text in the early summer of 1866. This did not occur.[186]

The third and final section of the Expatriation Act points directly to the influence of the continued debate over Irish American citizenship. That section stated that should it become known that American citizens were "deprived of . . . liberty by . . . the authority of any foreign government,"

> it shall be the duty of the President forthwith to demand of that government the reasons for such imprisonment, and if it appears to be wrongful and in violation of the rights of American citizenship, the President shall forthwith demand the release of such citizen, and if the release so demanded is unreasonably delayed or refused, it shall be the duty of the President to use such means, not amounting to acts of war, as he may think necessary and proper to obtain or effectuate such release, and all the facts and proceedings relative thereto shall as soon as practicable be communicated by the President to Congress.[187]

The connection is clear and is underlined by the fact that just three days earlier, in another report to Congress on the issue of John Warren's imprisonment (and that of Augustine Costello), Seward had again appealed "for a legislative declaration" supporting "an absolute equality and identity of civil rights between naturalized and native citizens of the United States when sojourning in foreign countries."[188] In fact, the original bill contained far stronger language that empowered the president "to . . . detain in custody any subject or citizen" of a foreign power "who might be found within the jurisdiction of the United States" if that power had denied the rights of naturalized U.S. citizens.[189] Penned by Nathaniel Banks, this "wholesome reprisal clause" was struck out in the Senate by Sumner's Committee on Foreign Affairs on the ground that it was tantamount to a declaration of war.[190]

The passage of the Expatriation Act underlines two important factors that shaped U.S. diplomacy during this period. The first is the value that congressional action could have for the executive. On numerous occasions, as in this instance, Seward could point to the actions of Congress and paint himself to a British audience as a moderate who was acting as a brake on a more belligerent, legislature-led policy. Second, it highlights the value of Charles Sumner to the executive (and, paradoxically, to his congressional opponents). His consistency in restraining rash action in Congress—or, in the instance of his belligerent speech on Civil War reparations, his desire to assert his own influence on the country's diplomatic course—meant that legislators such as Banks could introduce radical measures, thereby gaining electoral capital, without the responsibilities that would follow should such measures become law. By a similar logic, Sumner's stonewalling of legislation in sympathy with the Fenians absolved Seward and Johnson from the same task.

Comity Secured

As historian Nancy Green has argued, the 1868 Expatriation Act was "a sign of new international times," but as a response to the ferment generated by imprisoned naturalized citizens, it was more than this.[191] Provoked by the complications growing out of the arrest of naturalized Irish Americans, the British and U.S. governments inched toward a settlement regarding the issue of naturalized citizens. With this, they intended to close off a transatlantic category of citizen—the migrant Irishman, adopted as a citizen of the United States—whose allegiance was claimed by Great Britain but who demanded the protection of the United States. That dissonance had produced great tension in the three years following the Civil War, allowing actors that we would traditionally see as beyond the purview of high diplomacy to shape relations between Britain and the United States.

With U.S. law suitably amended, a protocol outlining British intentions "to come to an agreement with the United States" on naturalization followed in October 1868.[192] Parliament finally passed the legislation necessary to make a concrete agreement on naturalization in May 1870. On May 13, Lord Clarendon, who again was secretary of state following Gladstone's elevation to prime minister, and John Motley, Ulysses S. Grant's appointment as minister to London, signed a convention, resolving a long-standing source of friction.[193] Around the same time, Congress debated refining U.S. naturalization law to prevent abuses, to allow naturalized citizens to regain their original citizenship, and thereby to increase respect for the process of American naturalization abroad.[194] An act that extended federal oversight of the issuance of naturalization papers passed Congress on July 14, 1870.[195]

Gladstone sought to use his premiership to "show [Ireland] that there was no reasonable demand which the Westminster parliament could not fill" in order to marginalize the worrying strain of Fenianism in Irish political life.[196] "Our purpose & duty is to endeavour to draw a line between the Fenians & the people of Ireland, & to make the people of Ireland indisposed to cross it," he wrote to Charles Grey, the queen's private secretary.[197] One way the new government demonstrated its sensitivity was with a selective amnesty for Fenian prisoners, who had come to symbolize "the grievances of the Irish Catholic community at large."[198] Clemency also had international ramifications. In March 1869, William Seward reported to Congress that John Warren and another prisoner, Augustine Costello, had been released from their terms at Chatham prison.[199] Reverdy Johnson stated his belief that "these acts of clemency . . . are owing to the amicable spirit manifested by our government, as exhibited in the protocol and conventions now before our Senate," highlighting the link between developing comity between Britain and the United States and the status of Irish American prisoners.[200] In the newly confederated Canada, too, commutations and clemency were used as a means of demonstrating the justice of the state and conciliating Irish immigrants who might otherwise have been attracted to the Fenian cause.[201]

Another forty-nine Fenian internees, including some American citizens, were released at the same time as Warren and Costello.[202] Six Americans—William Halpin, John McCafferty, Charles Underwood O'Connell, Edward O'Meagher Condon (alias Shore), Richard Burke, and John McClure—remained in English jails because of their direct involvement in the Fenian uprisings of 1867. A number remained incarcerated in Canada, though by January 1872, they too had been released.[203] All were convicted for crimes that were clearly committed within British jurisdiction. Though William Seward and Hamilton Fish, his long-term successor at the State Department, continued to request clemency for them, the British government refused. Ironically, it was the conduct of Warren and Costello after their release that made clemency less likely.[204] At a St. Patrick's Day celebration in Cork, John Warren gave an intemperate speech in which he declared himself "a believer in the sabre as a means of uplifting downtrodden nations."[205] Likewise, at the same celebration, Augustine Costello made a series of "inflammatory remarks."[206] "The Fenians shouted before they were fairly out of the wood," one British journal noted, "and now they have the satisfaction of knowing that they turned the locks securely on many of their friends."[207] Fish concurred: Warren and Costello's remarks could only have the effect of "prolong[ing] the imprisonment of other citizens."[208] With the substance of a treaty on naturalization imminent, both were reduced to being radical nationalist orators and no more.

In a final fulmination in Congress on the subject, William Robinson argued that "the protection we owe our citizens traveling abroad . . . is neither an Irish nor a Fenian, but a great American question."[209] American and Irish concerns were consonant. By making, first, the alleged arrest of suspects for acts committed in the United States, and second, the British distinction between native and naturalized citizens the subject of Anglo-American controversy Fenian nationalists succeeded in gaining great leverage with U.S. public opinion. British conduct constituted "an outrage against the comity of nations, [and] an insult to our adopted country," Fenians claimed.[210] The annexation of Irish nationalist goals to U.S. state power proved productive in drawing attention to Irish American citizens imprisoned in Britain and Ireland and in focusing American ire on the British doctrine of perpetual allegiance. But Irish American nationalists were ultimately the victims of a nascent rapprochement between Britain and the United States. That rapprochement was built on British and American willingness to negotiate a resolution to their disputes over citizenship, subjecthood, expatriation, and naturalization.

Chapter 5

Toward Home Rule

From the Fenians to Parnell's Ascendancy

The ability of Irish American nationalists to challenge stable relations between Britain and the United States decreased with the failures of the Fenian Brotherhood. As the Irish home rule movement grew more prominent in British politics, the place of the Irish question in U.S. politics and diplomacy changed. The resolution of Reconstruction-era tests of Anglo-American peace—through mediation and the establishment of comity on the subject of naturalization—closed off means of generating the international instability that many Irish American nationalists had looked to as a condition of Irish liberation. It was not simply that the Fenian Brotherhood had failed to provoke conflict or to take advantage of the seeming fluidity of the postbellum international order but rather that its own actions had brought about a hardening (even an institutionalization) of the structures of Anglo-American relations. They thus narrowed the field for future revolutionary efforts and made the alliance of Irish and American interests much less probable.

The failures of the Fenian Brotherhood had implications for the standing of Irish nationalism in the United States. Both native-born Americans and Irish Americans found reason to critique or repudiate the activities of the 1860s. In addition, critics of U.S. urban governance argued that twenty years of mass Irish migration had created an Irish question for the United States. This led them to doubt both the viability of the American democratic experiment and the desirability of Irish self-governance in Ireland. The Irish had corrupted the administration of New York City, critics argued, and just imagine what a disaster a national legislature in Dublin would be.

It was in this context that Charles Stewart Parnell sought to make his name as the transatlantic leader of the home rule campaign and head of the Irish National Land League. The "land war" that broke out in Ireland at the end of the 1870s prompted renewed U.S. attention, and as in the 1860s, returned Irish Americans were among those arrested during the agitation. This time, British and U.S. statesmen were successful in avoiding the kind of confrontation that had previously taken place over the status of incarcerated naturalized Americans. Though arrestees wrote public letters and indirectly placed pressure on Congress to intervene on their behalf, they failed to engineer the confrontation between Britain and the United States that they were hoping for.

From the perspective of U.S. diplomacy, the Irish question looked very different in the 1880s than it had in the 1860s. Historian Mike Sewell argues that during the 1880s, "Irish nationalism overlapped with domestic radicalism" and thus jarred with the conservative drift of U.S. politics. He is surely correct, but he tells only half the story.[1] In the early 1880s there was a significant struggle over the direction of Irish nationalism between those who would privilege a global campaign against land monopoly, of which Ireland was only a part, and those who would focus squarely on a national struggle and were blind to arguments against the fundamental unfairness of private ownership. Ultimately, Charles Stewart Parnell and the Irish National League (which by spring 1882 was in an informal alliance with the British Liberal Party) repudiated social radicalism in favor of constitutional nationalism and economic conservatism.[2] As Henry George, a leading proponent of land nationalization in Ireland, lamented in May 1882, "the conservative influences in the management of the [Land] League [came] out in full force" against more radical doctrines.[3] Undoubtedly there were changes in how U.S. statesmen conceived of the relationship between U.S. diplomacy and the Irish question between 1865 and 1880, but antipathy to radicalism cannot tell the whole story. It was far more complex than that.

From Fenianism to the Land League

The manifest failure of the 1867 uprising, the Canadian raids of 1866, and the gradual improvement in Anglo-American tempers after the Civil War diminished enthusiasm for the Fenian Brotherhood amongst Irishmen in North America.[4] A futile raid on Canada in May 1870 generated little interest among Irish Americans, and the Grant administration responded swiftly and firmly by arresting the leaders.[5] In Ireland, "Fenianism" was construed broadly and, acting as a "moral and passive force in Irish affairs," it continued to exercise a hold among sections of the Irish public.[6] This contrasted with the more strict construction of the term in the United States. Charles Wentworth Dilke, a young English writer (and future Liberal Party statesmen), who was traveling in North America in 1866, argued that "the Irish in Ireland are not Fenians in the American sense." Distinguishing the implacable hatred of the latter from the discontent of the former, he held out hope for the positive effects of reform.[7]

At the same time that William Gladstone was attributing his program of Irish reform—the 1869 Irish Church Act that disestablished the Church of Ireland, the 1870 Land Act, and a series of amnesties and releases for Fenian prisoners—to "the intensity of fenianism," John Devoy, a recipient of a conditional release in January 1871, disparaged it.[8] On his arrival in the United States, Devoy stated bluntly that "most of us are sick of the very issue of Fenianism, though as resolved as ever to work for the attainment of Irish independence."[9] Another Fenian ex-prisoner, John Boyle O'Reilly, complained in the United States that U.S. Fenianism was "as big a humbug as Mormonism."[10] Writing to Devoy in early 1871, he claimed "I hate that infernal name—Fenianism. . . . That meanly-sounding word, with its associations of defeat, dissension, and trickery has been a millstone on the neck of our Nationality for years past."[11] This was a consequence of the infighting among Fenians in the United States as well as the embarrassment associated with the quixotic Canadian adventures of the 1860s. A major appeal for funds in support of Irish nationalist activity in early 1871 asked only for a "collection of money" and made no mention of filibustering or mobilization of Irish Americans.[12]

By 1870, the Fenian Brotherhood was in dire straits. John Mitchel had shunned the possibility of taking over as president of a united organization, disavowing any intention of "knit[ting] up the two ragged fag ends of an organisation originally rotten."[13] The Fenians, he argued, were "right . . . in the main point—that the British Government must be overthrown by force," but were "in sad confusion with respect to the mode of action, the place and the opportunity."[14] Strategic disarray matched financial incompetence. As Sean McConville has noted, the $100,000 the brotherhood had collected in the mid-1860s was so depleted by March 1870 that only $70 remained.[15] Two years later Gladstone wrote to the Roman Catholic archbishop of Westminster that he "believe[d] the American influence . . . is now nearly dead."[16]

Keen to extirpate Fenianism, Gladstone's first term in office (1868–1874) was characterized by a sincere effort to reconcile Irishmen to the Union. The question of amnesty became the principal concern of Irish nationalists, and mass rallies were taking place weekly by the autumn of 1869. These meetings expressed support for "suffering brothers [in] English dungeons" and were led by Isaac Butt, a prominent Tory barrister who had defended many Fenian prisoners at state trials in the 1860s.[17] Irish MPs such as John Francis Maguire had made clear to Gladstone that prisoner releases were likely to prove the sine qua non of Irish pacification, and in November 1870, the cabinet finally settled on amnesty for the majority of Fenian prisoners.[18] Gladstone was convinced that Fenianism "had its root in bad laws," and with his ministry in the process of reforming or repealing those laws, "there [was] something of pain & scandal in prolonging" the imprisonment of those involved in the 1867 uprising.[19] Two beneficiaries of Gladstone's determination were John Devoy and Jeremiah O'Donovan Rossa, both of whom would play a significant role in Irish American nationalism through the rest of the century.[20] Along with three others they were released in January 1871 on the condition that they be exiled from the United Kingdom for the duration of their prison sentences. Gladstone anticipated the warm reception that these men would receive in the United States (Rossa, for instance, received an official welcome to the United States from the House of Representatives) but argued that a show of clemency would bind the U.S. government more closely to British interests.[21] He wrote to the Irish lord lieutenant:

> The sufferings of these Fenians . . . tend to place in sympathy with them multitudes of men who are not Fenians. . . . What appreciable reinforcements would [the exiles] form when exported to the Fenians of America? None[,] but even if they did, there would be more than a countervailing advantage in liberating the American Government from its difficulties, strengthening our case for urging on them a systematic repression of

hostile manifestations & emboldening them to face the clamours that have
made them at times slack in their duty.[22]

Though they were feted on their arrival in New York, the exiles soon
became embroiled in the factionalism of the city's Irish politics.[23] They
also involved themselves in radical nationalist politics. In 1876, O'Donovan
Rossa launched a "skirmishing fund" that was intended to underwrite the
cost of dynamite attacks in British cities.[24] John Devoy, by contrast, committed himself to the Clan na Gael, a North American body dedicated to
supporting revolution in Ireland that had largely superseded the Fenian
Brotherhood by the early 1870s. Under the direction of Devoy and others,
the Clan expanded to a membership of 11,000 by the middle of the decade,
though this was far short of the numbers attracted to the Fenian Brotherhood in the mid-1860s.[25]

Transatlantic Liberalism and the Irish Question

Gladstone's Irish reforms were important touchstones for an emergent
community of transatlantic liberals. As Robert Kelley, Leslie Butler, Frank
Ninkovich, and others have documented, critics, journalists, intellectuals, and politicians on both sides of the Atlantic were acutely interested in
Anglo-American relations and saw both countries as essential to the preservation and dissemination of orderly, progressive liberty.[26] Within these
networks the condition of Ireland seemed, as Liberal statesman John Morley noted, "a microcosm of the whole imperial question."[27] To these liberal
reformers, the failure to permanently reconcile Irish popular opinion to
British sovereignty was an indictment of British rule. With a specifically
American frame of reference, George William Curtis noted that "Ireland
is England's touchstone, as slavery was ours."[28] This was, in a strange way, a
restatement of the pro-slavery, Anglophobic, antebellum critique of British
abolitionism: that because of continued poverty and injustice in Ireland,
Britain lacked the legitimacy to contest the morality of other nations. Now,
in the mouth of a former abolitionist in the post-emancipation United
States, it served as an exhortation to British liberals to set their house in
order. For U.S. liberals, British rule in Ireland qualified Britain's claim to a
place in the vanguard of global liberalism.[29] Liberals, Charles Dilke noted
during his tour of North America, might hate the Irish themselves "but
sympathise profoundly with Ireland."[30]

Idealism meshed with practical concerns about stability in the North Atlantic world. Though the 1871 Treaty of Washington was hailed as an undoubted success in providing for the arbitration of international disputes—it was "a victory for modern civilization," in the words of one exuberant critic—it also proved the "high water mark" of that liberal ideal.[31] Numerous Liberal Party statesmen and intellectuals, including John Morley, Goldwin Smith, and Lord Rosebery, spent extended periods in the United States in the late 1860s and 1870s and were struck by the residual Anglophobia in U.S. public life. In particular, they noted its connection with the Irish question.[32] Morley saw British misgovernment as the root cause of the Irish corruption of American urban politics:

> The Irish who . . . do their best to spoil the great republican experiment are the direct products not of the American republican, but of the English oligarchic system. There is nothing more heroic about the Americans than the fortitude and resolution with which they encounter their annual floods of Irish who we send over, as a rule, without a shilling in their pockets, or two civilized and orderly ideas in their heads.[33]

The Irish vote in the booming industrial hubs of the United States was of increasing concern to U.S. and British statesmen alike. Charles Francis Adams and others fretted that public life in America was declining and that the urban Irish were both a symptom and a cause of that decline. "What with the Irish, and the negro, the grade of intelligence and of capacity bids fair to fall so far as to endanger the success of the whole of our grand experiment," Adams confided in his diary.[34] Reformers feared that ethnic politics undermined reasoned republican deliberation and might amplify the Irish American voice as a disruptive influence in Anglo-American relations.

The development of an urban Irish vote that was adept at the workings of machine politics was not an entirely new phenomenon in the 1870s and 1880s.[35] What was distinctive was the growing pessimism about the viability of democracy in the postbellum nation-state. The problems the Irish presented, who were caricatured as feckless and drunken in their private lives and as slavish and violent at the polling station, were complemented by problems in the South. New York's "Celtocracy" was matched by the South's "niggerocracy," complained George Templeton Strong, and America's democratic experiment suffered for it.[36] The mass migration from Ireland in the middle of the century, argued contemporary British historian James Anthony Froude, had resulted in an Irish Catholic nation "grafted in upon the American Constitution . . . [that is] as separate from the Anglo-Saxon as [it] is at home [in Ireland]."[37] The anti-Catholic Froude had visited the United States in 1872, where his attempts to justify British rule in Ireland met with a cool response. Writing in 1879, Froude rather bitterly concluded that Americans had "themselves an Irish problem of their own," caused by what he perceived as the fundamental inassimilability of the great mass of Irish Catholic citizens.[38] "It is America that Fenianism invades from Ireland," Charles Dilke coolly noted, "not England from America."[39]

Both historians and contemporaries have suggested intriguing parallels between Ireland and the U.S. South.[40] Historian Mitchell Snay suggests that throughout Reconstruction, Ireland served as a valuable analogy that was used by both white southerners and black freedmen. For the former, the South was denied self-determination by the sanctimonious Radical Republicans of the North just as the British government denied the same to Ireland. This echoed John Mitchel's conception of the U.S. South as a romantic, subnational region denied its natural rights by doctrinaire Anglo-Saxons who were inspired by evangelical zeal and the cash nexus.[41] For ex-slaves, the government of Ireland represented a comparable case of justice denied that was bound up with the relationship between landholding and political agency. Both comparisons had a longer tradition than this suggests—the Carlylean-Mitchelite lineage in the case of white southerners, Frederick Douglass's rhetorical framing in the case of black freedmen—but Snay rightly highlights how the contingent details of Reconstruction made an appeal to the image of Ireland attractive at that particular moment. For such constituencies, comparison with Ireland lent legitimacy to their own struggles against the denial of political rights. By contrast, Froude's later suggestion of an American Irish question drew on a presumption that the Catholic Irish could not be assimilated into the body politic. He argued that the intractable and irreconcilable Irish would confound U.S. statesmen just as they did the British.

Interpretations of Ireland and Irish governance were shaped, then, by what Americans perceived as the negative impact of Irish voters and urban political machines on the quality of civic life in the United States. They were also affected by the seemingly conclusive failure of Irish nationalism that the Fenian raids represented.[42] In May 1876, one New York newspaper took the suicide of a leading Fenian, Henry Mulleda, as an opportunity to reflect on the future of Irish nationalism. It was a "vain endeavor to secure independence for a thoroughly integral part of the British Empire," the paper noted, as

for over seventy years, modern Ireland has made desperate efforts to escape the rule of England, and yet in not one instance has the rising been a
reasonable or a hopeful one. Meanwhile the veritable Irish population has
been diminishing; many onerous and obnoxious laws have been repealed;
the rigidity of the land tenures has been somewhat mitigated; the hand
of the Anglican Establishment has grown less heavy; the reasons for a
repeal of the Union and for independence have become fewer and less
urgent; while the aid of foreign interference is no longer to be hoped
for.... Century after century the fortune of Irishmen has been nothing but
failure . . . [The rebellion of] 1867 but strengthened English power. The
prospect of an Irish Parliament is hardly a brilliant one.[43]

The anticipation of failure conditioned transatlantic responses to Irish nationalism. Increasing rural prosperity in Ireland and profound economic
dislocation among Irish Americans consequent on the depression of 1873
meant that, as historian Kerby Miller notes, "the 1870s was a decade of
relative inactivity" for organized Irish nationalism.[44] And just as Irish nationalism entered a more subdued period, so Anglo-American relations
lost much of the heat of the 1860s. After the conclusion of the arbitration
process established by the Treaty of Washington, U.S. affairs figured little in
British parliamentary life. Indeed, one historian has argued that "there has
rarely been a period . . . during which such little attention was given to
American diplomatic issues as between 1874 and 1880."[45]

In Ireland itself, political life was marked by the emergence of the
Home Government Association—later renamed the Irish Home Rule
League—under the "genteel sway" of Isaac Butt.[46] From 1874 onward, Butt
pressed the case for a federal solution to the question of Irish governance.
In his promotion of the idea he made a virtue of imperial precedent and
referred frequently to the Canadian confederation of 1867 (and rather less
to the 1787 formation of the United States).[47] In this he repeated Thomas
D'Arcy McGee's conviction that the reconciliation of Canadian liberal nationalism and British imperial rule offered important lessons that might be
implemented in Ireland. Butt was supported in his work by an auxiliary
organization, the Home Rule Confederation of Great Britain. The confederation represented more militant parliamentarians who were prepared to
obstruct parliamentary business in order to draw attention to Irish matters.
At a meeting in Dublin in August 1876, the confederation delegated two
MPs—Charles Stewart Parnell, a young Protestant landlord from County
Wexford, and John O'Connor Power, an IRB member recently elected to

Parliament—to travel to Washington on behalf of the Irish people to present a congratulatory address to President Grant on the centenary of U.S. independence.[48] "Handsomely engrossed on parchment" and illuminated with the "National shield and standard [and] an allegorical picture of the genius of Erin . . . welcoming the dawning day of Irish liberty," the confederation's address spoke of the "bonds of mystic brotherhood" and the "mysterious designs of Providence" that would one day extend the liberty that America enjoyed to Ireland.[49] Neither Parnell nor O'Connor Power was widely known in the United States, and the *New York Times* felt the need to provide its readers with biographies of both on their arrival in the city on September 30, 1876.[50] In a letter to Grant, Patrick Egan and other IRB members stated that acceptance of the address would allow the "Irish nation" the opportunity to "mingle its accents of congratulation with the exultant jubilation of a victorious, a great and a free nation."[51] Lest the president should miss the hint, Egan continued: "America has now enjoyed one hundred years of freedom. . . . Ireland has borne seven centuries of oppression without having for a single instant forfeited her fervent love of liberty."[52]

The presentation of an Irish address demanded diplomatic tact. President Grant, it seems, had been a little rash in promising to receive the address without consulting staff at the State Department.[53] Assistant Secretary of State John Cadwalader wrote to Hamilton Fish expressing his concern and suggested that it would be wise to consult with the British minister, Sir Edward Thornton, before agreeing to meet with "O'Connor Power and some one else."[54] Fish responded emphatically that "it may be rec.d *with reservations,* or disclaimer of political import," and only after the State Department had vetted the content of the address and any speech that might be given at its reception.[55] He agreed with Cadwalader that a conference with Minister Edward Thornton would be wise.[56] Having impressed upon Grant the impropriety of receiving the address without prior consultation, Cadwalader, as acting secretary of state, moved to deny Parnell and O'Connor Power the opportunity to meet with the president.[57] Instead, reported the *New York Times,* the address was to be "presented through the British Minister . . . in accordance with the etiquette usually observed on such occasions."[58] In all, the episode was distinguished by the lack of tension it generated in formal Anglo-American relations and by the close collaboration of Fish and Cadwalader with their British counterparts.[59]

Despite this brief convergence of Irish and American politics, the issue of Irish home rule was largely absent from the foreign policy calculations of the Grant and Hayes administrations. Neither president relied on the elusive "Irish vote" as part of his political coalition and neither was the victim of the partisan cross-currents that had so buffeted the Johnson administration. Historian Paul Bew describes the 1870s as generally a "decade of disappointment" for the Fenian movement as the more moderate nationalism of Butt's federalists took center stage.[60] Though Clan na Gael gained some celebrity from an audacious rescue of Fenian prisoners from western Australia, a friend reminded John Devoy that "the general opinion of our American friends [is that] while we are capable of brilliant, desperate, disconnected personal effort, there is no hope of our ever rising to the level of successful revolutionists."[61]

For insight into the complicated and complicating impact of Irish life in U.S. political life during this period, we might instead look to the history of labor in the United States. Historians Michael Gordon, Kevin Kenny, Eric Foner, and others have detailed how ethnic rivalries, intense localism, and evolving class consciousness shaped the emergent struggle over patterns of industrial production and urban governance.[62] In the histories of each, the motivating power of nationalist sentiment is slight—or in Foner's case, alloyed with an internationalist sense of economic injustice—underscoring the heterogeneous and conflicted composition of Irish social and economic life. Irish nationalism was not—and was never—the dominant force structuring the world of Irish America, and many lives were lived quite apart from the geopolitics of the transatlantic tangles of Britain, Ireland, and the United States. Yet in the last year of the decade, interest in Irish governance again spiked, as the famine conditions of the mid-1840s again loomed.

Depression, the Land League, and Parnell's Fund-Raising in the United States

Successive harvest failures in the late 1870s brought fear of renewed famine in Ireland, and the agricultural depression sparked the resistance of hard-pressed tenants.[63] In the spring and summer of 1879, they organized themselves to campaign for rent relief. Beginning in County Mayo, the movement was initially local in focus. Michael Davitt, an ex-Fenian organizer who had recently been released from Dartmoor prison, coordinated tenant activities through, first, the Land League of Mayo and, second, the Irish National Land League. From October 1879, the National Land League came under the "nominal dictatorship" of Charles Stewart Parnell.[64]

John Devoy recognized that Parnell, who had flirted publicly with Fenianism without committing himself to either the Irish Republican Brotherhood or Clan na Gael, was a politician who might prove a useful ally for a radical nationalist like himself.[65] In particular, Devoy was convinced of the need to use the land question as a way of generating the broad, nationally organized movement that could ultimately sustain a campaign for national independence. Specifically, he sought to demand more than a British government would grant, advocating "a more radical land settlement . . . which could really only be effected by an independent Ireland."[66] Under the banner of the "New Departure," Devoy proposed the cooperation of advanced nationalists, land agitators, and parliamentarians on both sides of the Atlantic.[67] Though his proposals were never formally accepted and the interlocking relationships underpinning the New Departure remained ambiguous throughout the 1880s, Devoy's overture, made in October 1878, set the vague terms of association for American-Irish collaboration under Parnell's leadership.[68]

In December 1879, Parnell set sail for the United States with the intention of raising money to extend the organization of the new Irish National Land League.[69] The prospect of renewed famine prompted a great frenzy of enthusiasm for Parnell's North American visit, and though he was initially more interested in raising money for political ends than in collecting funds for famine relief, he used the platforms afforded him to outline the connections between renewed scarcity, national self-determination, and the need for land reform.[70] This blurring of philanthropic and partisan motives upset some Irish nationalists, who believed that "charity should have been kept separate from politics."[71] More generally, as historian Alan O'Day has suggested, this blurring may have proved useful in masking the declining interest that Irish Americans felt in nationalist projects. Despite nationalist rhetoric, Irish America did not represent a coherent, disciplined "avenging wolfhound" of the Irish nation, and it proved far easier for Parnell to enlist support on philanthropic grounds.[72]

Among Americans who were not Irish, this philanthropy was a contested undertaking. Some sections of the American press were initially unhappy with Parnell's apparent privileging of political fund-raising over charitable collection. "In Europe," the *New York Tribune* noted, "America is regarded as a fat cow among nations, but she is not lacking in intelligence and does not submit to being milked by foreign politicians as readily as of old."[73] Moreover, the Land League was not the only game in town. Two rival relief committees were established in Dublin—one by the Duchess of

Marlborough and one under the presidency of Lord Mayor Edward Dwyer Gray—and these competed for donations in the United States, to the chagrin of Land League organizers.[74] A third fund was organized by the *New York Herald* in late January 1880.[75] In total, the *Herald* claimed to have collected $321,000, as against the approximately £72,000 ($349,000) Parnell's mission had raised (£12,000 [$58,100] of which was collected specifically for the Land League.)[76]

Perhaps the most illuminating commentary came from the New York *Nation*, whose editor, Edwin L. Godkin, was a proponent of Irish Home Rule and a prominent transatlantic liberal commentator.[77] He ruminated that

> twenty years ago there were very few editors indeed, and no politician, who would have ventured to avow a want of interests in the efforts of Irish patriots to free Ireland from connection with England, or express doubts as to their eventual success. To-day all the leading journals in the country seem to unite in ridiculing or throwing cold water on the political part of Mr. Parnell's mission, while ungraciously forcing on him, evidently much to his dissatisfaction, the role of collector of contributions for the relief of hungry peasantry.[78]

Refusing to address either the Anglo-Irish connection or Irish land law, these editors and politicians demonstrated that "the United States have evidently ceased to be a good field for Irish agitation, and this without any diminution of sympathy for all Irish suffering which Americans can see and understand."[79] Though Americans could appreciate the immediacy of poverty or a lack of shelter, they had less time for the intricacies of land law and the minutiae of constitutional politics. *The Nation* pointed to the conservatism that the Civil War had bred, noting that "people here are not nearly as hopeful as they were thirty years ago about political experiments begun in bloodshed," and highlighted the dubious consequences of New York's "Celtocracy":

> The Irish patriots who, during the last forty years have fled to these shores from British oppression have played a part in American politics which has naturally modified the views once held by the average American about the Irish Parliament which it is proposed to set up in Dublin. Very few Americans now feel that they would like to live under that legislature

themselves. . . . In fact, they now claim more knowledge with regard to its character and capacity than Englishmen possess.[80]

Godkin was no opponent of what he perceived as the progressive drift of liberal nationalism, but in the case of Ireland, his journal argued that "the world . . . has within the last half-century grown unmistakably harder in temper" because of Fenian efforts to engineer Anglo-American conflict.[81] And, as Godkin would later argue, because Irish liberal nationalism could be expressed in constitutional terms, with an eye to achieving a cession of home rule from the Parliament at Westminster, the language of revolution was redundant and even counterproductive.

Though Parnell's tour could not be considered an unalloyed success, money contributed for the Land League from the United States was significant. As historian Conor Cruise O'Brien has detailed, "in the first months of the league's existence," from November 1879 to the end of June 1880, "95 per cent. of its receipts came from America."[82] Of the £69,000 ($334,000) received during this period, £66,000 ($320,000) came from the United States, which presumably includes the £12,000 ($58,100) raised by Parnell during his tour in early 1880.[83] Money from the United States was essential: Land League agitation was maintained in part by traveling organizers who earned a living from their political activities, itself a marker of the increasing modernity of Irish politics.[84] The channeling of funds from the United States was notable enough to draw the attention of British authorities, who successfully placed pressure on the Land League's bank, Drexel, Morgan & Co., to cease acting on its behalf.[85]

Material support mattered, but so did the moral and institutional props of agitation. Parnell's tour echoed Daniel O'Connell's efforts to enlist the moral power of the United States with the goal of influencing British public and parliamentary opinion. In an institutional sense, Parnell was a more successful transnational statesman than O'Connell, and with Michael Davitt's assistance he succeeded in establishing a skeleton of auxiliary organizations that might support constitutional and extra-constitutional politics in Ireland beyond his own political lifetime. Eric Foner notes that 1,500 Land League branches were in existence by September 1881 and that the league successfully incorporated "the three great strands of protest that had emerged in nineteenth-century Ireland . . . revolutionary republicanism . . . constitutional and parliamentary protest . . . and the agrarian grievances hitherto expressed in rural secret societies."[86] And despite—or perhaps because of—his lack of international celebrity, Parnell moved more comfortably than O'Connell could in the waters of American popular opinion. By the autumn of 1882, the American organization had raised $500,000 (£103,000) for its parent body in Ireland.[87]

The philanthropic intervention of Americans was not simply a function of Land League activism: Americans independently took up the matter of famine relief. Replicating the mobilization of early 1847, congressmen debated the appropriate response to Irish scarcity. As then, Congress rejected various resolutions that proposed financial relief in favor of one that authorized the use of a naval vessel—the *Constellation*—to transport private donations to Ireland. This was approved by President Hayes on February 25, 1880, and the *Constellation* set sail on March 30.[88] The similarities with Forbes's mission extend to the general Anglo-American bonhomie that accompanied it and the awkward, halting intervention of nationalist politics, this time in the form of an address from the Irish National Land League that had to be vetted and edited before its presentation to the ship's commander.[89] Aside from a minor dispute about the payment of customs duties at Queenstown, County Cork, the voyage offers the historian little in the way of political contention.[90] Interestingly, the British government's note of "sincere and cordial thanks" lacked the racialized language of Palmerston's 1847 message, perhaps suggesting confidence in a more sober, settled, Anglo-American relationship.[91] Instead, Minister Edward Thornton simply passed on gratitude for the "generous and friendly conduct" of the United States in providing provisions "which were so much needed" and were accepted "as a proof of the friendly feelings entertained towards the subjects of Her Majesty in Ireland . . . by the Government and citizens of the United States."[92] Just as in the 1840s, famine relief could provide the context for the performance of Anglo-American amity.

Irish Arrests, U.S. Diplomacy, and the Travails of Henry George

Poet and critic James Russell Lowell, the U.S. minister in London, kept Washington appraised of the course of Irish agitation in Britain. Reporting on the opening of Parliament in January 1881, he wrote home of the "abnormal condition of Ireland" and the political dissensions it had wrought.[93] He reported that "not only has the law been rendered powerless and order disturbed . . . but the sensitive nerve of property has been rudely touched" as a consequence of the Land League's pioneering use of the boycott to resist landlord evictions.[94] It must be remembered that in January 1881, it was not apparent what course Irish agitation would take. Previous famines—most notably that of the mid- to late 1840s—had been accompanied by death and emigration on a mass scale. This famine was less severe, but it was accompanied by the novel growth of formidable and sophisticated agitation in and out of Parliament in which disparate demands for social, economic, and political reform revolved with centripetal force around the figure of Charles Stewart Parnell.

James Lowell's despatches from London charted Parnellite demands and placed faith in the incoming Gladstone ministry's willingness to address Irish wrongs. Lowell accepted the legitimacy of agitation for reform of landholding laws, though he was less enthusiastic about Irish separatism. The ills of Ireland being generally accepted, he thought, some program of reform would follow. "I am sure," he continued "that the reasonable leaders or representatives of Irish opinion see the folly of expecting that England would ever peaceably consent to the independence of Ireland."[95] The *New York Times* echoed this bifurcation of aspirations into legitimate land reform and illegitimate—even foolhardy—national separatism, denouncing Parnell as "a demagogue" and "a hypocrite" who was only interested in furthering his own career. "The very violence of his harangues shows that what he seeks is rebellion and not land law reform," the editorial opined, concluding that "the mantle of O'Connell will not descend to grace his unworthy shoulders."[96] Both Lowell and the *Times* offer evidence in support of Alan O'Day's contention that at this time, Americans offered greater support to land reform than to any scheme of political separatism for Ireland.[97] Yet political separatism and "home rule" were not synonymous, though they might bleed into one another. Later in his British career, Lowell would speak favorably of the call for home rule and the benefits that would follow from its implementation. This showed no inconsistency on the part of the U.S. minister, only an awareness that home rule could be framed as a reasonable demand for local self-government that was compatible with the maintenance of the empire—which, as Lowell realized, was essential for any British legislation that dealt with Irish matters.[98]

For all the clarity that historians have brought to the evolution of Parnell's campaign for home rule during the 1880s, it must be remembered that to the Gladstone ministry and the incoming administration of President Garfield, it appeared that a crisis in Ireland loomed in the spring of 1881. Pressure from the National Land League brought both remedial and coercive measures from the British government. In March 1881, Parliament passed the Protection of Person and Property Act, and a month later the ministry introduced a new land bill, which passed into law in August 1881.[99] The former, informally known as a coercion bill, raised the specter of indiscriminate arrests of Irish Americans that had so troubled previous administrations. Though competing claims of citizenship were no longer at issue, the arrest of U.S. citizens might provoke sympathy and generate demands for the more rigorous protection of Americans abroad. This possibility was made all the more disquieting, Lowell noted, by Parnell's rhetorical construction of the United States. Lowell referred Secretary of State William Evarts to "an extraordinary passage" in a recent speech in which the Irish MP "makes a distinction between 'the American people' and the 'Irish nation in America.' This double nationality is likely to be of great practical inconvenience whenever the coercion bill becomes law."[100]

That the fruits of coercive legislation proved no more than an "inconvenience" was partly a consequence of the commitment of Lowell and James G. Blaine, the new secretary of state, to conciliatory engagement with the British government. Belying his reputation as a fierce Anglophobe, Blaine framed his condemnation of coercion ("a conferment of arbitrary and irresponsible power . . . repugnant to the principles of civil liberty and personal rights") as a deviation from the values that underwrote "the common glory of British and American jurisprudence."[101] In private conversation with Edward Thornton, Blaine confided that he "had written confidentially to Mr. Lowell and had strongly recommended him not to take up too warmly the cause of American citizens."[102] Even in public, where one would expect a degree of rhetorical inflation, Blaine spoke a language of legalism: he noted the importance of adhering to the norms of international jurisprudence and emphasized the importance of strictly adhering to the citizenship framework negotiated in 1870.[103] For that framework to function, it was imperative that representatives of the United States—James Lowell and his consular subordinates—examine evidence of naturalization closely and correctly categorize individuals as British subjects or American citizens. Moreover, as historian Mike Sewell has noted, the secretary of state used the trappings of public diplomacy, including a salute of the British flag at a commemoration of the Battle of Yorktown, "to show the Irish [in the United States], the true feelings of the American government."[104]

Lowell was right to suspect that the passage of coercive legislation signified an impending increase in his work at the legation. During the period March 1881 to August 1882, at least nineteen American citizens were the subjects of correspondence between the minister and Lord Granville, Gladstone's foreign secretary, as a result of their arrest in Ireland.[105] Though rumors circulated that Irish officials were unduly zealous in targeting Americans sojourning in Ireland (particularly after the institution of even more stringent coercive legislation in July 1882), British authorities were firm in insisting that no distinction be made between U.S. citizens and British subjects under the suspension of habeas corpus.[106] Preempting possible American complaints, Lord Granville made this similarity of treatment clear to Lowell and bluntly asked why anyone would expect a British government to treat its own subjects worse than those who had come from abroad.[107]

Lowell himself was impressed by the honorable intentions of the British government and accepted that the Gladstone ministry was making sincere efforts to root out the sources of Irish alienation from British rule. In particular, he perceived—as more extreme Irish nationalists such as Jeremiah O'Donovan Rossa feared—that remedial reform might promote a conservative sentiment in Ireland that would undercut nationalist enthusiasm. By April 1885, Lowell had come to believe that some measure of Home Rule would "make Conservatives of every mother's son of them."[108] Small-c conservative reform was catalyzed by the informal arrangement Parnell and Gladstone reached under the rubric of the "Kilmainham Treaty," an informal agreement by which Parnell agreed to scale back agrarian violence and Gladstone agreed to deal with the issue of rent arrears.[109] Reporting on the opening of Parliament in February 1883, Lowell expressed his hope that the reform measures adopted "may at least serve to convince reasonable men [of] an honest desire to repair . . . the evil effects of past legislation," even though "the extreme Irish party" would in all likelihood never be satisfied.[110]

The U.S. minister's faith in Gladstonian good intentions was appreciated in London. In fact, the correspondence between Lowell, Granville, Lionel Sackville-West (the new British minister to Washington), and Frederick T. Frelinghuysen, Blaine's replacement at the Department of State, is remarkable for its cordiality and good temper. When the House of Representatives requested information about Americans arrested under the coercion legislation in Ireland in late January 1882, Frelinghuysen submitted a record of the "active negotiations" that had taken place, noting that they had been "carried on . . . [in a] spirit of entire friendship."[111] The secretary of state went so far as to share his intended communication to the House with Sackville-West so the British minister would be fully assured of the U.S. government's goodwill.[112]

This is particularly interesting when we consider that this transatlantic congeniality was happening at the same time that U.S. statesmen were articulating an economic pan-Americanism that was antithetical to British interests in the Western Hemisphere. Most notably, Blaine and Frelinghuysen intimated that this might involve the renegotiation (or wholesale repudiation) of the Clayton-Bulwer Treaty, an enterprise that would inevitably have increased Anglo-American tensions.[113] It was not the case, then, that the incarceration of Irish American prisoners and the developing struggle for home rule took place in the absence of Anglo-American diplomatic tension. Yet in contrast with previous cross-currents of the Irish question and transatlantic strain, exchanges over incarceration and coercion remained cordial. U.S. statesmen such as Lowell demonstrated sensitivity and tact in assessing the Gladstone ministry's response to Irish agitation.

This sensitivity was at odds with the predictably more combative attitude of several members of Congress, including the irrepressible William Erigena Robinson. Unsurprisingly, when arrests continued through the spring of 1882, New York Democrats such as Robinson and Abram Hewitt sought to embarrass the administration by pressing for the release of U.S. prisoners.[114] The most aggressive tactic was a resolution, introduced by Robinson, calling for the attorney general's opinion of a hypothetical scenario in which a number of prominent U.S. statesmen of Irish descent were arrested while traveling in Ireland.[115] As historian Mike Sewell has noted, what was striking about this resolution was not its introduction but its tabling (which was approved by a vote of 117 to 102).[116] The political environment of the early 1880s, then, was far less conducive to the radical posturing in Congress that had taken place in the mid-1860s at the height of Fenian agitation. Indeed, the *New York Tribune* contrasted the present Congress's state of mind with that of the 1868 Congress and argued that the 1868 Expatriation Act was "one of the most irrational acts passed by an incoherent Congress" and a dead letter to boot.[117]

Of course, the detention of U.S. citizens remained contentious, the amiable correspondence of statesmen notwithstanding. As in the case of the Fenian arrests of the 1860s, a number of prisoners chose to make an appeal to U.S. public opinion in the pages of U.S. newspapers. Michael Boyton, whose case was the first of an arrested American to come before James Lowell, presented his story in the pages of Patrick Ford's *Irish World and American Industrial Liberator*, one of the most widely read radical papers of the period.[118] Likewise, the case of Michael Hart, arrested in January 1882, came to the attention of the State Department via the Lawrence,

Massachusetts, *Catholic Herald*, and another prisoner, Daniel McSweeney, saw fit to use the pages of the *San Francisco Examiner* to argue that U.S. authorities were lax in securing his release.[119] In each instance, incarcerated Irish Americans sought to gain publicity for their case, just as Fenian prisoners had during the 1860s.

It was therefore important for the executive to retain control of a potentially explosive issue. Hamilton Fish, now in semi-retirement, noted that "demagogues" in Congress might work on "every timid Representative" to generate momentum for "embarrassing" and "very offensive" resolutions.[120] Despite the failure of Robinson's belligerent stance, both Senator George Hoar and Assistant Secretary of State Bancroft Davis stressed to Lowell the importance of securing some kind of compromise agreement on the release of Irish American prisoners before Fish's fears were realized.[121] Mass meetings "into which many were being drawn who might have been expected to abstain from inflammatory proceeding[s]" produced a corresponding political drift in the House of Representatives.[122] Pressure from Congress might still result in a collision between the executive and the legislature or, worse, force an embarrassing position on the executive in relation to the British government. As early as June 1881, Bancroft Davis had expressed concern that American domestic politics would generate demands in regard to the prisoners that would only irritate British opinion.[123]

The State Department used unofficial channels of communication to defuse a looming crisis. At the suggestion of Bancroft Davis, Hamilton Fish made contact with Sir John Rose, a prominent international financier and former Canadian politician who had been deeply involved in the resolution of the *Alabama* dispute after the Civil War.[124] Rose's close relationship with both Hamilton Fish and members of the Liberal government made him an ideal intermediary. Through Rose, Fish urged the British government to bring the prisoners to trial or to dismiss the charges against them with all due haste. Delay, Fish argued, "strains the relations between the two governments, and looks like throwing away the substance to grasp after the shadow."[125] In reporting his fruitful conversations with both Granville and William Forster, chief secretary of Ireland, Rose noted the "*most* difficult position" of the British government but confirmed that liberation would be offered on the condition that the prisoners left for the United States.[126]

The U.S. government thus built upon Charles Francis Adams's strategy of working with the British government in official and unofficial capacities to marginalize the agency of Irish American agitators. Rose noted the political pitfalls inherent in the presentation of even an essentially successful policy such as securing prisoner releases: they "must be done gradually & quietly—Else we should have indignation meetings here [in Britain] that the Ministry were as usual truckling to the Eagle!!"[127] Rose worked with Fish, Lowell, Granville, and Forster to preserve good Anglo-American relations in the spring of 1882. Bancroft Davis was less generous in his assessment of the episode, suggesting that Lowell had "failed utterly" as a diplomat, but this seems rather to miss the point.[128] It was precisely Lowell's position as the representative of his government that limited his latitude of movement on the subject; alternative modes of addressing the issue of arrested Americans were required to break the impasse.

In a further replication of the events of the 1860s, prisoners who were offered freedom sometimes refused it. In August 1882, for instance, Henry O'Mahoney, Daniel McSweeney, and Patrick Slattery rejected their release. "When I spoke of this to Justin McCarthy [leader of the Irish Parliamentary Party]," Lowell recalled, "he answered, cheerfully, 'Certainly; *they are there to make trouble!*'"[129] Their success in doing so was limited by the rough transatlantic consensus that the British government had the right to introduce coercive measures provided they did not bear any more harshly on U.S. citizens and by the conciliatory approach of U.S. representatives (Granville called Lowell "one of the most agreeable men I have ever met").[130] Hamilton Fish believed that U.S. public opinion was generally sympathetic toward Great Britain and was unreceptive to the agitation of Irish American citizens.[131] MP James Bryce, who was traveling in the United States in autumn 1881, attributed such sympathy to the long shadow cast by the resolution of the *Alabama* claim. That settlement, he believed, "brought about . . . a great change of sentiment [and] a sense of brotherhood between England and America exists . . . such as one would eleven years ago have wholly despaired of ever seeing."[132] However, Fish warned that it paid to be wary. The demographic weight of the "sensitive . . . & excitable" Irish in America meant that "a single worthless devil detained . . . may at any time become again the cause of the trouble."[133]

In August 1882, the arrest of U.S. political economist Henry George (hardly the "worthless devil" that Fish had in mind) stoked Lowell's fears. His case and that of another arrestee, a journalist with the *New York Star*, presented a different class of difficulties.[134] Because George was a widely known writer on both sides of the Atlantic, his case would be "even more likely than [previous cases] to enlist the sympathy of the American people," argued Lowell.[135] The effect was doubled when, after being arrested and released at Loughrea, County Galway, George was detained again ten miles away at Athenry.[136] George himself was unperturbed by his arrests—indeed, he had expected some trouble with the police ever since his arrival in Ireland—and he gleefully boasted to a friend on his return to the United States that "among other things I saw the inside of two 'British bastiles.'"[137]

George documented—and was himself emblematic of—the changes affecting transatlantic Irish nationalism in the late 1870s and 1880s. Already celebrated as a writer on the issue of Chinese exclusion and as the author of *Progress and Poverty*, a critique of the inequalities generated by the private ownership of land and other natural resources, George's interest in the Irish land question predated the formation of the County Mayo Land League in the autumn of 1879.[138] He forged a close relationship with Land League activist Michael Davitt and, in New York, with Patrick Ford, editor of the *Irish World*, both of whom interpreted the struggle in Ireland as symptomatic of a broader global struggle for the rights of labor.[139] Davitt and Ford found intellectual ballast in George's arguments regarding land ownership, though both came to their positions on land monopoly and social radicalism independently of his work.[140] With the publication of a pamphlet, *The Irish Land Question*, in March 1881, George engaged intellectually and politically with the controversy over Irish agitation and its corollary, Irish coercion.[141] By September 1881, George had agreed that he would enter into it physically, as he "concluded an arrangement with the Irish World, by which I will go to Ireland and England . . . for three months" in order to supply Ford's journal with authoritative commentary on land agitation there.[142] In an interview upon his arrival in Ireland he made his internationalism clear: "I do not think the Irish land question differs essentially from the land question in any other country. [It] is as important in England as it is in Ireland—in the United States as it is in Europe. It is the coming question of both continents."[143]

Historians have framed George's time in the British Isles as indicative of an international social radicalism that emerged in the 1870s and 1880s, and they have been right to do so. George's *Poverty and Property* sold 100,000 copies in England alone following its publication in 1881, and he is certainly a significant figure in the history of progressive politics during this period.[144] However, this should not obscure the particular dynamics of George's intervention in Anglo-Irish constitutional politics. The treatment of the Irish question as a microcosm of a global struggle was unpopular with nationalists who saw the emphasis on social and economic reform as antithetical to the generation of a class-blind national movement. George and his U.S. readership believed in 1881 that the Irish question was pregnant with possibilities for remaking the basis of society on more equitable premises. The suppression of economic difference in the interest of national separatism and antipathy to George's technocratic imperialism drew John Devoy's barbed attack on those who hoped "to use Ireland as a means of working out a social revolution in other countries."[145] George was disillusioned when the Kilmainham Treaty poured cold water on the Land League's agrarian agitation in favor of constitutional engagement and a path to some form of home rule. According to George, the agreement between Parnell and Gladstone proved that "the Irish Land League management" was not radical enough.[146]

The Kilmainham Treaty represented the ascendancy of transnational nationalist organization over George's transnational critique of monopoly in land. Irishmen such as Michael Davitt who promoted George's ideas within the Land League were increasingly painted as islands of U.S. radicalism in the sea of moderate Irish reform. After the release of Parnell and his associates from Kilmainham Gaol in May 1882, the Irish National League was founded to replace the proscribed Land League. This new body, unlike the old, was under the direct control of the leadership of the Irish Parliamentary Party. Out of the fluidity of 1881 emerged the hierarchical political machine of mid-1882, refined and responsive to a "conservative" leadership that led George to despair.[147] Though this transition was not conclusive— agrarian unrest did not die completely in the spring of 1882—it made Georgian radicalism dispensable, even irritating. Davitt, wary of a split in the Irish movement, was "sensitive to the taunt that he has been 'captured by Henry George and the Irish World,'" the American economist glumly noted.[148] "They have been all along afraid of the Irish World . . . without which they would be nothing."[149] By the time of his departure from Ireland in September 1882, Henry George was satisfied that his ideas about land nationalization were circulating in the ether of British and Irish politics but pessimistic about the drift of the Irish Parliamentary Party.

What impact did the shifting sands of the Parnellite coalition have on the perception of Irish agitation in the United States? According to George, very little. "Our people don't understand t[he] Irish question, nor for t[hat] matter t[he] English question either," he complained.[150] They "don't realize what the English tyranny in Ireland is, and look on Irishmen as traitorous."[151] Historian Owen Dudley Edwards has written of a certain "moral imperialism" in U.S. treatment of Anglo-Irish relations in the early 1880s, underwritten by a conviction that British rule was ethically questionable and deviated from the norms of good liberal governance. This idea of a departure from the normative tenets of "civilized" governance featured in the despatches of James Blaine and Frederick T. Frelinghuysen. Yet any moral imperialism was subtle and was qualified by an appreciation that the land agitation of 1879–1882 presented the Gladstone ministry with exceptional difficulties. In the absence of the conflicting citizenship regimes of earlier years, proponents of Irish independence found it difficult to make political capital out of the arrests of Irish Americans during the Land League agitation. U.S. statesmen were concerned about the domestic political *consequences* of such arrests, but there was little suggestion that the arrests themselves were anything but the prerogative of the British government.

Irish nationalism in the 1880s was not an inherently radical force, and antipathy to radicalism cannot wholly explain how Americans responded to the Land League and home rule movements. Rather, the response in the United States was conditioned by the broader contours of the relationship between Britain and the United States; by an emergent group of transatlantic liberal intellectuals, journalists, and statesmen; by the transatlantic profile of Gladstone; and by the evolving tactics of Irish nationalists. For those who invoked an ideology of civilized and enlightened statesmanship, a particular new invention augured something far more troubling than land agitation. That invention was dynamite.

Chapter 6

A Search for Order

The Decline of the Irish Question in
American Diplomacy

The history of the relationship between the Irish question and U.S. diplomacy during the 1880s is, in a sense, the history of a paradox. The use of
dynamite augured a new era of spectacular violence, but this coexisted with
the prosaic parliamentarianism of Parnell and the Irish Parliamentary Party.
Scenes of explosive urban terrorism—legitimizing a narrative of guerilla
activity that stretched through the twentieth century—came during the
period of greatest progress toward Irish national self-determination since,
at least, the days of O'Connell.[1] There were tensions between the "democratic" mode of warfare that dynamiting represented, free from the central
direction inherent to the Fenian and Irish Republican Brotherhoods, and
the strict hierarchical model of the home rule campaign Parnell and his
associates built.

Two separate dynamite campaigns were launched during the early
1880s. One was under the direction of Fenian exile Jeremiah O'Donovan
Rossa; the other was organized by a revolutionary directory attached to
Clan na Gael. Both caused loss of life, extensive injury, and damage to property in British cities, provoking alarm in the press and in Parliament. The
response of Chester A. Arthur's administration may have been sluggish, but
the systematic use of dynamite weakened any existing bonds of sympathy

between Irish nationalists and the American public. This was exactly what a number of Irish American nationalists—including some who advocated the use of force—had anticipated and feared.

The election of 1884 saw the most purposeful injection of the Irish question into U.S. electioneering since the 1860s. In particular, James Blaine's presidential campaign made a conscious attempt to reach out to Irish nationalist voters, though with limited success. Ironically, this very direct interposition of Anglo-Irish relations into electoral politics was followed by a sharp diminution in the engagement of U.S. statesmen with the Irish question. The incoming administration of Grover Cleveland—the first Democratic president since James Buchanan left office in 1861—had reasons grounded in both principle and good politics to keep the Irish question at arm's length in its conduct of domestic and international affairs. From 1885 to 1889 and again from 1893 to 1897, the conservative Cleveland and his administrations acted in favor of building international legal structures that would shelter transatlantic relations from the intrusion of the Irish question.

The absence of diplomatic correspondence on the subject of Ireland and Irish governance during this period suggests that the Irish question was of becoming less salient to the course of American statecraft. Put simply, following the tapering off of the dynamite campaign in the mid-1880s, the Irish question largely drops out of sight in the papers of statesmen and diplomats (though Democratic secretary of state Thomas Bayard, for one, continued to worry about a fifth column of Irishmen who voted for Blaine and were bent on undermining his attempts to improve the tone of Anglo-American relations). This is not to suggest that Americans ceased to be interested in the Irish question or that Irish nationalist sentiment disappeared in the 1890s.[2] Rather, during the mid- to late 1880s, the constitutional status of Ireland was simply not contested in a way that entangled U.S. diplomacy.

An Explosive Contest

The problem of Irish American dynamite missions was more spectacular and potentially more threatening to the stability of Anglo-American relations than the arrest of naturalized Irish Americans. Alfred Nobel's development of nitroglycerine, a stable and transportable explosive, in 1867 inadvertently opened the way to more mobile forms of political violence that were less dependent on centralized planning.[3] Its revolutionary potential was

well exemplified by the assassination of Tsar Alexander II in March 1881.
Zealous individuals, emancipated from the hierarchical structures that were
necessary to organize filibuster expeditions or sustain gun-running opera-
tions, could arm themselves at relatively low cost and travel without de-
tection across national borders. At least seventeen dynamite missions were
carried out from 1881 to 1885: bombs were detonated at Salford Barracks
in Manchester, a gas works in Glasgow, the House of Commons, and various other urban targets.[4] The principals involved were Clan na Gael and
Jeremiah O'Donovan Rossa, although, as historian Owen Dudley Edwards
notes, the latter was rather less involved than contemporaries asserted and
Rossa himself implied.[5]

Nonetheless, it was Rossa who launched the first dynamite attacks on
British targets in 1881. Driven by some unknowable compound of political
principle and instability of mind, Rossa's "theology of explosives" dictated
that any means might be justified in the name of liberating an oppressed
people.[6] "I believe in all things for the liberation of Ireland," he wrote in
his newspaper, the *United Irishmen*. "If dynamite is necessary ... then [it] is a
blessed agent.... I do not know how dynamite could be put to better use
than in blowing up the British Empire."[7] Such a justificatory "theology,"
of course, had a pedigree. The most obvious antecedent was John Mitchel
who, in detailing his failing faith in "all invasions & insurrections," wrote: "it
is not that I stand out for 'civilized' warfare. The Irish have the clear right to
strike at England anywhere or anyhow, in Canada, in Ireland, in London, by
steel or gunpowder or firewood."[8] Similarly, John McCafferty argued that
terrorism was "the lawful weapon of the weak against the strong."[9] A series
of dynamite missions directed by Rossa began with an attack on Salford
Barracks on January 14, 1881, and ended in August 1883 after the arrest
and imprisonment of several of his operatives.[10] Clan na Gael's bombing
campaign, which overlapped with that of Rossa but was orchestrated by
Alexander Sullivan and William Mackay Lomasney, was better organized
and better funded. As such it was more troubling to the British authorities (though as one recent study intricately details, British spies effectively
infiltrated the Clan and colluded in the planning of dynamite attacks in
order to discredit Parnell and his colleagues).[11] The Clan na Gael campaign,
which included several attacks on London's train network, culminated in
an attack on the Tower of London and the Palace of Westminster in January 1885.[12] Arrests, deaths, internal disputes, and the seeming inefficacy
of dynamite as an agent of political change led to the end of this second
dynamite campaign by the spring of 1886.[13]

The attitudes of leading nationalists illustrate the contingent and conflicted nature of Irish American engagement at the beginning of the 1880s. Patrick Ford initially promoted both the Skirmishing Fund and the New Departure of supporting parliamentary activity in Ireland but later barred Rossa from the pages of his *Irish World*; John Devoy initiated the New Departure but clashed with Rossa over the control of funds for "skirmishing"; and Rossa avidly promoted dynamite even though he opposed the Land League (he denied that it was a truly "national movement" and feared the conservatism that moderate reform might bring).[14] Rossa and the Clan na Gael leadership disputed control of funds, leadership, and the relationship between dynamite attacks and broader political objectives. The Clan, not unreasonably, believed that Rossa's dangerous impetuosity—his attacks were "imbecile and farcical," according to Lomasney—would draw the attention of the British authorities and thus undermine the efficacy of their own, more carefully planned attacks.[15]

More generally, the use of dynamite was criticized by numerous leading Fenians who found the disregard for life and property shocking and who thought that such methods were at odds with the Fenian goal of conducting honorable and dignified resistance to British rule in the name of the Irish nation. James Stephens, John O'Leary, and Thomas Clarke Luby all denounced dynamiting.[16] Rossa had no claim "to represent any appreciable section of the Fenians," O'Leary argued in June 1882.[17] John Boyle O'Reilly expressed a nihilistic faith that British coercion inevitably followed Irish "mildness," but he too opposed dynamiting.[18] "We are sick of denouncing our own people," he wrote. "We have tried to generate a public Irish-American sentiment of conservative and moral agitation [but] what good has been done by it?"[19] The advent of dynamite, then, initiated a further struggle for control of the direction of nationalist activity. There was a clear division between those who believed that the use of dynamite was advantageous and those who did not. Moreover, the factors that made it a potentially powerful threat against the British state—ease of transit, ease of use, relative cheapness, lack of the need for extensive advance planning—could simultaneously prevent a particular cadre of nationalists (Clan na Gael, for instance) from monopolizing its use.

Historians have documented the British response to the dynamite threat. In the United States, British authorities employed Pinkerton agents to report on the activities of Irish Americans, and Canadian John Rose, fresh from his mediation of the prisoner issue, traveled to the United States to report on the state of intelligence gathering there.[20] Across the Atlantic,

the British surveillance service was reorganized and greater funds were assigned to combat the threat from radical nationalists, though the discretion
afforded British agents produced a murky world of agents and counter-
agents.[21] At the same time, the British government repeatedly reproached
the Arthur administration about its tolerance of the recently christened
"dynamite press," which openly advocated of murder and arson in British
cities; in spring 1883, British authorities lodged a formal complaint with
the U.S. government.[22] James Russell Lowell, in conversation with Lord
Granville, could only offer action that respected constitutional guarantees
about the freedom of the press. Nothing could be done "until some overt
act had been committed or until some definite proof should connect the
violent language on the one side of the Atlantic with specific actions on
the other."[23] This remained Lowell's position from mid-1881 until the end
of his time in London in spring 1885. British complaints grew more vo-
ciferous in response to the intensification of the bombing campaign under
the direction of Clan na Gael's Alexander Sullivan in 1883, but again U.S.
authorities refused to limit the flow of Irish American funds or to muzzle
the dynamite press.[24]

Whether the Arthur administration's sluggish response was due to gen-
uine constitutional scruples or to simple political expediency cannot be
definitively stated, though it seems clear that the proximity of the 1884
election was an important factor. Sullivan, for one, was an important figure
in Republican Chicago. The Arthur administration's formal declaration on
the transportation of dynamite, which it issued in March 1884, was broad
enough to encompass both interpretations. In it, Arthur asserted that there
was "no proof" of American implication in such "heinous crimes," but directed officials to exercise "diligence" in enforcing the (largely ineffective)
regulations that governed the shipment of explosives.[25] In his final address
to Congress, Arthur's only comment on the state of Anglo-American relations was the banal observation that "our intercourse with Great Britain
continues to be of a most friendly character."[26]

In contrast with the government's dilatory approach to restraining the
continued bombing of British cities, commentary from the United States
became more vocal in its condemnation of the transatlantic dynamiters.
Henry Wade Rogers, a future dean of Yale Law School, wrote of the innate sympathy that Americans had with the Irish demand for home rule
(which would have been news to many Parnellites earlier in the 1880s)
but lamented the debasement of civilized values that the dynamite war announced.[27] Such "crimes against humanity . . . crimes of which no civilized

GORILLA WARFARE UNDER THE PROTECTION OF THE AMERICAN FLAG.

Figure 5. Jeremiah O'Donovan Rossa is here characterized as a wide-eyed ape, bringing his idiosyncratic brand of guerilla warfare to England. "Gorilla Warfare under the Protection of the American Flag," (1884) chromolithographic cartoon, *Puck*, March 19, 1884.

people is guilty of even in a state of war" did irreparable injury to the struggle for constitutional change.[28] Though some Clan na Gael dynamiters outlined a distinct policy of "bloodless terrorism," targeting monuments and buildings rather than individuals, such finessing did little to persuade the public that dynamiting was anything but a "dastardly crime."[29]

Both dynamiting and the return of Irish Americans to Ireland revived mass concern about the dismissive way in which adopted citizens thought about their new country. Complained one commentator in the *North American Review*, many Irish American citizens "are beginning to claim the right to jeopard [*sic*] the peace and quiet of the United States by aiding and abetting felonies intended to keep up national feuds in their former home....We want no divided allegiance."[30] Such complaints mirrored James Lowell's frustrations. "Naturalized Irishmen seem entirely to misconceive the process through which they have passed in assuming American citizenship," he groused.[31] They look "upon themselves as Irishmen who have acquired a right to American protection, rather than as Americans who have renounced a claim to Irish nationality."[32] The *Boston Daily Advertiser* argued that dynamiting was "[a] crime committed by Irishmen who came here as guests, but [who] have betrayed all that is honourable."[33]

The broad popular condemnation that dynamiters elicited contrasted with the limited legal response of the U.S. government. That the United States did not bear greater legal responsibility for the actions of Jeremiah O'Donovan Rossa and various Clan na Gael dynamiters was due to the fact that the Neutrality Act, still in its 1818 incarnation, did not apply to the novel crime of dynamite terrorism. Addressing Congress for the final time in December 1884, Chester Arthur noted that "modern ingenuity supplies means for the organization of hostilities without open resort to armed vessels or filibustering parties" and recommended that Congress broaden the scope of the country's neutrality legislation.[34] His end-of-term call for action was at odds with the inertia that had characterized his approach to the question during the previous three and a half years. A bill criminalizing the use of explosives to destroy property or "for the purpose of assassination or murder or the destruction of life" was introduced to a lame duck Congress by Republican senator George Edmunds in January 1885 but never made it out of the Senate Judiciary Committee.[35] The House considered and killed a similar bill.[36]

In addition, no extradition agreement was in place that covered the act of traveling to the United Kingdom with the intention of laying dynamite in British cities. The existing Anglo-American agreement on extradition formed part of the Webster-Ashburton Treaty of 1842, which made provision for it in the cases of "murder, or assault with intent to commit murder, or Piracy, or arson, or robbery, or Forgery, or the utterance of forged paper."[37] This did not cover incitement to violence or war, and it explicitly exempted political crimes. The Cleveland administration that took office in 1885 negotiated a new agreement on extradition, the Phelps-Rosebery convention, the following year. This well-intentioned arrangement narrowed the definition of a political crime and allowed extradition in the event of "malicious injuries to property whereby the life of any person shall be endangered."[38] However, the convention was deemed "practically . . . worthless" for the simple reason that it only provided for extradition after the crime had been committed, assuming the perpetrator could be found.[39] Under the simple headline "What the Treaty Lacks," the

New York Times reprinted without comment a short paragraph from the London *Standard*:

> The new extradition convention hardly justifies the interest with which its appearance was awaited. It fails to provide for the suppression of American societies in which horrible projects are hatched. . . . Public opinion in Great Britain will certainly look to the American Government for the suppression of so gross and palpable a conspiracy against the peace and prosperity of a friendly nation.[40]

British authorities had no problem identifying those who encouraged dynamite missions. Far greater was the problem of identifying perpetrators after the fact. The bill's failings were moot, moreover, as the convention died in the Senate.[41] Historian Jonathan Gantt has suggested the importance of considering how "Irish anti-imperial violence . . . reconfigured how Americans conceptualized non-conventional political violence in relation to nationalism and imperialism," but just as important was how indefinite and halting that process was.[42]

The U.S. government's inertia was challenged by some American commentators, particularly those who interpreted the use of arbitration as a tool of diplomacy as indicative of a more civilized approach to settling international disputes. For those who sought to conceptualize the dynamite missions as transnational crimes, the *Alabama* case cast a long shadow. Americans might look to that case—and British toleration of London-based European revolutionaries—as justification for doing nothing to hold back Irish American dynamiters. James Blaine hinted at the long-term influence of Britain's Confederate sympathies in his 1884 memoirs, noting that they "still shadow with distrust a national friendship that ought to be cordial and constant."[43] But others were more sanguine and looked not to British toleration of pro-Confederate feeling but to the ultimate Anglo-American reconciliation as the salient precedent. Both the House of Commons and the U.S. Congress had passed resolutions in the mid-1870s affirming their support for the principle of international arbitration, and this commitment, however abstract, shaped the norms of Anglo-American diplomatic engagement.[44] Henry Wade Rogers argued that toleration of dynamiters did a disservice to the moral authority of the United States and ignored the historic significance of the *Alabama* settlement. "We cannot justify ourselves in the eyes of English people by saying that the laws of the United States do not enable us to interfere," he claimed, going on to suggest that the neutrality laws required amendment so that the United States met its moral obligations as a state.[45] "The Alabama case settled the principle that a nation cannot relieve itself from its responsibility by pleading that its laws do not permit it to interfere in the given case."[46] Yet it was not immediately obvious how the sound principles established by the *Alabama* case could be institutionalized so as to restrain Irish American dynamiters, despite the best wishes of liberal commentators on both sides of the Atlantic.[47]

In contrast with the discussion of dynamite and terrorism in American journals, the policies and actual practices of the Irish Parliamentary Party under Parnell received limited coverage in the U.S. press. This is perhaps understandable: the drudgery of maintaining parliamentary discipline through the Irish National League and the Parliamentary Party was of little interest to U.S. readers when compared with the sound and fury of Jeremiah O'Donovan Rossa and the Clan na Gael. It also had fewer implications for U.S. statecraft. Historians tell a similar story of radical Land League agitation followed by the arrest of Irish American agitators and the various dynamite campaigns of Rossa and Clan na Gael, but this obscures an appreciation of the progress of Parnell's parliamentary activity and skates over the very real fractures between conservatives and radicals within the American-Irish nationalist movement. Tensions centered on the role of Patrick Ford and his *Irish World*, the propriety of "selling" the Irish as a bloc vote, the transmission (and use) of American funds, and, of course, the role of dynamite.[48] As noted, many former Fenians had voiced condemnation about the propriety of dynamiting as a political tactic on both ethical grounds—arguing that it was a morally indefensible practice—and political grounds, in that it cast a pall on Irish nationalism as a whole.[49] A number of these more conservative Fenians—most notably Patrick A. Collins and John Boyle O'Reilly—found prominence in the U.S. branches of the Irish National League and used their influence to push the organization in a more conservative direction.[50]

What is underappreciated—perhaps because it is an unpalatable truth— is how the destructive methods of dynamite nationalists polished Parnell's credentials as a moderate restraining force. Though he lacked the transatlantic celebrity of his earlier compatriot, Parnell replicated O'Connell's ability to shape the seemingly anarchic materials of Irish politics into a cohesive movement. For example, Henry Wade Rogers's article on "harboring conspiracy" cast home rule agitation as uncontentious and as the proper object of U.S. sympathy, in contrast to the inhumane and uncivilized dynamite campaign. Newspapers might write uncharitable things about Parnell, but the Irish leader was clearly no dynamite fiend.[51] It was evident by the spring of 1883 that even generally hostile journals such as the *New York Times* could identify clear blue water between advocates of dynamiting and Parnell and his fellow constitutional nationalists.[52]

"Blaine Irishmen" and Presidential Politics

Nonetheless, the frenzy of presidential politics did much to boost the voices of relatively radical nationalists at the expense of their more moderate comrades. Writing about the election of 1884, historian Mark Summers has convincingly argued that the Irish American vote was "more than myth, less than monolith."[53] For our purposes, it is worth noting that James Blaine, the Republican candidate, believed rather more in the monolith than the myth. He applied himself to capturing the Irish vote for the Republican Party.[54] The ambivalence of the Democratic Party toward labor radicalism—and the outright hostility to organized labor of its candidate, Grover Cleveland— brought to the fore a tension between "working-class" and "Irish" as descriptors of Irish American voters. As early as the 1870s, Patrick Ford had advocated that Irish American voters support the Greenback Labor Party.[55] Blaine recognized the potential for partisan realignment implicit in such disillusionment. One response was to marry class, patriotism, and Irish nationalism under the banner of Republican protectionism. In doing so, Blaine glossed over his antebellum flirtations with anti-Catholicism and a more recent effort to amend the Constitution to prevent state funding for religious schools, an endeavor that had whipped up anti-Catholic sentiment across the country.[56] A chapter of his 1884 campaign biography was dedicated to winning the support of adopted citizens. In it, the editors reprinted a letter from Blaine during the 1880 campaign in which he made political economy central to his plea for Irish American votes:

> Never . . . since the execution of Robert Emmet, has the feeling of Irish-men, the world over, been so bitter against England and Englishmen as at this hour. And yet the great mass of the Irish voters in the United States will . . . vote . . . for the interests of England. . . . The Irishmen of America use their suffrage as though they were Tories. The Free-traders of England . . . wish to break down the protective tariff and cripple our manufacturers. The prosperity of the Irish in this country depends as largely as

that of any other class upon the maintenance of the financial and industrial policy represented by the Republican party.[57]

In this context, Blaine calculated that the language of protectionism was also the language of anti-British nationalism.[58] Republicans framed their defense of the tariff as a weapon against British economic imperialism and as a means to develop U.S. industrial capacity. One pamphlet promoting Blain's candidacy went as far as to suggest that a vote for the Republican tariff was an attractive alternative to dynamiting public buildings. Both tactics were a way of expressing Irishmen's "just cause of complaint against England," but the ballot was a "power ten thousand times more powerful . . . than all the dynamite in the world."[59] Those who were skeptical of the threat posed by Britain's commercial and industrial power need only consider the decline of the Irish economy through the nineteenth century, argued Republicans. There but for the grace of Blaine would go the United States.[60]

A second response was more direct and more explicitly partisan. Blaine cultivated connections with Irish nationalist editors, including John Devoy and Patrick Ford. Devoy, in particular, sought to make himself an indispensable broker in the election, writing to a Blaine associate that "no man is better acquainted with that portion of the Irish people . . . who are at all likely to change sides . . . than I am."[61]

> It is from the "National element" in those who have taken an active part during the last few years in Irish patriotic movements—that anything at all can be expected. They are the active force in Irish politics, the only class who have shown independence of the politicians. . . . And, let me say here, that there is no chance of a bolt at all except on the express ground of national sentiment, or of the position and standing of the Irish race in America.[62]

Devoy's letter was replete with not-so-subtle suggestions for patronage appointments and included a request for funds for his own newspaper, the *Irish Nation*. This notwithstanding, the detail and carefully qualified nature of his suggestions makes clear the seriousness with which he treated an Irish bolt to the Republican Party. Devoy was representative of a broader trend of pro-Republican sentiment among his peers. Clan na Gael leader Alexander Sullivan reported that the Blaine-Logan ticket was "highly satisfactory" to the Irish National League of America, of which he had been president, on the basis of its commitment to "Protection and an improved tone in our foreign policy."[63] Patrick Egan, the former treasurer of the Land League, condemned Cleveland as "the pet candidate of . . . the entire English press."[64] Patrick Ford provided updates on the progress of the election in Brooklyn and New York City.[65] According to some reports, Blaine had even tried to use Parnell's name to secure votes, though the Irishman demurred.[66]

Blaine did not secure a lock on the support of Irish Americans, nor did he win the election. The ideas of demonstrating the independence of the Irish vote and the folly of Democratic Party managers of taking that vote for granted may have been good, but without electoral success they meant little. Moreover, the Irish vote was not monolithic; it diverged along regional, class, and personal lines. The "professional savers of Ireland" might have gone for Blaine, sneered the *Detroit Free Press*, but they were hardly representative: Blaine's pandering for votes had come to naught.[67] Blaine had hardly acted the part of the rabid Anglophobe while at the State Department and, indeed, as late as 1883 he himself had complained that "there had been of late too much 'demagogy' on the part of the Government in dealing with the Irish element in New York."[68] His line of policy during the 1884 campaign undoubtedly opened him to just these charges. This, though, should not blind the historian to the significance of *how* Blaine went about canvassing Irish support during the election. Significantly, his use of the language of protectionism indicates its capacity to capture or subsume the idiom of Irish nationalism and thus turn it to evidently American ends.

As for the president-elect, though Mugwump reformers complained about him sating the demands of "dynamite Democrats," Cleveland was really as free of Irish American power brokers as any contemporary Democrat could be.[69] Patrick Collins, the dependable and conservative home ruler, was suggested as a possible Cabinet member, but in general Cleveland found himself beholden more to the liberal reformers who had bolted the Republican Party on Blaine's nomination than to any urban Irish political machine.[70] In addition, Cleveland's appointment to secretary of state—the "conspicuously patrician" Thomas Bayard—had been an outspoken critic of Irish American dynamiters during his time in the Senate and had introduced a resolution of "indignation and profound sorrow . . . horror and detestation" at "such monstrous crimes against civilization."[71] One Democratic Party insider summarized what seemed to him to be the new state of play in a private letter to a British friend, writing "your wish and demand for Justice, will find a better and more fertile soil under Cleveland than you now dream of."[72] The new administration would be firm in dealing with Irish American dynamiters: "the feeling of the Democratic leaders . . . is to let the Irish element understand that the Democratic Party henceforth is their master and not their slave."[73]

Almost simultaneously with Cleveland's accession to the White House came the cessation of dynamite attacks in Britain. Historians have suggested that the U.S. government's attitude began to harden toward physical-force nationalism in the context of growing social conservatism after the Haymarket bombing, though the events in Chicago postdated all but the last, aborted dynamite mission (in June 1887).[74] An alternative interpretation that has been advanced by historian K. R. M. Short in what is still the best study of the bombastically named "dynamite war" suggests that the balance of power shifted within the New Departure coalition as Parnell's parliamentary attrition appeared to be on the cusp of bringing reward.[75] This strengthened the IRB, which had long been skeptical of dynamiting as a tactic, against those enthusiasts for dynamite in the Clan na Gael. This explanation seems the fuller and more useful one, particularly when set alongside the new administration's more open hostility toward what Secretary of State Bayard called "the Dynamite and Fenian elements" in the United States.[76] In short, the value of dynamiting as a political tactic diminished as Parnell's Ireland edged toward home rule.

Civilization, Irish America, and the Prospect of Home Rule

Though it was not immediately apparent, during Cleveland's first term in office the Irish question declined in salience as a subject of diplomatic correspondence. This is not to say that Irish nationalists ceased to shape U.S. diplomacy but that their influence became more exclusively a domestic political factor to be weighed rather than potential leverage for international confrontation. The most time-consuming topics of negotiation with the British government during Cleveland's first administration were those relating to U.S.-Canadian fishing rights and to extradition. In both instances Secretary of State Bayard sought to insulate diplomatic negotiations from the potential disruption of the Irish question. On the seemingly banal topic of the fisheries, which remained contentious throughout the 1880s, Bayard wrote confidentially to a friend that "nothing is more essential than to remove combustible matter from propinquity to fire," referring to the need to keep the issue out of the hands of Irish American nationalists. "There is a violent element in our body politic that would embroil us with Great Britain with or without reason—and I desire to guard against all such chances."[77] This was a matter of upholding the values of civilization, Bayard argued. Referring to the Phoenix Park murders of 1882 and the dynamite attacks on British cities, he wrote that the use of "assassination . . . Dynamite and . . . daggers" set "the Irish World class" against "the two Guardians of the World's Civilization," Britain and the United States.[78] Defining a transatlantic commonality, Bayard believed that these two nations had a duty to protect the values of "Civilization," which was vulnerable to attacks from, as he saw it, anarchic labor radicals (including Henry George), domestic jingoists, and violent transatlantic revolutionaries.[79] In expressing his anxiety at British foot-dragging about a fisheries agreement, Bayard expressed "the sincere intentions of this Administration to avoid collisions and to strengthen the united forces and elements of civilization and liberty which Great Britain and the U.S. chiefly contain and represent in the world."[80] Bayard's diplomacy was fundamentally shaped by the desire to remove transatlantic sources of traction for Irish nationalists.

Bayard's search for Anglo-American "civilizational" security mandated a diplomacy of structural assurances: formal agreements on potentially contentious issues would limit the political space in which Irish and Irish American nationalists might operate. To use his own analogy, such agreements would reduce the stock of combustible material that the flame of extreme nationalism might ignite. Bayard explained that he hesitated to conclude a deal on extradition in March 1886 "when the Tory administration was in power and the Irish question was so burning in England and of course here [in the United States]. . . . A treaty negotiated with Gladstone's Administration would be less likely to provoke challenge."[81] Bayard's assumption that a treaty negotiated with Gladstone was likely to be better insulated from political challenge than one negotiated with a Conservative administration sprang from his reading of the domestic scenes in Britain and the United States. By spring 1886, with Gladstone a convert to some form of Irish home rule, an agreement with the Liberals would be far less likely to generate Irish opposition in Parliament than an equivalent agreement with the Tories.[82] Bayard was keen to avoid concluding a deal with the Tory Party that criminalized the actions of transatlantic Irish dynamiters: such an agreement might give the impression that the Democratic Party was acquiescing to repressive Tory rule in Ireland. Bayard believed that Blaine had been largely successful in capturing the Irish vote in 1884 and was maintaining a disciplined anti-British line ("a diligent minority mustering of old prejudices") against any compromises that the administration might reach with the British government.[83] The secretary of state was outraged that articles promoting Blaine's heady brew of violent anti-British protectionism appeared alongside advertisements in the dynamite newspapers "for funds to be used in procuring . . . the assassination of British officers."[84] In general, Democrats, whom Republicans painted as advocating "'British free trade,'" had to be cautious about negotiating mutual concessions with the British government.[85]

By March 1886, Gladstone had been returned to power—briefly—in alliance with Parnell's Irish Parliamentary Party. The election of late 1885 gave the Liberal leader a plurality of votes, but he was dependent on the Parnellites for a majority. This humiliating position, commented the *New York Times*, was a sign that "'eight hundred years of wrong' are near being avenged. . . . The conquering nation cannot regulate even its own domestic affairs except by the permission of a representative of the conquered race."[86] The newspaper concluded that should Parnell demand it, repeal of the union would be a small price to pay to get rid of the disruptive Irish Parliamentary Party. The home rule crisis of late 1885 and early 1886 and Gladstone's timely conversion to the home rule cause spurred American interest. "The effect of Gladstone's speech of April 8, 1886 [introducing the Home Rule Bill] upon the Irish in America was simply intoxicating," wrote one commentator.[87] Commitment to parliamentarianism had depressed financial contributions from the United States; now money flooded into Parnellite coffers.[88] The "Irish nation in the United States" that so troubled British politicians largely welcomed the Home Rule Bill of April 1886.[89] Even radical nationalists were positive about Gladstone's proposed measure. Patrick Egan stated that the bill would "meet with the approbation of the Irish in America," while Alexander Sullivan believed it "a great step in the right direction."[90]

Not all were so enthused by the Home Rule Bill. Writing in London in November 1885, Edward Phelps, Lowell's replacement as U.S. minister to London, was less buoyant about Gladstone's conversion:

I am sorry to see countenance given in our country to the mischievous schemes of Parnell. He is like all the demagogues who have thriven on the distress of that unfortunate people. What he proposes he well knows to be impossible. Parnell's position at this point was to demand complete Irish

independence. Crime and outrage are credited in its support. . . . I fear we
shall have trouble with the business before it is concluded.[91]

Bayard alluded privately to successful efforts to suppress a resolution in
Congress praising the bill, presumably doubting the propriety of U.S. intervention in a matter of British domestic politics.[92] Moreover, intellectuals and commentators on both sides of the Atlantic were divided over the
rights and wrongs of home rule and its implications for the durability of
the British Empire.

In Britain, proponents of home rule turned to U.S. examples to support
their position. Even the Conservative Unionist Lord Blandford, a former
lord lieutenant of Ireland, saw "in the constitution of the American Republic . . . the most successful effort to preserve the national feeling of people
while at the same time conceding to them the most extended form of
local administration." Likewise, the radical MP Henry Labouchère called
for "separate assemblies for England, Scotland and Ireland, modeled upon
the United States' constitution," an argument echoed by Justin McCarthy,
a prominent Irish nationalist at Westminster, and Andrew Carnegie, who
believed British statesmen ought to look to the United States for a federal
solution to the Irish question.[93] Gladstone himself rejected the fully federal
proposal advocated by Joseph Chamberlain, but he rather curiously suggested that Ireland be granted "a measure of full autonomy similar to that
given to the Southern States during Reconstruction."[94]

This invocation of the American example had a U.S. counterpart. In
his contribution to the *Handbook of Home Rule* in 1887, Edwin Godkin
recognized that American analogies were being made both to support and
condemn the project of home rule. He himself explicitly viewed the question through the prism of the Union's experience of the Civil War and
Reconstruction and hoped to persuade others of the merits of his interpretation. He concluded his essay by describing the removal of federal troops
from the South under President Hayes and noted "that it is no less true in
politics than in physics, that if you remove what you see to be the cause, the
effect will surely disappear."[95] He continued,

> It is true, at least in the Western world, that if you give communities in a
> reasonable degree the management of their own affairs, the love of mate-
> rial comfort and prosperity which is now so strong among all civilized,
> and even partially civilized men, is sure in the long run to do the work of
> creating and maintaining order.[96]

"Home Rule is very popular with nearly all classes in the United States, as it is generally looked upon as an American idea," noted a prominent Irish American politician in 1903.[97] With respect to Anglo-Irish affairs, then, the lens of federalism proved persistent.

In addition, the transatlantic prestige of Gladstone went some way to limit criticism of home rule in the United States. As Godkin noted, "no living American, has as much hold as Gladstone on the American imagination today," and he was not alone in this assessment.[98] Historians Leslie Butler and Frank Ninkovich have noted how many U.S. commentators understood British partisan politics as a Manichean conflict between the reformer Gladstone and the arch-conservative Benjamin Disraeli.[99] "Gladstone worship" was stoked by the Grand Old Man himself, whose celebrated essay, "Kin beyond Sea" delineated the Anglo-American rapprochement that emerged toward the end of the 1870s.[100]

Gladstone's celebrity might soothe skeptics about the program of constitutional reform that he and Parnell now advocated, but Cleveland's administration was still concerned about the impact that a combination of Irish American radicals and Blaine Republicans might have on the foreign policy of the United States. Thomas Bayard's anxieties over the alliance of Republicans and what he termed the "interest of dynamite," led him to set his face against any perceived Irish influence in U.S. foreign affairs.[101] Yet it was the domestic opposition—domestic opportunism, as he saw it—that troubled him, rather than any resumption of the dynamite attacks that had occurred during Frelinghuysen's time at the State Department. In reality, during Bayard's tenure, the significance of the Irish question in American diplomacy weakened and some of the vocal, radical Irish American nationalists continued to drift to the Republican Party. (Of course, these factors were not independent of each other.) Blaine's appeal to Irish Americans in 1884—and again in 1888, as a supporter of Benjamin Harrison—was sound and fury, masking this diminution, as was the Clan na Gael's open support of Harrison's candidacy.[102] Bayard, though, continued to fret over the prospect of a "consolidated . . . Irish vote" that might do mischief to the republic's foreign affairs.[103]

The increasing hold that the language of nationalism and protectionism had on the framing of the Irish American nationalist vote muted its subversive transatlantic potential. Patrick Ford, for instance, said nothing about Parnell and constitutionalism or about dynamite and social radicalism in his appeals to voters in 1888 but instead proclaimed that "the issue today is the Tariff. It is the American system *versus* the British colonial system. . . . The

Lion and the Unicorn [Gladstone and Disraeli] have taken the stump for Cleveland and [vice presidential candidate Allen G.] Thurman."[104] The Republican platform itself was more muted, expressing an earnest hope "that we may soon congratulate our fellow-citizens of Irish birth upon the peaceful recovery of home rule for Ireland."[105] Cleveland was defeated and Benjamin Harrison was elected president. When Blaine returned to office as Harrison's secretary of state, he appointed Patrick Egan as the new administration's minister to Chile, but this seems to have been the only fruit of Blaine's Irish American strategy. Egan's Anglophobia perhaps appealed to Blaine's broader desire to squeeze British influence out of the Western Hemisphere, but this was hardly a profound recalibration of the Anglo-Irish American triangle that the Blaine propaganda of 1884 had espoused.[106]

High Hopes Frustrated

All of this points to a domestication of the Irish question in both countries—and the corresponding attenuation of its capacity to unsettle transatlantic relations. In the United Kingdom, Parnell's success in forcing home rule to the top of the parliamentary agenda came at the cost of considerable autonomy. The Liberal Party's adoption of home rule as a policy transformed the Irish Parliamentary Party into one wing of one of Britain's major political parties.[107] (It also led the most committed Unionists into desperate attempts to link Parnell with dynamite enthusiasts in the United States.)[108] By making the Irish question central to Westminster governance, Parnell appeared to settle the ambiguity of whether Ireland was a subject of imperial or domestic governance in favor of the latter. As historian Murney Gerlach has noted, Gladstone's effort to legitimize British rule in Ireland through the concession of home rule caused his popularity to plummet in England but to soar in the United States, ushering in "a new era of Anglo-American reconciliation."[109] This might overstate the ameliorative capacity of home rule at the expense of other factors, but certainly the prospect of a measure of Irish self-governance augured well for the removal of a persistent destabilizing factor in Anglo-American diplomacy. In 1888, the Democratic Party marked this domestication by naming individuals who were not U.S. citizens in a presidential party platform for the first time.[110] Noting their "cordial sympathy with the struggling people of all nations in their effort to secure for themselves the inestimable blessings of self-government and civil and religious liberty," party delegates resolved to "especially declare our sympathy with the efforts of those noble patriots who, led by Gladstone and Parnell, have conducted their grand and peaceful contest for home rule in Ireland."[111] A moment of epochal significance seemed at hand.

To prominent Irish American nationalists, Parnell's breakthrough in Parliament brought a welcome sense of inevitability: the Irish question was a matter of domestic British partisan competition and would eventually win out, associated as it was with the great liberal statesman of the age. The Irish National League of America, which had been damaged by the Republican politicking of Alexander Sullivan and others, came together in August 1885 to endorse Parnell's course.[112] John Boyle O'Reilly proclaimed that repeal of the union would finally come, by the end of 1889 at the very latest.[113] Parnell "stands today the representative of a people resolved to recover National independence," wrote Sullivan, and "he has nearly succeeded."[114]

Nearly, but not quite. After four years of maintaining party discipline, the Irish Parliamentary Party, sloping toward Gladstone's return to power and a second home rule bill, was divided by the O'Shea-Parnell divorce case, as were Irish-American supporters of the home rule movement.[115] It seemed, the *New York Times* reported, that Irish home rule was now a "lost cause," and it proclaimed that "ten years of work [had been] thrown away."[116] From an American perspective, though, the factionalism that followed this split was mere gloss on the declining salience of Irish nationalism in American political life between the mid-1880s and the end of the century. Writing in 1888, William Henry Hurlbert reflected on the Democratic Party platform's praise for Parnell and Gladstone, but he argued that

> the sympathy of the great body of the American people with Irish efforts for self-government has been diminished, not increased, since 1848, by the gradual transfer of the head-quarters and machinery of those efforts from Ireland to the United States. The recent refusal of the Mayor of New York, Mr. Hewitt, to allow what is called the "Irish National flag" to be raised over the City Hall . . . is vastly more significant of the true drift of American feeling on this subject than any number of sympathetic resolutions adopted at party conventions.[117]

Hurlbert, who was opposed to home rule, might be suspected of anti-Irish sentiment, but his views were echoed elsewhere. Another sage argued that young politicians would do well to note the declining percentages of the Irish-born in the U.S. census. "The decay of Irish influence in this country

is certain," he stated, "and will be the political destruction of those preach-
ers of sedition who build their hopes upon a bad foundation."[118] This was
not altogether wishful thinking. House Speaker Thomas B. Reed, reflecting
on the changing characteristics of American public life in the mid-1890s,
mused that "the Irish in the United States are no longer a political force."

> Time has been . . . when the effort to secure the Irish vote was one of the
> chief anxieties of politicians on both sides. This anxiety showed itself in
> Congress, in the Press, in State Legislatures, in political contests all over the
> country. That day is past. . . . The Press is free again, and we here in Wash-
> ington are free, and Americans and not Irish now govern this country.[119]

Reed, Hurlbert, and others no doubt had the political machines of Boston,
New York, and numerous urban centers—and their seemingly corrosive
effect on the nomination and election of national political candidates—on
their minds when speaking of the declining power of "the Irish" as a bloc
vote. The new immigration of the late decades of the nineteenth century
coupled with increasing Irish American prosperity and cultural "Ameri-
canization" gave the Irish in the United States a new social, economic, and
political profile.[120]

This trend had its counterpart in U.S. statecraft. As we have seen, Irish
nationalists in earlier decades sought to harness American anticolonial republicanism for their own ends. They also explored gaps in the legal structures of U.S. foreign policy, attempting to redefine the limits of national
neutrality in the case of republican insurrection, exploit diverging British
and American conceptions of citizenship, and disrupt amity between Britain and the United States. Their actions had the perverse effect of provoking the establishment of transatlantic comity with regard to emigration
and expatriation and provided incentive for settling outstanding Civil War
claims by arbitration, a precedent that profoundly shaped expectations regarding the future resolution of disputes between the United States and
Great Britain. Attempts to establish a transatlantic framework for arbitration
failed in May 1897 (in part due to the lobbying efforts of Irish nationalists, though rather more because of the opposition of silver Democrats and
those concerned about future U.S. policy in Central and South America),
but that "sense of brotherhood" Bryce identified in 1881 meant that statesmen on both sides of the Atlantic persisted in these attempts.[121]

Though historians have investigated Americans' growing (though
hardly absolute) acceptance of a logic of empire in the last decades of the
nineteenth century, it would be too strong to say that Americans had made

their peace with British rule in Ireland.[122] Gladstone's legislative programs of the late 1860s and early 1880s had gone a long way toward addressing the most egregious symbols of ascendancy rule in Ireland—the dominance of the landlord class and the anomalous Church of Ireland—that had provided the staple criticisms of British rule. Yet Ireland still represented a failure of British governance and appeared to be one of the most conspicuous impediments to a blossoming "civilizational" rapprochement of the late 1890s. As one contributor to *Atlantic Monthly* suggested, Britain's failure to instigate some form of federal home rule for Ireland suggested not only that the British political nation was inattentive to the beneficial lessons of U.S. political science but that the English were incapable of formulating the kind of rigorous imperial policy that would be required in the geopolitical struggles of the coming century.[123] Theodore Roosevelt, writing in 1899, expressed his general desire for a rapprochement among the English-speaking peoples but was perturbed by the continued denial of Irish home rule. Noting that to be too effusive in one's desire for friendly relations with England would defeat one's own ends, he wrote "I became a Homeruler in consequence of reading [the historian] Lecky, and have continued so partly because I thought it would be a good thing for Ireland, and partly because I should like to see the removal of the one great obstacle among the people who speak English all over the world."[124] In this interpretation of global relations, the interests of civilization were best protected—and best advanced—by Anglo-American harmony. Better that Britain put her house in order by coming to some federal arrangement with Ireland, not least because of the potential domestic force in the United States of a mobilized anti-British Irish vote. But this was a minor note in the evolution of U.S. diplomacy rather than a major theme.

Here was the Irish question as annoyance, an irritant in a world of civilized (and civilizing), stable sovereign states who sought to export the virtues of responsible governance, openness to capital, and manly self-restraint in international relations. The notion of an independent Ireland was fanciful and quixotic, and as the British and U.S. governments worked steadily to eliminate the grounds of potential conflict, the idea of annexing Irish goals to the power of the United States appeared ever more the stuff of romance.[125] In another twenty years or so, events in Dublin would drag the Irish question back toward the center ground of U.S. diplomatic conversations. By that time, the world would be at war and the cross-currents of American geopolitics and Irish nationalism would look very different indeed.

Rapprochement, Paris, and a Free State

Grover Cleveland's astringent politics offered little to Irish national-ists. Even an apparently fierce dispute over Venezuelan territory—perhaps the episode most conducive to a full-scale crisis in Anglo-American rela-tions in the final quarter of the nineteenth-century—resulted in peaceful arbitration.[1] In both his domestic and his foreign politics, Cleveland was a conservative, and his administration sought to limit the power of the central government and avoid American entanglement overseas. Though attempts to establish an international agreement on arbitration failed, the amicable settlement of the Venezuela crisis in October 1899 serves as a valuable gauge of British-U.S. relations, which became ever closer during the first decade of the twentieth century.[2]

These diplomatic developments did not occur in a cultural vacuum.[3] During the final years of the century, U.S. statesmen offered a notably more positive interpretation of the British Empire, often in the context of an assumed Anglo-Saxon kinship. Unsurprisingly, journalists, intellectuals, au-thors, and politicians espoused Anglo-Saxonist ideas in the context of U.S. imperial ambitions. Proponents of U.S. intervention in the Philippines, the Caribbean, and Central America spoke the language of imperial duty, all in the service of the amorphous concept of "civilization."[4] For Theodore

Roosevelt, "the spread of the English-speaking peoples" was "the most striking feature of world history."[5] "It was a good thing for Egypt and the Sudan, and for the world, when England took Egypt and the Sudan," he noted in 1904, "and so it is a good thing, a very good thing, for Cuba and for Panama and for the world that the United States has acted as it has actually done."[6] And even those who were more skeptical about the wisdom and morality of exuberant intervention elsewhere in the Western Hemisphere could subscribe to these notions of Anglo-American fraternity. Richard Olney, a secretary of state under Cleveland and a leading anti-imperialist, felt quite comfortable asserting that "the American people . . . feel themselves to be not merely in name but in fact, part of one great English-speaking family whose proud destiny is to lead and control the world."[7] Anglo-Saxon theorizing, wrote one Irish American critic, was "humbug," yet its brief popularity in the late nineteenth century is illustrative of strengthening Anglo-American ties.[8]

Roosevelt's "very good things" were aided by a recalibration of British geopolitics. At the end of the nineteenth century, British statesmen began to feel themselves isolated in an increasingly troubling world and, where feasible, they sought out international alliances. Few saw a formal alliance with the United States as a possibility. Instead, British officials focused on reducing their entanglements in the Western Hemisphere.[9] In December 1904, Roosevelt announced his famous corollary to the Monroe Doctrine, suggesting that that the United States might act as an "international police power" in response to "chronic wrongdoing, or an impotence that results in a general loosening of the ties of civilized society" among Latin American states.[10] Even before this, however, British statesmen and intellectuals had encouraged the United States to take a leading role in policing the Western Hemisphere, as much to limit the imperial ambitions of other European powers as to maintain order in the states concerned.[11] As one recent historian has noted, "No power applauded the Roosevelt Corollary more than did Britain."[12] And British plans to remove sources of contention in the Western Hemisphere appeared successful. At the conclusion of Roosevelt's term of office in 1909, the *London Review* wrote that "pretty nearly every issue of any moment of contentiousness has been wiped off the Anglo-American slate."[13]

For Irish American nationalists, Anglo-American congeniality was unsettling. John Hay, who served as ambassador to Britain and later as Roosevelt's first secretary of state, griped about the influence of Irish (and German) Americans on the conduct of U.S. diplomacy, but in truth Irish nationalists had very limited political influence in the United States.[14]

Opposition to the Boer War offered an opportunity to vent anti-British sentiments with some slight receptivity in American public life at large, but it would be hard to ascribe any broader significance to Irish American activities.[15] More intriguing and of greater importance in the long term were shaky but novel alliances forged with German American groups and the campaign launched by John Devoy's *Gaelic American* that sought to promote Indian nationalism in the United States.[16] But such collaboration was tentative and only a minor departure from the broader trend of closer Anglo-American relations. By the end of the long Republican tenure of 1897 to 1913, the State Department and the Foreign Office had developed a strong working relationship that was adept at dealing with the sporadic inflammation of Irish American sentiment.[17]

The Boer War had a far greater impact in Ireland itself. Its impact on Irish political organization in its many forms was "nearly as crucial and event for Irish nationalism as the death of Parnell," one leading historian has argued.[18] It was contemporaneous with the stitching up of old wounds: the Irish Parliamentary Party, which had been divided since Parnell's fall from grace, reunited in 1900. John Redmond, leader of the reconstituted party, fostered a recently established U.S. corollary, the United Irish League of America. This came play a crucial role in the party's finances (leading Redmond's opponents to mock him as a "Dollar Dictator" for his dependence on American revenue).[19] Learning from past mistakes, Redmond was careful to keep this organization subordinate to his own party.

Irish Americans were somewhat divided over Redmond's politics. More radical Irish American nationalists—such as members of Clan na Gael, which itself was restructured under the leadership of John Devoy and Daniel Cohalan—distrusted him and dismissed his moderate home rule stance.[20] But in this they were out of step with the tone of American public life. Redmond, argued historian Bradford Perkins, was "very popular in the United States" and was supported by the most prominent Irish American congressman of the day, William Bourke Cockran.[21] With the help of American funds, the Irish Parliamentary Party was able to contest successive general elections and, following the elections of January and December 1910, it appeared to hold the balance in British politics once again. A third Home Rule Bill followed in April 1912, though its provision for anti–home rule Ulster was left vague. Few Americans would have disagreed with the *New York Times* when it expressed happy surprise that "after the hot contest that has raged for so many years the outcome should be so moderate, so fair, and so much in the nature of a compromise."[22]

In retrospect it is easy to overlook Redmond's success in favor of identifying the ascendant forces in Irish politics: cultural nationalism; the political development of Arthur Griffith's Sinn Féin movement; radical separatism; Patrick Pearse's itch for martyrdom. And, when one looks through the wrong end of the telescope, John Devoy and his more radical followers appear prescient in rejecting home rule in favor of complete national independence. But the storm that broke in 1912 owed very little indeed to the stalwart nationalism of a handful of Irish American activists and rather more to the fierce and increasingly militarized opposition of Ulster Unionists and their supporters within the British Tory Party.[23] In May 1914, the Home Rule Bill made it onto the statute books with the impasse of Ulster's status no closer to resolution. Ominously, both unionist Ulster Volunteers and nationalist Irish Volunteers engaged in drill practice and imported weapons.[24]

The transnational implications of the Ulster crisis deserve further exploration by historians. We know that William Jennings Bryan, who was appointed as Wilson's secretary of state in March 1913, did not have the surest grasp on the intricacies of British and Irish politics.[25] Wilson himself had no overwhelming sentiment in favor of Irish nationalism, and Irish American nationalists found it hard to break into the world of cordial Anglo-American diplomacy during his presidency.[26] His reaction to Ulster's obduracy was that Edward Carson, leader of the Ulster Unionist Party, "ought to be hanged for treason . . . [else] the contagion of unrest and rebellion in Ireland will spread until only a major operation will save the Empire."[27] As a devotee of Gladstone, Wilson supported Irish home rule, and he believed that the question of Irish governance ought to be settled peacefully within the rubric of British party politics.[28] Like Theodore Roosevelt, he was convinced that "there never can be real comradeship between America and England until this [Irish] issue is definitely settled and out of the way."[29]

Wilson's was perhaps a rather strong reaction to Carson's politics, although many Americans had little sympathy with Ulster intransigence.[30] Most likely his opinion was shaped by his views on secession and resistance to state authority in the U.S. context. But Wilson, Roosevelt, and others acted in a geopolitical environment in which the older existential anxieties about the security of the United States in a world dominated by British power no longer prevailed to the same extent. To them, the story of Irish American nationalism was one of failure; it was the liberal progressivism of Gladstone, Asquith, and Lloyd George that would shape future Anglo-American relations. The paradox of Irish American nationalist agency was that it demonstrated to statesmen on both sides of the Atlantic the virtues of limiting the political space in which it operated. The consequence of nationalist activity was not an independent Ireland or even an Ireland that enjoyed greater self-determination within the overarching structures of the British constitution. Instead, the fruits of Irish nationalist actions were Anglo-American comity with respect to citizenship and naturalization, greater codification of the duties of neutrality, and attempts to redefine extradition legislation. By the first decade of the twentieth century, transatlantic politics were decidedly less favorable to the kind of transnational nationalist movement that Irish Americans sought to build than they had been in the middle decades of the nineteenth century. Ironically, Irish American activism had been a significant factor in bringing about this change.

Hopes and Grievances

In Ireland, the First World War changed everything. Redmond's pledge in September 1914 that the Irish Volunteers would support the war effort wherever needed prompted a split between nationalists who saw the conflict as an opportunity to demonstrate that home rule was compatible with imperial loyalty and nationalists who considered it to be a British war that Ireland should have no part in.[31] In the United States, Irish Americans largely acquiesced to Wilson's neutral response to the conflict, though John Devoy and the Clan na Gael sought to make contact with German intermediaries with a view to further internationalizing Irish politics.[32] Wilson aroused little warmth among Irish Americans, be they Democrats or Republicans, but they, like the population at large, broadly supported U.S. neutrality.[33]

Wilson's response to British repression in the wake of the doomed Easter Rising did nothing to improve his reputation among Irish Americans. On April 24, 1916, a force of approximately 1,600 seized various strategically and symbolically important buildings in Dublin. Patrick Pearse, calling on the support of Ireland's "exiled children in America and [her] gallant allies in Europe," issued a proclamation declaring the "sovereign and indefeasible" right of the Irish people "to the ownership of Ireland and to the unfettered control of Irish destinies."[34] A week later, 450 people lay dead and the British had resumed control of the city. Though the rising itself provoked little sympathy in the United States, Irish Americans—and not just those of a more zealous nationalist persuasion—were dissatisfied with Wilson's failure to speak out against the British government's draconian response. (Wilson thought such intervention would be "inexcusable.")[35] Though the president secured reelection in 1916, he assumed that he had lost the Irish vote en masse as a result of both this and his heated condemnation of 'hyphenated' Americans during the election campaign.[36]

In April 1917, following months of deteriorating U.S.-German relations, Wilson addressed Congress to request a declaration of war.[37] Though the United States joined the war on the side of Great Britain, Irish American nationalists' hopes were fired by Wilson's speeches on the new international order that would be built in the conflict's aftermath.[38] Like the representatives of other "small nationalities," by 1918 they had come to see in Wilson's plans a window of opportunity. In his "Peace without Victory" address of January 1917, Wilson had argued that "no peace can last, or ought to last, which does not recognize and accept the principle that governments derive all their just powers from the consent of the governed."[39] Later, in February 1918, he spoke for the first time of the guiding principle of "self-determination" and argued that in any postwar settlement, "national aspirations must be respected."[40] Wilson's words prompted resolutions of support from Irish nationalists in both Ireland and the United States. Sinn Féin missives praised the president's "noble words regarding the rights of small nations," and John Devoy urged people to support Wilson and to lobby the president to get Ireland included in any postwar settlement.[41] These efforts were bolstered by the presence of republicans who had taken part in the 1916 uprising and who sought to hold Wilson to his rhetorical promises.[42]

Up to the armistice of November 1918, the Wilson administration successfully contained radical Irish American nationalist agitation. The wartime emphasis on public loyalty, the use of new Espionage and Sedition Acts, and the exposure of links between Irish American agitators and pro-German groups might have made the articulation of nationalist aspirations trickier, but at least one nationalist organizer was surprised at the relative absence of imprisonment and deportations.[43] The lack of repression notwithstanding, the administration gave free reign to British intelligence agents, who monitored the activities of both Clan na Gael and a newer organization, the Friends of Irish Freedom, which had been established in March 1916 to support "any movement that will tend to bring about the National Independence of Ireland."[44] Wilson combined such collaboration with conciliation: his speeches—and a January 1918 meeting with Sinn Féin activist Hanna Sheehy-Skeffington—implied that he was conscious of the need to address Irish nationalist aspirations when circumstances permitted.[45]

Wilson had no intention of pressing Irish claims to nationhood in the peace negotiations that commenced in Paris on January 12, 1919. He was prepared to raise Irish American concerns in an unofficial way both during and after the war, and he was sincere in his hope that Lloyd George's government would find some conciliatory home rule solution to the problem of Irish governance, but he was entirely candid when he assured Lloyd George that he "would not allow Ireland to be dragged into the Peace Conference."[46] What Wilson saw as key to the peace negotiations was not the adjustment of specific territorial claims but the development of international structures that would deal with these claims in the future. The establishment of the League of Nations was thus his primary concern, and discussion about its covenant dominated the early debates at the Paris conference.[47] It seemed to Wilson that Irish governance was a matter for deliberation at Westminster and that any formal discussion of an independent Ireland would alienate his British partners; Lloyd George was, after all, head of a coalition government that relied on Conservative unionist support.[48]

As the Paris Peace Conference met, however, Irish politics were radicalizing. A crisis over extending conscription to Ireland, the British reaction to the 1916 Easter Rising, and the rearrest of a number of leading republicans in May 1918 nourished the Sinn Féin movement.[49] The party triumphed at the British general election of December 1918, winning 73 of 101 seats (only 76 of which they contested). Rather than taking their seats at Westminster, Sinn Féiners who were not imprisoned met at Dublin on January 21, 1919, to declare Ireland independent and to establish a new Irish Parliament, the Dáil Éireann.[50] An Anglo–Irish war followed that was characterized by IRA guerrilla attacks and British military reprisals. Its escalation was slow but grisly. British actions alienated many and did much to bolster popular support for republican separatists.[51]

Promoters of Irish independence sought to keep Wilson true to the principles outlined in his speeches on the postwar settlement. As early as January 1918 the president of Sinn Féin, Éamon de Valera, gave a frank speech in Dublin in which he stated that "those who go about mouthing about self-determination" had to support an independent Ireland.[52] If they did not, "then they are hypocrites, and we tell President Wilson . . . if he does not take that view of it, he is as big a hypocrite as Lloyd George."[53] To focus political pressure on Wilson as the representative of aspiring nations at the Paris conference, Irish American nationalists staged mass meetings, petitioned the president, and designated the week before Wilson's departure for Europe "Self-Determination for Ireland Week."[54] In both Washington and Paris, Wilson was the recipient of repeated pleas for Ireland to have a hearing at the conference; none of these were successful.[55] In addition, Irish American nationalists made connections between their own ambitions and those of other national groups that lacked statehood. Daniel Cohalan, a leader of the Friends of Irish Freedom, drew on Wilsonian language to compare the Irish position with a wide variety of small European nationalities.[56] Finally, as historian Erez Manela notes, Irish American nationalists were particularly conspicuous amongst U.S. supporters of Indian and Egyptian self-determination.[57]

An alternative strategy was to focus on Congress. Prior to the opening of the Paris Peace Conference, numerous members of Congress presented resolutions requesting that the case for an independent Ireland be heard by the delegates in Paris.[58] From Wilson's point of view, the most troublesome was that brought forward by Thomas Gallagher of Illinois. Gallagher requested that the American delegation present "the right of Ireland to freedom, independence and self-determination" to the conference.[59] It took significant pressure from the White House to persuade the House Committee on Foreign Affairs not to report favorably on the resolution.[60] A diluted version that urged the conference to "favorably consider" Ireland's claims passed the House on March 4, 1919, just before Wilson's return to Europe after a brief stint in the United States.[61] Congressional pressure became an even more appealing strategy as the full provisions of the League of Nations covenant became known in the United States. Republicans who were alarmed at Wilson's concessions proved useful allies for groups such as the Friends of Irish Freedom, whose nationalist aspirations were not met by a final draft of the covenant that made no mention of the principle of self-determination.[62] Joining the anti–League of Nation forces in person was Éamon de Valera, who had arrived covertly in the United States in late June. His first public statement reads as a masterful piece of political cornering:

> I am in America as the official head of the Republic established by the will of the Irish people in accordance with the principle of self-determination. We shall fight for a real democratic League of Nations, not the present unholy alliance which does not fulfil the purposes for which the democracies of the world went to war. . . . I am sure that if [Wilson] is sincere, nothing will please him more than being pushed from behind by the people for this will show him that the people of America want the United States government to recognise the Republic of Ireland.[63]

Despite his attempts to remain above the partisan fray, De Valera's presence did much to stiffen the resolve of anti-treaty Republicans.[64] Furthermore, the escalation of the Anglo-Irish conflict greatly increased the attention being given to Irish matters, though it left Wilson unmoved.[65] As he toured the country seeking to promote his vision of the postwar world, the president attempted to characterize Irish American opposition as disloyal, much as he had during the war. In a speech in late September in Denver, Colorado, Wilson claimed that there was no opposition to the treaty "outside the people who tried to defeat the purpose of this government in the war," adding that "hyphens are the knives that are being stuck into this document."[66] The strain of campaigning severely affected the president's health, and he suffered a stroke the following night and a second, more debilitating stroke a week later, on October 2, 1919.[67] Even had his health held, Wilson might not have been able to broker the conclusion he sought to the covenant debates. In any event, the Senate struck down both the original covenant and a second, amended version that softened the obligation of the United States to intervene in international disputes.[68]

In his more contemplative moments Wilson dwelled on the bind his rhetoric of self-determination had created. En route to Paris in November 1918, he had confided to George Creel, head of the Committee on Public Information, that he feared that the dissemination of his speeches had "unconsciously spun a net" from which he would not be able to escape:

> It is to America that the whole world turns to-day, not only with its wrongs, but with its hopes and grievances. . . . People will endure tyrants for years, but they will tear their deliverers to pieces if a millennium is not created immediately. Yet you know, and I know, that these ancient wrongs . . . are not to be remedied in a day or with a wave of the hand. What I seem to see—with all my heart I hope that I am wrong—is a tragedy of disappointment.[69]

It was a view that he returned to when meeting with an Irish American delegation in Paris on June 11, 1919. When pushed on the rights of small nations and the applicability of his own rhetoric to the case of Ireland, Wilson conceded that the delegates had "touched on the great metaphysical tragedy of today":

> When I gave utterance to those words, I said them without the knowledge that nationalities existed, which are coming to us day after day. Ireland's

case . . . is the outstanding case of a small nationality. You do not know and
cannot appreciate the anxieties that I have experienced as a result of the
many millions of people having their hopes raised by what I have said.[70]

War, the Paris conference, and the subsequent contest over ratification
opened up a brief, novel space in which Irish American nationalists could
attempt to further internationalize their claims to statehood. Over time,
these nationalists became disillusioned with Wilson, and their dalliance
with Republican politicians was brief, if superficially, successful in terms
of preventing the United States from joining the League of Nations. With
the protracted defeat of the covenant—a final, amended formulation failed
to secure the necessary two-thirds vote in March 1920—few Republican
politicians were left with an abiding interest in the Irish question.[71] Irish
American nationalists had limited contact and even more limited leverage
with the administration of Warren G. Harding, who was elected in November 1920, though the Ohioan did cause a brief flurry of agitation when he
voiced his support for humanitarian aid for those suffering in Ireland as
a consequence of the Anglo-Irish conflict. His secretary of state, Charles
Evans Hughes, quickly assured his British counterparts that both he and
the president believed "that there must be no interference by the United
States in a purely British internal affair."[72] In this, if in little else, Harding
took a Wilsonian line.

Franklin Redivivus

The Irish Free State, established by the 1921 Anglo-Irish Treaty, finally secured formal recognition from the United States in October 1924.[73] The
Free State did not represent the complete consummation of Irish nationalist ambitions—one need only to look at the civil war that broke out over
the legitimacy of the new, pro-treaty provisional government for evidence
of this. But if, as Michael Collins noted in a neat formulation, the treaty
did not give Ireland the "ultimate freedom that all nations desire," it at least
gave Ireland "the freedom to achieve it."[74] Just over three years after formal
recognition, the first president of the Free State, William Cosgrave, visited
the United States. His address to Congress spoke of the "gratitude and
good-will" of the people of Ireland towards their American counterparts.[75]
He continued:

Benjamin Franklin in 1771 told the Irish people . . . that America's weight would be thrown in their scale in order that Irish and American liberty might be achieved. His promise has been nobly fulfilled. . . . Ireland's freedom has been obtained not merely by American advocacy of noble principles, but by the intense, devoted and constant support of the American people for the application of those principles to the Irish nation. . . . I come to thank the American people for the part they have played in the achievement of our liberty and I bear to them . . . a message of good-will and brotherly affection from the Irish people.[76]

Little in the tangled history of Irish American nationalism justified Cosgrave's claims. If anything, American sympathies with Irish separatism had declined over time as revolutionary republican sympathies gave way to contemplation of the United States' own "Irish question" in the late nineteenth century. In a pattern that late-twentieth-century observers might have recognized, insurgent Irish nationalism served over time to push the U.S. and British governments into negotiations on a range of contentious issues. Despite this, a largely autonomous Irish state had been conjured into being. Taken all together, that was a pretty surprising outcome.

Notes

Introduction

1 "Ireland," *New-York Daily Times* (later the *New York Times*), October 31, 1851.

2 Ibid.

3 "Meeting in Behalf of Smith O'Brien," *New-York Daily Times*, October 31, 1851.

4 See, for instance, the essays in *The New York Irish*, edited by Timothy J. Meagher and Ronald H. Bayor (Baltimore, MD: Johns Hopkins University Press, 1996); Joseph Lee and Marion R. Casey, eds., *Making the Irish American: History and Heritage of the Irish in the United States* (New York: New York University Press, 2006); David T. Gleeson, ed., *The Irish in the Atlantic World* (Columbia: University of South Carolina Press, 2010); and Kevin Kenny, ed., *New Directions in Irish-American History* (Madison: University of Wisconsin Press, 2003).

5 Roy Foster, *Modern Ireland, 1600–1972* (London: Penguin, 1989), 282–286; Brian Jenkins, *Irish Nationalism and the British State: From Repeal to Revolutionary Nationalism* (Montreal: McGill-Queen's University Press, 2006), 3–42.

6 Owen Dudley Edwards, "The American Image of Ireland: A Study of Its Early Phases," *Perspectives in American History* 4 (1970): 199–241.

7 "Address to the People of Ireland," July 28, 1775, in *Journals of the Continental Congress, 1774–1789*, 34 vols., edited by J. C. Fitzpatrick, W. C. Ford, and R. R. Hill (Washington, D.C.: Government Printing Office, 1904–37), 2:212–218; Edwards, "American Image of Ireland," 228–232; Foster, *Modern Ireland*, 241–258.

8 John Adams quoted in John Thaxter to the President of [the Continental] Congress, no. 34, April 4, 1780, The Adams Papers Digital Edition, edited by C. James Taylor, http://rotunda.upress.virginia.edu/founders/ADMS-06-09-02-0080 (accessed January 4, 2011).

9 Ibid.

10 David A. Wilson, *United Irishmen, United States: Immigrant Radicals in the Early Republic* (Ithaca, NY: Cornell University Press, 1998); Edwards, "American Image of Ireland," 241–255; Alan Taylor, *The Civil War of 1812: American Citizens, British Subjects, Irish Rebels, and Indian Allies* (New York: Alfred A. Knopf, 2010), 75–100; Michael Durey, *Transatlantic Radicals and the Early American Republic* (Lawrence: University of Kansas Press, 1997), chapters 4–7.

11 Uriah Tracy quoted in Wilson, *United Irishmen*, 1.

12 Foster, *Modern Ireland*, 296–302; Jenkins, *Irish Nationalism and the British State*, 29–35; Thomas F. Moriarty, "The Irish American Response to Catholic Emancipation," *Catholic Historical Review* 66, no. 3 (1980): 353–373.

13 Richard Davis, *The Young Ireland Movement* (Dublin: Gill and Macmillan, 1987); Jenkins, *Irish Nationalism and the British State*, 63–67.

14 Maurice O'Connell, "O'Connell, Young Ireland, and Negro Slavery: An Exercise in Romantic Nationalism," *Thought* 64 (1989): 130–136.

15 Edward L. Widmer, *Young America: The Flowering of Democracy in New York City* (New York: Oxford University Press, 1999).

16 See Roy Foster, *The Irish Story: Telling Tales and Making It Up in Ireland* (London: Penguin, 2002), esp. xi–xx, 1–22; Foster, *Modern Ireland*; Alan O'Day, "Irish Nationalism and Anglo-American Relations in the Late Nineteenth and Early Twentieth Centuries," in *Anglo-American Attitudes: From Revolution to Partnership*, edited by Fred M. Leventhal and Ronald Quinault (Aldershot: Ashgate, 2000), 168–194; R. V. Comerford, *The Fenians in Context: Irish Politics and Society, 1848–82* (Dublin: Wolfhound Press, 1998); Owen McGee, *The IRB: The Irish Republican Brotherhood, from the Land League to Sinn Féin* (Dublin: Four Courts Press, 2005); Oliver P. Rafferty, *The Church, the State, and the Fenian Threat, 1861–75* (Basingstoke: Palgrave Macmillan, 1999); and Marta Ramón, *A Provisional Dictator: James Stephens and the Fenian Movement* (Dublin: University College Dublin Press, 2007).

17 An incomplete initial draft with deletions and half of a final draft are extant in Seward's private papers. William Henry Seward to William Stokes, June 23, 1842, reel 26, in *The Papers of William H. Seward*, 198 reels (Woodbridge, CT: Research Publications, 1981) (hereafter *The Papers of William H. Seward*).

18 Ibid.

19 Ibid.

20 Richard Carwardine, *Evangelicals and Politics in Antebellum America* (New Haven, CT: Yale University Press, 1993), 209; Michael Feldberg, *The Philadelphia Riots of 1844: A Study of Ethnic Conflict* (Westport, CT: Greenwood Press, 1975).

21 Hereward Senior, *The Fenians and Canada* (Toronto: Macmillan of Canada, 1978), 24.

22 Christy Campbell, *Fenian Fire: The British Government Plot to Assassinate Queen Victoria* (London: HarperCollins, 2003), part 4.

23 David Noel Doyle, "The Remaking of Irish America, 1845–1880," in *Making the Irish American: History and Heritage of the Irish in the United States*, edited by Joseph Lee and Marion R. Casey (New York: New York University Press, 2006), 213–224; and Irene Whelan, "Religious Rivalry and the Making of Irish-American Identity," in ibid., 271–285.

24 Donal McCartney, "The Church and Fenianism," *University Review: A Journal of Irish Studies* 4, no. 3 (1967): 209.

25 Richard Franklin Bensel, *The American Ballot Box in the Mid-Nineteenth Century* (New York: Cambridge University Press, 2004), 289–290.

26 Daniel Walker Howe, *The Political Culture of the American Whigs* (Chicago: University of Chicago Press, 1979), 108–122, 137–139; Nicholas Onuf and Peter Onuf, *Nations, Markets, and*

War: Modern History and the American Civil War (Charlottesville: University of Virginia Press, 2006); and David C. Hendrickson, *Union, Nation, or Empire: The American Debate over International Relations, 1789–1941* (Lawrence: University Press of Kansas, 2009), 278–307.

27 See, for instance, Henry C. Carey, "British Free Trade in Ireland," *The Plough, the Loom, and the Anvil* (Philadelphia), September 1852; and, more generally, Henry C. Carey, *The Harmony of Interests, Agricultural, Manufacturing, and Commercial* (Philadelphia: J. S. Skinner, 1851). Carey wrote a series of articles on the subject in his journal *The Plough, the Loom, and the Anvil*.

28 Henry C. Carey, "The Way for Irishmen to Avenge Ireland," *The Plough, the Loom, and the Anvil*, May 1852.

29 Ibid.

30 William Henry Seward, *An Oration on the Death of Daniel O'Connell: Delivered at Castle Garden, New-York, September 22, 1847* (Auburn, NY: J. C. Derby & Co., 1847), 7.

31 "Interchange: The Global Lincoln," *Journal of American History* 96, no. 2 (2009): 479–480, 487–490 (contributions from Jay Sexton, Adam Smith, Vinay Lal, and Carolyn Boyd).

Chapter 1

1 Brian A. Jenkins, *Irish Nationalism and the British State: From Repeal to Revolutionary Nationalism* (Montreal: McGill-Queen's University Press, 2006), 35–40.

2 This section draws on R. V. Comerford, "O'Connell, Daniel (1775–1847)," *Oxford Dictionary of National Biography* (online edition, ed. Lawrence Goldman) (hereafter *Oxford Dictionary of National Biography*); Alvin Jackson, *Ireland 1798–1998: Politics and War* (Oxford: Blackwell, 1999), chapter 3; and Oliver MacDonagh, *The Emancipist: Daniel O'Connell, 1830–1847* (New York: St. Martin's Press, 1989), chapters 6–7.

3 Oliver MacDonagh, "Ambiguity in Nationalism: The Case of Ireland," *Australian Historical Studies* 19, no. 76 (1981): 341.

4 Though it seems fair to note, as historian Brian Jenkins does, that O'Connell's idealized Ireland would really have been ethnically exclusivist and unambiguously Catholic. Jenkins, *Irish Nationalism and the British State,* 43–46.

5 On the theorizing of a diasporic "Greater Ireland," see Adrian N. Mulligan, "A Forgotten 'Greater Ireland': The Transatlantic Development of Irish Nationalism," *Scottish Geographical Journal* 118, no. 3 (2002): 219–234.

6 David Noel Doyle, "The Irish in North America, 1776–1845," in *Making the Irish American: History and Heritage of the Irish in the United States*, edited by Joseph Lee and Marion R. Casey (New York: New York University Press, 2006), 201.

7 Nini Rodgers, *Ireland, Slavery and Anti-Slavery: 1612–1865* (Basingstoke: Palgrave Macmillan, 2007), 259.

8 O'Connell quoted in Angela Murphy, *American Slavery, Irish Freedom: Abolition, Immigrant Citizenship, and the Transatlantic Movement for Irish Repeal* (Baton Rouge: Louisiana State University Press, 2010), 33. See also Howard Temperley, "The O'Connell-Stevenson Contretemps: A Reflection of the Anglo-American Slavery Issue," *Journal of Negro History* 47, no. 4 (1962): 217–233.

9 Hershel Parker, *Herman Melville: A Biography*, 2 vols. (Baltimore, MD: Johns Hopkins University Press, 1996–2002): 1:318.

10 In 1845, this "eloquent Repealer" was, perhaps surprisingly, made secretary of the legation in London in recognition of his efforts on James Polk's behalf during the 1844 election. "Letters from America No. LIX," *Nation* (Dublin), November 1, 1845; Hershel Parker,

ed., *Gansevoort Melville's 1846 London Journal and Letters from England, 1845* (New York: Public Library, 1966), 7–14. Melville died in May 1846 at the age of 30.

11 George W. Potter, *To the Golden Door: The Story of the Irish in Ireland and America* (Boston: Little, Brown, 1960), 388–390; John F. Quinn, "The Rise and Fall of Repeal: Slavery and Irish Nationalism in Antebellum Philadelphia," *Pennsylvania Magazine of History and Biography* 130, no. 1 (2006): 52–53.

12 Lawrence J. McCaffrey, *The Irish Diaspora in America* (Bloomington: Indiana University Press, 1976), 112.

13 John O'Connell quoted in "Loyal National Repeal Association," *Nation* (Dublin), March 9, 1844.

14 Thomas Mooney, quoted in Doyle, "The Irish in North America, 1776–1845," 200.

15 Quotations from an October 1843 meeting of Albany repealers. The proceedings were printed as a pamphlet, *The Wrongs and Rights of Ireland*, that was distributed with the *Albany Democratic Recorder*, January 8, 1844. Quotation at p. 5; see also McCaffrey, *Irish Diaspora in America*, 138, 148.

16 The *Nation's* coverage detailed letters and remittances from the United States as they were read into the minutes at the Dublin meeting. Doyle, "The Irish in North America, 1776–1845," 200–201.

17 Angela Murphy, "Abolition, Irish Freedom, and Immigrant Citizenship: American Slavery and the Rise and Fall of American Associations for Irish Repeal" (PhD diss., University of Houston, 2006).

18 Kerby A. Miller, *Emigrants and Exiles: Ireland and the Irish Exodus to North America* (New York: Oxford University Press, 1985), 278.

19 Michael Feldberg, The *Philadelphia Riots of 1844: A Study of Ethnic Conflict* (Westport, CT: Greenwood Press, 1975), 28.

20 Lawrence J. McCaffrey, *Daniel O'Connell and the Repeal Year* (Lexington: University of Kentucky Press, 1966).

21 See, for instance, the account of a large-scale repeal meeting held in New York, reported in "Repeal the Union!" *Truth Teller* (New York), June 10, 1843, quote in same.

22 Miller, *Exiles and Emigrants*, 193–279.

23 Miller argues persuasively that various groups actively perpetuated the motif of exile, including Irish nationalists, the Catholic Church, and so on. That exile might be a politicized (and contested) construct should not, of course, obscure the fact that many migrants were victims of events far outside their control.

24 Though Jacksonian Democrats were strongly associated with anti-British rhetoric, in power the party was noticeably conciliatory in its relations with Great Britain. See John Belohlavek, *"Let the Eagle Soar!" The Foreign Policy of Andrew Jackson* (Lincoln: University of Nebraska Press, 1985), 54–73.

25 Duff Green to John C. Calhoun, August 2, 1843, in *The Papers of John C. Calhoun*, 28 vols., edited by Robert L. Meriwether et al. (Columbia: University of South Carolina Press, 1959–2003), 17:329 (hereafter *The Papers of John C. Calhoun*); John Quincy Adams quoted in Robert Kagan, *Dangerous Nation: America and the World, 1600–1898* (New York: Knopf, 2006), 220; Daniel Walker Howe, *What Hath God Wrought: The Transformation of America, 1815–1848* (New York: Oxford University Press, 2007), 677–678. Green was sincere in his portrayal of British designs, though he was largely mistaken. On the limits of British interest in Texas, see Leila M. Roeckell, "Bonds over Bondage: British Opposition to the Annexation of Texas," *Journal of the Early Republic* 19, no. 2 (1999): 257–278.

26 Edward B. Rugemer, "Robert Monroe Harrison, British Abolition, Southern Anglophobia and Texas Annexation," *Slavery and Abolition* 28, no. 2 (2007): 169–191; Steven Heath

Mitton, "The Upshur Inquiry: Lost Lessons of the Great Experiment," *Slavery and Abolition* 27, no. 1 (2006): 89–124.

27 Abel P. Upshur to Edward Everett, September 28, 1843, despatch no. 61, reel 74, *Diplomatic Instructions of the Department of State, 1801–1906*, 175 reels (Washington, D.C.: National Archives and Records Service, 1945–1946) (hereafter *Diplomatic Instructions of the Department of State*); Thomas Hietala, *Manifest Design: American Exceptionalism and Empire* (Ithaca, NY: Cornell University Press, 2003), 22–23. Upshur's despatch was accompanied by a private letter reaffirming his concern that the British ministry was driven by commercial imperatives to destroy American slavery.

28 "Speech of Robert Tyler," *Truth Teller*, September 16, 1843. Emphasis in original.

29 Ibid.

30 Howe, *What Hath God Wrought*, 588–594; Richard Carwardine, *Evangelicals and Politics in Antebellum America* (New Haven, CT: Yale University Press, 1993), 71.

31 Quinn, "The Rise and Fall of Repeal," 67–68.

32 *Truth Teller*, February 18, 1843, 16.

33 Doyle, "The Irish in North America, 1775–1845," 195.

34 *Truth Teller*, February 18, 1843, 16.

35 Sidney George Fisher, *A Philadelphia Perspective: The Diary of Sidney George Fisher Covering the Years, 1834–1871* (Philadelphia: Historical Society of Pennsylvania, 1967), 171.

36 Ibid.

37 John Tyler, quoted in Quinn, "The Rise and Fall of Repeal," 63.

38 Thomas P. Cope, diary entry for June 11, 1843, in *Philadelphia Merchant: The Diary of Thomas P. Cope, 1800–1851*, edited by Eliza Cope Harrison (South Bend, IN: Gateway Editions, 1978), 390.

39 George Bancroft to Martin Van Buren, October 1843, and Van Buren to Bancroft, July 24, 1843, in "Van Buren–Bancroft Correspondence, 1830–1845," *Proceedings of the Massachusetts Historical Society* 42 (October 1908–June 1909): 417, 412. Van Buren's correspondence suggests that it was his second attempt to address the issue. Most likely an earlier letter to the repealers of Massachusetts was too subtle to be of any real political value.

40 Van Buren to the Albany Repealers, December 27, 1843, in *The Wrongs and Rights of Ireland*, 15.

41 Van Buren had criticized Tyler's diplomacy on the Texas issue, though he suggested that he would accept annexation of Texas should the people strongly favor it.

42 Thomas Fitnam to John Calhoun, September 16, 1843, in Meriwether et al., *The Papers of John C. Calhoun*, 17:452.

43 Calhoun to Messrs. Emmitt, McNevin, and O'Connor of the Society of the Friendly Sons of St. Patrick of New York, March 1843, in Meriwether et al., *The Papers of John C. Calhoun*, 17:124; Andrew Jackson to Thomas Mooney, May 23, 1842, in *Niles' National Register* (Washington, D.C.), July 16, 1842.

44 Jackson to Mooney, May 23, 1842.

45 "Irish Repeal in Washington," *Liberator* (Boston), December 29, 1843, 1. Clay described Johnson as "extremely needy"; Henry Clay to John M. Berrien, September 22, 1843, in *The Papers of Henry Clay*, 11 vols., edited by James F. Hopkins et al. (Lexington: University of Kentucky, 1959–1992), 9:858 (hereafter *The Papers of Henry Clay*); Quinn, "The Rise and Fall of Repeal," 64; Philip Hone, diary entry for November 4, 1843, in *The Diary of Philip Hone, 1828–1851*, 2 vols., edited by Bayard Tuckerman (New York: Dodd, Mead, 1889), 2:199.

46 "Letters from America," *Truth Teller*, June 3, 1843; Owen Dudley Edwards, "The American Image of Ireland: A Study of Its Early Phases," *Perspectives in American History* 4 (1970): 199–282.

47 Ibid.

48 Ibid., 256–257; Doyle, "The Irish in North America," 202–203.

49 Carwardine, *Evangelicals and Politics*, 67, 209, 262; Doyle, "The Irish in North America," 199; Martin Meenagh, "Archbishop John Hughes and the New York Schools Controversy of 1840–43," *American Nineteenth Century History* 5, no. 1 (2004): 34–65; Glyndon G. Van Deusen, *William Henry Seward* (New York: Oxford University Press, 1967), 69–71.

50 John M. Taylor, *William Henry Seward: Lincoln's Right Hand* (Washington, D.C.: Brassey's, 1996), 31, 66.

51 George E. Baker, ed., *The Works of William H. Seward*, 4 vols. (New York: Redfield, 1853–1861), 1:xv.

52 Thurlow Weed to William Henry Seward, various letters, July 1843, reel 29, *The Papers of William H. Seward*.

53 Weed quoted in Edwards, "American Image of Ireland," 254.

54 Seward to Daniel O'Connell, March 31, 1842, reel 25, *The Papers of William H. Seward*.

55 Seward to Stokes et al., June 23, 1842, reel 26, *The Papers of William H. Seward*.

56 Ibid. On contemporary ambiguities in the racialization of the Irish, see Dale Knobel, *Paddy and the Republic: Ethnicity and Nationality in Antebellum America* (Middletown, CT: Wesleyan University Press, 1986).

57 Seward to William Cassidy and Matthew Jordan [incomplete], July 3, 1843, reel 29, *The Papers of William H. Seward*.

58 Ibid.

59 Clay to William Erigena Robinson, November 6, 1843, in Hopkins et al., *The Papers of Henry Clay*, 9: 883. Emphasis added.

60 George C. Collins, *Fifty Reasons Why the Honorable Henry Clay Should Be Elected President of the United States, by an Adopted Citizen* (Baltimore, MD: Printed for the author by "Murphy," 1844), 31, quoted in Carwardine, *Evangelicals and Politics*, 88.

61 Clay to Thomas Worthington, June 24, 1843, and Clay to Calvin Colton, September 2, 1843, in Hopkins et al., *The Papers of Henry Clay*, 9:828, 853.

62 The *New Orleans Bee* quoted in the *Daily Atlas* (Boston), March 31, 1842.

63 William Seward to William Cassidy and [first name unknown] Jordan, July 3, 1843, *The Papers of William H. Seward*.

64 Seward quoted in *The Wrongs and Rights of Ireland*, 12.

65 Thurlow Weed to William Seward, July 30, 1843, reel 29, *The Papers of William H. Seward*.

66 Edward Everett to Abel P. Upshur, August 28, 1843, despatch no. 51, reel 47, *Despatches from United States Ministers to Great Britain, 1791–1906*, 200 reels (Washington, D.C.: National Archives and Records Service, 1954) (hereafter cited as *Despatches from United States Ministers to Great Britain*).

67 "The Irish Repeal Question," *The United States Magazine, and Democratic Review* 13, no. 62 (1843): 115.

68 Seward quoted in *The Wrongs and Rights of Ireland*, 9.

69 *New York Herald* quoted in "The Repeal Agitation and Its Tendencies," *Truth Teller*, June 17, 1843.

70 Van Deusen, *William Henry Seward*, 65–67. On O'Connell, see Bruce Nelson, "'Come Out of Such a Land, You Irishmen': Daniel O'Connell, American Slavery, and the Making of the 'Irish Race,'" *Éire-Ireland* 42, nos. 1–2 (2007): 58–81; and Oliver MacDonagh, "O'Connell's Ideology," in *a Union of Multiple Identities: The British Isles, 1750–1950*, edited by Laurence W. B. Brockliss and David Eastwood (Manchester: Manchester University Press, 1997), 149.

71 Nelson, "'Come Out of Such a Land, You Irishmen,'" 63.

72 D. C. Riach, "Daniel O'Connell and American Anti-Slavery," *Irish Historical Studies* 20, no. 77 (1976): 5, 7, 12–13.

73 Garrison quoted in Caleb W. McDaniel, "Repealing Unions: American Abolitionists, Irish Repeal, and the Origins of Garrisonian Disunionism," *Journal of the Early Republic* 28, no. 2 (2008): 244.

74 Ibid., 246, 260–263; Gilbert Osofsky, "Abolitionists, Irish Immigrants, and the Dilemmas of Romantic Nationalism," *American Historical Review* 80, no. 4 (1975): 889–912.

75 *Liberator* (Boston), September 10, 1841, quoted in Osofsky, "Dilemmas of Romantic Nationalism," 898; Riach, "Daniel O'Connell," 10–12; R. J. M. Blackett, "'And There Shall Be No More Sea': William Lloyd Garrison and the Transatlantic Abolitionist Movement," in *William Lloyd Garrison at Two Hundred*, edited by James Brewer Stewart (New Haven, CT: Yale University Press, 2008), 25–27.

76 William Lloyd Garrison to George W. Benson, March 22, 1842, quoted in Osofsky, "Dilemmas of Romantic Nationalism," 900.

77 Ibid., 901; John F. Quinn, "'Three Cheers for the Abolitionist Pope!': American Reaction to Gregory XVI's Condemnation of the Slave Trade, 1840–1860," *Catholic Historical Review* 90, no. 1 (2004): 82–83.

78 See, for instance, the response of a meeting of Irish miners in Pottsville, Pennsylvania, described in Osofsky, "Dilemmas of Romantic Nationalism," 902.

79 Nelson, "'Come Out of Such a Land, You Irishmen,'" 66.

80 Riach, "Daniel O'Connell," 4.

81 Rodgers, *Ireland, Slavery and Anti-Slavery*, 270.

82 Ibid., 276–278.

83 Nelson, "'Come Out of Such a Land, You Irishmen,'" 68. O'Connell was prepared to accept the financial assistance of slaveholders, but he was not prepared to accept assistance that arrived accompanied by pro-slavery sentiments. Such parsing, as will be seen, was not welcomed by all members of the Dublin Loyal National Repeal Association.

84 Murphy, "Abolition, Irish Freedom, and Immigrant Citizenship," 154.

85 "Vote of Thanks to Mr. Tyler, Son of the President of the United States," *Nation* (Dublin), March 25, 1843.

86 James Haughton to the Editor, *Nation* (Dublin), March 1, 1845.

87 Nelson, "'Come Out of Such a Land, You Irishmen,'" 70.

88 Quinn, "Rise and Fall of Repeal," 46.

89 Murphy, "Abolition, Irish Freedom, and Immigrant Citizenship," 214–220.

90 Quinn, "Rise and Fall of Repeal," 65.

91 Ibid., 70; Murphy, "Abolition, Irish Freedom, and Immigrant Citizenship," 189. David Gleeson notes that the interest of southerners in Ireland increasingly existed independently of interest in Daniel O'Connell, likely a result of a practical dissociation of home rule and abolitionism. David T. Gleeson, *The Irish in the South, 1815–1877* (Chapel Hill: University of North Carolina Press, 2001), 131–132.

92 "Loyal National Repeal Association," *Nation* (Dublin), October 14, 1843; Murphy, "Abolition, Irish Freedom and Immigrant Citizenship," 235; Riach, "Daniel O'Connell," 15–17.

93 *Liberator* (Boston), November 10, 1843; Murphy, "Abolition, Irish Freedom, and Immigrant Citizenship," 262.

94 MacDonagh, *The Emancipist*, 238–240.

95 Robert Tyler to the Dublin LNRA, "American Remittances," *Nation* (Dublin), May 25, 1844. Tyler sent £200 with his letter. This equaled around $970 (somewhere between $20,000 and $25,000 in present-day terms). This and subsequent conversions calculated using Lawrence

H. Officer and Samuel H. Williamson, "Computing 'Real Value' over Time with a Conversion between U.K. Pounds and U.S. Dollars, 1830 to Present," Measuring Worth website, www. measuringworth.com (accessed April 15, 2013).

96 MacDonagh, *The Emancipist*, 262–265.

97 *New York Herald*, January 4, 1844, and New York *Journal of Commerce*, August 11, 1843, both cited in Murphy, "Abolition, Irish Freedom, and Immigrant Citizenship," 273–274, 269.

98 Feldberg, *Philadelphia Riots*, ix; Ray Allen Billington, *The Protestant Crusade 1800–1860: A Study of the Origins of American Nativism* (New York: Rinehart, 1938), 220–234; Carwardine, *Evangelicals and Politics*, 81–83; Cope, diary entries for February 26, May 7, and May 11, 1844, in Harrison, *Philadelphia Merchant*, 427, 437–440.

99 Carwardine, *Evangelicals and Politics*, 75–76, 85–87, quote at 76. The selection of Frelinghuysen mollified evangelical and anti-Catholic constituencies within the Whig Party.

100 Cope, diary entry for April 12, 1844, in Harrison, *Philadelphia Merchant*, 434.

101 Murphy, "Abolition, Irish Freedom, and Immigrant Citizenship," 276, 290–292; Carwardine, *Evangelicals and Politics*, 218; Billington, *Protestant Crusade*, 208–211.

102 Feldberg, *Philadelphia Riots*, 28.

103 John Hancock Lee, *The Origin and Progress of the American Party in Politics* (Philadelphia: Elliott & Gihon, 1855), 105. See also *The Truth Unveiled, or a Calm and Impartial Exposition of the Origin and Immediate Cause of the Terrible Riots in Philadelphia* (Philadelphia: M. Fithian, 1844), quoted in Philip H. Bagenal, *The American Irish and Their Influence on Irish Politics* (London: Kegan, Paul, Trench & Co., 1882), 50; Feldberg, *Philadelphia Riots*, 29.

104 "Lewis Charles Levin," Biographical Directory of the United States Congress, index at http://bioguide.congress.gov/biosearch/biosearch.asp (hereafter Biographical Directory of the United States Congress).

105 Potter, *To the Golden Door*, 419, 421; Lewis C. Levin, *A Lecture on Irish Repeal, in Elucidation of the Fallacy of Its Principles, and in Proof of Its Pernicious Tendency, in Its Moral, Religious, and Political Aspects* (Philadelphia: n.p., 1844).

106 Ibid., 7.

107 Ibid., 8.

108 Ibid.

109 Ibid.

110 Ibid., 7.

111 David R. Roediger, *The Wages of Whiteness: Race and the Making of the American Working Class* (London: Verso, 1991), 134–137; Theodore W. Allen, *The Invention of the White Race*, 2 vols. (London: Verso, 1994), 1:167–199.

112 Murphy, "Abolition, Irish Freedom, and Immigrant Citizenship," 292. The Boston Repeal Association, for instance, transmitted £1,000 (about $4,860) with the explicit purpose of underwriting the costs of O'Connell and his companions' defense; "Letters from America, No. XXXI," *Nation* (Dublin), June 1, 1844. The New York Repeal Association sent £2,000 (about $9,720); "Loyal National Repeal Association," *Nation* (Dublin), July 20, 1844.

113 O'Connell commented that slaveholders who sent money to Dublin for repeal "must love Ireland more than they loved slavery," because they could hardly be unaware of his own abolitionism. O'Connell quoted in Riach, "Daniel O'Connell," 14.

114 Edward Everett to Hugh Legaré, Acting Secretary of State, June 1, 1843, no. 40, reel 46, *Despatches from United States Ministers to Great Britain*.

115 Edward Everett to Abel P. Upshur, August 1, 1843, no. 49, reel 47, *Despatches from United States Ministers to Great Britain*.

116 Everett to Legaré, June 1, 1843.

117 W. Stephen Belko, *The Invincible Duff Green: Whig of the West* (Columbia: University of Missouri Press, 2006), 332–381.

118 Everett, diary entry for November 6, 1843, Diaries, 1825–1865, reel 37, Edward Everett Papers, Massachusetts Historical Society (hereafter Edward Everett Papers). Despite the concerns of southerners, Everett proved more than capable of protecting the interests of American slaveholders. See John O. Geiger, "A Scholar Meets John Bull: Edward Everett as United States Minister to England, 1841–1845," *New England Quarterly* 49, no. 4 (1976): 583–586.

119 Abel P. Upshur to John C. Calhoun, November 8, 1843, in Meriwether et al., *The Papers of John C. Calhoun*, 17:535.

120 Ibid.

121 Ibid.

122 Hietala, *Manifest Destiny*, 38.

123 Duff Green to John C. Calhoun, August 2, 1843, in Meriwether et al., *The Papers of John C. Calhoun*, 17:329.

124 Everett, diary entry for November 13, 1843, Diaries, 1825–1865, reel 37, Edward Everett Papers.

125 Duff Green to Abel P. Upshur, October 17, 1843, enclosed in Upshur to John C. Calhoun, November 30, 1843, in Meriwether et al., *The Papers of John C. Calhoun*, 17:575–578.

126 Duff Green to Abel P. Upshur, November 16, 1843, enclosed in Upshur to John C. Calhoun, November 18, 1843, in Meriwether et al., *The Papers of John C. Calhoun*, 17:549.

127 Duff Green to Abel P. Upshur, August 3, 1843, in Frederick Merk, *Slavery and the Annexation of Texas* (New York: Knopf, 1972), 224–225.

128 Ibid., 58–59.

129 Howe, *What Hath God Wrought*, 680.

130 Edward Everett to John C. Calhoun, August 19, 1844, despatch no. 181, reel 49, *Despatches from United States Ministers to Great Britain*.

131 John Hogan to John C. Calhoun, September 15, 1844, in Meriwether et al., *The Papers of John C. Calhoun*, 19:788.

132 Jenkins, *Irish Nationalism*, 71–72.

133 "The United States and Canada," *Nation* (Dublin), November 30, 1844.

134 "Letters from America, No. XXVI," *Nation* (Dublin), February 24, 1844.

135 Charles Gavan Duffy to Daniel O'Connell, October 18, 1844, in *Nation* (Dublin), October 19, 1844.

136 Hietala, *Manifest Design*, 47–54; Howe, *What Hath God Wrought*, 698–700.

137 James Haughton to the Editor, February 21, 1845, *Nation* (Dublin), March 1, 1845. Emphasis Haughton's.

138 Ibid.

139 James Haughton to Daniel O'Connell, January 29, 1845, in *The Correspondence of Daniel O'Connell*, 8 vols., edited by Maurice R. O'Connell (Dublin: Irish University Press, 1972–1977), 8:1845.

140 Daniel O'Connell to James Haughton, February 4, 1845, Gilder Lehrman Center for the Study of Slavery, Resistance, and Abolition, www.yale.edu/glc/archive/1117.htm (accessed December 28, 2009).

141 James K. Polk, "Inaugural Address," March 4, 1845, in *A Compilation of the Messages and Papers of the Presidents,* vol. 4, part 3, *James K. Polk, March 4, 1845 to March 4, 1849,* edited by James D. Richardson (Washington, D.C.: Government Printing Office, 1897), available at www.gutenberg.org/etext/12463 (accessed January 24, 2010); Murphy, "Abolition, Irish Freedom, and Immigrant Citizenship," 307.

142 *Liberator* (Boston), May 2, 1845, quoted in Nelson, "'Come Out of Such a Land, You Irishmen,'" 78; and Riach, "Daniel O'Connell," 19.

143 "Letters from America No. L," *Nation* (Dublin), February 15, 1845; "American Remittances," *Nation* (Dublin), February 22, 1845; Murphy, "Abolition, Irish Freedom, and Immigrant Citizenship," 309.

144 "Ireland's Neutrality," *Nation* (Dublin), April 5, 1845, and "America and England," *Nation* (Dublin), March 29, 1845.

145 "Ireland's Neutrality," *Nation* (Dublin), April 5, 1845; "Our First Triumph," *Nation* (Dublin), April 26, 1845.

146 "America and England," *Nation* (Dublin), March 29, 1845.

147 Nelson, "'Come Out of Such a Land, You Irishmen,'" 78–79; Noel Ignatiev, *How the Irish Became White* (New York: Routledge, 1995), 31. O'Connell was practicing multiple forms of self-delusion: there was little British appetite for intervention over Texas and there was little prospect that people of Irish descent in America (and perhaps even in Ireland) would take his prescriptions to heart.

148 Murphy, "Abolition, Irish Freedom, and Immigrant Citizenship," 300–324.

149 "Letters from America No. LIV," *Nation* (Dublin), June 21, 1845.

150 Ibid.

151 "Letters from America No. LV," *Nation* (Dublin), July 12, 1845.

152 Ignatiev, *How the Irish Became White*, 31.

153 Murphy, "Abolition, Irish Freedom, and Immigrant Citizenship," 317–321.

154 O'Connell quoted in ibid., 328.

155 Hietala, *Manifest Destiny*, 231–234; Louis McLane to John C. Calhoun, April 10, 1846, in Meriwether et al., *The Papers of John C. Calhoun*, 23:40. Emphasis McLane's.

156 Howe, *What Hath God Wrought*, 719–720. McLane reported home that the Peel ministry was making military preparations: Louis McLane to James Buchanan, January 3, 1846, no. 30, and McLane to Buchanan, February 3, 1846, no. 34, both reel 52, *Despatches from United States Ministers to Great Britain*.

157 Cong. Globe, 29th Cong., 1st Sess., January 6, 1846, 146. A Boston Whig newspaper described McConnell as "a drunken, profane bully and blackguard"; "The Congressional Blackguard," *Daily Atlas*, December 29, 1845.

158 Cong. Globe, 29th Cong., 1st Sess., January 6, 1846, 146. The idea was taken up by the Brooklyn Repeal Association, which was still meeting in January 1846 and was considering petitioning Congress for Ireland's admission to the Union. "Repeal! Oregon! Ireland a Nation, Not a Province," *Brooklyn Daily Eagle*, January 19, 1846.

159 Cong. Globe, 29th Cong, 1st Sess., January 6, 1846, 146.

160 Ibid., 146–147.

161 "Loyal National Repeal Association," *Nation* (Dublin), February 7, 1846.

Chapter 2

1 James S. Donnelly Jr., *The Great Irish Potato Famine* (Stroud: Sutton, 2005), 41.

2 Kerby A. Miller, *Emigrants and Exiles: Ireland and the Irish Exodus to North America* (New York: Oxford University Press, 1985), 284.

3 Donnelly, *Great Irish Potato Famine*, 41; David A. Wilson, *Thomas D'Arcy McGee*, 2 vols. (Montreal: McGill-Queen's University Press, 2008–2011), 1:97.

4 The Irish population increased from around 2.6 million to 8.5 million between 1750 and 1845. Donnelly, *Great Irish Potato Famine*, 1–4, 42; Roy F. Foster, *Modern Ireland 1600–1972* (London: Penguin, 1989), 319–320; Brian A. Jenkins, *Irish Nationalism and the British State: From Repeal to Revolutionary Nationalism* (Montreal: McGill-Queen's University Press, 2006), 147–150.

5 Donnelly, *Great Irish Potato Famine*, 1.

6 Boston *Pilot*, November 1845, quoted in George W. Potter, *To the Golden Door: The Story of the Irish in Ireland and America* (Boston: Little, Brown, 1960), 451.

7 Potter, *To the Golden Door*, 455.

8 Ibid.

9 Donnelly, *Great Irish Potato Famine*, 44–47.

10 Foster, *Modern Ireland*, 320; Miller, *Emigrants and Exiles*, 281; Donnelly, *Great Irish Potato Famine*, 9.

11 Timothy J. Sarbaugh, "A Moral Spectacle: American Relief and the Famine, 1845–1849," *Éire-Ireland* 15, no. 4 (1980): 10.

12 Foster, *Modern Ireland*, 325–326; Miller, *Emigrants and Exiles*, 283–284; Donnelly, *Great Irish Potato Famine*, 44–56.

13 Frederick Merk, "The British Corn Crisis of 1845–46 and the Oregon Treaty," in Merk, *The Oregon Question: Essays in Anglo-American Diplomacy and Politics* (Cambridge, MA: Belknap Press of Harvard University Press, 1967), 312; Jay Sexton, *Debtor Diplomacy: Finance and American Foreign Relations in the Civil War Era, 1837–1873* (Oxford: Oxford University Press, 2005), 51; Donnelly, *Great Irish Potato Famine*, 49.

14 Miller, *Emigrants and Exiles*, 281–284, quote at 284.

15 Robin F. Haines, *Charles Trevelyan and the Great Famine* (Dublin: Four Courts Press, 2004), chapters 2–6.

16 Donnelly, *Great Irish Potato Famine*, 16–22.

17 James Henry McBoyd to James Buchanan, September 3, 1846, no. 2, reel 52, *Despatches from United States Ministers to Great Britain*.

18 Sean Wilentz, *The Rise of American Democracy: Jefferson to Lincoln* (New York: Norton, 2005), 579–580.

19 Louis McLane to James Buchanan, February 3, 1846, no. 34, reel 52, *Despatches from United States Ministers to Great Britain*.

20 Merk, "The British Corn Crisis," 309–336. The Oregon question was settled in June 1846, well before the more serious contraction in the supply of food that fall.

21 Bancroft replaced McLane in the summer of 1846. George Bancroft to James Buchanan, November 3, 1846, no. 1, reel 53, *Despatches from United States Ministers to Great Britain*; Timothy J. Sarbaugh, "'Charity Begins at Home': The United States Government and Irish Famine Relief 1845–1849," *History Ireland*, 4, no. 2 (1996): 31; Lilian Handlin, *George Bancroft: The Intellectual as Democrat* (New York: Harper & Row, 1984), 223–224.

22 Gilpin served as consul at Belfast from July 1845 to his death in January 1848. Sarbaugh, "'Charity Begins at Home'," 31–32; James Buchanan to Louis McLane, July 23, 1845, no. 3, reel 74, *Instructions* to *Diplomatic Instructions of the Department of State*; John Romeyn Brodhead to James Buchanan, January 11, 1848, unnumbered, reel 54, *Despatches from United States Ministers to Great Britain*.

23 George Bancroft to James Buchanan, November 3, 1846, no. 1, reel 53, *Despatches from United States Ministers to Great Britain*.

24 On the Jeffersonian lineage of such thought, see Drew R. McCoy, *The Elusive Republic: Political Economy in Jeffersonian America* (New York: Norton, 1982).

25 Senate Doc. No. 2, 29th Cong., 2nd Sess., December 9, 1846, *United States Congressional Serial Set* (Washington, D.C.: Government Printing Office, 1817–), 8–12, quote at 12 (hereafter *United States Congressional Serial Set*).

26 James Hamilton Jr. to John C. Calhoun, August 12, 1846, in Meriwether et al., *The Papers of John C. Calhoun*, 23:407.

27 "Practical Annexation of England," *The United States Magazine, and Democratic Review* 19, no. 97 (1846): 3–14, quote at 14.

28 George Bancroft to James Buchanan, May 3, 1847, no. 25, reel 53, *Despatches from United States Ministers to Great Britain*.

29 Miller, *Exiles and Emigrants*, 292; Foster, *Modern Ireland*, 353; Oliver MacDonagh, "The Irish Famine Emigration to the United States," *Perspectives in American History* 10 (1976): 394–395; Asenath Nicholson, *Annals of the Famine in Ireland, in 1847, 1848, and 1849* (New York: E. French, 1851), 69. On remittances more generally, see Gary B. Magee and Andrew S. Thompson, *Empire and Globalisation: Networks of People, Goods and Capital in the British World, c. 1850–1914* (Cambridge: Cambridge University Press, 2010), 64–116. Migration was also funded, on occasion, by Irish landowners eager to wed humanitarianism and reduced poor relief. See Tyler Anbinder, "From Famine to Five Points: Lord Lansdowne's Irish Tenants Encounter North America's Most Notorious Slum," *American Historical Review* 107, no. 2 (2002): 351–387.

30 MacDonagh, "Irish Famine Emigration," 394–395; Miller, *Emigrants and Exiles*, 293, citing Arnold Schrier, *Ireland and the American Emigration, 1850–1900* (Minneapolis: University of Minnesota Press, 1958), 167. These are contemporary figures. The conversion has been estimated using Lawrence H. Officer and Samuel H. Williamson, "Computing 'Real Value' over Time with a Conversion between U.K. Pounds and U.S. Dollars, 1830 to Present," Measuring Worth website, www.measuringworth.com (accessed April 18, 2013).

31 Miller, *Emigrants and Exiles*, 291.

32 William S. Balch, *Ireland, as I Saw It: The Character, Condition, and Prospects of the People* (New York: G. P. Putnam, 1850), 49–50.

33 John C. Calhoun, "Speech on the War with Mexico," January 4, 1848, in Meriwether et al., *The Papers of John C. Calhoun*, 25:78.

34 George Bancroft to James Buchanan, March 3, 1847, no. 22, reel 53, *Despatches from United States Ministers to Great Britain*.

35 Ibid.

36 George Bancroft to James Buchanan, February 3, 1847, no. 18, reel 53, *Despatches from United States Ministers to Great Britain*.

37 George Bancroft to James Buchanan, February 3, 1847, George Bancroft Papers, Massachusetts Historical Society (hereafter George Bancroft Papers).

38 George Bancroft to James Buchanan, January 4, 1847, no. 11, reel 53, *Despatches from United States Ministers to Great Britain*.

39 Ibid.

40 George Bancroft to James Buchanan, March 29, 1847, no. 23, reel 53, *Despatches from United States Ministers to Great Britain*.

41 Ibid.

42 George Bancroft to James Buchanan, February 3, 1847, George Bancroft Papers.

43 Ibid. Thomas Mooney reported that he had met with President Polk, who assured him that "he and his cabinet take her [Ireland's] discontent into account when penning their instructions to their Ambassadors at the Court of St. James." Even if this conversation did actually take place—it is plausible, given Polk's open door policy for White House visitors—neither Polk nor Mooney elaborated on its particular implications. *Nation* (Dublin), February 7, 1846.

44 George Bancroft to James Buchanan, March 3, 1847, no. 22, reel 53, *Despatches from United States Ministers to Great Britain.*

45 Benjamin Goluboff, "'Latent Preparedness': Allusions in American Travel Literature on Britain," *American Studies* 31, no. 1 (1990): 65–82; Margaret Kelleher, "The Female Gaze: Asenath Nicholson's Famine Narrative," in *"Fearful Realities": New Perspectives on the Famine,* edited by Chris Morash and Richard Hayes (Dublin: Irish Academic Press, 1996), 119; Jenkins, *Irish Nationalism and the British State,* 76.

46 Gilbert Selds, "Open Your Mouth and Shut Your Eyes," *North American Review* 225, no. 842 (1928): 425–434; Henry Cludr, "The Late Asenath Nicholson," *Water-Cure Journal* (August 1855); Kelleher, "Female Gaze," 121–122.

47 Maureen Murphy, "Introduction," in Asenath Nicholson, *Annals of the Famine in Ireland,* edited by Maureen Murphy (1851; repr., Dublin: Lilliput Press, 1998), 5.

48 Murphy, "Introduction," 10–11; Kelleher, "Female Gaze," 121. On Irish immigrants in Five Points, see Tyler Anbinder, *Five Points: The 19th-Century New York City Neighborhood That Invented Tap Dance, Stole Elections, and Became the World's Most Notorious Slum* (New York: Plume, 2001); and Anbinder, "From Famine to Five Points," 351–387.

49 Asenath Nicholson, *Lights and Shades of Ireland. In Three Parts* (London: Charles Gilpin, 1850); Nicholson, *Annals of the Famine in Ireland.*

50 Nicholson, *Annals of the Famine in Ireland,* 14–15, 60, 140–143, 152–154, 171.

51 Ibid., 56–57. In this, Nicholson foreshadowed the later and infamous thesis put forward by John Mitchel that "the Almighty, indeed, sent the potato blight, but the English created the famine." John Mitchel, *The Last Conquest of Ireland (Perhaps)* (Glasgow: Cameron & Ferguson, 1876), 219. See also Murphy, "Introduction," 14.

52 Balch had served in Providence, Rhode Island, and had embraced the anti-Catholic politics of that state's Dorr Rebellion in 1841–1842. Indeed, in March 1842 he went so far as to issue a pamphlet warning of the dangers of Catholic immigrants holding the balance of power in Rhode Island politics. Peter Hughes, "William Balch," Dictionary of Unitarian and Universalist Biography, www25.uua.org/uuhs/duub/articles/williamstevensbalch.html (accessed January 24, 2011); Mark S. Schantz, *Piety in Providence: Class Dimensions of Religious Experience in Antebellum Rhode Island* (Ithaca, NY: Cornell University Press: 2000), 200–202; Wilentz, *Rise of American Democracy,* 539–545; William S. Balch, *Native American Citizens: Read and Take Warning!* [broadside], n. d. ("March 1842" penciled in margin), Rider Collection, John Hay Library, Brown University, Rhode Island.

53 Balch, *Ireland, as I Saw It,* 9.

54 Ibid., 36, 103, 168, 182, 290, 352.

55 Nicholson, *Annals of the Famine in Ireland,* 154–155.

56 "Great Meeting for the Relief of Ireland," *Daily National Intelligencer* (Washington, D.C.), February 11, 1847.

57 "Distress in Ireland," *Daily Atlas* (Boston), February 13, 1847, and February 18, 1847.

58 Oliver MacDonagh, *A Pattern of Government Growth: The Passenger Acts and Their Enforcement* (London: MacGibbon and Kee, 1961), 186.

59 Sarbaugh, "Moral Spectacle," 8; Foster, *Modern Ireland,* 329.

60 *Transactions of the Central Relief Committee of the Society of Friends during the Famine in Ireland, in 1846 and 1847* (Dublin: Hodges and Smith, 1852); Rodgers, *Ireland, Slavery and Anti-Slavery,* 287–288.

61 In the midst of relief efforts, one leading Philadelphia Friend confided in his diary that "the Catholics are generally . . . an ignorant, blighted, idle race." Thomas P. Cope, diary entry for January 31, 1847, in *Philadelphia Merchant: The Diary of Thomas P. Cope, 1800–1851,* edited by Eliza Cope Harrison (South Bend, IN: Gateway Editions, 1978), 526.

62 On the growing institutional assertiveness of the Catholic Church in the late 1840s and early 1850s, whose numbers were swelled by migrants fleeing the famine, see Jenkins, *Irish Nationalism and the British State*, 235.

63 Jacob Harvey to Jonathan Pim, December 28, 1846, in *Transactions of the Central Relief Committee of the Society of Friends*, 217.

64 Merle Curti, *American Philanthropy Abroad: A History* (New Brunswick, NJ: Rutgers University Press, 1963), 41–42.

65 Jonathan Pim to Jacob Harvey, December 3, 1846, in *Transactions of the Central Relief Committee of the Society of Friends*, 216.

66 Ibid., 218.

67 Jacob Harvey to Jonathan Pim, January 5, 1847, in *Transactions of the Central Relief Committee of the Society of Friends*, 219–220.

68 Cope, reporting on a letter from Jacob Harvey to him in his diary entry for March 15, 1847, in Harrison, *Philadelphia Merchant*, 529.

69 Jenkins, *Irish Nationalism and the British State*, 79. Conversions via Officer and Williamson, "Computing 'Real Value' over Time," www.measuringworth.com (accessed April 23, 2013). Such conversions are inevitably somewhat imprecise.

70 William Lloyd Garrison to the Central Relief Committee, Dublin, February 26, 1847, in *Transactions of the Central Relief Committee of the Society of Friends*, 234.

71 Nicholson, *Annals of the Famine in Ireland*, 53–54.

72 John Francis Maguire, *The Irish in America* (1868; repr., New York: Arno Press, 1969), 313.

73 Miller, *Emigrants and Exiles*, 284.

74 Nicholson, *Annals of the Famine in Ireland*, 54.

75 *Transactions of the Central Relief Committee of the Society of Friends*, 334.

76 *National Era* (Washington, D.C.), February 18, 1847, printed in ibid., 224.

77 Sir Richard Pakenham to Lord Palmerston, February 12, 1847, no. 12, FO 5/469, Public Record Office, National Archives, London (hereafter PRO).

78 Daniel Webster, E. A. Hannegan, Orville Dewey, Edward Curtis, and W. E. Robinson on behalf of the Washington meeting to the Society of Friends at Dublin[?], February 10, 1847, in *Transactions of the Central Relief Committee of the Society of Friends*, 226–227.

79 *National Era*, February 18, 1847, in *Transactions of the Central Relief Committee of the Society of Friends*, 225–226.

80 Ibid., 224–227.

81 "The Wail of Ireland," *North American* (Philadelphia), February 20, 1847.

82 See Pakenham's correspondence with the British Foreign Office for January and February 1847, FO 5/469, PRO.

83 James Adger, H. W. Conner, and Alexander Robinson to the Dublin Central Relief Committee, February 19, 1847 and February 23, 1847, in *Transactions of the Central Relief Committee of the Society of Friends*, 231.

84 *Distress in Ireland: Extracts from Sundry Reports* (Charleston: Burges & James, 1847), 30–31

85 David T. Gleeson, *The Irish in the South, 1815–1877* (Chapel Hill: University of North Carolina Press, 2001), 65–66; *Distress in Ireland*, 31–33.

86 Sarbaugh, "Moral Spectacle," 10.

87 Ibid., 11.

88 Ibid.

89 Cong. Globe, 29th Cong., 2nd Sess., February 25, 1847, 511.

90 Sarbaugh, "Moral Spectacle," 11. On Venezuela, see Curti, *American Philanthropy Abroad*, 10–13; and Cong. Globe, 29th Cong., 2nd Sess., February 26, 1847, 512.

91 Ibid.

92 Ibid., 533.

93 Cong. Globe, 29th Cong., 2nd Sess., February 27, 1847, 534–535.

94 Sarbaugh, "Moral Spectacle," 12.

95 Ibid., 12–13, quote at 13. The Democrats held a commanding majority in the House; there were only three Whigs on the nine-member Ways and Means Committee.

96 Some Whigs used the term *Locofoco* in a derogatory fashion to refer to Democrats. The term originally referred to a radical faction of the New York Democracy. "National Relief for Ireland," *North American* (Philadelphia), March 4, 1847.

97 Sarbaugh, "Moral Spectacle," 13.

98 Polk, diary entry for March 3, 1847, in *The Diary of James K. Polk during His Presidency, 1845 to 1849*, 4 vols., edited by Milo Milton Quaife (Chicago: A. C. McClurg, 1910), 2:397–398.

99 Polk's veto message for the Irish and Scottish relief bill, March 3, 1847, reel 60, *James K. Polk Papers* (Washington, D.C.: Library of Congress, 1964). Highland Scotland suffered from the same potato blight as Ireland, with similar consequences. The proposed U.S. relief bill encompassed distress in both areas.

100 Ibid.

101 Ibid.

102 Frederick M. Binder, *James Buchanan and the American Empire* (Selinsgrove, PA: Susquehanna University Press, 1994), 87–90. For instance, Polk was annoyed by Buchanan's reticence about offering a clear opinion on the proposed negotiation of the Oregon boundary with Great Britain in June 1846 because he was afraid of alienating pro-expansionist northerners.

103 Buchanan's draft of a veto message for the Irish and Scottish relief bill, March 3, 1847, reel 60, *James K. Polk Papers*.

104 Robert Bennet Forbes, *The Voyage of the Jamestown on Her Errand of Mercy* (Boston: Eastburn's Press, 1847), 7.

105 John Fairfield, a Democrat from Maine, quoted in Sarbaugh, "Moral Spectacle," 14; Cong. Globe, 29th Cong., 2nd Sess., Mach 3, 1847, 572.

106 William Lloyd Garrison to the Central Relief Committee, Dublin, February 26, 1847, in *Transactions of the Central Relief Committee of the Society of Friends*, 234–235.

107 For instance, Robert Bennet Forbes to Joshua Bates, February 27, 1847, Robert Bennet Forbes Papers, Massachusetts Historical Society, Box 2, Folder 2 (hereafter Robert Bennet Forbes Papers); Forbes to William Rathbone, November 14, 1847, Box 2, Folder 13, Robert Bennet Forbes Papers.

108 John Young Mason to Robert Bennet Forbes, March 8, 1847 and March 10, 1847, Box 2, Folder 2, Robert Bennet Forbes Papers; Forbes to Bates, February 27, 1847.

109 Edward Everett to Henry Labouchere, Chief Secretary for Ireland, March 26, 1847, Box 2, Folder 6, Robert Bennet Forbes Papers; Forbes, *Voyage of the Jamestown*, 8; Robert Bennet Forbes to Launcelot Dent, "18 1/2 days out" [April 15, 1847?], Robert Bennet Forbes Letterbook, Boston Athenaeum (hereafter Forbes Letterbook); Forbes, speech to the Irish Charitable Society, Boston, March 17, 1848, Box 2, Folder 3, Robert Bennet Forbes Papers. Interestingly, the *Macedonian* had been captured from the British during the War of 1812. Richard Pakenham felt the need to assure Lord Palmerston that no slight was intended by the selection of this vessel. It was chosen simply because almost all the other ships available were likely to be required in the prosecution of the Mexican-American War. Sir Richard Pakenham to Lord Palmerston, March 4, 1847, despatch no. 21, FO 5/469, PRO.

110 Robert Bennet Forbes to William Rathbone, March 11, 1847, Robert Bennet Forbes Papers; Forbes to Dent, "18 1/2 days out."

111 Robert Bennet Forbes to "John," April 20, 1847, Forbes Letterbook; Forbes, *Voyage of the Jamestown*, 20–21.

112 Forbes, *Voyage of the Jamestown*, xl–xli.

113 Michael P. Quinlin, *Irish Boston* (Guildford: Globe Pequot Press, 2004), 54–55.

114 Robert Bennet Forbes to M. Perkins, April 17, 1847, Forbes Letterbook; Forbes to "John." Father Mathew was the leader of a major temperance movement in Ireland in the 1830s and 1840s. In 1849, he traveled to the United States, where he was received by both Congress and President Zachary Taylor. See John F. Quinn, *Father Mathew's Crusade: Temperance in Nineteenth-Century Ireland and Irish America* (Amherst: University of Massachusetts Press, 2002).

115 As in, for instance, Bancroft's intercession to ensure the effective distribution of aid from New Orleans and Natchez; George Bancroft to "Crossman" et al., May 1, 1847; George Bancroft to Lord Kildare, July 13, 1847; George Bancroft to A. Fisk, July 29, 1847, all George Bancroft Papers.

116 Edward Everett to Robert Bennet Forbes, March 26, 1847, Robert Bennet Forbes Papers.

117 Robert Bennet Forbes to Emma Forbes, 11 days out from Boston [April 8, 1847], Robert Bennet Forbes Papers.

118 Alexander Gordon, "Rathbone, William (1757–1809)," rev. M. W. Kirby, *Oxford Dictionary of National Biography*.

119 Susan Pedersen, "Rathbone, William (1819–1902)," *Oxford Dictionary of National Biography*.

120 Bates was a key mediating figure in Anglo-American diplomacy. Sexton, *Debtor Diplomacy*, 20–69; Forbes to Bates, February 27, 1847; Forbes to Bates, March 11, 1847, Robert Bennet Forbes Papers.

121 Robert Bennet Forbes to William Rathbone, March 11, 1847; Forbes to Rathbone, April 17, 1847; Forbes to Charles Edward Trevelyan, April 22, 1847, all in Robert Bennet Forbes Papers.

122 George Bancroft to Robert Bennet Forbes, April 19, 1847, Robert Bennet Forbes Papers; Forbes, *Voyage of the Jamestown*, 9–10. The *HMS Crocodile* under Rear Admiral Sir Hugh Pigot was allocated to expedite the *Jamestown*'s visit.

123 Central Relief Committee Secretary to Jacob Harvey, May 16, 1847, in *Transactions of the Central Relief Committee of the Society of Friends*, 291.

124 A Brooklyn relief meeting worried that the Irish would waste money on politicking, Philadelphia philanthropist Thomas Cope worried that they would spend it on firearms, and Frederick Douglass worried that that they would drink it away in whiskey. Cope, diary entry for January 31, 1847, in Harrison, *Philadelphia Merchant*, 526; Douglass to Garrison, February 26, 1846, in *The Life and Writings of Frederick Douglass*, 5 vols., edited by Philip S. Foner (New York: International Publishers, 1950), 1:138–139; "Enthusiastic Meeting for the Relief of Ireland," *Brooklyn Daily Eagle*, February 27, 1847.

125 M. Van Schiack et al., the Irish Relief Committee of New York, to the Dublin Committee, February 24, 1847, in *Transactions of the Central Relief Committee of the Society of Friends*, 222–223.

126 J. [or S.?] Wilkinson to Pakenham, February 26, 1847, enclosed in Sir Richard Pakenham to Lord Palmerston, March 6, 1847, despatch no. 23, FO 5/469, PRO; Charles Trevelyan to Elihu Burritt and James Warren, enclosed in same; Trevelyan to William Rathbone, April 9, 1847, and April 12, 1847, in Forbes, *Voyage of the Jamestown*, ci–ciii; Cope, diary entry for March 4, 1847, in Harrison, *Philadelphia Merchant*, 528.

127 Lord Palmerston to Sir Richard Pakenham, appended to Pakenham to Palmerston, February 12, 1847, despatch no. 12, FO 5/469, PRO.

128 John Russell to William Rathbone, April 10, 1847, Robert Bennet Forbes Papers.

129 George Bancroft to James Buchanan, March 29, 1847, no. 23, reel 53, *Despatches from United States Ministers to Great Britain*. See also George Bancroft to Robert Bennet Forbes, April 19, 1847, Robert Bennet Forbes Papers.

130 George Bancroft to Robert Bennet Forbes, April 19, 1847, Robert Bennet Forbes Papers.

131 Sarah Mytton Maury to John C. Calhoun, February 18, 1847, in Meriwether et al., *The Papers of John C. Calhoun*, 24:164.

132 Lord Palmerston's note, appended to Sir Richard Pakenham to Palmerston, February 12, 1847, despatch no. 12, FO 5/469, PRO. Privately Pakenham had expressed his belief that philanthropy was more welcome when expressed through private donations than it would be as a national gift from the United States. Pakenham to Palmerston, February 25, 1847, despatch no. 14, FO 5/469, PRO.

133 Lord Bessborough's views communicated via the under-secretary for Ireland, Thomas Redington, to Robert Bennet Forbes, April 14, 1847, Robert Bennet Forbes Papers.

134 Reginald Horsman, *Race and Manifest Destiny: The Origins of American Racial Anglo-Saxonism* (Cambridge, MA: Harvard University Press, 1981), 116–157.

135 Ralph Waldo Emerson, "The Anglo-American," 1853 lecture, quoted in Nell Irvin Painter, "Ralph Waldo Emerson's Saxons," *Journal of American History* 95, no. 4 (2009): 982; Horsman, *Race and Manifest Destiny*, 160–162.

136 Thomas Hart Benton quoted in Horsman, *Race and Manifest Destiny*, 164; see also Horsman, *Race and Manifest Destiny*, 250–253.

137 Ibid., 292–293.

138 Lawrence quoted in ibid., 292. Emphasis Lawrence's.

139 Forbes, *Voyage of the Jamestown*, 10–20.

140 Address of the Citizens of Cork to Robert Bennet Forbes, [April 17, 1847], Robert Bennet Forbes Papers. Emphasis added.

141 Address of the Tenant League of Cork, April 17, 1847, Robert Bennet Forbes Papers. Emphasis in original.

142 Robert Bennet Forbes to W. H. Trenwith, April 17, 1847, in Forbes, *Voyage of the Jamestown*, lxxvii–lxxviii. On Trenwith, see Thomas P. O'Neill, "From Famine to Near Famine 1845–1879," *Studia Hibernica* 1 (1961): 161–171.

143 Forbes to Trenwith, April 17, 1847.

144 Ibid.

145 Robert Sloan, *William Smith O'Brien and the Young Ireland Rebellion of 1848* (Dublin: Four Courts, 2000), 180–181. O'Connell died in May 1847 while on a pilgrimage to Rome.

146 Robert Bennet Forbes to Thomas Francis Meagher, April 21, 1847, Robert Bennet Forbes Papers. Emphasis in original.

147 Forbes, Address to the Irish Charitable Society, [Boston?], March 17, 1848, Robert Bennet Forbes Papers.

148 Edward Everett to George Bancroft, May 31, 1847, George Bancroft Papers.

149 Ibid.

150 Forbes, *Voyage of the Jamestown*, 21.

151 Ibid.

152 "Repeal! Repeal!" *Brooklyn Daily Eagle*, March 7, 1846; Kathleen Neils Conzen, *Immigrant Milwaukee 1836–1860: Accommodation and Community in a Frontier City* (Cambridge, MA: Harvard University Press, 1976), 171.

153 "Enthusiastic Meeting for the Relief of Ireland," *Brooklyn Daily Eagle*, February 27, 1847.

154 "Great Meeting in Aid," *North American* (Philadelphia), February 18, 1847.

155 Balch, *Ireland, as I Saw It,* 88.

156 Ibid.

157 Ibid.

158 "On the Relief Sent to Ireland," *Daily National Intelligencer,* June 24, 1847.

159 "Arrival of the 'Jamestown' at Cork," *Arkansas State Democrat,* May 28, 1847.

160 "On the Relief Sent to Ireland," *Daily National Intelligencer,* June 24, 1847.

161 "Duke of Bessborough," *New York Herald,* July 4, 1847.

162 Quoted in Miller, *Emigrants and Exiles,* 284.

163 *Nation* (Dublin), April 3, 1847, cited in "The Effects of American Sympathy in Ireland," *Tri-Weekly Flag & Advertiser* (Montgomery, AL), May 4, 1847.

164 William Smith O'Brien, Thomas Francis Meagher, and Richard O'Gorman to George Dallas, "Gratitude of Ireland," *Mississippi Free Trader and Natchez Gazette,* May 11, 1847.

165 Balch, *Ireland, as I Saw It,* 47–49, 52. Asenath Nicholson reported a similar experience in *Annals of the Famine in Ireland,* 71.

166 James Haughton quoted in Maurice R. O'Connell, "O'Connell, Young Ireland, and Negro Slavery," 135; James Haughton to Henry C. Wright, July 15, 1847, in "Letters from Henry C. Wright," *Liberator* (Boston), August 6, 1847.

167 "Great Meeting," *Daily Atlas* (Boston), February 19, 1847.

168 Cope, diary entry for April 1, 1847, in Harrison, *Philadelphia Merchant,* 530.

169 "The Wail of Ireland," *North American* (Philadelphia), February 20, 1847.

170 "The Jamestown at Cork," *New-Hampshire Statesman and State Journal,* May 14, 1847.

171 "Speech in Lexington, Kentucky," November 13, 1847, in Hopkins et al., *The Papers of Henry Clay,* 10:361.

172 Ibid.; David C. Hendrickson, *Union, Nation, or Empire: The American Debate over International Relations, 1789–1941* (Lawrence: University Press of Kansas, 2009), 180–181.

173 "Speech on the War with Mexico," January 4, 1848, in Meriwether et al., *The Papers of John C. Calhoun,* 25:75. Hendrickson, *Union, Nation, or Empire,* 182–183.

174 Balch, *Ireland, as I Saw It,* 9.

175 Nicholson, *Annals of the Famine in Ireland,* 154.

176 Balch, *Ireland, as I Saw It,* 9; Cong. Globe, 29th Cong., 2nd Sess., February 27, 1847, 534.

177 Foster, *Modern Ireland,* 316; Miller, *Emigrants and Exiles,* 309–310.

178 Gavan Duffy also ended up in Britain's antipodean colonies, though not as an exile. Acquitted at trials in 1848 and 1849, he ultimately emigrated to Australia in 1855, where he entered politics and rose to become premier of Victoria in 1871.

179 Ibid., 310–344; Jenkins, *Irish Nationalism and the British State,* 84, 89, 140–142, 218–224, 255–286.

180 George Bancroft to James Buchanan, September 8, 1848, no. 85, and August 4, 1848, no. 83, both reel 54, *Despatches from United States Ministers to Great Britain.*

181 Balch, *Ireland, as I Saw It,* 102–103, 273; Nicholson, *Annals of the Famine in Ireland,* 134–135.

182 Everett, speech at Faneuil Hall reported in "Grain for Ireland," *Vermont Chronicle* (Bellows Falls), March 3, 1847.

183 "England," November 12, 1851; "Depopulation of Great Britain," November 28, 1851; "The Depopulation of Ireland," November 28, 1851, all *New-York Daily Times.* The population of the United States did indeed overtake that of Great Britain at the beginning of the decade.

Martin Crawford, *The Anglo-American Crisis of the Mid-Nineteenth Century: The Times and America, 1850–1862* (Athens: University of Georgia, 1987), 7.

184 Balch, *Ireland, as I Saw It,* 75–76, 139.

185 Sloan, *William Smith O'Brien and the Young Ireland Rebellion,* 284–296.

186 Daniel Webster to Abbott Lawrence, December 26, 1851, Abbott Lawrence Papers, Houghton Library, Harvard University, Cambridge, Massachusetts (hereafter Abbott Lawrence Papers).

187 *The Papers of Daniel Webster,* series 3, *Diplomatic Papers,* 2 vols., edited by Kenneth E. Shewmaker (Lebanon, NH: University Press of New England, 1983–1987), 2:124–126; Webster to Lawrence, December 26, 1851.

188 Wilson, *Thomas D'Arcy McGee,* 274.

189 Hendrickson, *Union, Nation, or Empire,* 185–191; Michael A. Morrison, "American Reaction to European Revolution, 1848–1852: Sectionalism, Memory and the Revolutionary Heritage," *Civil War History* 49, no. 2 (2003): 111–132; Daniel Webster to Abbott Lawrence, December 26, 1851, and December 29, 1851, Abbott Lawrence Papers. On Kossuth's visit, see David S. Spencer, *Louis Kossuth and Young America: A Study of Sectionalism and Foreign Policy, 1848–1852* (Columbia: University of Missouri Press, 1977).

190 Abbott Lawrence to John M. Clayton, October 11, 1849, no. 2, reel 56, *Despatches from United States Ministers to Great Britain.*

191 Abbott Lawrence to John M. Clayton, May 3, 1850, Abbott Lawrence Papers.

192 Abbott Lawrence to John M. Clayton, May 17, 1850, Abbott Lawrence Papers. Lawrence, like Webster, was prone to racialize Anglo-American relations in terms of a shared Anglo-Saxonism. See Sexton, *Debtor Diplomacy,* 55–56.

193 Abbott Lawrence to Daniel Webster, February 15, 1852; Lawrence to Fillmore, March 4, 1852; Abbott Lawrence to Daniel Webster, March 19, 1852, all Abbott Lawrence Papers.

194 Abbott Lawrence to Daniel Webster, January 14, 1852, Abbott Lawrence Papers; Cong. Globe, 32nd Cong., 1st Sess., January 28, 1852, 408.

195 Hamilton Fish quoted in William E. Gienapp, *The Origins of the Republican Party, 1852–1856* (New York: Oxford University Press, 1987), 14.

196 Cong. Globe, 32nd Cong., 1st Sess., December 2, 1851, 11.

197 Cong. Globe, 32nd Cong., 1st Sess., January 29, 1852, 418.

198 Ibid.; Cong. Globe, 32nd Cong., 1st Sess., February 7, 1852, appendix, 177.

199 Ibid., 177–178.

200 Ibid.

201 Ibid., 179. Shields is also notable for his dismissal of "this drivel about races," which he felt obfuscated the serious political (and moral) dimensions of Anglo-American relations. See Horsman, *Race and Manifest Destiny,* 262.

202 Abbott Lawrence to Daniel Webster, January 15, 1852, Abbott Lawrence Papers.

203 Abbott Lawrence to Daniel Webster, February 17, 1852; Lawrence to Fillmore, March 4, 1852; Abbott Lawrence to Daniel Webster, March 19, 1852, all in Abbott Lawrence Papers.

204 Abbott Lawrence to Daniel Webster, April 23, 1852, Abbott Lawrence Papers. As it transpired, Derby was correct.

205 The Clayton-Bulwer Treaty (1850), The Avalon Project: Documents in Law, History and Diplomacy, http://avalon.law.yale.edu/19th_century/br1850.asp (accessed March 18, 2010).

206 Abbott Lawrence to Daniel Webster, December 2, 1851, no. 144, reel 59, *Despatches from United States Ministers to Great Britain.*

207 Ibid. Galway eventually received a subsidy for a transatlantic packet line in 1859. Jenkins, *Irish Nationalism and the British State,* 119.

Chapter 3

1 In the antebellum United States, the word *filibustering* referred to people who "raised or participated in private military forces that either invaded or planned to invade foreign countries with which the United States was formally at peace." Robert E. May, *Manifest Destiny's Underworld: Filibustering in Antebellum America* (Chapel Hill: University of North Carolina Press, 2002), xi.

2 Jenkins, *Irish Nationalism and the British State: From Repeal to Revolutionary Nationalism* (Montreal: McGill-Queen's University Press, 2006) 94; John Belchem, "Republican Spirit and Military Science: The 'Irish Brigade' and Irish-American Nationalism in 1848," *Irish Historical Studies* 29, no. 113 (1994): 46; David A. Wilson, *Thomas D'Arcy McGee*, 2 vols. (Montreal: McGill-Queen's University Press, 2008–2011), 1:227.

3 Timothy Mason Roberts, *Distant Revolutions: 1848 and the Challenge to American Exceptionalism* (Charlottesville: University of Virginia Press, 2009), 25–27; May, *Manifest Destiny's Underworld*, 1–58.

4 Belchem, "Republican Spirit," 46–49; David T. Gleeson, *The Irish in the South, 1815–1877* (Chapel Hill: University of North Carolina Press, 2001), 69.

5 Belchem, "Republican Spirit," 49, 56–57; Jenkins, *Irish Nationalism and the British State*, 217–218, 254; W[illiam?] Kent to Hamilton Fish, Hamilton Fish Papers, folder 30, Library of Congress Manuscript Division, Washington, D.C. (hereafter Hamilton Fish Papers). Greeley had previously been a member of the Brooklyn Repeal Association; "City Intelligence," *Brooklyn Daily Eagle*, April 6, 1846.

6 Alan Taylor, *The Civil War of 1812: American Citizens, British Subjects, Irish Rebels, and Indian Allies* (New York: Alfred A. Knopf, 2010), 354; Wilson, *Thomas D'Arcy McGee*, 1:248.

7 Kerby A. Miller, *Emigrants and Exiles: Ireland and the Irish Exodus to North America* (New York: Oxford University Press, 1985), 334–335; Thomas Brown, *Irish-American Nationalism, 1870–1890* (Philadelphia: Lippincott, 1966), 19–24; Belchem, "Republican Spirit," 63.

8 Wilson, *Thomas D'Arcy McGee*, 1:228–229.

9 Joseph Denieffe, *A Personal Narrative of the Irish Revolutionary Brotherhood* (1906; repr., Shannon: Irish University Press, 1969), v.

10 Wilson, *Thomas D'Arcy McGee*, 1:215–229.

11 David Noel Doyle, "The Remaking of Irish America, 1845–1880," in *Making the Irish American: History and Heritage of the Irish in the United States*, edited by Joseph Lee and Marion R. Casey (New York: New York University Press, 2006), 212–216, 220–224. Doyle notes that even without the famine, the booming U.S. economy would have led to a considerable increase in the population of Irish America, though "on a less imposing scale and with a less dramatic transition" (215–216).

12 Ibid., 218.

13 McGee quoted in Wilson, *Thomas D'Arcy McGee*, 1:223.

14 Jenkins, *Irish Nationalism and the British State*, 84–87, 128–129.

15 Miller, *Emigrants and Exiles*, 335; Jenkins, *Irish Nationalism and the British State*, 218–219.

16 Jenkins, *Irish Nationalism and the British State*, 221.

17 Miller, *Emigrants and Exiles*, 280–344; Jenkins, *Irish Nationalism and the British State*, 206–209, 218; Laurence Fenton, "Charles Rowcroft, Irish-Americans, and the 'Recruitment Affair,' 1855–1856," *Historical Journal* 53, no. 4 (2010): 973; Cian McMahon, "Ireland and the Birth of the Irish-American Press, 1842–1861," *American Periodicals* 19, no. 1 (2009): 9–18; and William Leonard Joyce, *Editors and Ethnicity: A History of the Irish-American Press, 1848–1883* (New York: Arno Press, 1976), 74–93.

18 For the tensions between 1848 exiles and the Catholic Church, see Jenkins, *Irish Nationalism and the British State*, 55–67, 80–81.

19 Ibid., 98–101.

20 John Hughes, "The Tyrant and His Famine," cited in ibid., 210; see also 209–212.

21 John Hughes, "Speech at the Meeting for the Independence of Ireland," in *Complete Works of the Most Rev. John Hughes, D.D.*, 2 vols., edited by Lawrence Kehoe (New York: Richardson & Son, 1864), 2:791.

22 Richard Carwardine, *Evangelicals and Politics in Antebellum America* (New Haven, CT: Yale University Press, 1993), 199–207; and, more generally, Tyler Anbinder, *Nativism and Slavery: The Northern Know Nothings and the Politics of the 1850s* (New York: Oxford University Press, 1992), 3–126.

23 This thesis is most forcefully developed by Thomas Brown, though he focuses on a later period; *Irish-American Nationalism, 1870–1890* (Philadelphia: Lippincott, 1966). See also Jenkins, *Irish Nationalism and the British State*, 239–243, 247; and Oliver P. Rafferty, *The Church, the State, and the Fenian Threat, 1861–75* (Basingstoke: Palgrave, 1999), 52–53.

24 R. J. M. Blackett, *Building an Antislavery Wall: Black Americans in the Atlantic Abolitionist Movement, 1830–1860* (Baton Rouge: Louisiana State University Press, 1983); Van Gosse, "'As a Nation, the English Are Our Friends': The Emergence of African American Politics in the British Atlantic World, 1772–1861," *American Historical Review* 113, no. 4 (2008): 1003–1028; and Nini Rodgers, *Ireland, Slavery, and Anti-Slavery: 1612–1865* (Basingstoke: Palgrave, 2007), 281–286. An equivalence between American slavery and the Irish nation was a "well-established tradition in Irish patriotic discourse"; Pauline Collombier-Lakeman, "Ireland and the Empire: The Ambivalences of Irish Constitutional Nationalism," *Radical History Review* 104 (Spring 2009): 60.

25 For an excellent summary of those structures and their significance in mediating (though not eliminating) Anglo-American tensions, see Crawford, *Anglo-American Crisis*, 3–11.

26 Frederick Douglass, "Slavery and the Slave Power," speech delivered December 1, 1850, in *The Frederick Douglass Papers*, Series 1, *Speeches, Debates, and Interviews*, 5 vols., edited by John W. Blassingame (New Haven, CT: Yale University Press, 1979–1992), 2:258–259. Douglass attacked John Mitchel as a "traitor to humanity" for his outspoken support of slavery and his Irish sympathies cooled through the 1850s; *The Frederick Douglass Papers*, 2:486n; Rodgers, *Ireland, Slavery, and Anti-Slavery*, 285.

27 On Douglass and the Irish, see Richard Hardack, "The Slavery of Romanism: The Casting Out of the Irish in the Work of Frederick Douglass," in *Liberating Sojourn: Frederick Douglass & Transatlantic Reform*, edited by Alan J. Rice and Martin Crawford (Athens: University of Georgia Press, 1999), 115–140.

28 Sarah Mytton Maury to John Calhoun, August 15, 1858, in *The Papers of John C. Calhoun*, 28 vols., edited by Robert L. Meriwether et al. (Columbia: University of South Carolina Press, 1959–2003), 26:4.

29 Mitchel was invited to speak at numerous places in the South in his first few months in the United States. John Mitchel, *Jail Journal* (1854; repr., London: Sphere, 1983), 370–371, 376–378; Gleeson, *Irish in the South*, 70; Bryan McGovern, "John Mitchel: Ecumenical Nationalist in the Old South," *New Hibernia Review* 5, no. 2 (2001): 100; David T. Gleeson, "Securing the 'Interests' of the South: John Mitchel, A. G. Magrath, and the Reopening of the Transatlantic Slave Trade," *American Nineteenth Century History* 11, no. 3 (2010): 282–283.

30 Wilson, *Thomas D'Arcy McGee*, 1:317. Quotation from Mitchel, *Jail Journal*, 379. Mitchel agreed to become the Paris-based financial agent of the Fenian Brotherhood in November 1865; John O'Mahony to Mitchel, November 10, 1865, Fenian Brotherhood Collection, available via the American Catholic History Research Center and University Archives, The Catholic

University of America, www.aladin0.wrlc.org/gsdl/collect/fenian/fenian.shtml (accessed April 29, 2010). Hereafter Fenian Brotherhood Collection.

31 On the origins of the Irish Republican and Fenian Brotherhoods, see Owen McGee, *The IRB: The Irish Republican Brotherhood, from the Land League to Sinn Féin* (Dublin: Four Courts Press, 2005), 15–33; and Marta Ramón, *A Provisional Dictator: James Stephens and the Fenian Movement* (Dublin: University College Dublin Press, 2007), 70–75, 83–97.

32 Charles Rowcroft to John Crampton, January 5, 1856, telegram enclosed in Crampton to Lord Clarendon, January 14, 1856, despatch no. 8, FO 5/640, PRO. The incident is sometimes mentioned in passing in accounts of Irish American nationalism. See, for instance, Oliver Mac-Donagh, *States of Mind: A Study of the Anglo-Irish Conflict, 1780–1980* (London: Allen & Unwin, 1983), 81–82; Jenkins, *Irish Nationalism and the British State*, 257; and Brown, *Irish American Nationalism*, 28. It features a little more heavily in Fenton, "Charles Rowcroft, Irish-Americans, and the 'Recruitment Affair,'" 963–982.

33 A Robert Emmet Club, "a social organization," had been formed in Cincinnati in 1848. It isn't clear whether the two associations were related. Steven J. Ross, *Workers on the Edge: Work, Leisure, and Politics in Industrializing Cincinnati, 1788–1890* (New York: Columbia University Press, 1985), 178.

34 James M. McPherson, *Battle Cry of Freedom: The Civil War Era* (New York: Oxford University Press, 1988), 145–146; Ramón, *Provisional Dictator*, 64. On the use of "emigration" as a mask for filibustering, see May, *Manifest Destiny's Underworld*, 153–154. See also David Murphy, *Ireland and the Crimean War* (Dublin: Four Courts Press, 2002), 10–11.

35 "Letter from Robert Tyler," *New-York Daily Times*, December 15, 1855.

36 Ibid. Emphasis in original.

37 Fenton, "Charles Rowcroft, Irish-Americans, and the 'Recruitment Affair,'" 966–967; Lawrence to Rufus King, June 17, 1852, Abbott Lawrence Papers.

38 Details on arrests taken from *United States vs. W. G. Halpin, David Reidy, Edward Kenifeck, Samuel Lumsden, et al.: Charged with Conspiracy for Exciting Insurrection in Ireland* (Cincinnati: Moore, Wilstach, Keys & Overend, 1856) (hereafter *U.S. vs. Halpin*); Fenton, "Charles Rowcroft, Irish-Americans, and the 'Recruitment Affair,'" 977.

39 *U.S. vs. Halpin*, 20.

40 Samuel Lumsden to Robert Tyler, December 27, 1855, Box 4, Folder 3, Tyler Family Papers, Earl Gregg Swem Library, College of William and Mary, Williamsburg, Virginia (hereafter Tyler Family Papers).

41 Rowcroft to Crampton, January 5, 1856; Peter Michael Toner, "The Rise of Irish Nationalism in Canada, 1858–1884" (PhD diss., National University of Ireland, 1974), 17–19. In total, nineteen men were held for trial by the authorities in Cincinnati: William G. Halpin, John Kinney, Joseph W. Burke, Edward Kenifeck, Samuel Lumsden, William Lumsden, John M. C. MacGroarty, Thomas Hite, Thomas Heath, Bartholomew O'Keefe, David Reidy, Michael Noonan, Daniel Campbell, Thomas Tiernan, James Murphy, James Kelly, James O'Halloran, Owen B. Farley, and a man named Russell, first name unknown. An account of the trial—the account principally relied upon here—was published in 1856. Records are scant, as much of Cincinnati's municipal and criminal records were burned in a courthouse fire in 1884. See Nikki M. Taylor, *Frontiers of Freedom: Cincinnati's Black Community, 1802–1868* (Athens: Ohio University Press, 2005), 6–7.

42 *U.S. vs. Halpin*, 11–28.

43 Ibid., 3, 14. *William's Cincinnati Directory, City Guide, and Business Mirror, or Cincinnati in 1856* (Cincinnati: C. S. Williams, 1856), 184. Barber was born at Omagh, County Tyrone, and was brought up as a Presbyterian. According to his testimony, he came to the United States in

1845 and was naturalized as a U.S. citizen in Boston. He claimed to have been a member of the American Protestant Association for the previous eighteen months. *U.S. vs. Halpin*, 25.

44 Ibid., 28. On Irish Protestants and the APA, see Cecil J. Houston and William J. Smyth, "Transferred Loyalties: Orangeism in the United States and Ontario," *American Review of Canadian Studies* 14, no. 2 (1984): 206–207.

45 James E. Lewis, *The American Union and the Problem of Neighborhood: The United States and the Collapse of the Spanish Empire, 1783–1829* (Chapel Hill: University of North Carolina Press, 1998), 108–109.

46 "An Act in Addition to the 'Act for the Punishment of Certain Crimes against the United States' and to Repeal the Acts Therein Mentioned (a)," 15th Cong., 1st Sess., 1818, chapter 88, in *The Public Statutes at Large of the United States of America*, vol. 3 (Boston: Charles C. Little and James Brown, 1850), 449.

47 *U.S. vs. Halpin*, 55–56; Foster, *Modern Ireland*, 264–282.

48 *U.S. vs. Halpin*, 20–21, 84–93. Barber was described by the prosecution as an "overzealous Protestant," though with the best of intentions (84). Rowcroft was convinced that Ohio's Roman Catholic hierarchy was implicated in the filibuster's designs, particularly Archbishop Purcell. Rowcroft to Lord Clarendon, August 4, 1855, no. 20, FO 5/629, PRO. See also Fenton, "Charles Rowcroft, Irish-Americans, and the 'Recruitment Affair,'" 974.

49 Ross, *Workers on the Edge*, 163–192, esp. 178–179.

50 Ibid., 67–68; Taylor, *Frontiers of Freedom*, 19–21.

51 Ibid.; Ross, *Workers on the Edge*, 72–74.

52 Fenton, "Charles Rowcroft, Irish-Americans, and the 'Recruitment Affair,'" 970.

53 Taylor, *Frontiers of Freedom*, 23–24.

54 Stephen Middleton, "The Fugitive Slave Crisis in Cincinnati, 1850–1860: Resistance, Enforcement, and Black Refugees," *Journal of Negro History* 72, nos. 1–2 (1987): 9.

55 William E. Gienapp, "Salmon P. Chase, Nativism, and the Formation of the Republican Party in Ohio," *Ohio History* 93 (Winter–Spring 1984): 21.

56 *U.S. vs. Halpin*, 44, 83.

57 Taylor, *Frontiers of Freedom*, 25–26.

58 *U.S. vs. Halpin*, 14–16, 19.

59 Ibid., 26–27, 89.

60 John Crampton to Lord Clarendon, October 14, 1855, no. 216, and October 21, 1855, no. 222, FO 5/639, and Crampton to Clarendon, January 28, 1856, no. 12, FO 5/640, all PRO; and Caleb Cushing to B. F. Hallett and Hugh Q. Jewett, December 8, 1855, in *Official Opinions of the Attorneys General of the United States: Advising the President and Heads of Departments, in Relation to their Official Duties* (Washington, D.C.: Dept. of Justice, 1873–), 8:472–473.

61 *U.S. vs. Halpin*, 11.

62 Pierce had offered tacit endorsement to filibusters and would-be expansionists in his inaugural address, stating that the administration "would not be controlled by any timid forebodings of evil from expansion." Franklin Pierce, "Inaugural Address," March 4, 1853, The American Presidency Project, www.presidency.ucsb.edu/ws/index.php?pid=25816#axzz1FwajiJqS (accessed March 7, 2011); *U.S. vs. Halpin*, 86.

63 Ibid., 74–75. Probasco's claim that naturalized Irishmen were "no longer subjects of England" was not technically correct. The British doctrine of perpetual allegiance dictated that there was no legal right of expatriation. This was not modified by the British Parliament until 1870, in large part as a consequence of the Fenian agitation of the mid-1860s. See chapter 4.

64 *U.S. vs. Halpin*, 86.

65 Crampton quoted in Edward L. Widmer, *Young America: The Flowering of Democracy in New York City* (New York: Oxford University Press, 1999), 194; May, *Manifest Destiny's Underworld*, 218–219.

66 Arthur James May, "Contemporary American Opinion of the Mid-Century Revolutions in Central Europe" (PhD diss., University of Pennsylvania, 1927), 116–118.

67 Fenton, "Charles Rowcroft, Irish-Americans, and the 'Recruitment Affair,'" 978.

68 Trevor Royle, *Crimea: The Great Crimean War 1854–1856* (London: Little, Brown, 1999), 367.

69 Fenton, "Charles Rowcroft, Irish-Americans, and the 'Recruitment Affair,'" 967–968, quote at 967.

70 Charles Rowcroft to Lord Clarendon, July 11, 1855, no. 17, FO 5/629, PRO.

71 Charles Rowcroft to Lord Clarendon, August 4, 1855, no. 20, FO 5/629, PRO.

72 Fenton, "Charles Rowcroft, Irish-Americans, and the 'Recruitment Affair,'" 965; Olive Anderson, "Early Experiences of Manpower Problems in an Industrial Society at War: Great Britain, 1854–1855," *Political Science Quarterly* 82, no. 4 (1967): 541–542; Royle, *Crimean War*, 365–369; Mitchel, *Jail Journal*, 373–374.

73 Fenton, "Charles Rowcroft, Irish-Americans, and the 'Recruitment Affair,'" 966–968.

74 Rowcroft's trial was repeatedly postponed until the British government revoked his credentials as consul in May 1856. Charles Rowcroft to Clarendon, July 17, 1855, no number, FO 5/629; *U.S. vs. Halpin*, 145; "Violation of the Neutrality Laws," *New-York Daily Times*, July 18, 1855.

75 *U.S. vs. Halpin*, 70.

76 Leavitt had served as a congressman from 1830 to 1834, when he was appointed as a U.S. judge for the District of Ohio. "Humphrey Howe Leavitt," Biographical Directory of the United States Congress.

77 *U.S. vs. Halpin*, 101–102.

78 J. J. Berne, testimony, ibid., 41–42, my italics.

79 Ibid., 42.

80 Ibid., 95.

81 Ibid.

82 Ibid., 66.

83 Ibid., 71. On the links between Irish and abolitionist disunionism, see chapter 1.

84 Ibid., 66–67.

85 Caleb Cushing to William Marcy, December 2, 1856, in *Official Opinions of the Attorneys General of the United States*, 8:216.

86 *U.S. vs. Halpin*, 87.

87 Ibid., 24.

88 Robert E. May, *The Southern Dream of a Caribbean Empire, 1854–1861* (Gainesville: University Press of Florida, 2002), 65–67.

89 John Crampton to Lord Clarendon, February 11, 1856, no. 27, FO 5/640, PRO.

90 Samuel Lumsden to Robert Tyler, January 13, 1856, Box 4, Folder 4, Tyler Family Papers.

91 Ramón, *Provisional Dictator*, 84–90; Samuel Lumsden to Robert Tyler, December 28, 1855, Box 4, Folder 3, and John M'Clenahan to Tyler, January 5, 1856, Box 4, Folder 4, both in Tyler Family Papers. M'Clenahan succeeded John Mitchel as editor of the *New York Citizen* newspaper in December 1854; Mitchel, *Jail Journal*, 393.

92 McGovern, "John Mitchel," 100–102; Jenkins, *Irish Nationalism and the British State*, 218.

93 Robert G. Athearn, *Thomas Francis Meagher: An Irish Revolutionary in America* (Boulder: University of Colorado Press, 1949), 28–71.

94 Wilson, *Thomas D'Arcy McGee*, 1:271-360.

95 Samuel Lumsden to Robert Tyler, December 27, 1855, Box 4, Folder 3, and John J. McGowan to Tyler, August 14, 1856, Box 4, Folder 4, both in Tyler Family Papers.

96 John Crampton to Lord Clarendon, February 11, 1856, no. 27, FO 5/640, PRO.

97 J. J. McGowan to Robert Tyler, May 19, 1856, Box 4, Folder 4, Tyler Family Papers.

98 Ibid.

99 Samuel Lumsden to Robert Tyler, June 5, 1856, Box 4, Folder 4, Tyler Family Papers.

100 Craig M. Simpson, *A Good Southerner: A Life of Henry A. Wise of Virginia* (Chapel Hill: University of North Carolina Press, 1985), 111, 114–115.

101 Lumsden to Tyler, June 5, 1856. Wise argued that both nativism and abolitionism were English imports that ought to be rejected by U.S. citizens. Gleeson, *Irish in the South*, 111.

102 This political formula, Unionism excepted, is explored in McGovern's intellectual history of John Mitchel in the United States: McGovern, "John Mitchel," 99–110. David Gleeson notes that in the South, this fierce pro-Unionism could lead Irish voters, traditionally stalwart Democrats, to make common cause with Unionist Whigs; Gleeson, *Irish in the South*, 136.

103 Lumsden to Tyler, June 5, 1856.

104 There is too little scholarship on the composition and organization of pro–Fugitive Slave Law mobs to make a firm judgment on the extent of the involvement of "conservative armed force[s] of loyal [Irish-American] citizens". One of the most notorious trials of a fugitive slave, that of Margaret Garner, who was charged with murdering her daughter, took place in Cincinnati and was contemporaneous with the trial of Irish filibusters. A leading historian of the Garner case notes that the Democratic governor of Ohio had equipped Irish American militias with rifles so they would be available to enforce the Fugitive Slave Law in the event of violence breaking out, though there seems to have been no overlap of personnel between the militia units and the Irish filibusters. Steven Weisenburger, *Modern Medea: A Family Story of Slavery and Child-Murder from the Old South* (New York: Hill & Wang, 1998), 98, 145.

105 Charles Rowcroft to John Crampton, February 6, 1856, enclosed with Crampton to Clarendon, February 11, 1856, no. 27, FO 5/640, PRO.

106 Sen. Ex. Doc. No. 80, May 29, 1856, 34th Cong., 1st Sess., 38–99; H. Ex. Doc. No. 107, May 22, 1856, 34th Cong., 1st Sess., 1, both in *United States Congressional Serial Set*.

107 Ibid., 79.

108 Ironically, the British government was increasingly accepting of U.S. influence in the Western Hemisphere. See Crawford, *Anglo-American Crisis*, 7; and May, *Manifest Destiny's Underworld*, 244.

109 Buchanan to William Marcy, October 30, 1855, no. 98, reel 64, *Despatches from United States Ministers to Great Britain*.

110 "Charge against the British Consul," in *U.S. vs. Halpin*, 112.

111 This section draws upon Ramón, *Provisional Dictator*, 70–97.

112 IRB oath, quoted in ibid., 98.

113 Wilson, *Thomas D'Arcy McGee*, 2:54.

114 Stephens quoted in Rafferty, *Church, the State, and the Fenian Threat*, 41, Stephens's italics.

115 Jenkins, *Irish Nationalism and the British State*, 261; James Stephens to John O'Mahony, December 16, 1861, Box 9, Folder 3, Jeremiah O'Donovan Rossa Papers, Maloney Collection of Irish Historical Papers, New York Public Library (hereafter Rossa Papers). Stephens was not alone in his dislike of the United States. As David Wilson notes, it is a well-kept secret that many leading Irish American nationalists hated the United States. Wilson, *Thomas D'Arcy McGee*, 1:11, 237.

116 Jenkins, *Irish Nationalism and the British State*, 256.

117 Ramón, *Provisional Dictator*, 94–96; Toner, "Rise of Irish Nationalism," chapter 2.

118 James Stephens to John O'Mahoney, February 25, 1861, Box 9, Folder 3, Rossa Papers; Jenkins, *Irish Nationalism and the British State*, 270.

119 Denieffe, *Personal Narrative*, 77–81.

120 Crawford, *Anglo-American Crisis*, 103–105.

121 Ibid., 111.

122 Howard Jones, *Blue and Gray Diplomacy: A History of Union and Confederate Foreign Relations* (Chapel Hill: University of North Carolina Press, 2010); Jay Sexton, *Debtor Diplomacy: Finance and American Foreign Relations in the Civil War Era, 1837–1873* (Oxford: Oxford University Press, 2005), 82–189; Crawford, *Anglo-American Crisis*, 75–138.

123 William Henry Seward to Charles Francis Adams, March 1, 1865, no. 1282, in *Papers Relating to Foreign Relations of the United States* (Washington, D.C.: Government Printing Office, 1870–1946), *1865*, 1:190–192 (hereafter *FRUS*).

124 Jones, *Blue and Gray Diplomacy*, 83–111.

125 Hughes quoted in Jenkins, *Irish Nationalism and the British State*, 277.

126 James Stephens, by contrast, claimed to be unimpressed by such "legal" agitation and was wary of making Anglo-American conflict fundamental to nationalist organization. Ramón, *Provisional Dictator*, 123–126; Stephens to O'Mahony, February 25, 1861.

127 Jones, *Blue and Gray Diplomacy*, 191–201; William Henry Seward to Charles Francis Adams, January 16, 1865, *FRUS 1865*, 1:91–92; Jennifer L. Weber, *Copperheads: The Rise and Fall of Lincoln's Opponents in the North* (Oxford: Oxford University Press, 2006), 124–125, 128, 192–193; Sexton, *Debtor Diplomacy*, 111–112; Seán McConville, *Irish Political Prisoners, 1848–1922: Theatres of War* (London: Routledge, 2003), 143; Wilson, *Thomas D'Arcy McGee*, 2:208. On the *Alabama* controversy, see Jay Sexton, "The Funded Loan and the *Alabama* Claims," *Diplomatic History* 27, no. 4 (2003): 453–457.

128 Lord Clanricarde's speech in the House of Lords reported in Adams to Seward, March 3, 1864, no. 607, *FRUS 1864*, 1:247–252. Clanricarde described Pierce's actions in confronting British recruitment as decisive, drawing an unfavorable comparison with Palmerston's actions. Joseph M. Hernon Jr., *Celts, Catholics, and Copperheads: Ireland Views the Civil War* (Columbus: Ohio State University Press, 1968), 24; Rafferty, *Church, the State, and the Fenian Threat*, 62; Charles Francis Adams to William Henry Seward, April 1, 1864, no. 639, *FRUS 1864*, 1:431–560.

129 William Henry Seward to Charles Francis Adams, February 25, 1864, no. 855, *FRUS 1864*, 1:201.

130 Lord Palmerston to Queen Victoria, January 20, 1865, quoted in Brian A. Jenkins, *Fenians and Anglo-American Relations during reconstruction* (Ithaca, NY: Cornell University Press, 1969), 41–42.

131 Wilson, *Thomas D'Arcy McGee*, 2:116–164, 196–220.

132 Ramón, *Provisional Dictator*, 136–139; Consul William B. West to William Henry Seward, May 26, 1862, quoted in Hernon, *Celts, Catholics, and Copperheads*, 6.

133 Ibid., 17–19; Susannah Ural Bruce, *The Harp and the Eagle: Irish-American Volunteers and the Union Army, 1861–1865* (New York: New York University Press, 2006), 82–232.

134 David T. Gleeson, "Parallel Struggles: Irish Republicanism in the American South, 1798–1877," *Éire-Ireland* 34 (Summer 1999): 97–116; Hernon, *Celts, Catholics, and Copperheads*, 53.

135 Gleeson, *Irish in the South*, 133, 140–141; Rafferty, *Church, the State, and the Fenian Threat*, 62.

136 Jenkins, *Irish Nationalism and the British State*, 273.

137 John Michel quoted in Gleeson, *Irish in the South*, 155.

138 Hernon, *Celts, Catholics, and Copperheads,* 56.

139 John O'Leary quoted in McConville, *Irish Political Prisoners*, 143.

140 Hernon, *Celts, Catholics, and Copperheads,* 37; Bruce, *Harp and the Eagle*, 200.

141 On this, see Christian G. Samito, *Becoming American under Fire: Irish Americans, African Americans, and the Politics of Citizenship during the Civil War Era* (Ithaca, NY: Cornell University Press, 2009). Quotation from Bruce, *Harp and the Eagle*, 232; see also 254–262. Military experience during the Civil War must, of course, be set against the strength of Copperhead politics within Irish American communities and Irish American involvement in the horrific Draft Riots of 1863. See Weber, *Copperheads*, esp. 103–133; Iver Bernstein, *The New York City Draft Riots: Their Significance for American Society and Politics in the Age of the Civil War* (New York: Oxford University Press, 1990); and David Quigley, *Second Founding: New York City, Reconstruction and the Making of American Democracy* (New York: Hill & Wang, 2004), 3–13.

142 Ramón, *Provisional Dictator*, 162–166.

143 Ibid., 177; McConville, *Irish Political Prisoners,* 122.

144 *Times* (London), October 4, 1865, p. 6.

145 McConville, *Irish Political Prisoners*, 123–124; Brian A. Jenkins, *The Fenian Problem: Insurgency and Terrorism in a Liberal State, 1858–1874* (Liverpool: Liverpool University Press, 2009), 34–42.

146 Ibid., 46, Ramón, *Provisional Dictator*, 195–197. On the internal politics of the Fenian Brotherhood, see Timothy D. Lynch, "Erin's Hope: The Fenian Brotherhood of New York City, 1858–1866" (PhD diss., City University of New York, 2004); and Rafferty, *Church, the State, and the Fenian Threat*, 65, 84–105.

147 McConville, *Irish Political Prisoners*, 126; Denieffe, *Personal Narrative*, 126.

148 Wilson, *Thomas D'Arcy McGee*, 2:227–232, 247–248, 261–262.

149 Jenkins, *Fenians and Anglo-American Relations*, 40–69.

150 Eric Foner, *Reconstruction: America's Unfinished Revolution, 1863–1877* (New York: Perennial, 2002), 247–251, 260–261; Rafferty, *Church, the State, and the Fenian Threat*, 77.

151 Ibid., 78. Intriguingly, Peter Vronsky suggests that the U.S. government then attempted to reseize these arms before they could be used in any invasion plans. Peter Vronsky, *Ridgeway: The American Fenian Invasion and the 1866 Battle That Made Canada* (Toronto: Allen Lane Canada, 2011), 27.

152 Killian quoted in Wilson, *Thomas D'Arcy McGee*, 2:248; Ramón, *Provisional Dictator*, 193–194.

153 Wilson, *Thomas D'Arcy McGee*, 2:248; Vronsky, *Ridgeway*, 23–28.

154 Sweeny quoted in Bruce, *Harp and the Eagle*, 241.

155 Rafferty, *Church, the State, and the Fenian Threat*, 61.

156 Bruce quoted in Wilson, *Thomas D'Arcy McGee*, 2:268–269.

157 Ramón, *Provisional Dictator*, 196–198.

158 Ibid., 206–207; Wilson, *Thomas D'Arcy McGee*, 2:268–270; Jenkins, *Fenians and Anglo-American Relations*, 133–141.

159 Jenkins, *Fenians and Anglo-American Relations,* 139.

160 Wilson, *Thomas D'Arcy McGee*, 2:278; Vronsky, *Ridgeway*, 35–36.

161 Jenkins, *Fenians and Anglo-American Relations*, 142–150; Attorney-General James Speed, "Proclamation," June 5, 1866, in *A Compilation of the Messages and Papers of the Presidents*, vol. 6, *1861–1869,* edited by James D. Richardson (Washington, DC: Government Printing Office, 1897), available at Project Gutenberg, www.gutenberg.org/files/12755/12755-h/12755-h.htm (accessed April 21, 2010).

162 William Roberts, "To the Officers and Soldiers of the Irish Republican Army," June 13, 1866, in Lynch, "Erin's Hope," 166, O'Neill quoted in Wilson, *Thomas D'Arcy McGee*, 2:279.

163 Michael Scanlan quoted in Lynch, "Erin's Hope," 166.

164 Cong. Globe, 39th Cong., 1st Sess., June 11, 1866, 3085.

165 Ibid., July 23, 1866, 4047–4048.

166 House Report No. 100, July 25, 1866, 39th Cong., 1st Sess., 2–4, quote at 7, *United States Congressional Serial Set*.

167 Ibid., quote at 1.

168 Ibid., 7.

169 Ramón, *Provisional Dictator*, 212–214; Jenkins, *Fenians and Anglo-American Relations*, 181–182.

170 Ibid., 183–184; Wilson, *Thomas D'Arcy McGee*, 2:291.

171 Mabel Gregory Walker, *The Fenian Movement* (Colorado Springs, CO: R. Myles, 1969), 165–173.

172 *Times* (London), October 4, 1865, 6.

173 Frederick Bruce to Lord Stanley, October 30, 1866, FO 5/1340, PRO.

174 Charles Francis Adams, diary entry for September 19, 1866, reel 80, *Microfilms of the Adams Papers Owned by the Adams Manuscript Trust and Deposited in the Massachusetts Historical Society*, microfilm, 608 reels (Boston: Massachusetts Historical Society, 1954–1959) (hereafter *Adams Papers*).

175 Adams, diary entry for March 1, 1866, reel 79, *Adams Papers*.

176 Seward to Adams, March 28, 1867, no. 1852, *FRUS 1867*, 1:75.

177 Seward quoted in Vronsky, *Ridgeway*, 26.

178 Ibid., 75–76.

179 William Gladstone to Lord Clarendon, June 13, 1870, in *The Gladstone Diaries*, 14 vols., edited by M. R. D. Foot and H. C. G. Matthew (Oxford: Clarendon Press, 1968–1994), 7:306.

180 Ibid.

181 "International Policy," *North American Review* 103, no. 213 (1866): 609.

182 Ibid.

183 Doris W. Dashew, "The Story of an Illusion: The Plan to Trade the Alabama Claims for Canada," *Civil War History* 15 (December 1969): 332–348.

184 See Wilson, *Thomas D'Arcy McGee*, 2:196–241.

185 Ramón, *Provisional Dictator*, 206–207.

186 Wilson, *Thomas D'Arcy McGee*, 2:276.

187 McGee, *IRB*, 16–17.

188 James Stephens to John O'Mahony, December 16, 1861, Box 9, Folder 3, Rossa Papers.

189 Ramón, *Provisional Dictator*, 172–180.

190 This was the *Jacmel* expedition of April 1867. See chapter 4.

191 Jenkins, *Fenians and Anglo-American Relations*, 304. The selection of Schuyler Colfax as Grant's vice president may have been a nod to Fenian voters; Colfax had been an active speaker at Fenian events. See Walker, *The Fenian Movement*, 167; Charles Wentworth Dilke, *Greater Britain: A Record of Travel in English-Speaking Countries, during 1866 and 1867*, 2 vols. (London: Macmillan & Co., 1868), 1:296.

192 Jenkins, *Fenians and Anglo-American Relations*, 295–296.

193 Rafferty, *Church, the State, and the Fenian Threat*, 78. It should be noted, though, that the British minister in Washington, Edward Thornton, complained that the State Department also leaked information to the Fenians; ibid.

194 Charles G. Fenwick, *The Neutrality Laws of the United States* (Washington, D.C.: Carnegie Endowment for International Peace, 1913), 53.

195 Jay Sexton, "The Funded Loan and the *Alabama* Claims," 460, 477.

196 Sexton, *Debtor Diplomacy*, 215. For the treaty, see *Treaties, Conventions, International Acts, Protocols, and Agreements between the United States of America and Other Powers*, 4 vols., edited by William Malloy (Washington, D.C.: U.S. Government Printing Office, 1910–1938), 1:700–716; "The Treaty of Washington," *Harper's New Monthly Magazine* 45, no. 270 (1872): 931–932.

197 William Gladstone to Goldwin Smith, June 13, 1871, in Foot and Matthew, *The Gladstone Diaries*, 7:508.

198 See, for instance, Jonathan W. Gantt, "Irish-American Terrorism and Anglo-American Relations," *Journal of the Gilded Age and Progressive Era* 5, no. 4 (2006): 325–357.

Chapter 4

1 Alan Taylor, *The Civil War of 1812: American Citizens, British Subjects, Irish Rebels, and Indian Allies* (New York: Alfred A. Knopf, 2010), 3–5, 102–123.

2 Ibid., 358–362.

3 John T. Morse, "Expatriation and Naturalization," *North American Review* 106, no. 219 (1868): 612–613.

4 Nancy L. Green, "Expatriation, Expatriates, and Expats: The American Transformation of a Concept," *American Historical Review* 114, no. 2 (2009): 314–315.

5 This legislation became informally known as the Warren and Costello Act, named for two imprisoned Fenians whose cases provoked intense interest in both Britain and the United States. Alexander M. Sullivan, *New Ireland: Political Sketches and Personal Reminiscences* (London: Sampson Low, Marston, Searle & Rivington, 1878), 283–284; Naturalisation Act 1870, 33 & 34 Vict. cap. 14.

6 George Bancroft to James Buchanan, September 8, 1848, no. 85, reel 54, *Despatches from United States Ministers to Great Britain*.

7 John Romeyn Brodhead to James Buchanan, August 25, 1848, private, enclosed with ibid.; Senator Edward Allen Hannegan to George Bancroft, May 16, 1848, enclosed with George Bancroft to James Buchanan, September 22, 1848, no. 86, reel 54, *Despatches from United States Ministers to Great Britain*. John Belchem describes both as "leading figures" in the New York Irish Republican Union, and Bergen had been prominent among New York repealers in the mid-1840s. See Belchem, "Republican Spirit and Military Science: The 'Irish Brigade' and Irish-American Nationalism in 1848," *Irish Historical Studies* 29, no. 113 (1994): 60–62; and *Truth Teller* (New York), June 10, 1843.

8 Thomas Redington to George Bancroft, n.d., enclosed with George Bancroft to James Buchanan, September 8, 1848.

9 Ibid.

10 George Bancroft to James Buchanan, September 22, 1848; Lord Palmerston to George Bancroft, September 30, 1848, enclosed with George Bancroft to James Buchanan, October 6, 1848, no. 92, reel 54, *Despatches from United States Ministers to Great Britain*.

11 Unknown correspondent to George Bancroft, September 7, 1848, enclosed with George Bancroft to James Buchanan, October 6, 1848.

12 George Bancroft to James Buchanan, November 10, 1848, no. 100, reel 54, *Despatches from United States Ministers to Great Britain*.

13 George Bancroft to James Buchanan, November 23, 1848, no. 102, and December 1, 1848, no. 104, both reel 54, *Despatches from United States Ministers to Great Britain.*

14 George Bancroft to James Buchanan, December 1, 1848, no. 104, reel 54, *Despatches from United States Ministers to Great Britain.*

15 George Bancroft to James Buchanan, January 12, 1849, no. 122, reel 54, *Despatches from United States Ministers to Great Britain;* Buchanan to Bancroft, December 18, 1848, no. 44, and February 12, 1849, no. 47, both reel 74, *Diplomatic Instructions of the Department of State.*

16 George Bancroft to Lord Palmerston, January 26, 1849, FO 5/506, PRO.

17 Brian A. Jenkins, *The Fenian Problem: Insurgency and Terrorism in a Liberal State, 1858–1874* (Liverpool: Liverpool University Press, 2009), 46–48.

18 John Wodehouse, Lord Lieutenant of Ireland, quoted in ibid., 47.

19 Adams to Seward, September 22, 1865, despatch no. 1054, *FRUS 1865,* 1:561–563; Brian A. Jenkins, *Fenians and Anglo-American Relations during Reconstruction* (Ithaca, NY: Cornell University Press, 1969), 74–75.

20 Charles Francis Adams to William Seward, September 22, 1865, *FRUS 1865,* 1:562–563.

21 Cong. Globe, 39th Cong., 1st Sess., June 18, 1866, 3241; H. Ex. Doc. No. 139, 39th Cong., 1st Sess., *United States Congressional Serial Set.* Of these twenty-six, two were committed for trial. All had been released by the time of Seward's report.

22 William West to William Seward, September 20, 1865, in H. Ex. Doc. No. 157, February 10, 1868, 40th Cong., 2nd Sess., part 2, 8–9, *United States Congressional Serial Set.*

23 The description is in Charles Francis Adams's diary entry for August 15, 1865, reel 79, *Adams Papers.* West stated that he was a lawyer in a letter to Seward, November 25, 1865, despatch no. 132, in H. Ex. Doc. No. 157, 40th Cong., 2nd Sess., part 2, 20.

24 George Archdeacon to William West, January 10, 1866, in H. Ex. Doc. No. 157, 40th Cong., 2nd Sess., part 2, 137.

25 Archdeacon claimed that his certificate of citizenship had been taken from him by a Dublin detective. George Archdeacon to William West, n.d., and West to Archdeacon, September 26, 1865, in H. Ex. Doc. No. 157, February 10, 1868, 40th Cong., 2nd Sess., part 2, 115–116.

26 George Archdeacon to William West, October 10, 1867, in H. Ex. Doc. No. 157, 40th Cong., 2nd Sess., part 2, 117. Charles O'Conor was a conservative Democrat and a very able lawyer whose father had been involved in the 1798 Irish rebellion.

27 George Archdeacon to William West, October 20, 1867, in H. Ex. Doc. No. 157, 40th Cong., 2nd Sess., part 2, 120.

28 Seán McConville, *Irish Political Prisoners, 1848–1922: Theatres of War* (London: Routledge, 2003), 149; Jenkins, *Fenian Problem,* 48.

29 William West to George Archdeacon, January 15, 1866, in H. Ex. Doc. No. 157, 40th Cong., 2nd Sess., part 1, 17.

30 Thomas Larcom to William West, January 10, 1866, and West to Larcom, January 11, 1866, in H. Ex. Doc. No. 157, 40th Cong., 2nd Sess., part 2, 137–138.

31 William West to Thomas Larcom, February 20, 1866, in H. Ex. Doc. No. 157, 40th Cong., 2nd Sess., part 2, 144.

32 Thomas Larcom to William West, April 13, 1866, in H. Ex. Doc. No. 157, 40th Cong., 2nd Sess., part 2, 206.

33 West defended his course of action in William West to President Johnson, November 7, 1866, enclosed with Adams to Seward, November 23, 1867, despatch no. 1276, in H. Ex. Doc. No. 157, 40th Cong., 2nd Sess., part 1, 16–19, quote at 19. On his return to the United States, Archdeacon wrote to the president to complain of West's complacency and to request that the U.S. government plainly state the rights of naturalized citizens, "so that adopted citizens may

know their real standing in foreign countries, and the value from home of that citizenship of which they are so proud here." George Archdeacon to President Andrew Johnson, n.d., enclosed in Archdeacon to William Seward, September 29, 1866, in H. Ex. Doc. No. 157, 40th Cong., 2nd Sess., part 1, 9–11, quote at 11.

34 Adams diary entry for September 20, 1865, reel 79, *Adams Papers.*

35 R.V. Comerford, *The Fenians in Context: Irish Politics and Society, 1848–82* (Dublin: Wolf-hound Press, 1998), 133–134; James Stephens to the Head Centre and Central Council of the Fenian Brotherhood, October 14, 1865, Box 9, Folder 4, Rossa Papers; Marta Ramón, *A Provisional Dictator: James Stephens and the Fenian Movement* (Dublin: University College Dublin Press, 2007), 200–202.

36 Joseph Denieffe, *A Personal Narrative of the Irish Revolutionary Brotherhood* (1906; repr., Shannon: Irish University Press, 1969), 126–138.

37 Adams diary entry for January 14, 1866, reel 79, *Adams Papers.*

38 Ibid.

39 Adams diary entry for February 17, 1866, reel 79, *Adams Papers*; William West to Charles Francis Adams, February 18, 1866, H. Ex. Doc. No. 157, 40th Cong., 2nd Sess., part 2, 140.

40 Trials took place between late November 1865 and early February 1866. William West to William Seward, February 17, 1866, H. Ex. Doc. No. 157, 40th Cong., 2nd Sess., part 2, 138; William West to Charles Francis Adams, February 18, 1866, H. Ex. Doc. No. 157, 40th Cong., 2nd Sess., part 2, 140; McConville, *Irish Political Prisoners, 1848–1922*, 153.

41 William Halpin to John O'Mahony, October 6, 1865, and October 18, 1865, Fenian Brotherhood Collection; O'Mahony to Messrs. Paul, Barry and Morrison, Committee of the Council of the Fenian Brotherhood, January 5, 1870, Box 9, Folder 2, Rossa Papers.

42 William Halpin to William West, February 18, 1866, enclosed with West to Adams, February 18, 1866.

43 M. C. Taylor to William Seward, November 13, 1867, H. Ex. Doc. No. 157, 40th Cong., 2nd Sess., part 1, 334–335; Halpin's travails with the regiment are detailed in Kirk C. Jenkins, *The Battle Rages Higher: The Union's Fifteenth Kentucky Infantry* (Lexington: University Press of Kentucky, 2003), esp. 24–47.

44 John Savage to William Seward, November 11, 1867, H. Ex. Doc. No. 157, 40th Cong., 2nd Sess., part 1, 334.

45 William Seward to Charles Francis Adams, August 7, 1867, despatch no. 2032, *FRUS 1867*, 1:120. See also Christian G. Samito, *Becoming American under Fire: Irish Americans, African Americans, and the Politics of Citizenship during the Civil War Era* (Ithaca, NY: Cornell University Press, 2009), esp. 172–193.

46 Adams diary entry for February 19, 1866, reel 79, *Adams Papers.*

47 Thomas Larcom to William West, February 20, 1866, and West to Charles Francis Adams, February 21, 1866, both in H. Ex. Doc. No. 157, 40th Cong., 2nd Sess., part 2, 145–146.

48 William West to Charles Francis Adams, March 1, 1866, H. Ex. Doc. No. 157, 40th Cong., 2nd Sess., part 2, 162.

49 William West to Charles Francis Adams, March 6, 1866, H. Ex. Doc. No. 157, 40th Cong., 2nd Sess., part 2, 168.

50 Adams diary entries for February 24 and 25, 1866, reel 79, *Adams Papers.* Adams was frequently frustrated by the slight regard that British statesmen had for good Anglo-American relations. Indeed, he was often amazed at the limited knowledge that they had of events in the United States.

51 Adams diary entry for February 27, 1866, reel 79, *Adams Papers*; William West to William Seward, March 10, 1866, in H. Ex. Doc. No. 157, 40th Cong., 2nd Sess., part 2, 146.

52 Martin B. Duberman, *Charles Francis Adams, 1807–1886* (Boston: Houghton Mifflin, 1961), 323–330.

53 Adams diary entry for March 5, 1866, reel 79, *Adams Papers*.

54 Charles Francis Adams to William Seward, March 8, 1866, despatch no. 1165, *FRUS 1866*, 1:76.

55 Ibid.

56 Charles Francis Adams to William Seward, February 22, 1866, despatch no. 1158, *FRUS 1866*, 1:70.

57 William Seward to Charles Francis Adams, March 31, 1866, despatch no. 1729, *FRUS 1866*, 1:94.

58 Clarendon quoted in Jenkins, *Fenian Problem*, 48.

59 Adams diary entry for March 13, 1866, reel 79, *Adams Papers*; Rising Lake Morrow, "The Negotiation of the Anglo-American Treaty of 1870," *American Historical Review* 39, no. 4 (1934): 665.

60 Charles Francis Adams to William Seward, May 10, 1866, despatch no. 1195, *FRUS 1866*, 1:119.

61 Ibid.

62 William West to William Seward, March 31, 1866, despatch no. 150, H. Ex. Doc. No. 157, 40th Cong., 2nd Sess., part 2, 54. By contrast, Edwin G. Eastman, consul at Queenstown, County Cork, reported that all prisoners held there had been conditionally released by the end of April; Edwin G. Eastman to William Seward, April 28, 1866, despatch no. 175, H. Ex. Doc. No. 157, 40th Cong., 2nd Sess., part 2, 56.

63 Patrick Condon to President Johnson, August 7, 1866, H. Ex. Doc. No. 157, 40th Cong., 2nd Sess., part 1; Michael Cavanagh, *Memoirs of Thomas Francis Meagher* (Worcester, MA: Messenger Press, 1892), appendix, 28. It is not clear whether or not this is the same Patrick Condon who was active in Fenian circles in and around New Orleans after the Civil War. Gleeson, *Irish in the South*, 71.

64 Patrick Condon to William West, March 9, 1866, H. Ex. Doc. No. 157, 40th Cong., 2nd Sess., part 1, 12.

65 William West to Patrick Condon, April 28, 1866, H. Ex. Doc. No. 157, 40th Cong., 2nd Sess., part 1, 12.

66 Patrick Condon to William West, April 30, 1866, H. Ex. Doc. No. 157, 40th Cong., 2nd Sess., part 1, 12.

67 Thomas Larcom to William West, July 3, 1866, H. Ex. Doc. No. 157, 40th Cong., 2nd Sess., part 1, 21.

68 Thomas Larcom to the Governor of Mountjoy Prison, July 3, 1866, H. Ex. Doc. No. 157, 40th Cong., 2nd Sess., part 1, 23.

69 Patrick Condon to William West, in H. Ex. Doc. No. 157, 40th Cong., 2nd Sess., part 1, 14.

70 Patrick Condon, affidavit, July 17, 1866, H. Ex. Doc. No. 157, 40th Cong., 2nd Sess., part 1, 23; "News from Washington," *Bangor Daily Whig & Courier*, August 11, 1866.

71 Condon to Johnson, August 7, 1866, 11–12.

72 William West to William Seward, July 28, 1866, despatch no. 156, H. Ex. Doc. No. 157, 40th Cong., 2nd Sess., part 2, 60.

73 Adams diary entry for June 16, 1866, reel 79, *Adams Papers*.

74 Charles Francis Adams to William Seward, December 7, 1866, despatch no. 1287, *FRUS 1867*, 1:35.

75 Charles Francis Adams to William Seward, February 6, 1867, despatch no. 1316, *FRUS 1867*, 1:62–63.

76 Adams to William Seward, February 19, 1867, despatch no. 1323, *FRUS 1867*, 1:64.

77 Jenkins, *Fenian Problem*, 78–84.

78 Charles Francis Adams to William Seward, March 8, 1867, despatch no. 1334, *FRUS 1867*, 1:67.

79 Ibid.

80 Thomas Kelly had served with the 10th Ohio Infantry during the Civil War; John Savage, *Fenian Heroes and Martyrs* (Boston: P. Donahoe, 1868), 165–167. Halpin and Massey (Condon's alias) also served on the directory and played a prominent part in the March 1867 uprising. Ramón, *Provisional Dictator*, 221–228; Jenkins, *Fenian Problem*, 78–86; Comerford, *Fenians in Context*, 137.

81 Ibid., 137–139; Ramón, *Provisional Dictator*, 230–232; Jenkins, *Fenian Problem*, 85–86.

82 The description is Adams's, quoted in Jenkins, *Fenians and Anglo-American Relations*, 230.

83 William Seward to Charles Francis Adams, March 28, 1867, despatch no. 1952, *FRUS 1867*, 1:75.

84 Ibid.

85 Jenkins, *Fenian Problem*, 93.

86 William Seward to Charles Francis Adams, May 15, 1867, despatch no. 1981, telegram, *FRUS 1867*, 1:87–88.

87 Charles Francis Adams to William Seward, May 28, 1867, despatch no. 1375, *FRUS 1867*, 1:96.

88 James J. Rogers to William Seward, May 13, 1867, H. Ex. Doc. No. 157, 40th Cong., 2nd Sess., part 1, 40; Charles Francis Adams to William Seward, May 18, 1867, despatch no. 1369, *FRUS 1867*, 1:91. McCafferty had been arrested on a previous visit to Ireland in September 1865 but was released for want of evidence. Savage, *Fenian Heroes*, 177–193; McConville, *Irish Political Prisoners, 1848–1922,* 129; Jenkins, *Fenian Problem*, 81. He is briefly mentioned in David A. Wilson, "Swapping Canada for Ireland: The Fenian Invasion of 1866," *History Ireland* 16, no. 6 (2008): 26.

89 Adams diary entries for May 21 and 25, 1867, reel 80, *Adams Papers*.

90 Charles Francis Adams to William Seward, May 28, 1867, *FRUS 1867*, 1:96.

91 Lord Stanley to Charles Francis Adams, May 26, 1867, in H. Ex. Doc. No. 157, 40th Cong., 2nd Sess., part 1, 50; Adams to Seward, April 8, 1868, despatch no. 1568, *FRUS 1868*, 1:187; Jenkins, *Fenian Problem*, 93–95. While both Liberal and Conservative British statesmen criticized the others' policies while in opposition, both were attentive to the diplomatic ramifications of their actions.

92 Morrow, "Treaty of 1870," 665–666; *Report of the Trial of John Warren, for Treason-Felony: At the County Dublin Commission, Held at the Court-house, Green-street, Dublin, commencing the 30th October, 1867* (Dublin: A. Thorn, 1867), 25–26.

93 Charles Francis Adams to William Seward, with newspaper enclosure, August 23, 1867, despatch no. 1428, *FRUS 1867*, 1:129; *Report of the Trial of John Warren*, 27.

94 Kerrigan's career prior to the *Jacmel* expedition again demonstrates the connections between Central American and transatlantic filibustering. Born in New York City, he had served as a volunteer in the Mexican War and later accompanied William Walker on one of his expeditions to Nicaragua. On his return to the United States he sought elective office, and from 1861 he served one undistinguished term as an Independent Democrat representing New York's 4th Congressional District. May, *Manifest Destiny's Underworld*, 282, 286; "James Kerrigan (1828–1899)," Biographical Directory of the United States Congress.

95 McConville, *Irish Political Prisoners, 1848–1922,* 130.

96 *Report of the Trial of John Warren,* 29, 44–46.

97 Comerford, *Fenians in Context,* 139.

98 *Report of the Trial of John Warren,* 29–30.

99 Jenkins, *Fenian Problem,* 118.

100 William West to John Lawless, July 30, 1867, H. Ex. Doc. No. 157, 40th Cong., 2nd Sess., part 2, 497.

101 William Seward to Charles Francis Adams, September 24, 1867, despatch no. 2058, *FRUS 1867,* 1:152; and William West to Adams, July 27, 1867, H. Ex. Doc. No. 157, 40th Cong., 2nd Sess., part 2, 496.

102 Seward initially believed that Warren was a native Bostonian; William Seward to Charles Francis Adams, August 7, 1867, despatch no. 2032, *FRUS 1867,* 1:120; Henry Liebenau to William Seward, September 23, 1867, H. Ex. Doc. No. 157, 40th Cong., 2nd Sess., part 1, 83; *Report of the Trial of John Warren,* 13.

103 William Erigena Robinson quoting the *New York Tribune,* Cong. Globe, 40th Cong., 1st Session, November 25, 1867, 788. Like Nagle, Warren had served in the Union army, with the 63rd Massachusetts volunteers; William Seward to Charles Francis Adams, August 7, 1867, despatch no. 2032, *FRUS 1867,* 1:120.

104 William Nagle to his father, D. M. Nagle, July 4, 1867, H. Doc. Ex. No. 157, 40th Cong., 2nd Sess., part 1, 56–57.

105 Ibid.

106 Warren to the *Dublin Weekly News,* August 1867, in H. Ex. Doc. No. 157, 40th Cong., 2nd Sess., part 1, 70.

107 Cong. Globe, 40th Cong., 1st Session, November 25, 1867, 787–788; Fernando Wood to Andrew Johnson, August 16, 1867, H. Ex. Doc. No. 157, 40th Cong., 2nd Sess., part 1, 320.

108 Jenkins, *Fenian Problem,* 75. See also McConville, *Irish Political Prisoners, 1848–1922,* 146–147, 153, on conditions for Irish American prisoners.

109 John Warren to the *Dublin Weekly News,* August 1867. The "Massey" referred to was actually the alias of Patrick J. Condon, the Fenian who had been arrested the previous year and had caused problems for Charles Francis Adams by refusing the terms of his conditional release; Adams to Seward, April 30, 1867, despatch no. 1359, in H. Ex. Doc. No. 157, 40th Cong., 2nd Sess., part 1, 37. Warren, in fact, had served as a leading Fenian organizer in Massachusetts; *Report of the Trial of John Warren,* 83.

110 John Warren to the *Dublin Weekly News,* August 1867, in H. Ex. Doc. No. 157, 40th Cong., 2nd Sess., part 1, 70.

111 Ibid.

112 Charles Francis Adams to William Seward, September 3, 1867, no. 1438, *FRUS 1867,* 1:133.

113 Frederick Bruce to Lord Stanley, August 22, 1867, telegram, H. Ex. Doc. No. 157, 40th Cong., 2nd Sess., part 1, 64; William Seward to Charles Francis Adams, September 11, 1867, telegram, H. Ex. Doc. No. 157, 40th Cong., 2nd Sess., part 1, 72.

114 "An Irish-American Idea for the Use of the Atlantic Telegraph Cable," *Frank Leslie's Illustrated Newspaper,* July 24, 1858, 15.

115 Arnold Schrier, *Ireland and the American Emigration, 1850–1900* (Minneapolis: University of Minnesota Press, 1958), 105–123.

116 See chapter 2.

117 Walter J. Meade O'Dwyer to William Seward, May 14, 1867, in H. Ex. Doc. No. 157, 40th Cong., 2nd Sess., part 1, 43.

118 Cong. Globe, 40th Cong., 3rd Session, March 2, 1869, appendix, 259.

119 For Robinson's activities during the repeal movement, see chapter 1.

120 Cong. Globe, 40th Cong., 1st Session, November 25, 1867, 786. Historian James Paul Rodechko claims that as late as 1865, Robinson was a Republican. Though he gives no definite reason for Robinson's move toward the Democrats in 1866, it is possible that he was responding to broader trends in New York City politics during the late 1860s. See Rodechko, *Patrick Ford and His Search for America: A Case Study of Irish-American Journalism 1870–1913* (New York: Arno Press, 1976), 124–125.

121 Cong. Globe, 40th Cong., 1st Session, November 25, 1867, 786.

122 At an 1878 meeting welcoming Patrick Condon to New York after his release by the British authorities, William Erigena Robinson, who was between stints as a congressman from Brooklyn, described Adams as "virtually a murderer." The *New York Tribune* reported that "hisses and a howl of execration followed the mention of the name of Mr. Adams"; "Sympathizing with the Fenians," *New York Tribune*, October 22, 1878.

123 Adams diary entry for May 28, 1867, reel 80, *Adams Papers*.

124 The correspondent was Patrick A. Collins, an active Fenian who was later elected to Congress from Massachusetts and, surprisingly, was selected for the London consulate. Sister M. Jeanne D'Arc O'Hare, "The Public Career of Patrick Andrew Collins" (PhD diss., Boston College, 1959), 86.

125 Adams diary entries, April 15 and May 30, 1867, reel 80, *Adams Papers*.

126 For Adams's pessimism about civic life in the United States, see chapter 5.

127 Adams diary entry for December 4, 1867, reel 81, *Adams Papers*.

128 Walter J. Meade O'Dwyer to William Seward, May 14, 1867, in H. Ex. Doc. No. 157, 40th Cong., 2nd Sess., part 1, ibid., 43; "The Arrest of Cols. Nagle and Warren—Meeting on the Subject Last Evening," *New York Times*, July 16, 1867.

129 William Seward to Charles Francis Adams, September 20, 1867, despatch no. 2056, *FRUS 1867*, 1:144.

130 Ibid.

131 Ibid.; Charles Francis Adams to Lord Stanley, September 13, 1867, H. Ex. Doc. No. 157, 40th Cong., 2nd Sess., part 1, 74.

132 William Seward to Charles Francis Adams, October 3, 1867, despatch no. 2069, *FRUS 1867*, 1:156–157.

133 Charles Francis Adams to William Seward, October 19, 1867, despatch no. 1466, *FRUS 1867*, 1:159.

134 Charles Francis Adams to William Seward, November 5, 1867, despatch no. 1476, *FRUS 1867*, 1:171. William E. Robinson seized on this distinction as a demonstration of the contempt of the British authorities for Warren's adopted citizenship; Cong. Globe, 40th Cong., 3rd Session, December 8, 1868, 22.

135 *Report of the Trial of John Warren*, 6.

136 Ibid.

137 Charles Francis Adams to William Seward, November 1, 1867, despatch no. 1472, *FRUS 1867*, 1:165.

138 *Report of the Trial of John Warren*, 20.

139 Ibid. By contrast, Fenians tried in Canada after the 1866 raids were, where possible, granted mixed juries when they requested them. See R. Blake Brown, "'Stars and Shamrocks Will Be Sown': The Fenian State Trials, 1866–1867," in *Canadian State Trials*, edited by Barry Wright and Susan Binnie, vol. 3, *Political Trials and Security Measures, 1840–1914* (Toronto: University of Toronto Press, 2009), 54.

140 William Seward to U.S. Attorney General Henry Stanberry, November 18, 1867, H. Ex. Doc. No. 157, 40th Cong., 2nd Sess., part 1, 186.

141 *Report of the Trial of John Warren,* 121.

142 Ibid., 105.

143 Ibid.

144 Henry Stanbery to William Seward, November 26, 1867, H. Ex. Doc. No. 157, 40th Cong., 2nd Sess., part 1, 190–192.

145 *Report of the Trial of John Warren,* 132. William G. Halpin received the same sentence simultaneously, bringing to a close his long career as a transatlantic nationalist agitator.

146 John Warren to the Honorable Members of the United States Congress in Session Assembled, n.d., H. Ex. Doc. No. 157, 40th Cong., 2nd Sess., part 1, 196.

147 Ibid.

148 William Seward to Charles Francis Adams, December 14, 1867, despatch no. 2108, *FRUS 1868*, 1:49.

149 Ramón, *Provisional Dictator*, 234–235; John Savage to William Seward, November 11, 1867, H. Ex. Doc. No. 157, 40th Cong., 2nd Sess., part 1, 334.

150 John Savage to William Seward, November 26, 1867, H. Ex. Doc. No. 157, 40th Cong., 2nd Sess., part 1, 342.

151 Patrick Collins to Andrew Johnson, December 7, 1867, H. Ex. Doc. No. 157, 40th Cong., 2nd Sess., part 1, 343.

152 Ibid., 343–344.

153 Jenkins, *Fenian Problem*, 108; Jenkins, *Fenians and Anglo-American Relations*, 241–243.

154 The *Anglo-American Times*, quoted in Jenkins, *Fenian Problem*, 109.

155 The prisoner was Ricard Burke, an Irish-born veteran of the Union army who had served as a Fenian organizer for southern England. Jenkins, *Fenians and Anglo-American Relations*, 254; and Jenkins, *Fenian Problem*, 148–149.

156 Ibid., 149–161, 177–178; James H. Adams, "The Negotiated Hibernian: Discourse on the Fenian in England and America," *American Nineteenth Century History* 11, no. 1 (2010): 47–48; Jenkins, *Fenians and Anglo-American Relations*, 255; McConville, *Irish Political Prisoners, 1848–1922*, 136–138.

157 Charles Francis Adams to William Seward, December 24, 1867, despatch no. 1502, *FRUS 1868*, 1:130.

158 William Seward to Charles Francis Adams, December 9, 1867, despatch no. 2106, *FRUS 1868*, 1:37–38; and Seward to Adams, January 13, 1868, despatch no. 2119, *FRUS 1868*, 1:141–143.

159 "The Fenian Mode of Warfare," *New York Times*, December 29, 1867.

160 Ibid.

161 "Editorial: Fenian Trials at Manchester," *Times* (London), November 5, 1867.

162 Ibid. Henry Halleck's writings on this point can be found in his *International Law: Or, Rules Regulating the Intercourse of States in Perpetual Peace and War* (New York: D. Van Nostrand, 1861), 694–695. See also Charles Francis Adams to William Seward, November 5, 1867, despatch no. 1476, *FRUS 1867*, 1:171–173; and Jenkins, *Fenians and Anglo-American Relations*, 250–251.

163 Andrew Johnson, "Third Annual Message," December 3, 1867, in *A Compilation of the Messages and Papers of the Presidents*, 20 vols., edited by James D. Richardson (New York: Bureau of National Literature, 1927), 8:3778.

164 Ibid.

165 Ibid. The subject of expatriation in connection with throwing off the obligations of military service (for instance, in Prussia) had been raised in Johnson's message of December 1866. Of Great Britain, he noted that while she "has never acknowledged the right of expatriation,

she has not for some years past insisted upon the opposite doctrine." Andrew Johnson, "Seccond Annual Message," December 3, 1866, The American Presidency Project, www.presidency.ucsb. edu/ws/index.php?pid=29507 (accessed May 7, 2013).

166 Andrew Johnson, "Fourth Annual Message," December 9, 1868, in Richardson, *A Compilation of the Messages and Papers of the Presidents*, 8:3888.

167 Handlin, *George Bancroft*, 296–297.

168 Adams diary entry for December 11, 1867, reel 81, *Adams Papers*.

169 Harcourt would eventually become the Whewell Professor of International Law at Cambridge. Peter Stansky, "Harcourt, Sir William George Granville Venables Vernon (1827–1904)," *Oxford Dictionary of National Biography*; Murney Gerlach, *British Liberalism and the United States: Political and Social Thought in the Late Victorian Age* (Basingstoke: Palgrave, 2001), 4, 8–11.

170 Harcourt quoted in Jenkins, *Fenian Problem*, 95.

171 Historicus [Harcourt], "Who Is a British Subject?" *Times* (London), December 11, 1867; Gerlach, *British Liberalism*, 12.

172 Ibid.

173 Adams quoted in Jenkins, *Fenians and Anglo-American Relations*, 259.

174 Ibid., 268; Morrow, "Treaty of 1870," 671; Lord Stanley to Sir Edward Thornton, June 16, 1866, H. Ex Doc. No. 66, February 2, 1869, 40th Cong., 3rd Session, 8–9, *United States Congressional Serial Set*. Thornton was appointed as minister to Washington following the death of Frederick Bruce in September 1867.

175 Stanley to Thornton, June 16, 1868, 8.

176 William Seward to Reverdy Johnson, July 20, 1868, quoted in Morrow, "Treaty of 1870," 675.

177 William Seward to Reverdy Johnson, September 23, 1868, despatch no. 20, *FRUS 1868*, 1:355.

178 Cong. Globe, 40th Cong., 3rd Session, December 8, 1868, 26.

179 Robinson speeches, November 25 and December 2, 1867, in *Rights of American Citizens Abroad: Speeches of William E. Robinson . . . in the House of Representatives* (Washington, D.C.: Congressional Globe Office, 1867). Robinson was not reelected, a fact he blamed—perhaps disingenuously—upon his "talking so much on Ireland and Fenianism"; Cong. Globe, 40th Cong., 3rd Session, March 2, 1869, 264.

180 1868 Democratic Party platform, American Presidency Project, www.presidency.ucsb. edu/ws/index.php?pid=29579 (accessed September 20, 2010).

181 1868 Republican Party platform, American Presidency Project, www.presidency.ucsb. edu/ws/index.php?pid=29622 (accessed September 21, 2010).

182 Ibid.

183 Ibid.

184 "An Act Concerning the Rights of American Citizens in Foreign States," chapter 249, 40th Cong., 2nd Sess., in *Statues at Large, Treaties, and Proclamations of the United States of America, from December 1867, to March 1869*, vol. 15 (Boston: Little, Brown and Company, 1869), 223–224.

185 Peter Schuck and Rogers Smith, *Citizenship without Consent: Illegal Aliens in the American Polity* (New Haven, CT: Yale University Press, 1985), 87–88. Nancy Green seems to accept this link, though she expands on the international context of the act; Green, "Expatriation, Expatriates, and Expats," 314–315.

186 On Congress and the Fourteenth Amendment, see Foner, *Reconstruction*, 251–261.

187 "An Act Concerning the Rights of American Citizens in Foreign States," 224.

188 H. Ex. Doc. No. 312, June 24, 1868, 40th Cong., 2nd Sess., 1, *United States Congressional Serial Set*.

189 H. Report No. 44, March 2, 1869, 40th Cong., 3rd Session, 4, *United States Congressional Serial Set*.

190 The phrase is Robinson's; Cong. Globe, 40th Cong., 3rd Session, December 8, 1868, 22. For Sumner's speech discussing the committee's amendment, see Cong. Globe, 40th Cong., 2nd Sess., July 18, 1868, 4205–4206.

191 Green, "Expatriation, Expatriates, and Expats," 315.

192 Lord Stanley to Sir Edward Thornton, September 19, 1868, quoted in Jenkins, *Fenians and Anglo-American Relations*, 278–279, quote at 278.

193 Ibid., 280.

194 Cong. Globe, 41st Cong., 2nd Sess., June 9, 1870, 4266–4279.

195 Ibid., July 14, 1870, 5607; Steven P. Erie, *Rainbow's End: Irish-Americans and the Dilemmas of Urban Machine Politics, 1840–1985* (Berkeley: University of California Press 1988), 36.

196 H. C. G. Matthew, "Gladstone, William Ewart (1809–1898)," *Oxford Dictionary of National Biography*.

197 William Gladstone to General C. Grey, March 28, 1869, in *The Gladstone Diaries*, 14 vols., edited by M. R. D. Foot and H. C. G. Matthew (Oxford, UK: Clarendon Press, 1968–1994), 7:45.

198 McConville, *Irish Political Prisoners, 1848–1922*, 226–252; Comerford, *Fenians in Context*, 145–146, 164–166. For more on the amnesty movement, see chapter 5.

199 Seward's report, in H. Ex. Doc. No. 66, February 2, 1869, 40th Cong., 3rd Session, *United States Congressional Serial Set*. Costello was released first, in January 1869. Warren's release followed on March 4. Jeremiah O'Donovan Rossa, *My Years in English Jails* (Tralee: Anvil Books, 1967), 210; "The Pardoned Political Prisoners," *Freeman's Journal and Daily Commercial Advertiser* (Dublin), March 12, 1869.

200 Reverdy Johnson to William Seward, February 23, 1869, despatch no. 120, in H. Ex. Doc. No. 170, March 2, 1870, 41st Congress, 2nd Sess., 6, *United States Congressional Serial Set*.

201 Brown, "Fenian State Trials," 36.

202 Ibid.; and Reverdy Johnson to William Seward, March 1, 1869, despatch no. 126, H. Ex. Doc. No. 170, 41st Congress, 2nd Sess., 7; John Lothrop Motley to Hamilton Fish, October 5, 1869, despatch no. 114, H. Ex. Doc. No. 170, 41st Congress, 2nd Sess., 33.

203 Reverdy Johnson to Hamilton Fish, April 24, 1869, despatch no. 159, H. Ex. Doc. No. 170, 41st Congress, 2nd Sess., 12.

204 Reverdy Johnson to Elihu B. Washburne, March 24, 1869, despatch no. 145, H. Ex. Doc. No. 170, 41st Congress, 2nd Sess., 11. Washburne was President Grant's surprise appointment as secretary of state; he served only twelve days in the post.

205 "The Liberated Political Prisoners," *Freeman's Journal* (Dublin), March 18, 1869.

206 McConville, *Irish Political Prisoners, 1848–1922*, 231.

207 *Pall Mall Gazette* quoted in Jenkins, *Fenian Problem*, 231.

208 Hamilton Fish to Reverdy Johnson, April 13, 1869, despatch no. 100, in H. Ex. Doc. No. 170, 41st Congress, 2nd Sess., 11.

209 Cong. Globe, 40th Cong., 3rd Session, March 2, 1869, appendix, 262.

210 Augustine Costello to William West, September 16, 1867, in H. Ex. Doc. No. 157, 40th Cong., 2nd Sess., part 2, 520.

Chapter 5

1 Mike J. Sewell, "Rebels or Revolutionaries? Irish-American Nationalism and American Diplomacy, 1865–1885," *Historical Journal* 29, no. 3 (1986): 723–733, quote at 730.

2 Conor Cruise O'Brien, *Parnell and His Party 1880–1890* (Oxford: Clarendon Press, 1964), 72–118; Eric Foner, *Politics and Ideology in the Age of the Civil War* (New York: Oxford University Press, 1980), 166–168, 189–194.

3 Henry George to Francis G. Shaw, May 30, 1882, reel 2, Henry George Papers, microfilm, 15 reels, Manuscripts and Archives Division, New York Public Library, New York, New York (hereafter Henry George Papers).

4 Brian A. Jenkins, *Fenians and Anglo-American Relations during Reconstruction* (Ithaca, NY: Cornell University Press, 1969), 292–294.

5 Ibid., 305–308. Peter Michael Toner, "The Rise of Irish Nationalism in Canada, 1858–1884," (PhD diss., National University of Ireland, 1974), 233–235, 238.

6 Roy F. Foster, *Modern Ireland, 1600–1972* (London: Penguin, 1989), 395; R. V. Comerford, *The Fenians in Context: Irish Politics and Society, 1848–82* (Dublin: Wolfhound Press, 1998), esp. 210–212.

7 Charles Wentworth Dilke, *Greater Britain: A Record of Travel in English-Speaking Countries during 1866 and 1867*, 2 vols. (London: Macmillan and Co., 1868), 1:297.

8 Devoy's release was conditional on his leaving the United Kingdom for the duration of his prison sentence. Comerford, *Fenians in Context*, 145–146, 151–152; Foster, *Modern Ireland*, 395–396; Seán McConville, *Irish Political Prisoners, 1848–1922: Theatres of War* (London: Routledge, 2003), 209.

9 John Devoy quoted in Charles Callan Tansill, *America and the Fight for Irish Freedom 1866–1922: An Old Story Based upon New Data* (New York: Devin-Adair, 1957), 40.

10 John Boyle O'Reilly to Jeremiah O'Donovan Rossa, March 2, 1872, quoted in Oliver P. Rafferty, *The Church, the State and the Fenian Threat, 1861–75* (Basingstoke: Palgrave, 1999), 80.

11 John Boyle O'Reilly to John Devoy, January 28, 1871, in *Devoy's Post Bag 1871–1928*, 2 vols., edited by William O'Brien and Desmond Ryan (Dublin: Academy Press, 1979), 1:13 (hereafter *Devoy's Post Bag*).

12 "The Unity of the Irish Race in America, February 8, 1871," in *Devoy's Post Bag*, 1:26.

13 John Mitchel to John Martin, February 1868, quoted in *Devoy's Post Bag*, 1:3.

14 Ibid.

15 McConville, *Irish Political Prisoners*, 139; Brian A. Jenkins, *The Fenian Problem: Insurgency and Terrorism in a Liberal State, 1858–1874* (Liverpool: Liverpool University Press, 2009), 227.

16 William Gladstone to Archbishop Manning, August 26, 1872, in *The Gladstone Diaries*, 14 vols., ed. M. R. D. Foot and H. C. G. Matthew (Oxford, UK: Clarendon Press, 1968–1994), 8:201.

17 Jenkins, *Fenian Problem*, 278–285, quote at 279.

18 McConville, *Irish Political Prisoners*, 214–275.

19 William Gladstone to Earl Spencer, Lord Lieutenant of Ireland, September 3, 1870, in Foot and Matthew, *The Gladstone Diaries*, 7:352.

20 R. V. Comerford, "Isaac Butt and the Home Rule Party, 1870–1877," in *Ireland under the Union, 1870–1921*, 2 vols., edited by W. E. Vaughan (Oxford: Oxford University Press, 1996), 2:2.

21 Mark F. Ryan, *Fenian Memories* (Dublin: M. H. Gill & Son, 1945), 88; McConville, *Irish Political Prisoners*, 271. William Halpin was released and returned to the United States in late 1871. "Irish Confederation Moves," *Devoy's Post Bag*, 1:45.

22 William Gladstone to Earl Spencer, September 14, 1870, in Foot and Matthew, *The Gladstone Diaries*, 7:360.

23 Jeremiah O'Donovan Rossa, *My Years in English Jails* (1874; repr., Tralee: Anvil Books, 1967), 227–237; John Mitchel to O'Donovan Rossa, January 21, 1871, Box 8, Folder 14, Rossa Papers; Owen Dudley Edwards, "Rossa, Jeremiah O'Donovan (*bap.* 1831, *d.* 1915)," *Oxford Dictionary of National Biography*.

24 Edwards, "Rossa, Jeremiah O'Donovan"; Jonathan W. Gantt, "Irish-American Terrorism, and Anglo-American Relations," *Journal of the Gilded Age and Progressive Era* 5, no. 4 (2006): 330–332. For more on these attacks, see chapter 6.

25 Ibid., 329; Comerford, "Isaac Butt and the Home Rule Party," 21–22; McConville, *Irish Political Prisoners*, 209–213; Foster, *Modern Ireland*, 393; Kerby A. Miller, *Emigrants and Exiles: Ireland and the Irish Exodus to North America* (New York: Oxford University Press, 1985), 539.

26 Robert Kelley, *The Transatlantic Persuasion: The Liberal-Democratic Mind in the Age of Gladstone* (New York: Knopf, 1969); Leslie Butler, *Critical Americans: Victorian Intellectuals and Transatlantic Liberal Reform* (Chapel Hill: University of North Carolina Press, 2007), 221–241; Frank A. Ninkovich, *Global Dawn: The Cultural Foundation of American Internationalism, 1865–1890* (Cambridge, MA: Harvard University Press, 2009), 79–94.

27 John Morley quoted in Tom Dunne, "La Trahison des Clercs: British Intellectuals and the First Home-Rule Crisis," *Irish Historical Studies* 23, no. 90 (1982): 135.

28 Curtis quoted in Butler, *Critical Americans*, 233.

29 Ninkovich, *Global Dawn*, 232–262.

30 Dilke, *Greater Britain*, 1:300.

31 The "high water mark" phrase is from Frank Ninkovich, *Global Dawn*, 303; the earlier quote is from G. E. Ponded, quoted in ibid., 91.

32 David Hamer, "Morley, John, Viscount Morley of Blackburn (1838–1923)," *Oxford Dictionary of National Biography*; and Christopher A. Kent, "Smith, Goldwin (1823–1910)," *Oxford Dictionary of National Biography*.

33 Morley quoted in Murney Gerlach, *British Liberalism and the United States: Political and Social Thought in the Late Victorian Age* (Basingstoke: Palgrave, 2001), 23.

34 Adams diary entry for January 4, 1867, reel 80, *Adams Papers*; Butler, *Critical Americans*, 233.

35 See Steven P. Erie, *Rainbow's End: Irish-Americans and the Dilemmas of Urban Machine Politics, 1840–1985* (Berkeley: University of California Press, 1988), esp. 25–66.

36 Strong quoted in Stephen G. N. Tuck, *We Ain't What We Ought to Be: The Black Freedom Struggle from Emancipation to Obama* (Cambridge: Belknap Press, 2010), 63.

37 James Anthony Froude, "Romanism and the Irish Race in the United States. Part I," *North American Review* 129, no. 277 (1879): 523.

38 Ibid., 523, 525. On Froude's visit to the United States, see Mary C. Kelly, *The Shamrock and the Lily: The New York Irish and the Creation of a Transatlantic Identity, 1845–1921* (New York: Peter Lang, 2005), 94–96.

39 Dilke, *Greater Britain*, 1:44–45.

40 Mitchell Snay, *Fenians, Freedmen, and Southern Whites: Race and Nationality in the Era of Reconstruction* (Baton Rouge: Louisiana State University Press, 2007). James Belich writes of "the South/Ireland, deeply split within itself into black/white and Catholic/Protestant" as a "junior partner" to "a wealthy and populous senior partner, England/Mid-Atlantic states." Each junior partner might be governed by its senior equivalent, and its incorporation into the larger whole—the United Kingdom/the United States—was halting and incomplete. Belich, *Replenishing the Earth: The Settler Revolution and the Rise of the Angloworld* (Oxford: Oxford University Press, 2009), 68.

41 As Mitchel succinctly put it, "the North is England; the South is Ireland"; quoted in David T. Gleeson, "Securing the 'Interests' of the South: John Mitchel, A. G. Magrath, and the Reopening of the Transatlantic Slave Trade," *American Nineteenth Century History* 11, no. 3 (2010): 286.

42 Miller, *Emigrants and Exiles*, 538.

43 "An Exile of Erin," *New York Tribune*, May 16, 1876, 4.

44 Miller, *Emigrants and Exiles*, 538.

45 Gerlach, *British Liberalism and the United States,* 40; See also Jay Sexton, *Debtor Diplomacy: Finance and American Foreign Relations in the Civil War Era, 1837–1873* (Oxford: Oxford University Press, 2005), 212–229.

46 Comerford, "Isaac Butt and the Home Rule Party," 11–17. Butt saw federation as a means of strengthening the British Empire.

47 Isaac Butt, *Irish Federalism! Its Meaning, Its Objects, and Its Hopes*, 4th ed. (Dublin: The Irish Home Rule League, 1874); Toner, "Rise of Irish Nationalism," 262.

48 Donald Jordan, "John O'Connor Power, Charles Stewart Parnell and the Centralisation of Popular Politics in Ireland," *Irish Historical Studies* 25, no. 97 (1986): 55; "Ireland to America," *New York Times*, September 26, 1876.

49 "Ireland to America," *New York Tribune*, October 2, 1876.

50 "A Congratulatory Address from Ireland," *New York Times*, October 1, 1876. Power was described as "a self-made man" who had reached his current position "by mere force of ability." Parnell, by contrast, was described as being merely "a member of an old aristocratic family, and a large landed proprietor," although the newspaper noted that his grandfather had "voted steadfastly against the Union" as a member of the Irish House of Commons. Interestingly, no mention was made of Parnell's American mother.

51 Patrick Egan, James Kavanagh, and Robert J. Dunne to Ulysses S. Grant, n.d., in *The Papers of Ulysses S. Grant*, 28 vols., edited by John Y. Simon (Carbondale: Southern Illinois University Press, 1967–), 27:337. Hereafter *Papers of Ulysses S. Grant*.

52 Ibid.

53 John L. Cadwalader to Hamilton Fish, October 13, 1876, letterbook 116, Hamilton Fish Papers; Charles Stewart Parnell and John O'Connor Power to Hamilton Fish, *Papers of Ulysses S. Grant*, 27:337.

54 Cadwalader to Fish, October 13, 1876.

55 Hamilton Fish to John Cadwalader, October 16, 1876, letterbook 192, Hamilton Fish Papers.

56 Ibid.

57 Grant, "Note," October 17, 1876, *Papers of Ulysses S. Grant*, 27:336; Culver C. Sniffen to Charles Stewart Parnell and John O'Connor Power, October 17, 1876, *Papers of Ulysses S. Grant*, 27:336, Parnell and O'Connor Power to Sniffen, October 23, 1876, *Papers of Ulysses S. Grant*, 27:337.

58 "Notes from Washington," *New York Times*, October 22, 1876.

59 Grant's apparent snub had an effect on his 1879 world tour. When he visited Ireland, he was warmly welcomed in Dublin but the Cork Corporation made it known that should he visit the city, "he would receive neither public reception nor municipal honours." "Cork Snubs General Grant," *Devoy's Post Bag*, 1:390.

60 Paul Bew, *Land and the National Question in Ireland* (Dublin: Gill and Macmillan, 1978), 46.

61 William Carroll to John Devoy, March 29, 1876, quoted in ibid., 46; "The Escaped Fenians," *New York Tribune*, August 21, 1876.

62 Michael A. Gordon, *The Orange Riots: Irish Political Violence in New York City, 1870 and 1871* (Ithaca, NY: Cornell University Press, 1993); Kevin Kenny, *Making Sense of the Molly Maguires* (New York: Oxford University Press, 1998); Foner, *Politics and Ideology in the Age of the Civil War*; Victor A. Walsh, "'A Fanatic Heart': The Cause of Irish-American Nationalism in Pittsburgh during the Gilded Age," *Journal of Social History* 15, no. 2 (1981): 187–204; Alexander

Saxton, *The Indispensable Enemy: Labor and the Anti-Chinese Movement in California* (Berkeley: University of California Press, 1971).

63 Bew, *Land and the National Question*, 25–33; Foster, *Modern Ireland*, 402–403.

64 Foster, *Modern Ireland*, 354; Comerford, "The Land War and the Politics of Distress, 1877–1882," in *Ireland under the Union, 1870–1921*, 2 vols., edited by W. E. Vaughan (Oxford: Oxford University Press, 1996), 2:33–34; O'Brien, *Parnell and His Party*, 33–34; Davitt quoted in Foster, *Modern Ireland*, 401.

65 Comerford, "Land War and the Politics of Distress," 29–33. Paul Bew argues that Parnell did eventually take the IRB oath, though this was not made public. Paul Bew, "Parnell, Charles Stewart (1846–1891)," *Oxford Dictionary of National Biography*.

66 Bew, *Land and the National Question*, 48–50, Devoy quoted at 50.

67 The significance—or otherwise—of the phrase "new departure" is unclear. It would have been a phrase with currency in American political culture during the 1870s, referring to southern states' acceptance of the terms of Reconstruction, the end of federal occupation of the South, and the reinstatement of (Democratic) home rule, another term with clear resonance in Irish and Irish-American politics.

68 Comerford, "Land War and the Politics of Distress," 30–33; Foster, *Modern Ireland*, 403; Bew, *Land and the National Question*, 46–54.

69 R. V. Comerford, "Land War and the Politics of Distress," 36; David M. Pletcher, *The Awkward Years: American Foreign Relations under Garfield and Arthur* (Columbia: University of Missouri Press, 1962), 237.

70 Comerford, "Land War and the Politics of Distress," 37–38; Alan O'Day, "Irish Nationalism and Anglo-American Relations in the Late Nineteenth and Early Twentieth Centuries," in *Anglo-American Attitudes: From Revolution to Partnership*, edited by Fred M. Leventhal and Ronald Quinault (Aldershot: Ashgate, 2000), 181–182. As in the United States, so in Canada (which Parnell also visited), where donations for charitable purposes dwarfed those for political ends. In fact, as historian D. C. Lyne has noted, private philanthropic contributions—i.e., money that was not sent to support parliamentary organizations for the period 1879–1880 probably equaled or exceeded the total donations for Irish causes from 1880 to the end of the century. Lyne, "Irish-Canadian Financial Contributions to the Home Rule Movement in the 1890s," *Studia Hibernica*, no. 7 (1967): 183; Toner, "Rise of Irish Nationalism," 315–318.

71 William O'Carroll quoted in O'Day, "Irish Nationalism and Anglo-American Relations," 181.

72 O'Day, "Irish Nationalism and Anglo-American Relations," 181–183; and Alan O'Day, "Imagined Irish Communities: Networks of Social Communication of the Irish Diaspora in the United States and Britain in the Late Nineteenth and Early Twentieth Centuries," *Immigrants and Minorities* 23, nos. 2–3 (2005): 415–418. The phrase is Michael Davitt's, quoted in O'Day, "Irish Nationalism and Anglo-American Relations," 168; "Parnell's Noisy Hearers," *New York Times*, January 5, 1880; Merle Curti, *American Philanthropy Abroad: A History* (New Brunswick, NJ: Rutgers University Press, 1963), 88.

73 *New York Tribune*, January 12, 1880, quoted in Curti, *American Philanthropy Abroad*, 87.

74 Ibid., 86; Comerford, "Land War and the Politics of Distress," 37–38.

75 The editor of the *Herald*, James Gordon Bennett Jr., was cynical about Parnell's tour. Parnell, for his part, saw the *Herald's* activities as no more than a promotional scheme to increase the paper's circulation. Curti, *American Philanthropy Abroad*, 87–94.

76 O'Day, "Irish Nationalism and Anglo-American Relations," 182. Even in absolute terms, that £72,000 (approximately $349,000) compares unfavorably with the £133,000 ($637,000) worth of donations collected during 1847. Conversions estimated using Lawrence H. Officer and Samuel H. Williamson, "Computing 'Real Value' over Time with a Conversion between

U.K. Pounds and U.S. Dollars, 1830 to Present," Measuring Worth website, www.measuring-worth.com (accessed May 7, 2013).

77 Godkin even contributed to the *Handbook of Home Rule*, an 1887 Liberal Party publication that made the case for Irish home rule. He had little patience with Irish Americans who returned to Ireland to take place in nationalist agitation. William M. Armstrong, *E. L. Godkin and American Foreign Policy, 1865–1900* (New York: Bookman, 1957), 151–158; William M. Armstrong, ed., *The Gilded Age Letters of E. L. Godkin* (Albany: State University of New York Press, 1974), 380; Butler, *Critical Americans*, 234, 236–237, 239.

78 "Mr. Parnell's Mission," *The Nation* (New York), January 8, 1880, 23.

79 Ibid.

80 Ibid.

81 Ninkovich, *Global Dawn*, 264–267; "Mr. Parnell's Mission," *The Nation* (New York), 23.

82 O'Brien, *Parnell and His Party*, 134.

83 All conversions estimated Officer and Williamson, "Computing 'Real Value' over Time."

84 Comerford, "Land War and the Politics of Distress," 42–43.

85 John Dillon to Patrick A. Collins, February 5, 1880, Series 1, Subseries A, Box 1, Patrick A. Collins Papers, John J. Burns Library, Boston College, Boston, Massachusetts (hereafter Patrick A. Collins Papers); O'Hare, "Patrick Andrew Collins," 147–148. The bank served as the financial agent for both the Land League and the Irish Famine Relief Fund; O'Day, "Irish Nationalism and Anglo-American Relations," 182.

86 Foner, *Politics and Ideology in the Age of the Civil War*, 155–157, quote at 157.

87 Ibid., 156.

88 *Congressional Record*, 46th Cong., 2nd Sess., February 17–18 and February 27, 1880, 938, 963, 1175; Curti, *American Philanthropy Abroad*, 95–96.

89 Ibid., 96.

90 William J. Hoppin to William Evarts, April 24, 1880, despatch no. 180, *FRUS 1880*, 1:476–478.

91 Edward Thornton to William Evarts, May 14, 1880, despatch no. 340, *FRUS 1880*, 1:514.

92 Ibid.

93 James Russell Lowell to William Evarts, January 7, 1881, despatch no. 115, *FRUS 1881*, 1:492.

94 The idea being that should a tenant take up a lease that had previously been that of an evictee, that man or woman would be shunned by the community at large. By maintaining disciplined opposition to the filling of empty leases, Land Leaguers hoped to exercise some control over the behavior of landlords; O'Brien, *Parnell and His Party*, 44–65. At least one commentator in the American press condemned the undercurrent of violence that underpinned the boycott strategy as "terrorism"; H. O. Arnold-Forster, "The Gladstone Government and Ireland," *North American Review* 133, no. 301 (1881): 566, 570.

95 Lowell to Evarts, January 7, 1881, 493.

96 "Ireland," *New York Times*, November 16, 1880. Owen Dudley Edwards notes that "after the Civil War, when a record against slavery was a desideratum instead of a source of obloquy, the memory of O'Connell proved highly advantageous to the cause of Ireland." Edwards, "The American Image of Ireland," 267.

97 O'Day, "Imagined Irish Communities," 417.

98 For more on the home rule movement, see chapter 6.

99 Comerford, "Land War and the Politics of Distress," 47; Pletcher, *Awkward Years*, 237–238.

100 James Russell Lowell to William Evarts, February 26, 1881, despatch no. 132, reel 137, *Despatches from United States Ministers to Great Britain*. Parnell did not have an American audience

in mind. More likely, he sought to impress a British public with the existence—and power—of an Irish diaspora and to reassure an Irish audience that they were not isolated in their participation in agrarian agitation. O'Brien, *Parnell and His Party*, 63–64.

101 James G. Blaine to James Russell Lowell, May 26, 1881, despatch no. 166, *FRUS 1881*, 1:530; and Blaine to Lowell, June 2, 1881, despatch no. 172, *FRUS 1881*, 1:532. For characterizations of Blaine as an Anglophobe, see Pletcher, *Awkward Years*, 238; and Edward P. Crapol, *America for Americans: Economic Nationalism and Anglophobia in the Late Nineteenth Century* (Westport, CT: Greenwood Press, 1973), 7. For an important corrective, see Mike J. Sewell, "Political Rhetoric and Policy-Making: James G. Blaine and Britain," *Journal of American Studies* 24, no. 1 (1990): 61–84.

102 Edward Thornton to Lord Granville, June 27, 1881, quoted in Sewell, "Rebels or Revolutionaries?" 726.

103 Sen. Ex. Doc. No. 5, May 20, 1881, 47th Cong., Special Session No. 1, 5, *United States Congressional Serial Set*.

104 Blaine quoted in Victor Drummond to Lord Granville, November 1, 1881, in K. R. M. Short, *The Dynamite War* (Dublin: Gill & Macmillan, 1979), 69; Sewell, "Political Rhetoric and Policy-Making", 66.

105 The nineteen here referred to are Michael Boyton, Joseph D'Alton, Joseph P. Walsh, John McEnery, Dennis H. O'Connor, Michael Hart, Daniel McSweeney, M. B. Fogarty, Henry O'Mahoney, James F. Daly, Philip O'Sullivan, James L. White, John McCormack, Patrick Slattery, William Brophy, John Leonard Gannon, James Lynam, Stephen J. Meany, and Henry George. These are the names that appear in the *Foreign Relations of the United States* series for 1881 and 1882, but *FRUS* is not a complete diplomatic record.

106 James Russell Lowell to Lord Granville, August 29, 1882, enclosed in Lowell to Frederick Frelinghuysen, August 30, 1882, despatch no. 434, *FRUS 1882*, 1:292; Frelinghuysen to Lowell, September 22, 1882, *FRUS 1882*, 1:294; and Lowell to Frelinghuysen, July 14, 1882, despatch no. 398, *FRUS 1882*, 1:285.

107 James Russell Lowell to James G. Blaine, June 4, 1881, despatch no. 193, *FRUS 1881*, 1:533.

108 Lowell quoted in Pletcher, *Awkward Years*, 238. An early biographer claimed "that Mr. Lowell's sympathies were with the Irish, and that he looked upon home-rule for Ireland as, in some form, inevitable," and historian Owen Dudley Edwards has highlighted Lowell's long-term appreciation of the need for Irish reform, which dated back to at least 1870. George W. Smalley, "Mr. Lowell in England," *Harper's New Monthly Magazine* 92, no. 551 (1896): 793; Edwards, "American Diplomats and Irish Coercion, 1880–1883," *Journal of American Studies* 1, no. 2 (1967): 226.

109 Bew, "Parnell."

110 James Russell Lowell to Frederick Frelinghuysen, February 16, 1883, despatch no. 498, *FRUS 1883*, 1:413.

111 Frederick Frelinghuysen to President Arthur, April 4, 1882, copy enclosed with James Russell Lowell to Frelinghuysen, May 6, 1882, despatch no. 351, *FRUS 1882*, 1:262.

112 Lionel Sackville-West to Lord Granville, April 6, 1882, enclosed with Lowell to Frelinghuysen, May 6, 1882.

113 Walter LaFeber, *The New Empire: An Interpretation of American Expansion, 1860–1898* (Ithaca, NY: Cornell University Press, 1963), 46–53.

114 Pletcher, *Awkward Years*, 241.

115 Robinson's resolution quoted in Lionel Sackville-West to Lord Granville, February 15, 1882, *FRUS 1882*, 1:251.

116 Sewell, "Rebels or Revolutionaries?" 726.

117 *New York Tribune*, April 5, 1882, enclosed in Lionel Sackville-West to Lord Granville, April 8, 1882, *FRUS 1882*, 1:263. As Mike Sewell notes, this piece of legislation was invoked frequently in congressional debates on the release of Irish American prisoners, but to no avail. Sewell, "Rebels or Revolutionaries?" 727.

118 Patrick Ford to William G. Blaine, March 25, 1881, Sen. Ex. Doc. No. 5, May 20, 1881, 20, *United States Congressional Serial Set*. Patrick Ford's paper attacked economic privilege, especially the evils of land monopolies. Though it was printed in the United States, it circulated widely in Ireland. Such was the size of its Irish readership that the British government moved to ban it in late 1882. On Ford, see James Paul Rodechko, *Patrick Ford and His Search for America: A Case Study of Irish-American Journalism 1870–1913* (New York: Arno Press, 1976); and Foner, *Politics and Ideology in the Age of the Civil War*, 157–160. Boyton was a key Land League organizer in County Tipperary. He had grown up in Pennsylvania and had returned to Ireland in 1867; Bew, *Land and the National Question*, 237–238; Arnold-Forster, "The Gladstone Government and Ireland," 566; Henry George to Patrick Ford, December 28 [December 30], 1882, reel 7, Henry George Papers; Rodechko, *Patrick Ford and His Search for America*, 186–188.

119 Peter McCorry to Frederick Frelinghuysen, January 26, 1882, enclosed in Frelinghuysen to James Russell Lowell, January 31, 1882, despatch no. 313, *FRUS 1882*, 1:194–195; John Chandler Bancroft Davis to Lowell, February 10, 1882, despatch no. 316, *FRUS 1882*, 1:197–198.

120 Hamilton Fish to Sir John Rose, April 18, 1882, letterbook 194, Hamilton Fish Papers.

121 Pletcher, *Awkward Years*, 242.

122 Fish to Rose, April 18, 1882.

123 Bancroft Davis to Hamilton Fish, June 16, 1881, letterbook 132, Hamilton Fish Papers.

124 Sexton, *Debtor Diplomacy*, 212–229.

125 Fish quoted in Pletcher, *Awkward Years*, 242–243.

126 Sir John Rose to Hamilton Fish, April 4, 1882, letterbook 135, Hamilton Fish Papers.

127 Ibid.; and Sir John Rose to Hamilton Fish, April 6, 1882, letterbook 135, Hamilton Fish Papers.

128 Bancroft Davis to Hamilton Fish, April 9, 1882, Hamilton Fish Papers; Edwards, "American Diplomats and Irish Coercion," 228.

129 James Russell Lowell to Oliver Wendell Holmes, December 28, 1884, quoted in Smalley, "Mr. Lowell in England," 792. McCarthy was leader of the Irish Parliamentary Party during Parnell's time in Kilmainham Gaol. James Russell Lowell to Frederick Frelinghuysen, August 8, 1882, despatch no. 417, *FRUS 1882*, 1:286.

130 Gerlach, *British Liberalism and the United States*, 74–75, quote at 75.

131 Fish to Rose, April 18, 1882.

132 James Bryce quoted in Gerlach, *British Liberalism and the United States*, 80.

133 Fish to Rose, April 18, 1882.

134 The journalist, Stephen J. Meany, had seemed somewhat less respectable fifteen years previously, when he had been arrested "on charges of participation in Fenian movements." William Henry Seward to Charles Francis Adams, August 7, 1867, *FRUS 1867*, 1:121. His case was noted in Congress at the time by William Robinson; see Cong. Globe, 40th Cong., 1st Sess., November 25, 1867, 787; Bancroft Davis to James Russell Lowell, August 16, 1882, despatch no. 439, *FRUS 1882*, 1:289.

135 Lowell to Granville, August 29, 1882, 292; Frederick Frelinghuysen to James Russell Lowell, October 3, 1882, despatch no. 466, *FRUS 1882*, 1:296.

136 Henry George to Annie George, August [?], 1882, reel 2, Henry George Papers; Davis to Lowell, August 16, 1882; Davis to Lowell, August 18, 1882, despatch no. 445, *FRUS 1882*, 1:291; Edwards, "American Diplomats," 223.

137 Henry George to Patrick Ford, November 10, 1881, and December 28, 1881, both reel 7, Henry George Papers; and Henry George to [Francis G.?] Shaw, August 15, 1882, reel 2, Henry George Papers.

138 Henry George to Charles Nordhoff, January 31, 1879, reel 2, Henry George Papers.

139 "The cause of Ireland," Davitt argued, "was also that of humanity and labour throughout the world"; quoted in O'Brien, *Parnell and His Party*, 62; Rodechko, *Patrick Ford and His Search for America*, 7:187–188; Foner, *Politics and Ideology in the Age of the Civil War*, 161.

140 Davitt and George had met during Davitt's tour of the United States in 1878, though most likely he did not read *Progress and Poverty* until his time in Portland Prison in the spring of 1881. Foster, *Modern Ireland*, 354; draft of a "Letter in defense of Michael Davitt and the Irish Land League," reel 8, Henry George Papers.

141 "Notice of publication, *Irish Land Question*," March 10, 1881, reel 2, Henry George Papers.

142 Henry George to "Doctor," September 12, 1881, reel 2, Henry George Papers; Rodechko, *Patrick Ford and His Search for America*, 77–78.

143 Henry George, interview in the *Newcastle-on-Tyne Chronicle*, reprinted in Kenneth C. Wenzer, ed., *Henry George, the Transatlantic Irish, and Their Times* (Bingley: Emerald JAI, 2009), 41.

144 Foner, *Politics and Ideology in the Age of the Civil War*, 184–200; Gerlach, *British Liberalism and the United States*, 94–101.

145 John Devoy to James Reynolds, April 11, 1881, quoted in Rodechko, *Patrick Ford and His Search for America*, 188–189.

146 Henry George to Francis G. Shaw, April 28, 1882; and Henry George to Annie George, May [?] and May 4, 1882, all reel 2, Henry George Papers.

147 Henry George to Francis G. Shaw, May 30, 1882; O'Brien, *Parnell and His Party*, 119–149.

148 George to Shaw, May 30, 1882.

149 Letter fragment, likely Henry George to Francis G. Shaw, possibly May 30 or 31, 1882, reel 2, Henry George Papers.

150 Henry George to Patrick Ford, March 9, 1882, reel 7, Henry George Papers.

151 Henry George to Patrick Ford, April 20, 1882, reel 7, Henry George Papers.

Chapter 6

1 Owen Dudley Edwards, "Rossa, Jeremiah O'Donovan (*bap.* 1831, *d.* 1915)," *Oxford Dictionary of National Biography*.

2 On the negotiation of Irish American identity during this period, see Úna Ní Bhroiméil, *Building Irish Identity in America, 1870–1915: The Gaelic Revival* (Dublin: Four Courts, 2003); and Timothy J. Meagher, *Inventing Irish America: Generation, Class, and Ethnic Identity in a New England City, 1880–1928* (Notre Dame, IN: University of Notre Dame Press, 2001).

3 Seán McConville, *Irish Political Prisoners, 1848–1922: Theatres of War* (London: Routledge, 2003), 326–327.

4 K. R. M. Short, *The Dynamite War* (Dublin: Gill & Macmillan, 1979), 50, 104–105, 206–208, 259–260; Campbell, *Fenian Fire: The British Government Plot to Assassinate Queen Victoria* (London: HarperCollins, 2003), 109–148.

5 Edwards, "Rossa."

6 McConville, *Irish Political Prisoners*, 339–341, quote at 339.

7 Rossa quoted in Tom Corfe, *The Phoenix Park Murders: Conflict, Compromise and Tragedy in Ireland, 1879–1882* (London: Hodder & Stoughton, 1968), 60.

8 John Mitchel to M[?]. Moynahan, January 28, 1867, Fenian Brotherhood Collection, American Catholic History Research Center and University Archives, The Catholic University of America, available at www.aladin0.wrlc.org/gsdl/collect/fenian/fenian.shtml (accessed February 21, 2010).

9 McCafferty quoted in Brian A. Jenkins, *The Fenian Problem: Insurgency and Terrorism in a Liberal State, 1858–1874* (Liverpool: Liverpool University Press, 2009), 114.

10 McConville, *Irish Political Prisoners*, 342–344, 346–347.

11 Lomasney had led a series of raids in and around Cork. He was tried for fatally wounding a policeman during his arrest in February 1868 but was acquitted. Prior to this he had spent time in Kilmainham Gaol for his Fenian activities. In diplomatic correspondence he is identified as a native of Baltimore, Maryland. See, for instance, William West to Thomas Larcom, March 5, 1866, and West to Charles Francis Adams, February 19, 1866, H. Ex. Doc. No. 157, February 10, 1868, 40th Cong., 2nd Sess., part 2, 47, 143, *United States Congressional Serial Set*. Lomasney died in December 1884 while attempting to blow up London Bridge. McConville, *Irish Political Prisoners*, 348, 353; Jenkins, *Fenian Problem*, 177, 331; Mark F. Ryan, *Fenian Memories* (Dublin: M. H. Gill & Son, 1945), 117–119; Campbell, *Fenian Fire*.

12 McConville, *Irish Political Prisoners*, 348–355.

13 Ibid., 355.

14 O'Donovan Rossa quoted in Eric Foner, *Politics and Ideology in the Age of the Civil War* (New York: Oxford University Press, 1980), 164; Campbell, *Fenian Fire*, 110.

15 Short, *Dynamite War*, 46–55; McConville, *Irish Political Prisoners*, 344–345, Lomasney quote on 345.

16 McConville, *Irish Political Prisoners*, 332, 340, 359–360.

17 O'Leary quoted in ibid., 340.

18 O'Reilly quoted in James Jeffrey Roche, *Life of John Boyle O'Reilly* (London: T. Fisher Unwin, 1891), 230.

19 Ibid.

20 Short, *Dynamite War*, 85–86, 97–101. The development of intelligence gathering in Great Britain built on the anti-Fenian work that had been done in the 1860s under Robert Anderson at the Home Office. Jenkins, *Fenian Problem*, 333–334.

21 This was partly prompted by the Phoenix Park murders in May 1882, when the chief secretary, Lord Cavendish, and the permanent under-secretary, Thomas Burke, were stabbed to death in broad daylight in a Dublin park by a group calling themselves the Invincibles. The murders provoked revulsion in Ireland, Britain, and the United States. Short, *Dynamite War*, 73–101, 112–115; David M. Pletcher, *The Awkward Years: American Foreign Relations under Garfield and Arthur* (Columbia: University of Missouri Press, 1962), 248; Murney Gerlach, *British Liberalism and the United States: Political and Social Thought in the Late Victorian Age* (Basingstoke: Palgrave, 2001), 85–87; Campbell, *Fenian Fire*, 149–363.

22 Pletcher, *Awkward Years*, 250; Jonathan W. Gantt, "Irish-American Terrorism and Anglo-American Relations," *Journal of the Gilded Age and Progressive Era* 5, no. 4 (2006): 328, 335, 341.

23 Lowell quoted in Gantt, "Irish-American Terrorism and Anglo-American Relations," 334.

24 Ibid., 341; Pletcher, *Awkward Years*, 250–251.

25 Attorney-General Benjamin Harris Brewster to the District Attorneys and Marshals of the United States, March 12, 1884, in *A Compilation of the Messages and Papers of the Presidents*, 20

vols., edited by James D. Richardson (New York: Bureau of National Literature, 1927), 10:4815; Pletcher, *Awkward Years*, 193–196.

26 Chester A. Arthur, "Fourth Annual Message," December 1, 1884, The American Presidency Project, www.presidency.ucsb.edu/ws/index.php?pid=29525 (accessed February 20, 2011).

27 Henry Wade Rogers, "Harboring Conspiracy," *North American Review* 138, no. 331 (1884): 521–534.

28 Ibid., 532.

29 Lomasney quoted in Gantt, "Irish-American Terrorism and Anglo-American Relations," 339; Lowell quoted in Mike J. Sewell, "Rebels or Revolutionaries? Irish-American Nationalism and American Diplomacy, 1865–1885," *Historical Journal* 29, no. 3 (1986): 729.

30 Edward Self, "The Abuse of Citizenship," *North American Review* 136, no. 319 (1883): 544, 554.

31 James Russell Lowell to Frederick Frelinghuysen, March 14, 1882, despatch no. 331, *FRUS 1882*, 1:206.

32 Ibid.

33 *Boston Daily Advertiser*, April 21, 1883, quoted in McConville, *Irish Political Prisoners*, 359.

34 Arthur, "Fourth Annual Message."

35 Jonathan Gantt, *Irish Terrorism in the Atlantic Community, 1865–1922* (New York: Palgrave Macmillan, 2010), 168.

36 The Senate had a Republican majority; the House a Democratic one. Jonathan Gantt attributes the bill's failure to "fear of offending the powerful Irish vote," though it might just as easily have been a more pragmatic aversion to increasing the power of the federal government under a law that Edmunds himself conceded was "imperfect." Gantt, *Irish Terrorism*, 168; Edmunds quoted in ibid., 1.

37 Webster-Ashburton Treaty (1842), Avalon Project: Documents in Law, History and Diplomacy, http://avalon.law.yale.edu/19th_century/br-1842.asp (accessed November 22, 2010); McConville, *Irish Political Prisoners*, 355.

38 William Harcourt was again central to the negotiation of the agreement. "Extradition," *New York Times*, July 21, 1886; Gerlach, *British Liberalism and the United States*, 89.

39 "Extradition"; Gantt, "Irish-American Terrorism and Anglo-American Relations," 352–353; "The Extradition of Dynamite Criminals," *North American Review* 141, no. 344 (1885): 47–59. Ireland was not the only country where the definition of "political crime" proved contentious; see Frederick C. Griffin, "Protesting Despotism: American Opposition to the U.S.-Russian Extradition Treaty of 1887," *Mid America* 70, no. 2 (1988): 91–99.

40 "What the Treaty Lacks," *New York Times*, July 21, 1886.

41 Sewell, "Rebels or Revolutionaries?" 727–728. Secretary of State Thomas Bayard attributed attacks on the extradition agreement to "the interest[s] of dynamite"; Thomas Bayard to Edward Phelps, July 27, 1886, Container 196, Thomas F. Bayard Papers, Manuscript Division, Library of Congress, Washington, D.C. (hereafter Thomas F. Bayard Papers).

42 Gantt, *Irish Terrorism*, 8.

43 Blaine quoted in Sewell, "Political Rhetoric," 64.

44 Nelson M. Blake, "The Olney-Pauncefote Treaty of 1897," *American Historical Review* 50, no. 2 (1945): 228.

45 Rogers, "Harboring Conspiracy," 529.

46 Ibid.

47 See, for instance, William M. E. L. Armstrong, *Godkin and American Foreign Policy, 1865–1900* (New York: Bookman, 1957), 151–161; Frank A. Ninkovich, *Global Dawn: The Cultural*

Foundation of American Internationalism, 1865–1890 (Cambridge, MA: Harvard University Press, 2009), 302–306.

48 See, for instance, Patrick Egan to Patrick Collins, March 7, 1881, and Fanny Parnell to Patrick Collins, September 25, 1881, both Series 1, Subseries A, Box 1, Patrick Collins Papers; John Finerty to Collins, November 11, 1881, and Patrick Egan to Patrick Collins, November 28, 1881, both Series 1, Subseries A, Box 2, Patrick Collins Papers; M. Jeanne D'Arc O'Hare, "The Public Career of Patrick Andrew Collins" (PhD diss., Boston College, 1959), 152–153, 164–168, 173–180.

49 McConville, *Irish Political Prisoners*, 359–360; Campbell, *Fenian Fire*, 154.

50 Foner, *Politics and Ideology in the Age of the Civil War*, 167–168.

51 "Boss Parnell," *New York Times*, August 1, 1883; "The Parnell Party," *New York Times*, August 15, 1883.

52 "Parnell and Dynamite," *New York Times*, April 18, 1883.

53 Mark W. Summers, *Rum, Romanism, & Rebellion: The Making of a President, 1884* (Chapel Hill: University of North Carolina Press, 2000), 210.

54 A similar effort had been made in 1880. Four years later, the anti-labor politics of Cleveland's administration made the project much more viable. Ibid., 211.

55 James Paul Rodechko, *Patrick Ford and His Search for America: A Case Study of Irish-American Journalism 1870–1913* (New York: Arno Press, 1976), 70–74.

56 Summers, *Rum, Romanism, & Rebellion*, 216; Steven K. Green, "The Blaine Amendment Reconsidered," *The American Journal of Legal History* 36, no. 1 (1992): 38–69.

57 H. J. Ramsdell, *Life and Public Services of James G. Blaine* (New York: J. S. Willey, 1884), 222–223.

58 On this connection between protectionism and nationalism, see Edward P. Crapol, *America for Americans: Economic Nationalism and Anglophobia in the Late Nineteenth Century* (Westport, CT: Greenwood Press, 1973); and Andrew Wender Cohen, "Smuggling, Globalization, and America's Outward State, 1870–1909," *Journal of American History* 97, no. 2 (2010): 371–398.

59 Thomas Dudley, *The Cobden Club of England and Protection in the United States* (New York: n.p., 1884), 21.

60 Summers, *Rum, Romanism, & Rebellion*, 95–97, 176.

61 John Devoy to Joseph Medill, July 26, 1884, forwarded with Medill to James G. Blaine, August 5, 1884, Container 15, James G. Blaine Papers, Library of Congress Manuscript Division, Washington, D.C. (hereafter James G. Blaine Papers).

62 Devoy to Medill, July 26, 1884.

63 Thomas Cooper to James G. Blaine, June 10, 1884, Container 14, James G. Blaine Papers.

64 Egan quoted in Summers, *Rum, Romanism, & Rebellion*, 212.

65 Patrick Ford to James G. Blaine, October 18, 1884, Container 14, James G. Blaine Papers.

66 "An Irish Boom for Blaine," *New York Times*, July 1, 1884. Parnell's mother, by contrast, accepted the prominent place afforded her at Democratic Party meetings. Summers, *Rum, Romanism, & Rebellion*, 220.

67 Ibid., 219–220.

68 This was in private conversation with the British minister, Lionel Sackville-West. Blaine may well have been trying to impress the British diplomat with his own anti-Irish credentials. Blaine quoted in Charles Callan Tansill, *Fight for Irish Freedom, 1866–1922: An Old Story Based upon New Data* (New York: Devin-Adair, 1957), 84.

69 Geoffrey Blodget, "Ethno-Cultural Realities in Presidential Patronage: Grover Cleveland's Choices," *New York History* 81, no. 2 (2000): 197–198, quote at 197. See also John T. Galvin, "Patrick J. Maguire: Boston's Last Democratic Boss," *New England Quarterly* 55, no. 3 (1982): 392, 411–412.

70 Collins eventually received an appointment in the second Cleveland administration. He served as consul-general in London, a lucrative post, for four years. Despite his Fenian credentials, his appointment was accepted by the British authorities. O'Hare, "Patrick Andrew Collins," 252–253; Galvin, "Patrick J. Maguire," 412.

71 Bayard quoted in Sewell, "Rebels or Revolutionaries?" 727. The description is in Summers, *Rum, Romanism, & Rebellion,* 109. According to the secretary of the American legation in London, Bayard's comments were well received; Gantt, "Irish-American Terrorism and Anglo-American Relations," 350.

72 J. S. Moore quoted in Gerlach, *British Liberalism and the United States,* 92.

73 Moore quoted in Short, *Dynamite War,* 199.

74 Niall Whelehan, "'Scientific Warfare or the Quickest Way to Liberate Ireland': The Brooklyn Dynamite School," *History Ireland* 16, no. 6 (2008): 45; Sewell, "Rebels or Revolutionaries?" 724, 730–733.

75 Short, *Dynamite War,* 225–228.

76 Thomas Bayard to Edward Phelps, July 1, 1885, Container 194, Thomas F. Bayard Papers.

77 Thomas Bayard to William Dorsheimer, January 8, 1885, Container 195, Thomas F. Bayard Papers; Sexton, *Debtor Diplomacy,* 216; Charles S. Campbell, *The Transformation of American Foreign Relations: 1865–1900* (New York: Harper & Row, 1976), 30–32, 122–139.

78 Thomas Bayard to Edward Phelps, November 6, 1886, Container 196, Thomas F. Bayard Papers.

79 Bayard's conception of civilization lacked the overtly imperialist punch of the later Rooseveltian concept. See Frank Ninkovich, "Theodore Roosevelt: Civilization as Ideology," *Diplomatic History* 10, no. 3 (1986): 221–245; Ninkovich, *Global Dawn,* 15–46; and Jay Sexton, *The Monroe Doctrine: Empire and Nation in Nineteenth-Century America* (New York: Hill & Wang, 2011), 201–211.

80 Thomas Bayard to Edward Phelps, December 17, 1886, Container 197, Thomas F. Bayard Papers.

81 Thomas Bayard to Edward Phelps, March 7, 1886, Container 195, Thomas F. Bayard Papers. Lord Salisbury, a Conservative, briefly headed a minority government from June 1885 to January 1886.

82 That Bayard was correct to fear the (U.S) domestic reception of an agreement with the Tory Party is suggested by the later characterization of the 1897 Olney-Pauncefote Treaty of Arbitration as "Secretary Olney's Mugwump-Tory scheme." Chicago *Tribune,* January 16, 1897, quoted in Blake, "The Olney-Pauncefote Treaty," 235.

83 Thomas Bayard to Edward Phelps, May 27, 1886, Container 195, Thomas F. Bayard Papers.

84 Thomas Bayard to Edward Phelps, July 3, 1886, Container 196, Thomas F. Bayard Papers.

85 Ibid.; Edward Phelps to Thomas Bayard, March 27, 1886, Container 86, Thomas F. Bayard Papers.

86 "Premier Parnell," *New York Times,* December 4, 1885. Any future Irish state, the paper deadpanned, would do well to look to New York City for a pool of Irish politicians and administrators from which to draw. Thus "they can introduce into their own land the political improvements they have brought to such perfection here." "A Call for Irish Patriots," *New York Times,* December 18, 1885.

87 William Henry Hurlbert, *Ireland under Coercion,* 2nd ed. (Edinburgh: n.p., 1888), l.

88 Conor Cruise O'Brien noted that whereas 95 percent of Land League funds came from the United States, contributions to the National League from the same source lagged, reaching £2,129 out of £11,068 ($10,300 of $53,700) in the first year of the National League (1882–1883)

and only £3,101 out of £11,508 ($15,100 of $55,900) in the second (1883–1884). "The proportion of American help had dwindled . . . to under 30 per cent. in the immediate aftermath of the Kilmainham treaty [of 1882]." O'Brien asserts that American support did not "return until the home rule crisis of 1885–6."Conor Cruise O'Brien, *Parnell and His Party, 1880–90* (Oxford: Clarendon Press, 1964), 133–136, quotes at 135. Murney Gerlach writes that from January to June 1886, subscriptions to the National League "jumped from £3340 ($16,200) to £66,420 ($323,000)" and that "90 percent" came from the United States; Gerlach, *British Liberalism and the United States*, 109. A similar pattern of a decrease in political contributions followed by a surge of donations in 1885–1886 occurred in Canada; D. C. Lyne, "Irish-Canadian Financial Contributions to the Home Rule Movement in the 1890s," *Studia Hibernica* 7 (1967): 184. See also "Patrick Egan on Home Rule," *New York Times*, December 24, 1885; and "Helping the Irish Cause," *New York Times*, December 29, 1885.

89 O'Brien, *Parnell and His Party*, 186–187.The phrase was William Harcourt's, then chancellor the exchequer (161). See also "Extradition."

90 Both quoted in O'Brien, *Parnell and His Party*, 187.

91 Edward Phelps to Thomas Bayard, November 14, 1885, Container 82,Thomas F. Bayard Papers.

92 Thomas Bayard to Edward Phelps, July 3, 1886, Container 196, Thomas F. Bayard Papers. Journalist William Henry Hurlbert concurred that strong pressure had been placed on the Foreign Affairs Committee in both the House and the Senate to pass such a resolution; Hurlbert, *Ireland under Coercion*, xxix. Hurlbert's account of his time in Ireland strongly suggested that American demagoguery was the source of Irish discontent during the 1880s.

93 Gerlach, *British Liberalism and the United States*, 102–104, Labouchère quote at 102.

94 Gladstone quoted in ibid., 108. Presumably he referred loosely to a limited measure of local authority circumscribed by central sovereignty.

95 E. L. Godkin, "American Home Rule," in *Handbook of Home Rule: Being Articles on the Irish Question*, edited by James Bryce (London: Kegan, Paul,Trench & Co., 1887), 23.

96 Ibid.

97 John F. Finerty quoted in Alan O'Day, "Irish Nationalism and Anglo-American Relations in the Late Nineteenth and Early Twentieth Centuries," in *Anglo-American Attitudes: From Revolution to Partnership*, edited by Fred M. Leventhal and Ronald Quinault (Aldershot: Ashgate, 2000), 187.

98 Godkin quoted in Leslie Butler, *Critical Americans: Victorian Intellectuals and Transatlantic Liberal Reform* (Chapel Hill: University of North Carolina Press, 2007), 232. See also George Washburn Smalley, *Anglo-American Memories*, 2 vols. (London: Duckworth & Co., 1911–1912), 2:195; and Hurlbert, *Ireland under Coercion*, xxxii. Here was Britain's own "problem of neighbourhood" replicating that faced by the early American republic. Were home rule to prove the thin end of the wedge, eventual Irish independence would follow. Ireland had the potential (to some observers, the inevitable propensity) to develop as a hostile power whose weakness might attract the intervention of other, stronger anti-British powers.This argument was advanced most clearly by the historian and anti-home ruler William Lecky in, for instance, "Why Home Rule Is Undesirable," *North American Review* 152, no. 412 (1891): 358.

99 Butler, *Critical Americans*, 227–229; Ninkovich, *Global Dawn*, 85–86.

100 Ibid., 96; Gerlach, *British Liberalism and the United States*, 48–52; Butler, *Critical Americans*, 148;W. E. Gladstone, "Kin beyond Sea," *North American Review* 127, no. 264 (1878): 179–212.

101 Thomas Bayard to Edward Phelps, July 27, 1886, and September 24, 1886, both Container 196,Thomas F. Bayard Papers.

102 Campbell, *Fenian Fire*, 306.

103 Thomas Bayard to Edward Phelps, December 17, 1886, Container 197, Thomas F. Bayard Papers.

104 Ford quoted in Hurlbert, *Ireland under Coercion*, xii. Emphasis in original.

105 Republican Party Platform of 1888, American Presidency Project, www.presidency.ucsb.edu/ws/index.php?pid=29627 (accessed February 24, 2011).

106 Joyce Goldberg, *The Baltimore Affair* (Lincoln: University of Nebraska Press, 1986), 30–32; Joyce Goldberg, "Patrick Egan: Irish-American Minister to Chile, 1889–1893," *Éire-Ireland* 14, no. 3 (1979): 83–95; Edward P. Crapol, *James G. Blaine: Architect of Empire* (Wilmington, DE: Scholarly Resources, 2000), 131. Egan was not the first Irish nationalist to receive a posting to Santiago. William Roberts, ex-president of one Fenian Brotherhood faction, was Egan's predecessor as U.S. minister to Chile. William Roberts to Thomas Bayard, February 5, 1886, Container 85, Thomas F. Bayard Papers.

107 O'Brien, *Parnell and His Party*, 192.

108 Campbell, *Fenian Fire*, 299–363.

109 Gerlach, *British Liberalism and the United States*, 109–110, quote at 110.

110 Lafayette was the first non-American to be named in a party platform, but he became a U.S. citizen during his lifetime.

111 Democratic Party Platform of 1888, American Presidency Project, www.presidency.ucsb.edu/ws/index.php?pid=29584 (accessed February 24, 2011).

112 "Irish National League," *New York Times*, August 15, 1885; "The Irish National League," *New York Times*, August 15, 1885.

113 John Boyle O'Reilly, "At Last!" *North American Review* 142, no. 350 (1886): 104–111.

114 Alexander Sullivan, "Parnell as Leader," *North American Review* 144, no. 367 (1887): 624.

115 Parnell and Katherine O'Shea had been in a relationship, apparently with the tacit consent of Katherine's husband, William, since the early 1880s. In December 1889, William O'Shea filed for divorce, naming Parnell as co-respondent. Parnell's implication in a divorce case caused serious dissension among both Irish Catholics and British nonconformists, and the latter constituted a core constituency of the Liberal Party. The Irish Parliamentary Party, concerned for the future of home rule legislation, split between Parnellite and anti-Parnellite factions. The two wings of the Parliamentary Party did not reunite until 1900 (and then only partially), nine years after Parnell's death in October 1891. See R. V. Comerford, "The Parnell Era, 1883–1891," in *A New History of Ireland,* vol. 5, *Ireland under the Union,* part 2, *1870–1921,* edited by W. E. Vaughan (Oxford: Oxford University Press, 1996), 56–57, 75–80; and F. S. L. Lyons, "The Aftermath of Parnell, 1891–1903," in *A New History of Ireland,* vol. 5, *Ireland under the Union,* part 2, *1870–1921,* edited by W. E. Vaughan (Oxford: Oxford University Press, 1996), 81–110. On the North American dimensions, see Lyne, "Irish-Canadian Financial Contributions," 205; and Alan O'Day, "Irish Diaspora Politics in Perspective: The United Irish Leagues of Great Britain and America, 1900–1914," *Immigrants & Minorities* 18, no. 2 (1999), 227–234.

116 "Home Rule a Lost Cause," *New York Times*, December 14, 1890.

117 Hurlbert, *Ireland under Coercion*, xxiii–xxv; "Hewitt Is Their Choice," *New York Times*, October 7, 1888. Mayor Hewitt also produced a stinging article about the effects of Irish "home rule" on the city he administered; Abram S. Hewitt, "Twenty Years of Irish Home Rule in New York," *Quarterly Review* (London) 171, no. 341 (1890): 260–286.

118 Self, "The Abuse of Citizenship," 551.

119 Thomas B. Reed quoted in Smalley, *Anglo-American Memories*, 2:212.

120 Michael Doorley contends that by 1900, Irish Americans "had achieved relative occupational parity with native-born Americans in most fields"; Doorley, *Irish-American Diaspora Nationalism: The Friends of Irish Freedom, 1916–1935* (Dublin: Four Courts, 2005), 21–23.

121 Blake, "The Olney-Pauncefote Treaty," 238–241; Howard K. Beale, *Theodore Roosevelt and the Rise of America to World Power* (Baltimore, MD: Johns Hopkins University Press, 1956), 89–91, 349–350; O'Day, "Irish Nationalism and Anglo-American Relations," 186; Stuart Anderson, *Race and Rapprochement: Anglo-Saxonism and Anglo-American Relations, 1895–1904* (Rutherford, NJ: Fairleigh Dickinson University, 1981), 105–111; Doorley, *Diaspora Nationalism*, 25–26, 28–30. On Bryce, see chapter 5.

122 Ninkovich, *Global Dawn*, 232–244, 253–262; Paul A. Kramer, "Empires, Exceptions, and Anglo-Saxons: Race and Rule between the British and United States Empires, 1880–1910," *Journal of American History* 88, no. 4 (2002): 1315–1353.

123 George Benton Adams, "The United States and the Anglo-Saxon Future," *Atlantic Monthly* 78, no. 465 (1896): 39.

124 As Alan O'Day has detailed, this interpretation was reiterated by prominent statesmen on both sides of the Atlantic through the first decades of the twentieth century. O'Day, "Irish Nationalism and Anglo-American Relations," 170–171; Theodore Roosevelt to William Archer, August 31, 1899, in *The Letters of Theodore Roosevelt*, 8 vols., edited by Elting E. Morison (Cambridge, MA: Harvard University Press, 1951–1954), 2:1064. Roosevelt referred to William Lecky, a notable anti–home ruler. It was probably not Lecky's arguments against home rule that Roosevelt drew on, however freely available they were in the United States, but his description of the Anglo-Irish Union as essentially fraudulent.

125 Bradford Perkins, *The Great Rapprochement: England and the United States, 1895–1914* (London: Gollancz, 1969), chapter 1.

Epilogue

1 Jay Sexton, *The Monroe Doctrine: Empire and Nation in Nineteenth-Century America* (New York: Hill & Wang, 2011), 208–209; Bradford Perkins, *The Great Rapprochement: England and the United States, 1895–1914* (London: Gollancz, 1969), 12–30, 160.

2 Perkins, *Great Rapprochement*, 156–208.

3 Ibid., 64–88; Paul A. Kramer, "Empires, Exceptions, and Anglo-Saxons: Race and Rule between the British and United States Empires, 1880–1910," *Journal of American History* 88, no. 4 (2002): 1315–1335; Stuart Anderson, *Race and Rapprochement: Anglo-Saxonism and Anglo-American Relations, 1895–1904* (Rutherford, NJ: Fairleigh Dickinson University Press, 1981).

4 Sexton, *Monroe Doctrine*, 216; Kramer, "Empires, Exceptions, and Anglo-Saxons," 1331.

5 Roosevelt quoted in Kramer, "Empires, Exceptions, and Anglo-Saxons," 1325.

6 Roosevelt quoted in Sexton, *Monroe Doctrine*, 223.

7 Olney quoted in Perkins, *Great Rapprochement*, 29; Michael Patrick Cullinane, *Liberty and American Anti-Imperialism 1898–1909* (New York: Palgrave Macmillan, 2012), 24.

8 J. D. O'Connell quoted in Gretchen Murphy, *Shadowing the White Man's Burden: U.S. Imperialism and the Problem of the Color Line* (New York: New York University Press, 2010), 54.

9 Perkins, *Great Rapprochement*, 8, 58–61, 156–158.

10 Theodore Roosevelt, "Fourth Annual Message," December 6, 1904, American Presidency Project, www.presidency.ucsb.edu/ws/index.php?pid=29545 (accessed December 7, 2012); Sexton, *Monroe Doctrine*, 229.

11 Perkins, *Great Rapprochement*, 156–161, 193–194.

12 Sexton, *Monroe Doctrine*, 237–238.

13 *London Review*, quoted in Perkins, *Great Rapprochement*, 172.

14 Bernadette Whelan, *United States Foreign Policy and Ireland: From Empire to Independence 1913–29* (Dublin: Four Courts Press, 2006), 30–31.

15 Perkins, *Great Rapprochement*, 90–93, 142–143; Kramer, "Empires, Exceptions, and Anglo-Saxons," 1341–1342; Alan J. Ward, *Ireland and Anglo-American Relations 1899–1921* (London: Weidenfeld and Nicolson, 1969), 32–39.

16 Ward, *Ireland and Anglo-American Relations*, 59–61; Harald Fischer-Tiné, "Indian Nationalism and the 'World Forces': Transnational and Diasporic Dimensions of the Indian Freedom Movement on the Eve of the First World War," *Journal of Global History* 2, no. 3 (2007): 333–335. On earlier, tentative links with anti-imperialist groups outside Ireland, see H. V. Brasted, "Irish Nationalism and the British Empire in the Late Nineteenth Century," in *Irish Culture and Nationalism, 1750–1950*, edited by Oliver MacDonagh, W. F. Mandle, and Pauric Travers (Dublin: Gill and Macmillan, 1983), esp. 91–98. On Irish nationalism and ideas about the breakup of the empire, see Naomi Lloyd-Jones, "The Irish Home Rule Paradox," The I. B. Tauris Blog, October 8, 2012, http://theibtaurisblog.com/2012/10/08/the-home-rule-paradox (accessed December 17, 2012).

17 Whelan, *United States Foreign Policy*, 18, 30.

18 Roy F. Foster, *Modern Ireland, 1600–1972* (London: Penguin, 1989), 456–458, quote at 448; Owen McGee, *The IRB: The Irish Republican Brotherhood, from the Land League to Sinn Féin* (Dublin: Four Courts Press, 2005), 279–283; Bruce Nelson, "'From the Cabins of Connemara to the Kraals of Kaffirland': Irish Nationalists, the British Empire, and the 'Boer Fight for Freedom,'" in *The Irish in the Atlantic World*, edited by David T. Gleeson (Columbia: University of South Carolina Press, 2010), 154–175.

19 Ward, *Ireland and Anglo-American Relations*, 18; David Brundage, "'In Time of Peace, Prepare for War': Key Themes in the Social Thought of New York's Irish Nationalists, 1890–1916," in *The New York Irish*, edited by Timothy J. Meagher and Ronald H. Bayor (Baltimore, MD: Johns Hopkins University Press, 1996), 325–326, quote at 326.

20 Unsurprisingly, Redmond tailored his rhetoric to his audience. By and large, he was more radical in front of Irish American audiences than he was in Ireland. McGee, *The IRB*, 294; Ward, *Ireland and Anglo-American Relations*, 9–10, 15. Francis M. Carroll, *American Opinion and the Irish Question 1910–1923* (Dublin: Gill and Macmillan, 1978), 20.

21 Ibid., 21–22; Perkins, *Great Rapprochement*, 284–285, quote at 284.

22 *New York Times,* quoted in Perkins, *Great Rapprochement*, 284.

23 Foster, *Modern Ireland*, 462–471.

24 An Irish National Volunteer Fund was established in the United States to help support the Irish Volunteers, and the Clan na Gael donated $100,000 (approximately £21,000) to foster revolutionary organization in Ireland in the years 1913 to 1916. Ward, *Ireland and Anglo-American Relations*, 72–73. Conversions estimated using Lawrence H. Officer and Samuel H. Williamson, "Computing 'Real Value' over Time with a Conversion between U.K. Pounds and U.S. Dollars, 1830 to Present," Measuring Worth website, www.measuringworth.com (accessed May 8, 2013).

25 Whelan, *United States Foreign Policy*, 50–51.

26 Ibid., 59–177. On the spread of information about events in Ireland, see Maurice Walsh, *The News from Ireland: Foreign Correspondents and the Irish Revolution* (London: I. B. Tauris, 2008).

27 Woodrow Wilson quoted in Whelan, *United States Foreign Policy*, 57.

28 Ibid., 29.

29 Wilson quoted in ibid., 57.

30 Perkins, *Great Rapprochement*, 285–286.

31 Foster, *Modern Ireland*, 471–476.

32 Whelan, *United States Foreign Policy*, 60–66; Foster, *Modern Ireland*, 479.

33 Michael Hopkinson, "President Woodrow Wilson and the Irish Question," *Studia Hibernica* 27 (1993): 89–90; Whelan, *United States Foreign Policy*, 39.

34 "Proclamation of the Irish Republic," April 24, 1916, The 1916 Uprising: Personalities & Perspectives: An Online Exhibition, www.nli.ie/1916/pdf/1.intro.pdf (accessed September 15, 2012); Foster, *Modern Ireland*, 477–484.

35 Carroll, *American Opinion and the Irish Question*, 70–78; Wilson quoted in Whelan, *United States Foreign Policy*, 110.

36 Whelan, *United States Foreign Policy*, 120–123.

37 David M. Kennedy, *Over Here: The First World War and American Society* (New York: Oxford University Press, 2004), 10–30.

38 Erez Manela, *The Wilsonian Moment: Self-Determination and the International Origins of Anticolonial Nationalism* (New York: Oxford University Press, 2009), 19–26, 37–53, 215–225; Whelan, *United States Foreign Policy*, 179.

39 Wilson quoted in Manela, *Wilsonian Moment*, 24.

40 Wilson quoted in ibid., 41.

41 Whelan, *United States Foreign Policy*, 179; Sinn Féin resolution, 129.

42 Ibid., 125, 129, 157–158.

43 Ibid., 144–148, 157; Hopkinson, "President Woodrow Wilson and the Irish Question," 91–92.

44 Whelan, *United States Foreign Policy*, 146, 157; quote in Carroll, *American Opinion and the Irish Question*, 52. On the Friends of Irish Freedom, see Michael Doorley, *Irish-American Diaspora Nationalism: The Friends of Irish Freedom, 1916–1935* (Dublin: Four Courts, 2005); and Hopkinson, "President Woodrow Wilson and the Irish Question," 92.

45 Whelan, *United States Foreign Policy*, 158.

46 Ibid., 136–139, 176–177, 186, Wilson quoted at 184; Hopkinson, "President Woodrow Wilson and the Irish Question," 99.

47 Manela, *Wilsonian Moment*, 60.

48 Whelan, *United States Foreign Policy*, 184–185, 189.

49 Adrian Gregory, "'You Might As Well Recruit Germans': British Public Opinion and the Decision to Conscript the Irish in 1918," in *Ireland and the Great War: 'A War to Unite Us All?'* edited by Adrian Gregory and Senia Paseta, 113–132 (Manchester: Manchester University Press, 2002); Foster, *Modern Ireland*, 484–493, quote at 488.

50 Whelan, *United States Foreign Policy*, 185–186.

51 Ibid., 203; Walsh, *News From Ireland*, 58–151.

52 Éamon de Valera quoted in Whelan, *United States Foreign Policy*, 180.

53 Ibid.

54 Ibid., 176, 183.

55 Ibid., 190–199; Hopkinson, "President Woodrow Wilson and the Irish Question," 94–96; Manela, *Wilsonian Moment*, 59–60.

56 Whelan, *United States Foreign Policy*, 180–181.

57 Manela, *Wilsonian Moment*, 172.

58 Carroll, *American Opinion and the Irish Question*, 124–131.

59 Thomas Gallagher quoted in ibid., 124.

60 Whelan, *United States Foreign Policy*, 190–191.

61 Ibid., 196–197.

62 Ibid., 211–219; Manela, *Wilsonian Moment*, 61; Hopkinson, "President Woodrow Wilson and the Irish Question," 104–105.

63 De Valera quoted in Whelan, *United States Foreign Policy*, 218.

64 Ibid., 218–220.

65 Ibid., 223.

66 Wilson quoted in Hopkinson, "President Woodrow Wilson and the Irish Question," 107.

67 John Milton Cooper, *Breaking the Heart of the World: Woodrow Wilson and the Fight for the League of Nations* (New York: Cambridge University Press, 2001), 85–192, 198–200.

68 Whelan, *United States Foreign Policy*, 226; Kennedy, *Over Here*, 361–362.

69 Wilson quoted in Manela, *Wilsonian Moment*, 219.

70 Wilson quoted in Hopkinson, "President Woodrow Wilson and the Irish Question," 103–104. More generally, this is the subject of Erez Manela's excellent book *The Wilsonian Moment*.

71 Kennedy, *Over Here*, 362.

72 Whelan, *United States Foreign Policy*, 281–402, Harding quoted at 318; Hopkinson, "President Woodrow Wilson and the Irish Question," 111.

73 Whelan, *United States Foreign Policy*, 440–468.

74 Michael Collins quoted in "Debate on Treaty," Dáil Éireann, vol. 3, December 9, 1921, Díospóireachtaí Parlaiminte: Parliamentary Debates, http://historical-debates.oireachtas.ie/D/DT/D.T.192112190002.html (accessed December 17, 2012).

75 "Congress Honors Irish President," *New York Times*, January 26, 1928.

76 Ibid.

Bibliography

Manuscript Collections

Abbott Lawrence Papers. Houghton Library, Harvard University, Cambridge, Massachusetts.

Despatches from United States Ministers to Great Britain, 1791–1906. Microfilm. 200 reels. Washington, D.C.: National Archives and Records Service, 1954.

Diplomatic Instructions of the Department of State, 1801–1906. Microfilm. 175 reels. Washington, D.C.: National Archives and Records Administration, 1945–1946.

Edward Everett Papers. Massachusetts Historical Society, Boston, Massachusetts.

Fenian Brotherhood Collection. American Catholic History Research Center and University Archives, The Catholic University of America.

Foreign Office Archives. Public Record Office, National Archives, Kew Gardens, London.

George Bancroft Papers. Massachusetts Historical Society, Boston, Massachusetts.

Hamilton Fish Papers. Library of Congress Manuscript Division, Washington, D.C.

Henry George Papers. Microfilm. 15 reels. Manuscripts and Archives Division, New York Public Library, New York, New York.

James G. Blaine Papers. Library of Congress Manuscript Division, Washington, D.C.

James K. Polk Papers. Microfilm. 67 reels. Washington, D.C.: Library of Congress, 1964.

Jeremiah O'Donovan Rossa Papers. Maloney Collection of Irish Historical Papers, Manuscripts and Archives Division, New York Public Library, New York, New York.

Microfilms of the Adams Papers Owned by the Adams Manuscript Trust and Deposited in the Massachusetts Historical Society. Microfilm. 608 Reels. Boston: Massachusetts Historical Society, 1954–1959.

The Papers of William H. Seward. 198 reels. Woodbridge, CT: Research Publications, 1981.

Patrick A. Collins Papers. John J. Burns Library, Boston College, Boston, Massachusetts.

Robert Bennet Forbes Letterbook. Boston Athenæum, Boston, Massachusetts.

Robert Bennet Forbes Papers. Massachusetts Historical Society, Boston, Massachusetts.

Rider Collection, John Hay Library, Brown University, Rhode Island.

Thomas F. Bayard Papers. Manuscript Division, Library of Congress, Washington, D.C.

Tyler Family Papers. Special Collections Research Center, Swem Library, College of William and Mary, Williamsburg, Virginia.

Primary Sources

The 1916 Rising: Personalities and Perspectives. Online exhibition. National Library of Ireland. www.nli.ie/1916/. Accessed September 2012.

The American Presidency Project. www.presidency.ucsb.edu/. Accessed September 2012.

Armstrong, William M., ed. *The Gilded Age Letters of E. L. Godkin*. Albany: State University of New York Press, 1974.

The Avalon Project: Documents in Law, History and Diplomacy. http://avalon.law. yale.edu/. Accessed March 2010.

Bagenal, Philip H. *The American Irish and Their Influence on Irish Politics*. London: K. Paul, Trench & Co., 1882.

Baker, George E., ed. *The Works of William H. Seward*. 4 vols. New York: Redfield, 1853–1861.

Balch, William S. *Ireland, as I Saw It: The Character, Condition, and Prospects of the People*. New York: G. P. Putnam, 1850.

Blassingame, John W., ed. *The Frederick Douglass Papers*. Series 1. 5 vols. New Haven, CT: Yale University Press, 1979–.

Bryce, James, ed. *Handbook of Home Rule. Being Articles on the Irish Question*. London: K. Paul, Trench & Co, 1887.

Butt, Isaac. *Irish Federalism! Its Meaning, Its Objects and Its Hopes*. 4th ed. Dublin: The Irish Home Rule League, 1874.

Carey, Henry. *The Harmony of Interests, Agricultural, Manufacturing, and Commercial*. Philadelphia: J. S. Skinner, 1851.

Collins, George C. *Fifty Reasons Why the Honorable Henry Clay Should Be Elected President of the United States, by an Adopted Citizen*. Baltimore, MD: Printed for the author by "Murphy," 1844.

Congressional Globe. 46 vols. Washington, D.C.: Support of Documents, U.S.G.P.O, 1834–1873.

Congressional Record. Washington, D.C.: Government Printing Office, 1973–.

Denieffe, Joseph. *A Personal Narrative of the Irish Revolutionary Brotherhood*. 1906; repr., Shannon: Irish University Press, 1969.

Dilke, Charles Wentworth. *Greater Britain: A Record of Travel in English-Speaking Countries during 1866 and 1867*. 2 vols. London: Macmillan and Co., 1868.

Díospóireachtaí Parlaiminte: Parliamentary Debates. http://historical-debates. oireachtas.ie/. Accessed December 2012.

Distress in Ireland. Extracts from Sundry Reports. Charleston, SC: Burges & James, 1847.

Doheny, Michael. *The Felon's Track, or History of the Attempted Outbreak in Ireland*. 1867; repr., Dublin: M. H. Gill & Son, 1920.

Dudley, Thomas. *The Cobden Club of England and Protection in the United States*. New York: n.p., 1884.

Fisher, Sidney George. *A Philadelphia Perspective: The Diary of Sidney George Fisher Covering the Years, 1834–1871*. Philadelphia: Historical Society of Pennsylvania, 1967.

Fitzpatrick, J. C., W. C. Ford, and R. R. Hill, eds. *Journals of the Continental Congress, 1774–1789*. 34 vols. Washington, DC: Government Printing Office, 1904–1937.

Foner, Philip S., ed. *The Life and Writings of Frederick Douglass*. 5 vols. New York: International Publishers, 1950.

Foot, M. R. D., and H. C. G. Matthew, eds. *The Gladstone Diaries*. 14 vols. Oxford, UK: Clarendon Press, 1968–1994.

Forbes, Robert Bennet. *The Voyage of the Jamestown on Her Errand of Mercy*. Boston, MA: Eastburn's Press, 1847.

The Gilder Lehrman Center for the Study of Slavery, Resistance, & Abolition. Online archive. www.yale.edu/glc/index.htm. Accessed December 2009.

Halleck, Henry. *International Law: Or, Rules Regulating the Intercourse of States in Perpetual Peace and War*. New York: D. Van Nostrand, 1861.

Harrison, Eliza Cope, ed. *Philadelphia Merchant: The Diary of Thomas P. Cope, 1800–1851*. South Bend, IN: Gateway Editions, 1978.

Hopkins, James F. et al., eds. *The Papers of Henry Clay*. 11 vols. Lexington: University Press of Kentucky, 1959–1992.

Hurlbert, William Henry. *Ireland under Coercion*. 2nd ed. Edinburgh: Unknown publisher, 1888.

Kehoe, Lawrence, ed. *Complete Works of the Most Rev. John Hughes, D.D.* 2 vols. New York: Richardson & Son, 1864.

Lee, John Hancock. *The Origin and Progress of the American Party in Politics*. Philadelphia: Elliott & Gihon, 1855.

Levin, Lewis C. *A Lecture on Irish Repeal, in Elucidation of the Fallacy of Its Principles, and in Proof of Its Pernicious Tendency, in Its Moral, Religious, and Political Aspects*. Philadelphia: n.p., 1844.

Maguire, John Francis. *The Irish in America*. 1868; repr., New York: Arno Press, 1969.

Malloy, William, ed. *Treaties, Conventions, International Acts, Protocols, and Agreements between the United States of America and Other Powers*. 4 vols. Washington, D.C.: U.S. Government Printing Office, 1910–1938.

Meriwether, Robert L. et al., eds. *The Papers of John C. Calhoun*. 28 vols. Columbia: University of South Carolina Press, 1959–2003.

Mitchel, John. *Jail Journal*. 1854; repr., Dublin: M. H. Gill & Son, 1913.

——. *Jail Journal*. 1854; repr., London: Sphere, 1983.

——. *The Last Conquest of Ireland (Perhaps)*. Glasgow: Cameron & Ferguson, 1876.

Morison, Elting E., ed. *The Letters of Theodore Roosevelt.* 8 vols. Cambridge, MA: Harvard University Press, 1951–1954.

Nicholson, Asenath. *Annals of the Famine in Ireland, in 1847, 1848, and 1849.* New York: E. French, 1851.

——. *Lights and Shades of Ireland. In Three Parts.* London: Charles Gilpin, 1850.

O'Brien, William, and Desmond Ryan, eds. *Devoy's Post Bag 1871–1928.* 2 vols. Dublin: Academy Press, 1979.

O'Connell, Maurice R., ed. *The Correspondence of Daniel O'Connell.* 8 vols. Dublin: Irish University Press, 1972–1977.

Official Opinions of the Attorneys General of the United States: Advising the President and Heads of Departments, in Relation to Their Official Duties. Washington, D.C.: Dept. of Justice, 1873–.

Papers Relating to Foreign Relations of the United States. Washington, D.C.: Government Printing Office, 1870–1946.

Parker, Hershel, ed. *Gansevoort Melville's 1846 London Journal and Letters from England, 1845.* New York: Public Library, 1966.

Quaife, Milo Milton, ed. *The Diary of James K. Polk during His Presidency, 1845 to 1849.* 4 vols. Chicago, IL: A. C. McClurg & Co., 1910.

Ramsdell, H. J. *Life and Public Services of James G. Blaine.* New York: J. S. Willey, 1884.

Report of the Trial of John Warren, for Treason-Felony: At the County Dublin Commission, Held at the Court-House, Green-Street, Dublin, Commencing the 30th October, 1867. Dublin: A. Thorn, 1867.

Richardson, James D., ed. *A Compilation of the Messages and Papers of the Presidents.* 20 vols. New York: Bureau of National Literature, 1927.

Robinson, William Erigena. *Rights of American Citizens Abroad: Speeches of William E. Robinson in the House of Representatives, Nov. 25 and Dec. 2, 1867.* Washington, D.C.: Congressional Globe Office, 1867.

Roche, James Jeffrey. *Life of John Boyle O'Reilly.* London: T. Fisher Unwin, 1891.

Rossa, Jeremiah O'Donovan. *My Years in English Jails.* 1874; repr., Tralee: Anvil Books, 1967.

Ryan, Mark F. *Fenian Memories.* Dublin: M. H. Gill & Son, 1945.

Savage, John. *Fenian Heroes and Martyrs.* Boston: P. Donahoe, 1868.

Seward, William Henry. *An Oration on the Death of Daniel O'Connell: Delivered at Castle Garden, New-York, September 22, 1847.* Auburn: J. C. Derby & Co., 1847.

Shewmaker, Kenneth E., ed. *The Papers of Daniel Webster.* Series 3, *Diplomatic Papers.* 2 vols. Lebanon, NH: University Press of New England, 1983–1987.

Simon, John Y., ed. *The Papers of Ulysses S. Grant.* 28 vols. Carbondale: Southern Illinois University Press, 1967–.

Smalley, George Washburn. *Anglo-American Memories.* 2 vols. London: Duckworth & Co., 1911–1912.

Sullivan, Alexander M. *New Ireland: Political Sketches and Personal Reminiscences.* London: S. Low, Marston, Searle & Rivington, 1878.

Taylor, James, ed. *The Adams Papers Digital Edition.* http://rotunda.upress.virginia.edu/founders/ADMS.html. Accessed January 2011.

Transactions of the Central Relief Committee of the Society of Friends during the Famine in Ireland, in 1846 and 1847. Dublin: Hodges and Smith, 1852.

The Truth Unveiled, or a Calm and Impartial Exposition of the Origin and Immediate Cause of the Terrible Riots in Philadelphia. Philadelphia: M. Fithian, 1844.

Tucherman, Bayard, ed. *The Diary of Philip Hone, 1828–1851.* 2 vols. New York: Dodd, Mead, 1889.

United States Congressional Serial Set. Washington, D.C.: Government Printing Office, 1817–.

United States Statutes at Large. Washington, D.C.: Government Printing Office, 1937–.

United States vs. W. G. Halpin, David Reidy, Edward Kenifeck, Samuel Lumsden, et al. Charged with Conspiracy for Exciting Insurrection in Ireland. Cincinnati, OH: Moore, Wilstach, Keys & Overend, 1856.

"Van Buren–Bancroft Correspondence, 1830–1845." *Proceedings of the Massachusetts Historical Society* 42 (October 1908–June 1909): 381–443.

Wenzer, Kenneth C., ed. *Henry George, the Transatlantic Irish, and Their Times.* Bingley: Emerald JAI, 2009.

Williams, Calvin S. *Cincinnati Directory, City Guide, and Business Mirror; or Cincinnati in 1856.* Cincinnati, OH: C. S. Williams, 1856.

Secondary Sources

Adams, James H. "The Negotiated Hibernian: Discourse on the Fenian in England and America." *American Nineteenth Century History* 11, no. 1 (2010): 47–77.

Allen, Theodore W. *The Invention of the White Race.* 2 vols. London: Verso, 1994.

Anbinder, Tyler. *Five Points: The 19th-Century New York City Neighborhood That Invented Tap Dance, Stole Elections, and Became the World's Most Notorious Slum.* New York: Plume, 2001.

———. "From Famine to Five Points: Lord Lansdowne's Irish Tenants Encounter North America's Most Notorious Slum," *American Historical Review* 107, no. 2 (2002): 351–387.

———. *Nativism and Slavery: The Northern Know Nothings and the Politics of the 1850's.* New York: Oxford University Press, 1992.

Anderson, Olive. "Early Experiences of Manpower Problems in an Industrial Society at War: Great Britain, 1854–56." *Political Science Quarterly* 82, no. 4 (1967): 526–545.

Anderson, Stuart. *Race and Rapprochement: Anglo-Saxonism and Anglo-American Relations, 1895–1904.* Rutherford, NJ: Fairleigh Dickinson University Press, 1981.

Armstrong, William M. *E. L. Godkin and American Foreign Policy, 1865–1900.* New York: Bookman, 1957.

Athearn, Robert G. *Thomas Francis Meagher: An Irish Revolutionary in America.* Boulder: University Press of Colorado, 1949.

Beale, Howard K. *Theodore Roosevelt and the Rise of America to World Power.* Baltimore, MD: Johns Hopkins University Press, 1956.

Belchem, John. "Republican Spirit and Military Science: The 'Irish Brigade' and Irish-American Nationalism in 1848." *Irish Historical Studies* 29, no. 113 (1994): 44–64.

Belich, James. *Replenishing the Earth: The Settler Revolution and the Rise of the Angloworld.* Oxford: Oxford University Press, 2009.

Belko, W. Stephen. *The Invincible Duff Green: Whig of the West*. Columbia: University of Missouri Press, 2006.

Belohlavek, John. *"Let the Eagle Soar!" The Foreign Policy of Andrew Jackson*. Lincoln: University of Nebraska Press, 1985.

Bensel, Richard Franklin. *The American Ballot Box in the Mid-Nineteenth Century*. Cambridge, MA: Cambridge University Press, 2004.

Bernstein, Iver. *The New York City Draft Riots: Their Significance for American Society and Politics in the Age of the Civil War*. New York: Oxford University Press, 1990.

Bew, Paul. *Land and the National Question in Ireland*. Dublin: Gill and Macmillan, 1978.

——. "Parnell, Charles Stewart 1846–1891." *Oxford Dictionary of National Biography*. www.oxforddnb.com/view/article/21384. Accessed September 2012.

Billington, Ray Allen. *The Protestant Crusade 1800–1860: A Study of the Origins of American Nativism*. New York: Rinehart, 1938.

Binder, Frederick M. *James Buchanan and the American Empire*. Selinsgrove, PA: Susquehanna University Press, 1994.

Biographical Directory of the United States Congress, 1774–Present. http://bioguide. congress.gov/biosearch/biosearch.asp. Accessed September 2012.

Blackett, R. J. M. *Building an Antislavery Wall: Black Americans in the Atlantic Abolitionist Movement, 1830–1860*. Baton Rouge: Louisiana State University Press, 1983.

——. "'And There Shall Be No More Sea': William Lloyd Garrison and the Transatlantic Abolitionist Movement." In *William Lloyd Garrison at Two Hundred*, edited by James Brewer Stewart, 13–40. New Haven, CT: Yale University Press, 2008.

Blake, Nelson M. "The Olney-Pauncefote Treaty of 1897." *American Historical Review* 50, no. 2 (1945): 228–243.

Blodget, Geoffrey. "Ethno-Cultural Realities in Presidential Patronage: Grover Cleveland's Choices." *New York History* 81, no. 2 (2000): 189–210.

Brasted, H. V. "Irish Nationalism and the British Empire in the Late Nineteenth Century." In *Irish Culture and Nationalism, 1750–1950*, edited by Oliver MacDonagh, W. F. Mandle, and Pauric Travers, 83–103. Dublin: Gill and Macmillan, 1983.

Brown, Blake R. "'Stars and Shamrocks Will Be Sown': The Fenian State Trials, 1866–67." In *Canadian State Trials.* Vol. 3, *Political Trials and Security Measures, 1840–1914*, edited by Barry Wright and Susan Binnie, 35–84. Toronto: University of Toronto Press, 2009.

Brown, Thomas. *Irish-American Nationalism, 1870–1890*. Philadelphia: Lippincott, 1966.

Bruce, Susannah Ural. *The Harp and the Eagle: Irish-American Volunteers and the Union Army, 1861–1865*. New York: New York University Press, 2006.

Brundage, David. "'In Time of Peace, Prepare for War': Key Themes in the Social Thought of New York's Irish Nationalists, 1890–1916." In *The New York Irish*, edited by Timothy J. Meagher and Ronald H. Bayor, 321–334. Baltimore, MD: Johns Hopkins University Press, 1996.

Butler, Leslie. *Critical Americans: Victorian Intellectuals and Transatlantic Liberal Reform*. Chapel Hill: University of North Carolina Press, 2007.

Campbell, Charles S. *The Transformation of American Foreign Relations, 1865–1900*. New York: Harper & Row, 1976.

Campbell, Christy. *Fenian Fire: The British Government Plot to Assassinate Queen Victoria.* London: HarperCollins, 2003.

Carroll, Francis M. *American Opinion and the Irish Question, 1910–1923.* Dublin: Gill and Macmillan, 1978.

Carwardine, Richard. *Evangelicals and Politics in Antebellum America.* New Haven, CT: Yale University Press, 1993.

Cavanagh, Michael. *Memoirs of Thomas Francis Meagher.* Worcester, MA: Messenger Press, 1892.

Cohen, Andrew Wender. "Smuggling, Globalization, and America's Outward State, 1870–1909." *Journal of American History* 97, no. 2 (2010): 371–398.

Collombier-Lakeman, Pauline. "Ireland and the Empire: The Ambivalences of Irish Constitutional Nationalism." *Radical History Review* 104 (Spring 2009): 57–76.

Comerford, R. V. *The Fenians in Context: Irish Politics and Society, 1848–82.* Dublin: Wolfhound Press, 1998.

———. "Isaac Butt and the Home Rule Party, 1870–77." In *A New History of Ireland,* vol. 5, *Ireland under the Union,* part 2, *1870–1921,* edited by W. E. Vaughan, 1–25. Oxford: Oxford University Press, 1996.

———. "The Land War and the Politics of Distress, 1877–82." In *A New History of Ireland,* vol. 5, *Ireland under the Union,* part 2, *1870–1921,* edited by W. E. Vaughan, 26–52. Oxford: Oxford University Press, 1996.

———. "O'Connell, Daniel (1775–1847)." *Oxford Dictionary of National Biography.* www.oxforddnb.com/view/article/20501. Accessed September 2012.

———. "The Parnell Era, 1883–91." In *A New History of Ireland,* vol. 5, *Ireland under the Union,* part 2, *1870–1921,* edited by W. E. Vaughan, 53–80. Oxford: Oxford University Press, 1996.

Conzen, Kathleen Neils. *Immigrant Milwaukee, 1836–1860: Accommodation and Community in a Frontier City.* Cambridge, MA: Harvard University Press, 1976.

Cooper, John Milton. *Breaking the Heart of the World: Woodrow Wilson and the Fight for the League of Nations.* New York: Cambridge University Press, 2001.

Corfe, Tom. *The Phoenix Park Murders: Conflict, Compromise and Tragedy in Ireland, 1879–1882.* London: Hodder & Stoughton, 1968.

Crapol, Edward P. *America for Americans: Economic Nationalism and Anglophobia in the Late Nineteenth Century.* Westport, CT: Greenwood Press, 1973.

———. *James G. Blaine: Architect of Empire.* Wilmington: Scholarly Resources, 2000.

Crawford, Martin. *The Anglo-American Crisis of the Mid-Nineteenth Century: The Times and America, 1850–1862.* Athens: University of Georgia Press, 1987.

Cullinane, Michael Patrick. *Liberty and American Anti-Imperialism, 1898–1909.* New York: Palgrave Macmillan, 2012.

Curti, Merle. *American Philanthropy Abroad: A History.* New Brunswick, NJ: Rutgers University Press, 1963.

Dashew, Doris W. "The Story of an Illusion: The Plan to Trade the Alabama Claims for Canada." *Civil War History* 15 (December 1969): 332–348.

Davis, Richard. *The Young Ireland Movement.* Dublin: Gill and Macmillan, 1987.

Donnelly, James S. Jr. *The Great Irish Potato Famine.* Stroud: Sutton, 2005.

Doorley, Michael. *Irish-American Diaspora Nationalism: The Friends of Irish Freedom, 1916–1935.* Dublin: Four Courts, 2005.

Doyle, David Noel. "The Irish in North America 1776-1845." In *Making the Irish American: History and Heritage of the Irish in the United States*, edited by Joseph Lee and Marion R. Casey, 171–212. New York: New York University Press, 2006.

——. "The Remaking of Irish America, 1845–1880." In *Making the Irish American: History and Heritage of the Irish in the United States*, edited by Joseph Lee and Marion R. Casey, 213–254. New York: New York University Press, 2006.

Duberman, Martin B. *Charles Francis Adams, 1807–1886*. Boston: Houghton Mifflin, 1961.

Dunne, Tom. "La Trahison des Clercs: British Intellectuals and the First Home-Rule Crisis." *Irish Historical Studies* 23, no. 90 (1982): 134–173.

Durey, Michael. *Transatlantic Radicals and the Early American Republic*. Lawrence: University Press of Kansas, 1997.

Edwards, Owen Dudley. "American Diplomats and Irish Coercion, 1880–1883." *Journal of American Studies* 1, no. 2 (1967): 213–232.

——. "The American Image of Ireland: A Study of its Early Phases." *Perspectives in American History* 4 (1970): 199–282.

——. "Rossa, Jeremiah O'Donovan (*bap.* 1831, *d.* 1915)." *Oxford Dictionary of National Biography*. www.oxforddnb.com/view/article/46330. Accessed September 2012.

Erie, Steven P. *Rainbow's End: Irish-Americans and the Dilemmas of Urban Machine Politics, 1840–1985*. Berkeley: University of California Press, 1988.

Feldberg, Michael. *The Philadelphia Riots of 1844: A Study of Ethnic Conflict*. Westport, CT: Greenwood Press, 1975.

Fenton, Laurence. "Charles Rowcroft, Irish-Americans, and the 'Recruitment Affair,' 1855–1856." *The Historical Journal* 53, no. 4 (2010): 963–982.

Fenwick, Charles G. *The Neutrality Laws of the United States*. Washington, D.C.: Carnegie Endowment for International Peace, 1913.

Fischer–Tiné, Harald. "Indian Nationalism and the 'World Forces': Transnational and Diasporic Dimensions of the Indian Freedom Movement on the Eve of the First World War." *Journal of Global History* 2, no. 3 (2007): 325–344.

Foner, Eric. *Politics and Ideology in the Age of the Civil War*. New York: Oxford University Press, 1980.

——. *Reconstruction: America's Unfinished Revolution, 1863–1877*. New York: Perennial, 2002.

Foster, Roy F. *The Irish Story: Telling Tales and Making It up in Ireland*. London: Penguin, 2002.

——. *Modern Ireland, 1600–1972*. London: Penguin, 1989.

Galvin, John T. "Patrick J. Maguire: Boston's Last Democratic Boss." *New England Quarterly* 55, no. 3 (1982): 392–415.

Gantt, Jonathan W. "Irish-American Terrorism and Anglo-American Relations." *Journal of the Gilded Age and Progressive Era* 5, no. 4 (2006): 325–357.

——. *Irish Terrorism in the Atlantic Community, 1865–1922*. New York: Palgrave Macmillan, 2010.

Geiger, John O. "A Scholar Meets John Bull: Edward Everett as United States Minister to England, 1841–1845." *New England Quarterly* 49, no. 4 (1976): 577–595.

Gienapp, William E. *The Origins of the Republican Party, 1852–1856*. New York: Oxford University Press, 1987.

——. "Salmon P. Chase, Nativism, and the Formation of the Republican Party in Ohio." *Ohio History* 93 (Winter–Spring 1984): 5–39.

Gerlach, Murney. *British Liberalism and the United States: Political and Social Thought in the Late Victorian Age.* Basingstoke: Palgrave, 2001.

Gleeson, David T. *The Irish in the South, 1815–1877.* Chapel Hill: University of North Carolina Press, 2001.

——. "Parallel Struggles: Irish Republicanism in the American South, 1798–1877." *Éire-Ireland* 34 (Summer 1999): 97–116.

——. "Securing the 'Interests' of the South: John Mitchel, A. G. Magrath, and the Reopening of the Transatlantic Slave Trade." *American Nineteenth Century History* 11, no. 3 (2010): 279–297.

Gleeson, David T., ed. *The Irish in the Atlantic World.* Columbia: University of South Carolina Press, 2010.

Goldberg, Joyce. *The Baltimore Affair.* Lincoln: University of Nebraska Press, 1986.

——. "Patrick Egan: Irish-American Minister to Chile, 1889–93." *Éire-Ireland* 14, no. 3 (1979): 83–95.

Goluboff, Benjamin. "'Latent Preparedness': Allusions in American Travel Literature on Britain." *American Studies* 31, no. 1 (1990): 65–82.

Gordon, Alexander, and M. W. Kirby. "Rathbone, William (1757–1809)." *Oxford Dictionary of National Biography.* www.oxforddnb.com/view/article/23160. Accessed September 2012.

Gordon, Michael A. *The Orange Riots: Irish Political Violence in New York City, 1870 and 1871.* Ithaca, NY: Cornell University Press, 1993.

Gosse, Van. "'As a Nation, the English Are Our Friends': The Emergence of African American Politics in the British Atlantic World, 1772–1861." *American Historical Review* 113, no. 4 (2008): 1003–1028.

Green, Nancy L. "Expatriation, Expatriates, and Expats: The American Transformation of a Concept." *American Historical Review* 114, no. 2 (2009): 307–328.

Green, Steven K. "The Blaine Amendment Reconsidered." *The American Journal of Legal History* 36, no. 1 (1992): 38–69.

Gregory, Adrian. "'You Might As Well Recruit Germans': British Public Opinion and the Decision to Conscript the Irish in 1918." In *Ireland and the Great War: 'A War to Unite Us All?'* edited by Adrian Gregory and Senia Pašeta, 113–132. Manchester: Manchester University Press, 2002.

Griffin, Frederick C. "Protesting Despotism: American Opposition to the U.S.-Russian Extradition Treaty of 1887." *Mid America* 70, no. 2 (1988): 91–99.

Haines, Robin F. *Charles Trevelyan and the Great Famine.* Dublin: Four Courts Press, 2004.

Hamer, David. "Morley, John, Viscount Morley of Blackburn (1838–1923)." *Oxford Dictionary of National Biography.* www.oxforddnb.com/view/article/35110. Accessed September 2012.

Handlin, Lilian. *George Bancroft: The Intellectual as Democrat.* New York: Harper & Row, 1984.

Hardack, Richard. "The Slavery of Romanism: The Casting Out of the Irish in the Work of Frederick Douglass." In *Liberating Sojourn: Frederick Douglass & Transatlantic Reform,* edited by Alan J. Rice and Martin Crawford. Athens: University of Georgia Press, 1999.

Hendrickson, David C. *Union, Nation, or Empire: The American Debate over International Relations, 1789–1941.* Lawrence: University Press of Kansas, 2009.

Hernon, Joseph M. *Celts, Catholics & Copperheads: Ireland Views the Civil War.* Columbus: Ohio State University Press, 1968.

Hietala, Thomas. *Manifest Design: American Exceptionalism and Empire.* Ithaca, NY: Cornell University Press, 2003.

Hopkinson, Michael. "President Wilson and the Irish Question." *Studia Hibernica* 27 (1993): 89–111.

Horsman, Reginald. *Race and Manifest Destiny: The Origins of American Racial Anglo-Saxonism.* Cambridge, MA: Harvard University Press, 1981.

Houston, Cecil J., and William J. Smyth. "Transferred Loyalties: Orangeism in the United States and Ontario." *American Review of Canadian Studies* 14, no. 2 (1984): 193–211.

Howe, Daniel Walker. *The Political Culture of the American Whigs.* Chicago: University of Chicago Press, 1979.

——. *What Hath God Wrought: The Transformation of America, 1815–1848.* New York: Oxford University Press, 2007.

Hueston, Robert Francis. *The Catholic Press and Nativism, 1840–1860.* New York: Arno Press, 1972.

Hughes, Peter. "William Balch." *Dictionary of Unitarian and Universalist Biography.* http://www25.uua.org/uuhs/duub/articles/williamstevensbalch.html. Accessed September 2012.

Ignatiev, Noel. *How the Irish Became White.* New York: Routledge, 1995.

"Interchange: The Global Lincoln." *Journal of American History* 96, no. 2 (2009): 462–499.

Jackson, Alvin. *Ireland 1798–1998: Politics and War.* Oxford: Blackwell, 1999.

Jenkins, Brian A. *The Fenian Problem: Insurgency and Terrorism in a Liberal State, 1858–1874.* Liverpool: Liverpool University Press, 2009.

——. *Fenians and Anglo-American Relations during Reconstruction.* Ithaca, NY: Cornell University Press, 1969.

——. *Irish Nationalism and the British State: From Repeal to Revolutionary Nationalism.* Montreal: McGill-Queen's University Press, 2006.

Jenkins, Kirk C. *The Battle Rages Higher: The Union's Fifteenth Kentucky Infantry.* Lexington: University Press of Kentucky, 2003.

Jones, Howard. *Blue and Gray Diplomacy: A History of Union and Confederate Foreign Relations.* Chapel Hill: University of North Carolina Press, 2010.

Jordan, Donald. "John O'Connor Power, Charles Stewart Parnell and the Centralisation of Popular Politics in Ireland." *Irish Historical Studies* 25, no. 97 (1986): 46–66.

Joyce, William Leonard. *Editors and Ethnicity: A History of the Irish-American Press, 1848–1883.* New York: Arno Press, 1976.

Kagan, Robert. *Dangerous Nation: America and the World, 1600–1898.* New York: Knopf, 2006.

Kelleher, Margaret. "The Female Gaze: Asenath Nicholson's Famine Narrative." In *'Fearful Realities': New Perspectives on the Famine*, edited by Chris Morash and Richard Hayes, 119–130. Blackrock: Irish Academic Press, 1996.

Kelley, Robert. *The Transatlantic Persuasion: The Liberal-Democratic Mind in the Age of Gladstone.* New York: Knopf, 1969.

Kelly, Mary C. *The Shamrock and the Lily: The New York Irish and the Creation of a Transatlantic Identity, 1845–1921.* New York: Peter Lang, 2005.

Kenny, Kevin. *Making Sense of the Molly Maguires.* New York: Oxford University Press, 1998.

Kenny, Kevin, ed. *New Directions in Irish-American History.* Madison: University of Wisconsin Press, 2003.

Kent, Christopher A. "Smith, Goldwin (1823–1910)." *Oxford Dictionary of National Biography.* www.oxforddnb.com/view/article/36142. Accessed September 2012.

Knobel, Dale. *Paddy and the Republic: Ethnicity and Nationality in Antebellum America.* Middletown, CT: Wesleyan University Press, 1986.

Kramer, Paul A. "Empires, Exceptions, and Anglo-Saxons: Race and Rule between the British and United States Empires, 1880–1910." *Journal of American History* 88, no. 4 (2002): 1315–1353.

LaFeber, Walter. *The New Empire: An Interpretation of American Expansion, 1860–1898.* Ithaca, NY: Cornell University Press, 1963.

Lee, Joseph, and Marion R. Casey, eds. *Making the Irish American: History and Heritage of the Irish in the United States.* New York: New York University Press, 2006.

Lewis, James E. *The American Union and the Problem of Neighborhood: The United States and the Collapse of the Spanish Empire, 1783–1829.* Chapel Hill: University of North Carolina Press, 1998.

Lloyd–Jones, Naomi. "The Irish Home Rule Paradox." http://theibtaurisblog.com/2012/10/08/the-home-rule-paradox/. Accessed December 2012.

Lynch, Timothy D. "Erin's Hope: The Fenian Brotherhood of New York City, 1858–1866." PhD diss., City University of New York, 2004.

Lyne, D. C. "Irish-Canadian Financial Contributions to the Home Rule Movement in the 1890s." *Studia Hibernica* 7 (1967): 182–206.

Lyons, F. S. L. "The Aftermath of Parnell, 1891–1903." In *A New History of Ireland,* vol. 5, *Ireland under the Union,* part 2, *1870–1921,* edited by W. E. Vaughan, 81–110. Oxford: Oxford University Press, 1996.

McCaffrey, Lawrence J. *Daniel O'Connell and the Repeal Year.* Lexington: University Press of Kentucky, 1966.

——. *The Irish Diaspora in America.* Bloomington: Indiana University Press, 1976.

McCartney, Donal. "The Church and Fenianism." *University Review: A Journal of Irish Studies* 4, no. 3 (1967): 203–215.

McConville, Seán. *Irish Political Prisoners, 1848–1922: Theatres of War.* London: Routledge, 2003.

McCoy, Drew R. *The Elusive Republic: Political Economy in Jeffersonian America.* New York: Norton, 1982.

McDaniel, Caleb W. "Repealing Unions: American Abolitionists, Irish Repeal, and the Origins of Garrisonian Disunionism." *Journal of the Early Republic* 28, no. 2 (2008): 243–269.

MacDonagh, Oliver. "Ambiguity in Nationalism: The Case of Ireland." *Australian Historical Studies* 19, no. 76 (1981): 337–352.

——. *The Emancipist: Daniel O'Connell, 1830–1847*. New York: St. Martin's Press, 1989.

——. "The Irish Famine Emigration to the United States." *Perspectives in American History* 10 (1976): 357–446.

——. "O'Connell's Ideology." In *A Union of Multiple Identities: The British Isles, 1750–1950*, edited by Laurence W. B. Brockliss and David Eastwood, 147–161. Manchester: Manchester University Press, 1997.

——. *A Pattern of Government Growth: The Passenger Acts and Their Enforcement*. London: MacGibbon and Kee, 1961.

——. *States of Mind: A Study of the Anglo-Irish Conflict, 1780–1980*. London: Allen & Unwin, 1983.

McGee, Owen. *The IRB: The Irish Republican Brotherhood, from the Land League to Sinn Féin*. Dublin: Four Courts Press, 2005.

McGovern, Bryan. "John Mitchel: Ecumenical Nationalist in the Old South." *New Hibernia Review* 5, no. 2 (2001): 99–110.

McMahon, Cian. "Ireland and the Birth of the Irish-American Press, 1842–61." *American Periodicals* 19, no. 1 (2009): 5–20.

McPherson, James M. *Battle Cry of Freedom: The Civil War Era*. New York: Oxford University Press, 1988.

Manela, Erez. *The Wilsonian Moment: Self-Determination and the International Origins of Anticolonial Nationalism*. New York: Oxford University Press, 2009.

Matthew, H. C. G. "Gladstone, William Ewart (1809–1898)." *Oxford Dictionary of National Biography*. www.oxforddnb.com/view/article/10787. Accessed September 2012.

May, Arthur James. "Contemporary American Opinion of the Mid-Century Revolutions in Central Europe." PhD diss., University of Pennsylvania, 1927.

May, Robert E. *Manifest Destiny's Underworld: Filibustering in Antebellum America*. Chapel Hill: University of North Carolina Press, 2002.

——. *The Southern Dream of a Caribbean Empire, 1854–1861*. Gainesville: University Press of Florida, 2002.

Meagher, Timothy J. *Inventing Irish America: Generation, Class, and Ethnic Identity in a New England City, 1880–1928*. Notre Dame, IN: University of Notre Dame Press, 2001.

Meagher, Timothy J., and Ronald H. Bayor, eds. *The New York Irish*. Baltimore, MD: Johns Hopkins University Press, 1996.

Meenagh, Martin. "Archbishop John Hughes and the New York Schools Controversy of 1840–43." *American Nineteenth Century History* 5, no. 1 (2004): 34–65.

Merk, Frederick. *The Oregon Question: Essays in Anglo-American Diplomacy and Politics*. Cambridge, MA: Belknap Press of Harvard University Press, 1967.

——. *Slavery and the Annexation of Texas*. New York: Knopf, 1972.

Miller, Kerby A. *Emigrants and Exiles: Ireland and the Irish Exodus to North America*. New York: Oxford University Press, 1985.

Middleton, Stephen. "The Fugitive Slave Crisis in Cincinnati, 1850–1860: Resistance, Enforcement, and Black Refugees." *Journal of Negro History* 72, nos. 1–2 (1987): 20–32.

Mitton, Steven Heath. "The Upshur Inquiry: Lost Lessons of the Great Experiment." *Slavery & Abolition* 27, no. 1 (2006): 89–124.

Moriarty, Thomas F. "The Irish American Response to Catholic Emancipation." *The Catholic Historical Review* 66, no. 3 (1980): 353–373.

Morrison, Michael A. "American Reaction to European Revolution, 1848–1852: Sectionalism, Memory and the Revolutionary Heritage." *Civil War History* 49, no. 2 (2003): 111–132.

Morrow, Rising Lake. "The Negotiation of the Anglo-American Treaty of 1870." *American Historical Review* 39, no. 4 (1934): 663–681.

Mulligan, Adrian N. "A Forgotten 'Greater Ireland': The Transatlantic Development of Irish Nationalism." *Scottish Geographical Journal* 118, no. 3 (2002): 219–234.

Murphy, Angela. "Abolition, Irish Freedom, and Immigrant Citizenship: American Slavery and the Rise and Fall of American Associations for Irish Repeal." PhD diss., University of Houston, 2006.

——. *American Slavery, Irish Freedom: Abolition, Immigrant Citizenship, and the Transatlantic Movement for Irish Repeal*. Baton Rouge: Louisiana State University Press, 2010.

Murphy, David. *Ireland and the Crimean War*. Dublin: Four Courts Press, 2002.

Murphy, Gretchen. *Shadowing the White Man's Burden: U.S. Imperialism and the Problem of the Color Line*. New York: New York University Press, 2010.

Murphy, Maureen. "Introduction." In *Asenath Nicholson, Annals of the Famine in Ireland*, edited by Maureen Murphy. 1851; repr., Dublin: Lilliput Press, 1998.

Nelson, Bruce. "'Come Out of Such a Land, You Irishmen': Daniel O'Connell, American Slavery, and the Making of the 'Irish Race.'" *Éire-Ireland* 42, nos. 1–2 (2007): 58–81.

——. "'From the Cabins of Connemara to the Kraals of Kaffirland': Irish Nationalists, the British Empire, and the 'Boer Fight for Freedom.'" In *The Irish in the Atlantic World*, edited by David T. Gleeson, 154–175. Columbia: University of South Carolina Press, 2010.

Ní Bhroiméil, Úna. *Building Irish Identity in America, 1870–1915: The Gaelic Revival*. Dublin: Four Courts, 2003.

Ninkovich, Frank A. *Global Dawn: The Cultural Foundation of American Internationalism, 1865–1890*. Cambridge, MA: Harvard University Press, 2009.

——. "Theodore Roosevelt: Civilization as Ideology." *Diplomatic History* 10, no. 3 (1986): 221–245.

O'Brien, Conor Cruise. *Parnell and His Party, 1880–1890*. Oxford: Clarendon Press, 1964.

O'Connell, Maurice. "O'Connell, Young Ireland, and Negro Slavery: An Exercise in Romantic Nationalism." *Thought* 64, no. 2 (1989): 130–136.

O'Day, Alan. "Imagined Irish Communities: Networks of Social Communication of the Irish Diaspora in the United States and Britain in the Late Nineteenth and Early Twentieth Centuries." *Immigrants and Minorities* 23, nos. 2–3 (2005): 399–424.

——. "Irish Diaspora Politics in Perspective: The United Irish Leagues of Great Britain and America, 1900–14." *Immigrants & Minorities* 18, no. 2 (1999), 214–239.

——. "Irish Nationalism and Anglo-American Relations in the Late Nineteenth and Early Twentieth Centuries." In *Anglo-American Attitudes: From Revolution to Partnership*, edited by Fred M. Leventhal and Ronald Quinault, 168–194. Aldershot: Ashgate, 2000.

O'Hare, M. Jeanne D'Arc. "The Public Career of Patrick Andrew Collins." PhD diss., Boston College, 1959.

O'Neill, Thomas P. "From Famine to Near Famine 1845–1879." *Studia Hibernica* 1 (1961): 161–171.

Officer, Lawrence H., and Samuel H. Williamson. "Computing 'Real Value' over Time with a Conversion between U.K. Pounds and U.S. Dollars, 1830 to Present." Measuring Worth website. www.measuringworth.com. Accessed May 8, 2013.

Onuf, Nicholas, and Peter Onuf. *Nations, Markets, and War: Modern History and the American Civil War*. Charlottesville: University of Virginia Press, 2006.

Osofsky, Gilbert. "Abolitionists, Irish Immigrants, and the Dilemmas of Romantic Nationalism." *American Historical Review* 80, no. 4 (1975): 889–912.

Painter, Nell Irvin. "Ralph Waldo Emerson's Saxons." *Journal of American History* 95, no. 4 (2009): 977–985.

Parker, Hershel. *Herman Melville: A Biography*. 2 vols. Baltimore, MD: Johns Hopkins University Press, 1996–2002.

Perkins, Bradford. *The Great Rapprochement: England and the United States, 1895–1914*. London: Gollancz, 1969.

Pletcher, David M. *The Awkward Years: American Foreign Relations under Garfield and Arthur*. Columbia: University of Missouri Press, 1962.

Potter, George W. *To the Golden Door: The Story of the Irish in Ireland and America*. Boston: Little, Brown, 1960.

Quigley, David. *Second Founding: New York City, Reconstruction, and the Making of American Democracy*. New York: Hill & Wang, 2004.

Quinlin, Michael P. *Irish Boston*. Guildford: Globe Pequot Press, 2004.

Quinn, John F. *Father Mathew's Crusade: Temperance in Nineteenth-Century Ireland and Irish America*. Amherst: University of Massachusetts Press, 2002.

——. "Rise and Fall of Repeal: Slavery and Irish Nationalism in Antebellum Philadelphia." *Pennsylvania Magazine of History and Biography* 130, no. 1 (2006): 45–78.

——. "'Three Cheers for the Abolitionist Pope!' American Reaction to Gregory XVI's Condemnation of the Slave Trade, 1840–1860." *Catholic Historical Review* 90, no. 1 (2004): 67–93.

Rafferty, Oliver P. *The Church, the State and the Fenian Threat, 1861–75*. Basingstoke: Palgrave Macmillan, 1999.

Ramón, Marta. *A Provisional Dictator: James Stephens and the Fenian Movement*. Dublin: University College Dublin Press, 2007.

Riach, D. C. "Daniel O'Connell and American Anti-Slavery." *Irish Historical Studies* 20, no. 77 (1976): 3–25.

Roberts, Timothy Mason. *Distant Revolutions: 1848 and the Challenge to American Exceptionalism*. Charlottesville: University of Virginia Press, 2009.

Rodechko, James Paul. *Patrick Ford and his Search for America: A Case Study of Irish-American Journalism 1870–1913*. New York: Arno Press, 1976.

Rodgers, Nini. *Ireland, Slavery and Anti-Slavery: 1612–1865*. Basingstoke: Palgrave, 2007.

Roeckell, Leila M. "Bonds over Bondage: British Opposition to the Annexation of Texas." *Journal of the Early Republic* 19, no. 2 (1999): 257–278.

Roediger, David R. *The Wages of Whiteness: Race and the Making of the American Working Class*. London: Verso, 1991.

Ross, Steven J. *Workers on the Edge: Work, Leisure, and Politics in Industrializing Cincinnati, 1788–1890*. New York: Columbia University Press, 1985.

Royle, Trevor. *Crimea: The Great Crimean War, 1854–1856*. London: Little, Brown, 1999.

Rugemer, Edward B. "Robert Monroe Harrison, British Abolition, Southern Anglophobia and Texas Annexation." *Slavery & Abolition* 28, no. 2 (2007): 169–191.

Samito, Christian G. *Becoming American under Fire: Irish Americans, African Americans, and the Politics of Citizenship during the Civil War Era*. Ithaca, NY: Cornell University Press, 2009.

Sarbaugh, Timothy J. "'Charity Begins at Home': The United States Government and Irish Famine Relief, 1845–1849." *History Ireland*, 4, no. 2 (1996): 31–35.

——. "A Moral Spectacle: American Relief and the Famine, 1845–1849." *Éire-Ireland* 15, no. 4 (1980): 6–14.

Saxton, Alexander. *The Indispensable Enemy: Labor and the Anti-Chinese Movement in California*. Berkeley: University of California Press, 1971.

Schantz, Mark S. *Piety in Providence: Class Dimensions of Religious Experience in Antebellum Rhode Island*. Ithaca, NY: Cornell University Press, 2000.

Schrier, Arnold. *Ireland and the American Emigration, 1850–1900*. Minneapolis: University of Minnesota Press, 1958.

Schuck, Peter, and Rogers Smith. *Citizenship without Consent: Illegal Aliens in the American Polity*. New Haven, CT: Yale University Press, 1985.

Senior, Hereward. *The Fenians and Canada*. Toronto: Macmillan of Canada, 1978.

Sloan, Robert. *William Smith O'Brien and the Young Ireland Rebellion of 1848*. Dublin: Four Courts, 2000.

Sewell, Mike J. "Political Rhetoric and Policy-Making: James G. Blaine and Britain." *Journal of American Studies* 24, no. 1 (1990): 61–84.

——. "Rebels or Revolutionaries? Irish-American Nationalism and American Diplomacy, 1865–1885." *Historical Journal* 29, no. 3 (1986): 723–733.

Sexton, Jay. *Debtor Diplomacy: Finance and American Foreign Relations in the Civil War Era, 1837–1873*. Oxford: Oxford University Press, 2005.

——. "The Funded Loan and the Alabama Claims." *Diplomatic History* 27, no. 4 (2003): 449–478.

——. *The Monroe Doctrine: Empire and Nation in Nineteenth-Century America*. New York: Hill & Wang, 2011.

Short, K. R. M. *The Dynamite War*. Dublin: Gill & Macmillan, 1979.

Simpson, Craig M. *A Good Southerner: A Life of Henry A. Wise of Virginia*. Chapel Hill: University of North Carolina Press, 1985.

Snay, Mitchell. *Fenians, Freedmen, and Southern Whites: Race and Nationality in the Era of Reconstruction*. Baton Rouge: Louisiana State University Press, 2007.

Spencer, David S. *Louis Kossuth and Young America: A Study of Sectionalism and Foreign Policy, 1848–1852*. Columbia: University of Missouri Press, 1977.

Stansky, Peter. "Harcourt, Sir William George Granville Venables Vernon (1827–1904)." *Oxford Dictionary of National Biography*. www.oxforddnb.com/view/article/33693. Accessed September 2012.

Summers, Mark W. *Rum, Romanism, & Rebellion: The Making of a President, 1884*. Chapel Hill: University of North Carolina Press, 2000.

Tansill, Charles Callan. *America and the Fight for Irish Freedom, 1866–1922: An Old Story Based upon New Data*. New York: Devin-Adair, 1957.

Taylor, Alan. *The Civil War of 1812: American Citizens, British Subjects, Irish Rebels, &*
Indian Allies. New York: Alfred A. Knopf, 2010.

Taylor, John M. *William Henry Seward: Lincoln's Right Hand.* Washington, D.C.:
Brassey's, 1996.

Taylor, Nikki M. *Frontiers of Freedom: Cincinnati's Black Community, 1802–1868.*
Athens: Ohio University Press, 2005.

Temperley, Howard. "The O'Connell-Stevenson Contretemps: A Reflection of the
Anglo-American Slavery Issue." *Journal of Negro History* 47, no. 4 (1962): 217–233.

Toner, Peter Michael. "The Rise of Irish Nationalism in Canada, 1858–1884." PhD
diss., National University of Ireland, 1974.

Tuck, Stephen G. N. *We Ain't What We Ought To Be: The Black Freedom Struggle from*
Emancipation to Obama. Cambridge, MA: Belknap Press, 2010.

Van Deusen, Glyndon G. *William Henry Seward.* New York: Oxford University Press,
1967.

Vronsky, Peter. *Ridgeway: The American Fenian Invasion and the 1866 Battle That Made*
Canada. Toronto: Allen Lane Canada, 2011.

Walker, Mabel Gregory. *The Fenian Movement.* Colorado Springs: R. Myles, 1969.

Walsh, Maurice. *The News from Ireland: Foreign Correspondents and the Irish Revolution.*
London: I. B. Tauris, 2008.

Walsh, Victor A. "'A Fanatic Heart': The Cause of Irish-American Nationalism in
Pittsburgh during the Gilded Age." *Journal of Social History* 15, no. 2 (1981): 187–204.

Ward, Alan J. *Ireland and Anglo-American Relations, 1899–1921.* London: Weidenfeld
and Nicolson, 1969.

Weber, Jennifer L. *Copperheads: The Rise and Fall of Lincoln's Opponents in the North.*
Oxford: Oxford University Press, 2006.

Weisenburger, Steven. *Modern Medea: A Family Story of Slavery and Child-Murder from*
the Old South. New York: Hill & Wang, 1998.

Whelan, Bernadette. *United States Foreign Policy and Ireland: From Empire to Independence*
1913–29. Dublin: Four Courts Press, 2006.

Whelan, Irene. "Religious Rivalry and the Making of Irish-American Identity." In
Making the Irish American: History and Heritage of the Irish in the United States, edited
by Joseph Lee and Marion R. Casey, 271–285. New York: New York University
Press, 2006.

Whelehan, Niall. "'Scientific Warfare or the Quickest Way to Liberate Ireland': The
Brooklyn Dynamite School." *History Ireland* 16, no. 6 (2008): 42–45.

Widmer, Edward L. *Young America: The Flowering of Democracy in New York City.* New
York: Oxford University Press, 1999.

Wilentz, Sean. *The Rise of American Democracy: Jefferson to Lincoln.* New York: Norton,
2005.

Wilson, David A. "Swapping Canada for Ireland: The Fenian Invasion of 1866." *History*
Ireland 16, no. 6 (2008): 24–27.

——. *Thomas D'Arcy McGee.* 2 vols. Montreal: McGill-Queen's University Press,
2008–2011.

——. *United Irishmen, United States: Immigrant Radicals in the Early Republic.* Ithaca,
NY: Cornell University Press, 1998.

Index

Abercorn, Marquess of, 112
abolitionism, 25–31, 73, 83; American, 17, 80, 133; British, 4–5, 11–12, 17, 23, 32; Irish, 26–27, 34–35; opposition to, 77, 82–83
Adams, Charles Francis, 98, 104, 111, 116, 119, 134, 147; *Alabama* claims and, 105; calls to impeach, 115; Irish-Americans arrested in Ireland and, 105–107, 109, 120; the Fenian Brotherhood and, 92, 103, 121; John Warren case and, 114, 117–118; reports the 1867 Irish rebellion, 109–110; supports naturalization agreement, 121–122; tours Ireland, 101; William Nagle case and, 112
Adams, John, 3
Adams, John Quincy, 17; views on repeal of the Act of Union, 21
Alabama claims, 86–87, 92–93, 95–96, 122, 147–148, 160–161
Alexander II, Tsar, 155
American party, 29
American Protestant Association (APA), 75–77
American Revolution: analogy with Ireland, 3, 7, 16, 18, 79

American System, 18; Ireland and, 9
Ancona, Sydenham, 91
Anglo-Irish war, 181, 183
Anglophobia, 16, 29, 92, 134, 144, 163–164, 170
Anglo-Saxonism, 7, 96, 175–176; the Great Famine and, 57–58
anti-Catholicism, 6–7, 28–30, 58, 72, 135. *See also* nativism
anti-clericalism, 7, 72
arbitration, 93, 96, 134, 136, 160, 172, 175
Archdeacon, George, 99, 101–103, 107
Archer, William S., 53
Arthur, Chester A., administration of: responds to dynamiters, 153, 157, 159
Asquith, Herbert, 178
Atlantic telegraph, 114–115

Badger, George E., 53
Balch, William, 47, 61–62, 65
Bancroft, George, 55, 57, 61, 64, 121; Irish-Americans arrested in Ireland and, 99–100; reports on the Great Famine, 42–46, 68

Banks, Nathaniel, 92, 110; Expatriation Act and, 124; Neutrality Act revision proposed, 91–92, 94

Barber, John, 75–77

Baring Brothers, 41

Bates, Joshua, 56

Bayard, Thomas Francis, 154, 164–166, 168–169

Bergen, James, 99–100

Bessborough, Lord, 58

Blaine, James G., 146, 151, 160; appeals to Irish-American voters, 154, 162–164, 167, 169–170; land war and, 144

Blandford, Lord, 168

Boer war, 177

Bourke, Thomas, 110–111

Boyton, Michael, 146

British North America. *See* Canada

Brophy, William, 230n105

Bruce, Frederick Sir, 88–90, 92; Irish-Americans arrested in Ireland and, 114

Bryan, William Jennings, 178

Bryce, James, 148, 172

Buchanan, James, 44–45, 54, 74, 83; James Stephens criticizes, 85

Burke, Edmund, 3

Burke, Joseph W., 208n41

Burke, Richard, 126

Butt, Isaac, 132, 136, 138

Cadwalader, John, 137

Calhoun, John C., 16, 19, 31–33, 57, 73; compares Mexico and Ireland, 63–64; response to the Great Famine, 52–53

Campbell, Daniel, 208n41

Canada: Confederation of, 86–87, 94; as a model for Anglo-Irish federation, 136; possible annexation of, 34, 71, 86, 94, 97; release of Irish nationalist prisoners in, 126

Carey, Henry, 9

Carlyle, Thomas, 58

Carnegie, Andrew, 168

Carson, Edward, 178

Cass, Lewis: filibustering and, 78; response to the Great Famine, 52; support for repeal of the Act of Union, 21

Catholic Church, 6–7; relationship with Irish nationalism, 72

Catholic emancipation, 4, 13–15

Chamberlain, Joseph, 168

Civil War (Irish), 184

Civil War (U.S.), 70, 85–87, 90, 96; Federal recruitment in Ireland during, 86

Clan na Gael, 6, 133, 138–139, 161, 163, 165, 177, 179–180; election of 1884 and, 153, 155–159; election of 1888 and, 169

Clarendon, Lord, 77, 79, 93, 125; Irish-Americans arrested in Ireland and, 105–107, 115, 120

Clarke, Reader, 91

Clay, Henry, 18, 21; compares Mexico and Ireland, 63; views on repeal of the Act of Union, 22

Clayton, John M., 52, 66

Clayton-Bulwer Treaty, 67, 146

Clerkenwell prison, 119–120

Cleveland, Grover, 90, 154, 159, 162, 164–165, 169–170, 175

Cockran, William Bourke, 177

Cohalan, Daniel, 177, 182

Collins, Michael, 184

Collins, Patrick A., 161, 164

Condon, Edward O'Meagher, 126

Condon, Patrick J., 99, 106–108; involved in the 1867 rebellion, 110

Confederate States of America, 85–86; analogies drawn with Ireland, 87, 135

Conservative party. *See* Tory party

Constellation (ship), 142

Continental Congress, 3

Corn Laws, 31, 42

Cosgrave, William, 184–185

Costello, Augustine, 124, 126

Crampton, John, 77–82, 84

Creel, George, 183

Crimean War, 74, 78

Crittenden, John, 52–54

Curtis, George William, 133

Cushing, Caleb, 80

Dáil Éireann, 181

Dallas, George, 51, 62

D'Alton, Joseph, 230n105

Daly, James F., 230n105

Davis, John Bancroft, 147–148

Davis, Thomas, 33

Davitt, Michael, establishes Land League branches in the United States, 141; land war and, 138; relationship with Henry George, 149–150

de Korponay, Gabriel, 78

Democratic party, 18, 29, 162, 164–165, 170, 172; Irish immigrants and, 26, 34–35, 37; the Irish question and, 9, 19, 166–167; response to the Great Famine, 39, 42–43, 53–54; supports protection for naturalized citizens overseas, 122–123
Denieffe, Joseph, 71
Derby, Lord, 67
de Valera, Éamon, 181–183
Devoy, John, 87, 131–133, 138, 177–180; election of 1884 and, 163; on Henry George, 150; "new departure" and, 139;
Dilke, Charles Wentworth, 131, 133, 135
Disraeli, Benjamin, 169–170
Doheny, Michael, 70, 72, 77, 84
Dolan, Patrick, 110
Douglas, Stephen: filibustering and, 78
Douglass, Frederick, 73, 135
Drexel, Morgan and Company, 141
Duffy, Charles Gavan, 33–34, 64
dynamiting, 9, 153–163, 165–166, 169–170; British intelligence and, 155–157; skirmishing fund for, 133

Easter Rising, 179–181
Edmunds George, 159
Egan, Patrick, 137, 164; appointed U.S. minister to Chile, 170; home rule and, 167
elections: U.K., 1910, 177; U.K., 1918, 181; U.S., 1844, 17–23, 28–29, 34; U.S., 1852, 66; U.S., 1866, 88, 93; U.S., 1868, 122; U.S., 1884, 154, 157, 162–164, 167, 169; U.S., 1888, 169
Emerson, Ralph Waldo, 58
evangelicals: 1844 election and, 28–29; respond to the Great Famine, 48, 63
Evarts, William, 144
Everett, Edward, 17, 24, 31, 33, 56, 59, 62; views on the Great Famine, 64
expansionism, 32–38, 45
expatriation. *See* naturalization
Expatriation Act, 123–125, 146
extradition, 159–160, 165–166, 179

famine, 138–139, 143; American philanthropy in response to, 139–140, 142. *See also* Great Famine, the
Farley, Owen B., 208n41
federalism: possible Anglo-Irish, 34, 36, 136, 168–169, 173

Fenian Brotherhood, 6, 8, 64, 70, 74, 95, 97, 99–100, 103–104, 109, 129, 141, 153, 156; in Canada, 87–88; decline in support for, 95, 119–120, 131–136; established, 84–85; former members condemn use of dynamite, 161; Irish-Americans arrested in Ireland and, 102; issue of naturalization and, 98; raids on Canada, 8, 90–91, 93, 96, 107, 131; splits, 88; U.S. politics and, 88–95
filibustering, 85; antebellum Irish, 70, 73–84; Central American, 77, 81, 84; Cuban, 81; Fenian Brotherhood and, 92, 95, 111, 116
Fillmore, Millard, 65–66
First World War, 179–180, 184. *See also* Paris Peace Conference
Fish, Hamilton, 95, 137; Irish-Americans arrested in Ireland and, 126, 147–148
Fisher, Sidney George, 18
fisheries, 165–166
Fogarty, M. B., 230n105
Foote, Henry S., 66
Forbes, Robert Bennet, 54–57, 59–60, 68, 142; criticized by Democrats, 63
Ford, Patrick, 149, 156, 161–162; election of 1884 and, 163–164; election of 1888 and, 169–170
Forster, William, 147–148
Franco-Prussian War, 95
Franklin, Benjamin, 185
Frelinghuysen, Frederick T., 145–146, 151, 169
Frelinghuysen, Theodore, 28–29
Friends of Irish Freedom, 180, 182
Froude, James Anthony, 134–135
Fugitive Slave Act, 77, 81, 83

Gallagher, Thomas, 182
Gannon, John Leonard, 230n105
Garfield, James A., 143
Garrison, William Lloyd, 26, 49, 54
George, David Lloyd, 178, 181
George, Henry, 130, 166; arrested in Ireland, 148–149; Irish land reform and, 149–150
Gilpin, Thomas, 42
Gladstone, William Ewart, 96, 121, 143, 151, 171, 173, 178; the *Alabama* claims and, 93; Fenianism and, 125–126, 131–133; home rule and, 166–170; Kilmainham treaty and, 145, 150

Godkin, Edwin L. 140–141; home rule and, 168–169

Grant, Ulysses S., 96, 125, 137–138; administration of, and the Fenian Brotherhood, 95, 131

Granville, Lord, 145, 147–148, 157

Grattan, Henry, 3

Gray, Edward Dwyer, 140

Great Famine, the, 7, 13, 39–42, 78; American exports and, 43–45; American philanthropy in response to, 39–40, 45, 47–63, 68; British response to, 41–42, 44–45; Federal government response to, 52–54; Irish nationalism and, 71–72; knowledge of in the United States, 41, 46–48, 51

Greeley, Horace, 51, 71

Green, Duff, 16–17, 31–32

Greenback Labor party, 162

Grey, Charles, 125

Griffith, Arthur, 178

Groesbeck, William, 79–80

Halleck, Henry Wager, 120

Halpin, William G., 116–117, 126; arrested in Ireland, 104; support for antebellum Irish filibustering, 75

Hammond, James Henry, 43

Harcourt, William Vernon, 121–122

Harding, Warren G., 184

Harrison, Benjamin, 169–170

Harrison, William Henry, 17

Hart, Michael, 146–147

Harvey, Jacob, 48–49

Haughton, James, 27, 34–35; response to American philanthropy during the Great Famine, 62

Hay, John, 176

Hayes, Rutherford, 138, 142, 168

Heath, Thomas, 208n41

Hewitt, Abram, 146, 171

Hibernian Anti-Slavery Society, 26–27

Hite, Thomas, 208n41

Hoar, George, 147

Hogan, John, 33

Home Rule, 136, 146, 167–173, 177–179; American opinions regarding, 140–141, 143, 151, 157, 161, 167–171; comparison with Repeal, 15

Home Rule Confederation of Great Britain, 136

Hughes, Charles Evans, 184

Hughes, John, 21, 28, 48, 86; 1848 rebellion and, 71–72

Hunt, Washington, 52

Hurlbert, William Henry, 171–172

Ingersoll, Charles J., 52

Irish Confederation, 13, 59, 62, 70

Irish Emigrant Aid Society, 74, 76; intervenes in U.S. domestic politics, 82–83

Irish Free State, 184

Irish Home Rule League, 136

Irish immigrants, 30, 172; Great Famine relief efforts of, 48–49; racialization of, 22, 58, 63–64, 79; return to Ireland from the United States, 97, 144–145, 158; service during the American Civil War, 87, 104; support for repeal of the Act of Union amongst, 15

Irish nationalism: the American Civil War and, 86–87; Egyptian nationalism and, 182; Indian nationalism and, 177, 182; impact on Anglo-American relations, 2–3, 5, 84, 134, 157, 166, 172–173, 176, 178–179, 185; slavery and, 72–73; in the United States, 8, 10, 15, 40, 61, 62–85, 88–94, 97–99, 101, 119, 129–131, 134–137, 154, 156, 161–166, 169, 171–172, 176–177, 180

Irish National Land League, 130, 138–139, 143–144, 149–151, 156; branches in the United States, 141; U.S. funds for, 140–142

Irish National League, 130, 150, 161; branches in the United States, 164, 171; U.S. funds for, 167

Irish Parliament. *See* Dáil Éireann

Irish Parliamentary Party, 148, 150, 153, 161, 167, 170–171, 177

Irish Republican Army (I.R.A.), 181

Irish Republican Brotherhood (I.R.B.), 6, 8, 74, 84–85, 88, 92, 102–104, 119, 137, 153, 165; 1867 rebellion and, 110; "new departure" and, 139; suppressed by the British government, 101; U.S. funds for, 87, 95

Irish Volunteers, 178–179

Jackson, Andrew, 18; and views on repeal of the Act of Union, 19–20

Jacmel expedition, 111, 116–117

Jamestown (ship), 54–56, 59–60, 62, 65

Jefferson, Thomas, 43
Johnson, Andrew, 125; expatriation legislation and, 120; the Fenian Brotherhood and, 88–91, 93–94, 109; impeachment, 116; John Warren case and, 118
Johnson, Reverdy, 122; Irish-Americans arrested in Ireland and, 126
Johnson, Richard M., and support for repeal of the Act of Union, 19

Kelly, James, 208n41
Kelly, Thomas, 110, 119
Kenifeck, Edward, 75
Kent, James, 120
Kerrigan, James E., 111
Killian, Bernard Doran, 89–90, 94
Kinney, John, 208n41
Know Nothing party, 82–83
Kossuth, Lajos (Louis), 65

Labouchere, Henry, 45, 57
Labouchère, Henry, 168
Land League of Mayo, 138
land war, 130, 142–151
Larcom, Thomas, 102, 105, 107
Lawrence, Abbott, 62: Irish exiles and, 65–67; tours Ireland, 1–2, 58, 67–68, 114
League of Nations, 181–184
Leavitt, Humphrey, 75, 79, 81, 83
Lecky, William, 173
Levin, Lewis, 29–30; response to Great Famine relief efforts in the United States, 53
liberalism, 8–9, 133–136, 140–141, 151
Liberal party, 166; home rule and, 130, 167, 170
Liberator (newspaper), 21
Lomasney, William Mackay, 155–156
Lowell, James Russell, 158–159; dynamite and, 157; home rule and, 143, 145; Irish-Americans arrested in Ireland and, 146; 148; land war and, 142–145
Luby, Thomas Clarke, 84, 156
Lumsden, Samuel, 75, 81–83
Lumsden, William, 208n41
Lynam, James, 230n105

Macedonian (ship), 54, 62
MacGroarty, John M. C., 208n41
Maguire, John Francis, 49, 132
Marcy, William, 77, 80

Marlborough, Duchess of, 139–140
Mason, James Young, 54–55
Mathew, Theobald, 55–56
McBoyd, James Henry, 42
McCafferty, John, 110, 126, 155
McCarthy, Justin, 148, 168
McClure, John, 126
McConnell, Felix Grundy, 37–38
McCormack, John, 230n105
McEnery, John, 230n105
McGee, Thomas D'Arcy, 70–72, 82, 136
McLane, Louis, 37
McSweeney, Daniel, 147–148
Meade, George E., 91
Meagher, Thomas Francis, 33, 64–66, 72–73, 82; James Stephens criticizes, 85; offers address to Robert Bennet Forbes, 59–60
Meany, Stephen J., 230n105
Melbourne, Viscount, 12–13
Melville, Gansevoort, 14, 18
Mexican-American War, 40, 44, 51, 63; Irish veterans of returning to Ireland, 100
migration, 16, 44, 64, 71, 76–77, 130, 134, 140; of Irish-Americans from the United State to Ireland, 100–101, 103, 109; "new immigration," 172
Mitchel, John, 59, 64, 67, 77–78, 135, 155; disillusionment with Irish nationalism, 82, 131–132; impact on Irish nationalism, 70, 72–73; James Stephens criticizes, 85; support for the Confederacy, 87–89
Mooney, Thomas, 15, 34, 36
Morley, John, 133–134
Motley, John, 125
Mulleda, Henry, 135
Murphy, James, 208n41

Naas, Lord, 111
Nagle, William, 99, 111–112, 116–117
Nation (newspaper), 15, 34–36, 62
nativism, 9, 16, 21–22, 29–30, 36, 47–48, 72, 75–76. *See also* anti-Catholicism
naturalization, 8, 69, 81, 97–98, 103, 107, 114, 117–118, 120–125, 127, 144, 172, 179; Anglo-American agreement concerning, 99
Navigation Laws, 42
neutrality, 8, 70, 75, 84, 88, 95–96, 161, 172, 179; British, during the Civil War, 85–86, 109–110; the Fenian Brotherhood and, 91; the U.S. Neutrality Act and, 76, 79–83, 91–94, 159

"new departure," 139, 156, 165
Nicholson, Asenath, 46–47, 64
Nobel, Alfred, 154
Noonan, Michael, 208n41

O'Brien, William Smith, 2, 59, 66, 70–71
O'Connell, Charles Underwood, 126
O'Connell, Daniel, 4, 7, 10, 24–25, 29,
    33; abolitionism of, 12, 14, 25–31, 35,
    37; arrest of, 13, 28, 30; compared with
    Charles Stewart Parnell, 141–143, 161;
    death of, 13; Irish-Americans and, 26–28;
    loyalism of, 33–37, 61; the Repeal
    movement and, 11–14, 16; Young Ireland
    and, 36, 59
O'Connell, John, 15
O'Connor, Dennis H., 230n105
O'Conor, Charles, 102
O'Donovan Rossa, Jeremiah, 132–133,
    145, 161; dynamite and, 153, 155–156,
    158–159
O'Halloran, James, 208n41
O'Keefe, Bartholomew, 208n41
O'Leary, John, 87, 156
Olney, Richard, 176
O'Mahoney, Henry, 148
O'Mahony, John, 84–85, 90–91, 94
O'Neill, John, 91
O'Power, John Connor, 136–137
Oregon boundary dispute, 32, 34–37, 43
O'Reilly, John Boyle, 131, 161, 171; views on
    dynamiters, 156
O'Shea, Katharine, 171
O'Sullivan, Philip, 230n105

Pakenham, Sir Richard, 51, 56–57
Palmerston, Lord, 56–58, 86, 100, 142
Paris Peace Conference, 181–184
Parnell, Charles Stewart, 10, 130, 143–144,
    150, 153, 161–162, 164–165, 167,
    169–171, 177; compared with Daniel
    O'Connell, 141–143, 161; 1876 visit to
    the United States, 136–137; 1879–1880
    visit to the United States, 139–142;
    Kilmainham treaty and, 145, 150; land war
    and, 138–139
Pearse, Patrick, 178–179
Peel, Sir Robert, 13, 31–32; 41–42
perpetual allegiance, doctrine of, 99–100,
    102, 105, 119–123, 127

Philadelphia riots (1844), 28–30, 72
Philippines, 175
Pierce, Franklin, 77–78, 81, 84, 86
Pim, Jonathan, 48
Phelps, Edward, 167–168
Phelps-Roseberry convention, 159–160
Phoenix Park murders, 166
phytophthora infestans, 40
Polk, James K. 40, 100; opposes Federal relief
    efforts in response to the Great Famine,
    53–54, 62; support for repeal of the Act of
    Union, 21; U.S. expansionism and, 34–37
Poor Law: in Ireland, 41–42, 46
Probasco, John, 77–78
protectionism, 43, 162–164, 167, 169–170

Quakers: the Great Famine and, 48–51, 55
Quitman, John, 81

rapprochement, Anglo-American: antebellum,
    40, 52, 57–59, 66–67; late nineteenth-
    century, 173–179; naturalization
    agreement and, 125–127; Reconstruction
    era, 96, 129, 160, 169
Rathbone, William, 56
rebellion: 1798, 4, 76; 1848, 64–65, 70–71;
    1867, 95, 100, 109, 117, 126, 136; 1916, *see*
    Easter Rising
Redington, Thomas Nicholas, 99
Redmond, John, 177–179
Reed, Thomas B., 172
Reidy, David, 208n41
Religious Society of Friends. *See* Quakers
remittances, 44, 48–49
repeal movement. *See* Union, Act of,
    movement for Repeal of
Republican party: the Irish question and,
    9, 162–163, 167, 169–170, 184; opposes
    the League of Nations, 182–184; supports
    protection for naturalized citizens overseas,
    123
Ritchie, Thomas, 51
Robert Emmet Club, 74–80, 82, 84
Roberts, William R., 90–92, 94
Robinson, William Erigena, 22, 147; Irish-
    Americans arrested in Ireland and, 115,
    122, 126; land war and, 146; response to
    the Great Famine, 51; support for repeal of
    the Act of Union, 21
Rogers, Henry Wade, 157, 161

Roosevelt, Theodore, 175–176, 178; corollary to the Monroe Doctrine, 176; home rule and, 173
Rose, Sir John, 147–148, 156
Roseberry, Lord, 134
Rowcroft, Charles, 75–78; involved in enlistment scandal, 78–79, 83–84
Russell, Lord, 41, 45, 57
Ryan, Richard F., 99–100

Sackville-West, Lionel, 145
Savage, John, 72; on naturalization, 118–119
Schenck, Robert, 91
self-determination, 180–183
Seward, William Henry, 5, 10, 29, 104–105, 118–119, 123, 125; 1848 rebellion and, 71; 1867 rebellion and, 110; abolitionism and, 24; the *Alabama* claims and, 93; criticizes British neutrality during the Civil War, 85–86; the Fenian Brotherhood and, 89–90; George Archdeacon case and, 102; Irish-Americans arrested in Ireland and, 101, 106, 114, 116, 126; John Warren case and, 116, 118; opposes nativism, 22; support for repeal of the Act of Union, 21–22, 24–25; supports naturalization agreement, 122, 124; visits Ireland, 21
Sheehy-Skeffington, Hanna, 180
Shields, James, 66–67
Sinn Féin, 178, 180–181
skirmishing fund. *See* dynamiters
Slattery, Patrick, 148
Smith, Goldwin, 134
Society of Friends. *See* Quakers
Spalding, Martin John, 90
Spalding, Rufus, 91
Stanberry, Henry, 118
Stanley, Lord, 92, 120, 122; Irish-Americans arrested in Ireland and, 111–112, 115
Stephens, James, 84–85, 92, 95, 109; dynamite and, 156; ousted as head of I.R.B., 104, 110, 119; recruits in the United States, 87–88
Stevenson, Andrew, 14
Stokes, William, 5
Strong, George Templeton, 134
Sullivan, Alexander, 155, 157, 163–164; home rule and, 167, 171
Sumner, Charles, 92, 124–125
Sweeny, Thomas, 90–91, 94

Tenant League of Cork, 59
Ten Years' War, 95
Texas, 43; and British foreign policy, 17; and U.S. foreign policy, 11, 16–17, 31–36
Thornton, Edward, 137, 142, 144
Tiernan, Thomas, 208n41
Tory party, 12, 166, 178
Trent crisis, 86
Trenwith, William, 59
Tyler, John, 16–18, 31, 34; support for repeal of the Act of Union, 19
Tyler, Robert, 27, 34–35, 82; 1848 rebellion and, 71; support for antebellum Irish filibustering, 74–75; support for repeal of the Act of Union, 18–19, 23–24, 28

Ulster, 177–178
Ulster Unionists, 178
Ulster Volunteers, 178
Union, Act of, 11–12; discontent with movement for Repeal of, 28–30, 61; movement for Repeal of, 11–38, 40, 80
United Irish League of America, 177
United Irishmen, 4, 76
Upshur, Abel P., 17, 31–32

Van Buren, Martin, 23; support for repeal of the Act of Union, 19
Venezuelan boundary dispute, 175
Versailles, Treaty of, 183
Victoria, Queen, 85–86

Walker, Robert, 43, 58
Walsh, Joseph P., 230n105
War of 1812, 98
Warren, John, 99, 111–119, 124, 126
Washington, Treaty of, 8, 96, 134, 136
Webster, Daniel, 120; Irish exiles and, 65–67; response to the Great Famine, 52–53, 64
Webster-Ashburton Treaty, 159
Weed, Thurlow, 21, 24
Wentworth, John: response to the Great Famine, 53
West, William, 98, 109, 111; on the doctrine of perpetual allegiance, 103; George Archdeacon case and, 102–103; Irish-Americans arrested in Ireland and, 101, 104–106; John Warren case and, 114, 117; Patrick Condon case and, 107
Whig party (U.K.), 12–13, 41–42

Whig party (U.S.), 16–21, 28–29; the Great
    Famine and, 40, 53, 62–63; the Irish
    Question and, 9, 21
White, James L., 230n105
Wilmot Proviso, 51
Wilson, Woodrow, home rule and, 178; Irish
    nationalism and, 179–184
Winthrop, Robert C.: response to the Great
    Famine, 53

Wise, Henry, 83
Wodehouse, John, 101, 107
World War One. *See* First World War

Young America, 4, 24, 43; filibustering
    and, 78; Irish nationalism and,
    24–25
Young Ireland, 4, 8, 13, 68, 70–73, 77; and
    U.S. expansionism, 33–36